THE REVOLUTIONARY IMAGINATION

THE REVOLUTIONARY IMAGINATION

The Poetry and Politics of
John Wheelwright and Sherry Mangan

ALAN M. WALD

The University of North Carolina Press

Chapel Hill and London

Some portions of this book appeared in different form in
*International Socialist Review, Marxist Perspectives, Michigan Quarterly Review,
New Boston Review,* and *Pembroke Magazine.*
Permission to quote from the following selections is gratefully acknowledged.

LANGSTON HUGHES

"Share-Croppers." In *Selected Poems of Langston Hughes* (New York: Alfred A. Knopf, Inc., 1959).
Copyright 1942 by Alfred A. Knopf, Inc. and renewed 1970 by Arna Bontemps and George Houston Bass.
By permission of Alfred A. Knopf, Inc.

SHERRY MANGAN

"Activist Miliciano." *Western Review* 21, no. 1 (Autumn 1956).
By permission of the University of Iowa.
"Grade 5: Seven Dives: A Sensible Dead End." In *New Directions 24*
(New York: New Directions, 1948). By permission of New Directions Publishing Corporation.
"Walk Do Not Run." *The New Republic,* 14 August 1935.
By permission of *The New Republic.*

JOHN WHEELWRIGHT

"Canal Street," "D'Autre Temps," "Father," "The Huntsman,"
"In Poet's Defence," "Plantation Drouth," "Skulls as Drums,"
"Titanic Litany," "Village Hangover," and "Winter."
In *The Collected Poems of John Wheelwright,* edited by Alvin H. Rosenfeld
(New York: New Directions, 1972). Copyright © 1971 by
Louise Wheelwright Damon. Copyright © 1972 by New Directions Publishing Corporation.
By permission of New Directions Publishing Corporation.

Library of Congress Cataloging in Publication Data

Wald, Alan M., 1946–
The revolutionary imagination.

Includes bibliographical references and index.
1. American poetry—20th century—History and
criticism. 2. Politics and literature—United States.
3. Revolutionary poetry, American—History and criticism.
4. Radicalism in literature. 5. Socialism in literature.
6. Wheelwright, John, 1897–1940. 7. Mangan, Sherry,
1904–61. 8. Poets, American—20th century—Political
activity. I. Title.
PS310.P6W43 1983   811'.5'09358   82-8498
ISBN 0-8078-1535-7   AACR2

To My Mother, Ruth Jacobs Wald,
and in Memory of My Father,
Haskell Philip Wald (1916–1981)

So far as your career goes, consider it
your chief contribution to the cause and
no moral conflict will arise.
A conflict must have arisen to have
painting and socialism present a choice
in your mind.
Be a socialist painter, as another is a socialist cook,
mechanic, lemon picker or as with
Engels, manufacturer.

John Wheelwright in a letter
to Fairfield Porter, about 1936

Even though revolutionary politics are
an honorable occupation, it's poetry
I still love best.

Sherry Mangan in a letter
to Dudley Fitts, 15 June 1959

CONTENTS

Unlike biographers and critics of established figures, the author of a book about two minor and almost forgotten New England poets quite naturally finds himself asked to provide justification for such a project to friends, co-workers, family, research foundations, and, finally, his readers. They assume, understandably, that the motive for such an undertaking is the discovery of neglected geniuses whose achievements will profoundly change the literary canon as it is now conceived.

Certainly I believe these poets have made emancipatory advances in literary practice; but this book is not prompted by the hope that my discoveries will revise the canon in any remarkable way. Raymond Williams argued in *Marxism and Literature* (1977) that literary traditions are self-serving mechanisms by which a privileged elite ratifies a selective past. If he is right, then the canon needs more than a revision. That is why this book is not a plea for a new ranking of poets, but an intervention into the dominant literary culture. My object is to rectify the social amnesia that has caused us to forget the radical and Marxist heritage of American letters in our century. Simply by aspiring to accurate historical remembrance, this book aims to subvert the currently sanctified canon of letters and the vision of society legitimatized by its codification.

I first encountered the careers of John Wheelwright and Sherry Mangan in the early 1970s while preparing my study *James T. Farrell: The Revolutionary Socialist Years* (1978). They were identified to me by several radical intellectuals of the Great Depression era as authentic artists of exceptional character—men of high principle and classical learning, with modernist sensibilities and colorful personalities—who became disciples of Leon Trotsky during the 1930s. Intrigued by this combination of features, I began to gather information in my spare time about their lives and work, with the intention of publishing a critical essay about each. Then, in the summer of 1976, Austin Warren, who had known and written about both poets, encouraged me to prepare a short book about them. Because they were intimate friends and frequent collaborators on literary projects and because both graduated from the Harvard Poetry Society in the post–World War I era to become members of the Socialist party and the Socialist Workers party in the Great Depression, their careers seemed to cohere sufficiently to provide usefully contrasting illustrations of the choices made by members of their generation.

However, in the process of reconstructing their lives and art, I recognized that each poet's encounter with Marxism resonated with familiar themes from the history of literary radicalism. One theme is the psychic risk of ideological and organizational commitment itself. Confronted with drastic changes in American society between 1929 and 1931, Wheelwright attempted to break new ground for American letters, while Mangan found his energies frustrated and displaced by the demands of Marxist political activity and personal economic survival. In these two characteristic responses to social crisis, in which the poetic imagination becomes informed and influenced by revolutionary politics, I found the complex theme for a longer dual biography.

I accepted the task for another reason. The careers of these two writers afforded me the opportunity to extend the theory of American literary radicalism, particularly into such areas as the interaction of Marxism and modernism, the formal features of left-wing poetry in the United States, and the fate of 1930s revolutionaries who remained unrepentant during the Cold War epoch. Pioneering books—Walter B. Rideout's *Radical Novel in the U.S.* (1956), Daniel Aaron's *Writers on the Left* (1961), and James B. Gilbert's *Writers and Partisans* (1968)—not only disintegrated taboos that had previously obstructed authentic scholarship, but also charted a territory for inquiry. However, few subsequent researchers persevered with equal diligence to extend the exploration of the region.

Perhaps the most positive contribution of the last ten years to the study of literature and radicalism has not been about American literary radicalism at all but its British counterpart. Samuel Hynes's *The Auden Generation* (1977) is a book remarkable for its precise characterization of the alterations in forms and functions of poetry in England in the 1930s. It has strongly influenced my perception of the poetic process, even though it is sparse in details about the interaction of writers with the living Marxist movements of Britain and vague about the phenomenon of Soviet communism. Still, the book underscored my disappointment with American scholarship and elicited a sense that my own approach in *Farrell* had been incomplete. At the time I wrote *Farrell*, it seemed sufficient to compare the characteristics of an alternative tradition in American radical politics among writers—the political tradition of the anti-Stalinist left—to the traits associated with the Communist party and popular front liberalism. Now it seemed more urgent to explore the implications of that political tradition for literary creation itself.

By the time the general scope of the new book had been formulated, Wheelwright had begun to emerge as a significant figure who had the respect of many poets and scholars. Proof of continuing interest in his poetry from other poets came in 1972 when New Directions published his *Collected Poems* in one volume. Wheelwright was compared favorably with John Berryman, Robert Lowell, Ezra Pound, Sylvia Plath, and A. R. Ammons in leading literary journals. John Malcolm Brinnin observed that, because of the relatively small quantity of Wheelwright's work, "He cannot be accorded major status; yet, had he lived to expand the achievement of this volume, he would very likely share rank and status with his close contemporaries Allen Tate, E. E. Cummings and Hart Crane." As recently as 3 June 1979, John Ashbery named Wheelwright's *Collected Poems* in the Sunday *New York Times Book Review* as one of the hundred most important books of Western literature since the end of World War II. In the course of my research, I uncovered verse tributes to Wheelwright by Leonard Bacon, Howard Blake, Richard Eberhart, Robert Fitzgerald, Roger Hecht, Frank Merchant, Howard Nemerov, and Frank O'Hara.

The paucity of Wheelwright scholarship cannot be attributed exclusively to the difficulty of his poems; they are no less accessible than the much annotated works of Blake, Eliot, or Pound. Nor can his obscurity be blamed simply on antiradical prejudice. The absence of sustained critical and biographical material is more likely due to the inability of scholars to achieve a clear perspective on the evolution and significance of Wheelwright's thought and art in an era that has failed to be remembered in its full complexity. I am convinced that such a perspective can be attained only by reconstructing certain currents of thought within American literary radicalism of the interwar years, for reasons I shall indicate in the Introduction.

Despite the lesser importance of Mangan's poetry and prose, his life story is necessary for a rounded understanding of twentieth-century American literature. While his evolution is distinctive in his wholehearted commitment to Marxist politics, it is thematically connected with recent biographies of Delmore Schwartz, Winfield Townley Scott, Harry Crosby, and Robert McAlmon, books dramatizing the adversary relation many poets have maintained to contemporary American culture. Mangan, whose youthful literary promise was never realized, belongs in the company of these poets, as well as in that of revolutionary-minded figures like the young André Malraux, whose writings he sought to emulate in his later years. The exploration of Mangan's political engagement extends our comprehension of this central and enduring condition of the poet at war with modern American society.

Finally, I wrote this book because I believe that the poets and their work deserve to be lifted out of obscurity and given a hearing. Two friends had special convictions about the need for such a book, but did not live to see the results of my labor. Robert Langston and Larry Trainor believed, as I do, that Mangan and Wheelwright's message to their contemporaries is more relevant today than at any time since the end of the 1930s. Both poets were firmly convinced that the preservation and advancement of human culture is linked to the movement for a socialist society.

Those familiar with literature by and about the American literary left will recognize that the title of this book, *The Revolutionary Imagination*, echoes the titles of two books by well-known critics associated with American radicalism. In 1949 Lionel Trilling published *The Liberal Imagination* to counter the tendency of liberal politics to oversimplify cultural issues and to drift "toward a denial of the emotions and the imagination." In 1967 Irving Howe edited the collection *The Radical Imagination* to draw attention to the more "problematic" aspects of social democracy. *The Revolutionary Imagination* is intended, in part, to perform the analogous function of enriching the vision of the revolutionary Marxist political and cultural tradition.

Since this project led to an intense personal involvement with the poets and their lives, I have decided to refer to them by their first names (Jack and Sherry) when discussing their personal and political affairs and by their last names (Wheelwright and Mangan) when analyzing their fiction, poetry, and criticism. In some cases the spelling and punctuation of quoted materials have been corrected or made consistent.

I am grateful to the following libraries and private collections for assistance and in some cases for permission to quote from letters and manuscripts by Wheelwright, Mangan, and others: Alderman Library, University of Virginia; Amherst College Library; Archibald Stevens Alexander Library, Rutgers University; Collection of American Literature, Beinecke Rare Book and Manuscript Library, Yale University; Charles Patterson Van Pelt Library, University of Pennsylvania; Fourth International Archives, Paris; George Arents Research Library for Special Collections, Syracuse University; Harvard University Records Office; Harvard University Registrar's Office; Holy Cross College Records Office; Houghton Library, Harvard University; Brown University Library; John Marshall, Wilton, Connecticut; Dr. Edward Meilman, Long Island Jewish-Hillside Medical Center, New Hyde Park, New York; Joseph Regenstein Library, University of Chicago; Library of Social History, New York City; Lockwood Library, State University of New York at Buffalo; Lynn Public Library, Lynn, Massachusetts; Morris Library, University of Delaware; Newberry Library, Chicago; New Directions Archives, Norfolk, Connecticut; Princeton University Library; Richard De Rochemont, New York City; St. George's School, Rhode Island; Tamiment Library, New York University, New York City; University of Nanterre, France; and Virgil Thomson, New York City.

The following people cooperated in personal interviews, many of them tape recorded: John Archer, Mary Archer, Mary Baird, George Breitman, Pierre Broué, Nicholas Calas, Joel Carmichael, Bert Cochran, Ernest Costa, Malcolm Cowley, Muriel Cowley, Charles Curtiss, Lillian Curtiss, Richard De Rochemont, Sirio Di Giulomaria, Farrell Dobbs, John Dwyer, Joshua Epstein, James T. Farrell, Gerald R. Fitzgerald, Jr., Robert Fitzgerald, Pierre Frank, Albert Glotzer, George Goodspeed, Mildred Gordon,

Sam Gordon, Clement Greenberg, Horace Gregory, Jacques Gremblat, Rita Hammer, Joseph Hansen, Reba Hansen, Dorothy Haywood, Mirti Hugnet, Theodate Johnson, Pat Jordan, Matthew Josephson, Benjamin Kittridge, Jr., James Laughlin, Frank Lovell, Mary McCarthy, David McCord, Dwight Macdonald, John McDonald, Livio Maitan, Ernest Mandel, John Marshall, Raymond Molinier, Felix Morrow, Maurice Nadeau, George Novack, William Phillips, John Poulos, Rodolphe Prager, Michel Raptis, Louis Rigal, Waverly Root, Harry Roskolenko, Jean Rous, David Rousset, Susie Rousset, Muriel Rukeyser, Meyer Schapiro, Donald Starr, Polly Thayer Starr, John Tabor, Virgil Thomson, Gustie Trainor, Charles van Gelderen, Amelia Wheelwright Vickery, Austin Vickery, Austin Warren, Elroy Webber, George Weissman, Vera Wygod, and Marya Zaturenska. My research assistant, Howard Brick, transcribed a number of tapes and made many useful suggestions.

The following shared information with me about the poets through correspondence and phone conversations: John A. Abbott, Robert Alexander, Reginald Allen, Hannah Arendt, Regina Arroll, John Ashbery, Bernard Bandler, Pearl K. Bell, Leonard Bernstein, Elizabeth Mann Borgesse, Oliver Brooks, John N. Brown, Susan J. Brown, Kenneth Burke, James Burnham, Richard Carline, Virginia Chamberlain, Pedro Chartos, John Cheever, I. Bernard Cohen, Content Cowan, Yvan Craipeau, Robert Creeley, Mina Curtiss, Cuthbert Daniel, Robert Gorham Davis, Dorothy de Santillana, Babette Deutsch, Tamara Deutscher, Philip Dodge, Richard Eberhart, Rose Feitelson, Rae Ferren, Bruno Fischer, Cornelia Fitts, Walter Goldwater, C. Manfred Gottfried, Maurice Grosser, Allen Grover, John P. Hall, Mary Hall, Betty Hamilton, Frank Haskell, Jock Haston, Richard Haywood, Andrew Heisker, David Herreshoff, Doris Herreshoff, John Hersey, Henry Russell Hitchcock, Philip and Tessa Horton, John Houseman, Quincy Howe, Cornelia Iselin, Edward C. Johnson, Margot Johnson, H. J. Kaplan, Lincoln Kirstein, Annette Kraeutler, Kate Kurzke, Stefan Lamed, John Laurence, Denise Levertov, Alfred Baker Lewis, Janet Lewis, Morris Lewit, Sylvia Lewit, Peter Lynch, Nancy Macdonald, Archibald Macleish, Norman MacLeod, Ralph Manheim, Mary Marshall, J. T. Matthews, A. Hyatt Mayor, Edward Meilman, Frank Merchant, Franz Modlik, Brian Moore, Nahuel Moreno, Samuel French Morse, Lewis Mumford, Charles J. V. Murphy, Pierre Naville, Howard Nemerov, Helen Neville, Ron Padgett, Lyman Paine, George Anthony Palmer, Phoebe Palmer, Richard Parker, Miriam Patchen, Dudley Poore, Anne Porter, Fairfield Porter, Kenneth Porter, Oliver Prescott, Jr., Hart Preston, E. W. Raye, Kenneth Rexroth, Philip Reynolds, Philip Riesman, Mary Roberts, Olga Rodakiewicz, Gérard Rosenthal, George Santry, Frances Sarason, May Sarton, Anna Maria Satta, Edgar Scott, Mrs. William Ellery Sedgwick, B. F. Skinner, Sanford Smoller, Dorothy Snow, Dorle Soria, Peter Sourian, Ray Sparrow, Paula Sterner, Arne Swabeck, Allen Tate,

Lawrence Trainor, Eleanor Trimble, Gus Tyler, Jean van Heijenoort, Gunther von Fritsch, Jac Wasserman, Edward Weeks, Warren Wheelwright, and Alice D. Wolfson.

The following provided various kinds of technical assistance in obtaining manuscripts and offered suggestions about the content of the book: Naomi Allen, Robert W. Allison, Tom Banit, Clark L. Beck, Jr., Ronald Becker, James Bunn, Edward Butscher, Eric J. Carpenter, Jane Colokarthis, Carolyn Davis, Rodney G. Dennis, Stuart Dick, Henry Donagy, Eugenia Dooley, Michael Dreyfuss, Peter Dzwonkoski, Les Evans, Ann Farr, Fred Feldman, Russell Fraser, Donald Gallup, Eugene Genovese, Tom Goldwasser, Isadore Goralnick, Sibyl Goralnick, Barbara Greer, Ronald Grele, Mitzi Hamovitch, James Hoopes, Phyllis Hymoff, Clifton Jones, Gerald M. Kelly, James Kilroy, John King, Beverly Ruth Vander Kooy, Gaile Labelle, Berta Langston, Robert Langston, Ralph Levitt, Tracy Libros, Nat London, James McIntosh, David Martz, Richard Morgan, Patrick Quinn, Eric Rabkin, Lyman Riley, Gérard Roche, Alvin Rosenfeld, Byron Rushing, Brian Shannon, Stuart Sherman, George Shriver, Louis Sinclair, Henry Nash Smith, Ormond Smythe, Gwendolyn B. Suggs, Dorothy Swanson, Michael Tormey, Helen Troy, and Barbara West. At the University of North Carolina Press I received excellent editorial and other aid from Iris Tillman Hill, Pam Morrison, and Anne Tice.

For assistance with translations I am indebted to John Barzman, Jeff Beneke, Pierre Frank, Stuart McDougal, Joanna Misnik, and Cathy Mitten. My analysis of various poems was enhanced by the discussion in my seminar "Rebels, Poets, and Dissenters in the New England Cultural Tradition," taught at the University of Michigan in the winter of 1978, and to particular insights offered by Howard Brick, Margaret Donovan, Larry Francis, Mary Hendricksen, Robbie Lieberman, William Loizeaux, Beth Spencer, Ted Sylvester, and Mark Warnowitz. In my research into the circumstances surrounding John Wheelwright's death, I was aided by John F. Geagan, deputy superintendent, Boston Police; Walter Krasny, chief of police, Ann Arbor, Michigan; and Francis X. Orfanello, executive secretary to the chief justice, Massachusetts Supreme Court. Many of my theoretical formulations regarding cultural practice and radical modernism are influenced not only by the well-known work of Raymond Williams, but also by the recent Marxist criticism of Fredric Jameson, Terry Eagleton, and Tony Bennett. The impact of these scholars, whom I have taught in lectures and seminars at the University of Michigan, is so pervasive that it would be impossible for me to footnote every manifestation. Although it is conceivable that none would share my non-Althusserian applications of their work, I am indebted to the example of their theoretical rigor and hope that this book will assist in their receiving greater attention in connection with the study of American literature.

Funding for various aspects of this research was provided by the American Council of Learned Societies, a contribution from the Robert H. Langston Foundation to the University of Michigan, and a summer fellowship and two research grants from the Rackham School at the University of Michigan.

In the final stages of writing, drafts of the manuscript were given critical readings by George Breitman, William Chace, Robert Fitzgerald, Laurence Goldstein, James Kavanagh, Lemuel A. Johnson, Jay Martin, George Novack, Mark Shechner, Paul Siegel, Virgil Thomson, Celia Wald, and George Weissman. To these generous individuals I owe a special debt; but I alone am responsible for the interpretations and any errors or weaknesses in the book.

THE REVOLUTIONARY IMAGINATION

Marxism and Modernism in the 1930s

In the United States prior to World War I, poetry and socialism were frequent companions in the salons and studios of Greenwich Village, as well as in the pages of the *Masses* magazine, edited by the poet-revolutionaries Max Eastman, Floyd Dell, and John Reed. In the decades following the Russian Revolution, however, attempts to sustain a marriage between poetry and the new center of left-wing political activity, the American Communist party, met with only episodic success.

A good measure of the blame for this unsatisfactory union must be attributed to the literary approaches established by the Communist International in the late 1920s, in the aftermath of Joseph Stalin's consolidation of power through the defeat of the oppositional factions led by Leon Trotsky and Nikolai Bukharin. The Soviet Communists' slogan of that time, "Art is a Class Weapon," had two major liabilities for left-wing poetry: it encouraged the use of political criteria to judge the quality of literature, and it created a hostile and disparaging attitude toward the poetic achievements of the 1920s, one of the richest decades in modern times for the advancement of literary form. Stalinist theoreticians peremptorily categorized 1920s modernism as the bankrupt outlook of disoriented middle-class intelligentsia; modernism's characteristic literary techniques—complex symbolism, myth, abstruse argumentation, stream of consciousness, abstraction, mixture of genres, literary allusion, montage, and a problematic mood—were politically coded as expressions of a reactionary ideology that reproduced the fragmentation experienced in bourgeois society. For example, at the First All-Union Congress of Soviet Writers in August 1934, Karl Radek delivered a paper charging that the writings of James Joyce and Marcel Proust were trivial in both form and content, thus proving that capitalism had "shrivelled" intellectually.[1]

In spite of the official Communist dogma, the development of British poets W. H. Auden, Stephen Spender, C. Day-Lewis, Louis MacNeice, and Christopher Isherwood was intimately bound up with their left-wing experiences in the depression decade. Could no parallel phenomenon have existed among poets in the United States during the social dislocation and radicalization of the 1930s? This question cannot be fully answered yet because, with the notable exception of William Carlos Williams, American social poets who took their themes from the Great Depression have received only a small portion of the study they deserve. But perhaps this book can facilitate the process of resurrecting forgotten figures and reassessing undervalued ones, an objective shared by Jack Salzman and Leo Zanderer's recent anthology, *Social Poetry of the 30s* (1978), which presents previously uncollected work by Joy Davidman, Kenneth Fearing, Joseph Freeman, Sol Funaroff, Norman Macleod, Herman Spector, Genevieve Taggard, Richard Wright, and others. The relation of these political writers to modernism will be one of the central issues discussed when future scholars assign a place to 1930s poetry in the evolution of modern literature.

The two central figures of this present study, John Wheelwright (1897–1940) and Sherry Mangan (1904–61), were established poets at the time of the Great Depression, each with several books to his name. But in their literary styles, themes, and achievements, and in their very personalities, they defy all the stereotyped versions of 1930s literati. They were revolutionary Marxists but never Communists; their political convictions were not episodic but lifelong; they did not contribute to the *New Masses* but wrote for forgotten New England publications such as *Smoke, Anathema,* and *Housatonic,* and occasionally for the *New Republic, Poetry, Sewanee Review,* and *Partisan Review.* Their political commitments did not cause them to step outside the community of poets in Boston; instead, they were the mainstays of a regionally oriented poetry circle called "The Bards." This group met in Boston restaurants and its regulars included less politically involved writers such as Howard Blake, R. P. Blackmur, and Austin Warren, who at that time considered himself a "monarchist."

Furthermore, the pamphlets of poetry they jointly edited from 1934 to 1937, under the rubric of "Vanguard Verse," involved a new literary form that blended literary motifs of the 1920s with concerns of the 1930s. A central mode of expression in the previous decade had been the "little magazine," elegantly published in small quantities at high prices and containing literature that addressed itself to an international elite of cognoscenti. Wheelwright and Mangan adopted this form, producing small pamphlets of poetry on social and political themes. These were directed at intellectuals and educated workers in the Boston-area socialist movement and could be distributed inexpensively.

Wheelwright was a Harvard student from 1916 to 1920. During this time he earned a reputation as a charismatic eccentric—alternately charming and irascible, but always of interest. His family background was pure Brahmin. He was tenth in descent from the Reverend John Wheelwright, leader of the Antinomian rebellion against Puritan rule of Massachusetts Bay Colony in the 1630s and founder of many New England settlements. Wheelwright's father was the Boston city architect and designer of many of the city's bridges, school buildings, museums, hospitals, and homes. His mother was the great granddaughter of

Peter Chardon Brooks, wealthiest of the New England merchant princes. After leaving Harvard (he was expelled for a prank in his senior year), Wheelwright briefly sojourned among expatriates in Western Europe and edited a few issues of the avant-garde *Secession* magazine. In 1925 he began some studies in architecture at the Massachusetts Institute of Technology. Shortly after, his poetry and criticism began appearing regularly in *Hound and Horn*, and in the next decade he issued three volumes of verse: *Rock and Shell* (1933), *Mirrors of Venus* (1938), and *Political Self-Portrait* (1940).

Mangan, too, was perfectly suited for a career in letters. He graduated with honors in classics from Harvard in 1925 and came from a literary family: his father wrote the definitive two-volume study of Erasmus and believed himself to be a great nephew of the Irish poet James Clarence Mangan. To all his contributions as a poet, novelist, short-story writer, editor, printer, and book designer, Mangan brought wit, elegance, and cultivation. Between 1927 and 1928 his elaborately designed and hand-printed publication *larus* offered New England literati original writings from Paris by Gertrude Stein and Robert McAlmon. At the start of the 1930s, he assisted Richard Johns in producing *Pagany: A Native Quarterly*, one of the most creative magazines of the decade. His novel *Cinderella Married* was published by A. & C. Boni in 1932, and two years later his collected verse, *No Apology for Poetrie*, appeared under the imprint of the Boston firm of Bruce Humphries.

To understand the centrality of literary modernism for the Marxist poetry of Wheelwright, Mangan, and others during the Great Depression, a theoretical perspective on the problems involved in assimilating political doctrine or ideology to imaginative literature is required. Despite the existence of many politically committed modern poets—Neruda and Lowell, for example—the relation of politics to literature is often misunderstood. In *Politics and the Novel*, Irving Howe quotes the nineteenth-century novelist Stendhal as follows: "Politics in a work of literature is like a pistol-shot in the middle of a concert, something loud and vulgar, and yet a thing to which it is not possible to refuse one's attention."[2] This statement is a casual remark of Stendhal and it is not possible to determine its meaning in a precise sense. But the quotation might suggest to some a fundamental distinction or alleged incompatibility between political and literary discourse. The shot in the concert jars one from the aesthetic experience; it disrupts.

The distinction is persuasive but deceptive; it depicts art as absorbing, complex, and harmonious, while politics is a crude intruder. It is true, of course, that there are times when politics presents itself with an urgency that unmoors one from normal pursuits and cries out for immediate action; at such times, the poet may be pressured to hastily present undigested images. Yet how useful as a general rule is the distinction implied in the observation of Stendhal, whose own work is brimming with politics? In fact, it is not uncommon for modern poets aiming at a violent renewal of perception to use displacement, extreme condensation, and word surprises—techniques that can strike a reader or listener as a gunshot at a concert. On the other hand, political ideas can be experienced not only as vulgarized slogans, but also as subtle and sophisticated ideology, so that masterworks of political theory can be as absorbing, complex, and harmonious as a concert itself.

Thus it is naive to distinguish the discourses of art and politics by counterposing a complex medium to a crude one. Nor can literary and political discourse be differentiated by the former's use of literary devices, for both employ metaphors and allusions as well as factual statements. Nor can it be said that art restricts itself to the generation of emotions and sensations, whereas politics fosters a viewpoint. Politics is often emotive, and even the "purest" art can repress or manipulate but never avoid a social content.

Neither means nor ends alone, but the dialectical relationship between means and ends, distinguishes poetic discourse from political discourse. The logical exposition required by political ideology is integral to its intention of systematically explaining perceived reality. Ideally, political analysis is communicated by logical sequence; it at least has the pretense of appealing to the rational faculties of the reader in prose that reflects the "real world." Consequently, its appropriate forms of expression seem to be the essay, scholarly book, polemical pamphlet, and the oration.

Although poetry may seem unsuitable for expressing the category of systematic ideas presented in political analysis, it does not follow that poetic discourse is irrational, although it can be, just as politics can sometimes be irrational. Poetic discourse is not bound by the same limitations as political discourse. When it does involve rationality, its distinctive feature is that this rationality can be expressed in a greater variety of ways: through association, a sub-rosa pattern of logical symbolism, contradiction, the explosion of reified experience by dialectical images, constellations of meaning reassembled into fresh constellations, or shifts in the conventional relation between signifiers and things signified. Terry Eagleton refers to aesthetic effect as "the index of a certain bracketing, whereby the work dissolves and distantiates the real to produce its signification."[3] For example, a single poem might have passages that naturalistically describe facets of New York City's appearance, reflect the city as seen in the mind of the artist, or comment on the poem itself as a particular semiotically organized signification of the city.

Poetry appears to be a privileged means of access to reality because the emotional, aesthetic, imaginative, and moral senses are central to its discourse and effects, and these function on the terrain of the subconscious. For our purposes, it is sufficient to say that poetic discourse uses a range of devices to imaginatively rework experience in order to communicate a new form of consciousness to the reader. A socialist poet may wish to communicate a socialist vision. Such a poet need not use the "rationality" of prose found in political discourse, with its direct correspondence to the observed world. Instead, this poet has the option of using configurations of diction and metaphor to exert moral pressure, manipulate symbols to disintegrate conventionalized perceptions, or produce a burst of light that will disclose the outlines of the socialist future. In summary, a socialist poet may use all the devices of craft available and appropriate for the transformation of reality: narrative, drama, character, stanza, rime, refrain, assonance, synecdoche, metonymy, image, metaphor, myth, and other tropes for inducing the reader to relinquish at least partially his or her sense of immediate reality for the imaginative world of the literary text.

The distinctions I have made by no means account for the whole of the artistic experience nor for the equally complex hermeneutical matters faced by the critic; but they do indicate the areas of similarity and difference between the discourse of political thought and that of imaginative literature. It may not be impossible for a Marxist to write a poem arguing that Lenin's view of the state as class rule is superior to Rousseau's theory of the social contract, but this task would make special demands on the poet, demands quite different from those of a poem that recreates the emotions and thoughts experienced when hearing a nightingale or falling in love.

What happens when a poet fails to be expressive as a poet in responding to a political problem can be seen in the following excerpt from Maxwell Bodenheim's "To a Revolutionary Girl," his contribution to the Communist party's 1935 anthology, *Proletarian Literature in the United States*:

> In the Russia of the past
> Women once pinned flowers
> To their shoulders, chained to lovers,
> Flogged by snarling guards
> In the exile to Siberia,
> And in the Russia of today
> Men and women, proud of work-hours,
> Sturdy, far from blood-steeped tinsel,
> Take their summer vacations
> On the steppes, in cleaner games,
> In flowers, pledges, loyalties,
> Clear-growing, inevitable,
> Deepening in their youth.[4]

Art has been absorbed by agitational-didactic politics; Bodenheim would probably have been able to make his case more cogently in an entirely different literary genre.

"To a Revolutionary Girl" fails as poetry because of Bodenheim's conception of the poetic act in this instance, not because of his desire to produce simple lines or his choice of political subject matter, but because his imaginative reworking of experience wants cogency and discipline. The poem lacks adequate craft. The same volume contains another poem with short lucid lines that is also concerned with politics—Langston Hughes's "Share-Croppers." But Hughes's poem functions more in accordance with the appropriate modes of the poetic imagination:

> Just a herd of Negroes
> Driven to the field
> Plowing, planting, hoeing,
> To make the cotton yield.
>
> When the cotton's picked
> And the work is done
> Boss Man takes the money
> And we get none.
>
> Leaves us hungry, ragged
> As we were before,
> Year by year goes by
> And we are nothing more
>
> Than a herd of Negroes
> Driven to the field—
> Plowing life away
> To make the cotton yield.[5]

Using the simple meter of a nursery rhyme and the diction and perceptions of common people, Hughes presents the naturalist metaphor of the herd to depict how enforced servitude transforms humans into beasts. He thus makes the poem an ironic work song. The same metaphor illuminates a central lesson of Marx's *Wage-Labor and Capital*: the planter-capitalists' need to realize surplus value (through the cotton yield) requires that the population of workers be kept as close to subsistence living as possible. Although there is nothing extraordinary about "Share-Croppers," it is still an advance over Bodenheim's poem and presents one way of assimilating political ideas to poetic forms.

However, an entirely different order of the political-literary imagination is disclosed in John Wheelwright's 1935 poem "Skulls as Drums." While this poem also contains relatively simple language (except for the third stanza) and has an explicitly political emphasis, it contrasts with Hughes's poem in its self-conscious and complex experiments in form.

Wheelwright treats the Marxist themes of the 1930s in a wholly fresh and unique manner, appropriating from literary modernism such devices as sudden shifts in perspective, unidentified voices, and enigmatic symbols. Furthermore, in his "Argument" to the poem, Wheelwright explains that he "develops Lenin's grammatical example" by using the personal pronouns "*they*, for capitalists; *you*, for wage earners; *we*, for professionals."[6] In this explanatory note, which reveals a complication in the work while also affirming a political identity, he attempts to use a modernist strategy to resolve the tensions between political ideology and the creative act.

Dedicated to Malcolm Cowley, "Skulls as Drums" demonstrates the importance Wheelwright attached to a correct understanding of the economic and class features of American history. It is also one of several poems that Wheelwright wrote to "contradict" works by earlier writers on the same topic. In this case, his prototype is Walt Whitman's Civil War poem "Beat! Beat! Drums!" which reads as follows:

BEAT! beat! drums!—blow! bugles! blow!
Through the windows—through doors—burst like a ruthless force,
Into the solemn church, and scatter the congregation,
Into the school where the scholar is studying;
Leave not the bridegroom quiet—no happiness must he now have
    with his bride,
Nor the peaceful farmer any peace, ploughing his field or gathering
    his grain,
So fierce you whirr and pound you drums—so shrill you bugles
    blow.

Beat! beat! drums!—blow! bugles! blow!
Over the traffic of cities—over the rumble of wheels in the streets;
Are beds prepared for sleepers at night in the houses? no sleepers
    must sleep in those beds,
No bargainers' bargains by day—no brokers or speculators—would
    they continue?
Would the talkers be talking? would the singer attempt to sing?
Would the lawyer rise in the court to state his case before the judge?
Then rattle quicker, heavier drums—you bugles wilder blow.

Beat! beat! drums!—blow! bugles! blow!
Make no parley—stop for no expostulation,
Mind not the timid—mind not the weeper or prayer,
Mind not the old man beseeching the young man,
Let not the child's voice be heard, nor the mother's entreaties,
Make even the trestles to shake the dead where they lie awaiting the
    hearses,
So strong you thump O terrible drums—so loud you bugles blow.[7]

The point of view is surprising in a poem by Whitman. In "Beat! Beat! Drums!" Whitman does not celebrate himself or meditate on childhood experiences. He is totally preoccupied with social events. The theme of the poem is antisubjective: war demands perfect conformity on the part of the entire community. All personal interests must be subordinated to the common goal, which Whitman (according to Wheelwright's interpretation) believes to be military victory over the enemy outside the community. Scholars must stop studying and speculators must stop speculating. This drive for conformity is reflected in the technical simplicity and comparative regularity of the poem: there are three stanzas, each with seven lines and each beginning with the same six words. Whitman's drums pound heavily and the rhythm of his lines is harsh; discipline and conformist behavior crush idiosyncrasies and private concerns.

Wheelwright wrote in the "Argument" to his book *Political Self-Portrait* that he objected to "Beat! Beat! Drums!" because "naively he [Whitman] calls for a war enthusiasm so intense as to prevent any possibility of financial profit. The Author [Wheelwright] contrarywise calls for indifference so profound as to germinate the civil war against war."[8] This characterization of "Beat! Beat! Drums!" does not do justice to Whitman's complex view of the Civil War, nor to the irony and fascination present in the poem. Wheelwright interprets this particular poem so that it provides an opportunity to offer the series of political observations about the class nature of war that were to become the theme of his answer, "Skulls as Drums":

> When the *first* drumtaps sound and trumpets buzz
> through doors and windows, then may no one stir.
> May listeners keep their seats while orators
> fear to speak to the point. In chalky schoolrooms
> may schoolboys not look up; in bridal chambers
> heart clocks'll keep "Tick-Tock" although the drums
> beat to a different time; or the same time.
>
> In the plowed field, or field of ripened grain,
> may farmers look up,—and spit. However drums
> pound or whirr, however shrill horns blow,
> housewives'll make beds,—as usual.
> Let men and women sleep with deafened ears.
>   Only the timid fear not fear; only
> a coward stops his tears. Father, remember;
> remind the boy of 'bravery'! Mother,
> entreat your heart! You who are fond of talking,
> continue in conversation. You who are silent,
> silently close your window; while heavy drums'll
> rattle quicker to a wilder and wilder bugle.

When *more* drums beat and shriller bugles squeal;
armored hearses snarl around that tomb
where covered skeletons play with live corpses.
. . . Roll your great stone before the door.
(They will stifle breathing air
so foetal grey with funk.) Now, charge your wire
that'll bring a galvanic startle to their great
Jack-in-the-Box. Open the lid. Look in:
   Whoever stifles fear, he is the coward.
Gaze on the corpse, pre-mortified
—gas bloated—of Mars. And on the fearful
helm of Suicide, Inc., drum, drum, drum
drum louder to drum up more fear.
From fear *and* fear a sterner fear is born
whose name is Wrath,—a filament of light
in every man. O, snarling bugles!
Crack the great stone before the door.
Drill the fat corpses for a brave parade.
Send the brave skulls and bones under the yoke
with thump of muffled drum and trumpet blurr.[9]

To the drive for conformity urged by the patriotic propaganda of the drum and bugle in Whitman's poem, Wheelwright counterposes resistance and reflection by all citizens as the starting point for determining the appropriate response to war. Like Whitman, he divides his poem into three sections, but only the first adheres to Whitman's seven-line schema. Wheelwright eliminates the regular refrain about trumpets and drums, dispersing his references to these instruments irregularly throughout the poem. He also replaces Whitman's simplicity of diction and description with ideas and images that are increasingly complex and convoluted. By the third stanza, Wheelwright introduces many typical modernist features, including a surreal series of images that includes World War I battlefields, marching corpses, and a Roman god.

Wheelwright begins by urging the citizenry to turn their backs on the drum and bugle of war propaganda, to continue life as before. In the second half of the stanza, the aphorism "Only the timid fear not fear; only / a coward stops his tears" introduces a moral tenet intended as an antidote to Whitman's depiction of how individual consciousness and concerns become submerged in the larger ethos of patriotism. To achieve the perspective that it is cowardly to pretend one does not have fears and one is unable to cry, Wheelwright urges fathers to expose the sham rhetoric of "bravery" and mothers to express their true feelings.

In the third section, Wheelwright describes the second response, the action that should follow the period of emotional resistance, "the civil war against war" that is to be germinated by the profound indifference to the official battle call. This class war is to be fought under the moral guidance of a new Blake-like aphorism: "From fear *and* fear a sterner fear is born / whose name is wrath,—a filament of light / in every man." In the poem a collation of surrealist imagery, armored hearses, and an ancient tomb depict the capitalist war-makers, called "Suicide, Inc." Transcending the conventional barriers between reality and fantasy, Wheelwright likens the tomb to a jack-in-the-box that opens to reveal the Roman war-god Mars; capitalists are described as living corpses. Wheelwright rallies the workers to military action against the capitalist creators of war: in a complex counterresurrection image, the tomb is opened and the corpses of Suicide, Inc. are marched off to prison. This is done to the accompaniment of a "muffled drum" and "trumpet blurr," which symbolize military instruments that have been brought under the control of a just "wrath." The poem is antiwar, yet not pacifist; it is aimed at Whitman and others who, in Wheelwright's opinion, failed to learn the lessons of history about the class nature of war and American society.

Bodenheim and Hughes represent two different approaches to political poetry: one communicates by direct didacticism, the other by indirect didacticism. Hughes's technique is somewhat closer to the extreme form of indirect didacticism that W. H. Auden called "parabolic"—poetry that teaches not by interpretation but by rendering feeling. Wheelwright's techniques are even more parabolic, yet his "Argument" reminds us that his ends are too precise politically to qualify as parable in the conventional understanding of the term; he leans toward the use of modernist devices to try to overcome the limitations of dead-end agitational didacticism. The style of his poem is indicative of his attitude toward the reader, whom he wants to shake up, tease, entertain, and intrigue. This approach distinguishes the mood of Wheelwright's work from the melancholy complexion tinging the poetry of Crane and other 1920s modernists.

Wheelwright's techniques are appropriate because his intention is not to present a chunk of dogma, but to redeem the past by submitting it to new insights. The title of the poem itself, "Skulls as Drums," challenges the customary perceptions of the Civil War. The reference back to Whitman is crucial, for, as Wheelwright presents it, "Beat! Beat! Drums!" constructs the war experience from the viewpoint of bourgeois ideology, devoid of class conflicts. Wheelwright intends to disintegrate this depiction of the Civil War, not to prove that the experience is objectively unknowable, but to encourage a Marxist view of it. Consequently, Wheelwright cannot be labeled simply as a modernist; if he revolutionizes language or estranges the reader from experience, it is not to make a metaphysical point but to criticize society from a Marxist point of view. More accurately, Wheelwright contends with the problems of the literary-political imagination by drawing on strategies from a large part of the legacy of literary schools.

This aspect of literary radicalism of the 1930s—the role played by literary schools—requires careful attention. Distinctive schools express historic moments in the evolution of literature. Most works are hybrids to one degree or another, but, when the essential features are separated out, each school provides insight into the literary techniques used in various contexts. For example, the inception of the novel as a dominant literary form is usually linked to the movement of realism, which was then followed by naturalism and modernism. Most literary historians associate committed literature of the left with realism and naturalism and their corresponding literary strategies—density of detail in the former and social Darwinistic motifs in the latter. On the other hand, modernist literature of the 1920s is conventionally linked with apolitical literature, that is, with what Raymond Williams calls unconsciously aligned literature, or even with politics of the far right. The experimentalists are often depicted as subjective, mystical, and more interested in self-exploration than social regeneration.

Of course, one may accurately say that the first generation of committed writers of the left in the twentieth century employed realistic and naturalistic conventions; this was true of pioneer writers such as Upton Sinclair and Jack London. However, the mature committed writers of the 1930s actually learned their literary skills in the 1920s and were hardly immune to the attractions of literary modernism. Many of them passed through a period of expatriation and some had association with the most extreme offshoots of European modernism, Dadaism and surrealism.

As the 1920s ended and the 1930s began, the more farsighted novelists and poets did not jettison what they had learned from modernism. On the one hand, there was a natural tendency to try to adapt some of the techniques of modernism to more consciously social and political ends. On the other hand, this objective was complicated by the recognition that modernism, from its inception, was not oriented toward the oppressed classes, but was aimed at refining the sensibilities of the already literate—the intellectual elite—in ways that were simply not available to working people. No doubt this dilemma caused feelings of guilt; it was a genuine conundrum for every artist torn between social conscience and muse in the thirties, including those attracted to Trotskyism, social democracy, and other movements that had no precise cultural program. But those who allied themselves with the official Communist party— Horace Gregory and Josephine Herbst, for example, who made their criticisms public—found that the issue of literary diversity constituted a painful battleground, a terrain of contradiction and frustration. In Communist publications the leading party critics, such as Michael Gold in the United States and Georg Lukács in Europe, identified the experimental techniques of modernism as the literary counterpart of subjectivism and individualism, perhaps even an indicator of incipient fascism.

Nevertheless, the practice of many left-wing writers, both inside and outside the party and its literary appendages, regularly defied the orthodox pronouncements. An entire echelon of mediators, including Joseph Freeman, Malcolm Cowley, and Granville Hicks in the United States, developed to make palatable the party's cruder and less diplomatic declarations. Of course, the real issue for the party did not concern literary principle; the party's cultural orientation shifted in accordance with zigzags in the political line, moving from an ultraleft "proletarian" cultural perspective to a liberal "people's" outlook with the advent of the popular front in 1935. When a new literary line was announced in the Soviet Union and implemented by subordinate parties abroad, the decree was primarily a vehicle by which the party officialdom could politically police the writers on the left. If a writer's political standing with the party and its current orientation was satisfactory, gross literary heresies could be tolerated; but if a writer fell under suspicion of some sort of deviation—especially a left-wing deviation when the party was immersed in reformism—the quality of his or her writing and the motives animating it might be disparaged.

Thus, despite instances of writers who regressed to the simpler forms of realism and naturalism, modernism had left its stamp on a generation and could not be eradicated. Any student of the literary left in the 1930s can see at once that what existed between the Communist party and its most talented literary allies was a state of internecine warfare on the issues of style and technique. The public manifestations of this controversy are most famously represented by the debate between Georg Lukács and Bertolt Brecht in Europe and that between James T. Farrell and the Communist *New Masses* magazine in the United States. In *A Note on Literary Criticism* (1936), Farrell stated forthrightly that "any hierarchy of values in novels according to their form . . . is meaningless. Distinctions must be of another order."[10]

The pervasive impact of modernism on political writers of the decade is quite evident in a book like the *U.S.A.* trilogy (1932–38) by John Dos Passos, an experimental novel that interpolates stream of consciousness and "camera eye" with montage and segments of straight realism. Other outstanding prose works associated with the 1930s—Henry Roth's *Call It Sleep* (1935), Nathanael West's *Day of the Locust* (1939), and James Agee's *Let Us Now Praise Famous Men* (written between 1936 and 1939, but not published until 1941)—are spiritually akin to Wheelwright's work in that they are unquestionably animated by many surreal, symbolic, and experimental techniques partly inspired by such modernist "heroes" as Eliot, Joyce, and Freud.

Even Richard Wright's *Native Son* (1940), which appears to have many of the classical naturalist motifs, bears the marks of radical modernism. A careful reading of the book shows that the motifs of naturalism are intentionally used to indicate an ironic attitude toward the naturalist vision. In Wright's view, Bigger Thomas's debilitating defect is his perception of white society as a huge mountain, a force of nature, rather than as a complex of class relations that can be altered. Furthermore, in the creation of the character Bigger Thomas, Wright employs techniques of estrangement for the purpose of distancing the reader and preventing catharsis, that is, for aesthetic objectives that bear a striking resemblance to those championed by Bertolt Brecht's "epic theater."

In contrast, the so-called proletarian novel, which some critics fancifully present as the dominant school of the 1930s, was a short-lived and unsuccessful hothouse experiment fostered by the Communist party for political reasons after 1928–29 and abandoned in 1935 when the political line changed. This theory was declaimed more than practiced, and only a small number of works from the proletarian school can be called strictly proletarian in content and perspective, Jack Conroy's *Disinherited* (1933) being one example.

Many poets of the left were as resistant as the novelists to suppressing the lessons of the 1920s; Muriel Rukeyser, Kenneth Patchen, Kenneth Fearing, and others all employed modernist forms, techniques, and sensibilities in writing that was political in its concerns and objectives. Indeed, the literary venture from the 1930s with the strongest impact, *Partisan Review*, achieved distinction largely through its willingness to openly ratify modernism as a movement for Marxists to study and from which to learn new techniques.

However, it is crucial to recognize that this decision to openly champion modernism on the part of *Partisan Review* was interlocked with a reassessment of the politics of the Communist party and led ultimately to a partial and transitory acceptance of Leon Trotsky, the party's archenemy on the left. The literary views of *Partisan Review* editors William Phillips and Philip Rahv might have been tolerated by the party, but any sympathy for Trotskyism meant excommunication. As a consequence of the party's campaign of vilification against *Partisan Review*, experimental writers who feared isolation from the party—William Carlos Williams is the most famous example—kept their distance from the journal when it was reorganized on an anti-Stalinist basis in 1937 and inadvertently assisted in the identification of modernism with political deviation.

In Europe, resistance to the party's coding of literary techniques was significantly stronger. On the one hand stood Georg Lukács, the representative of the official party position, yet a thinker open to subtleties of reasoning and uncomfortable with socialist realist doctrine; on the other hand, the defenders of experimental techniques—Bertolt Brecht, Walter Benjamin, and Ernst Bloch—were more outspoken than modernists linked to the American Communist party and more daring in their theoretical pronouncements than the *Partisan Review* editors. The most fully developed defense of modernist techniques was that of Bertolt Brecht, who showed in practice how formalistic experimentation could be used to explode the reified illusions of capitalist ideology and to agitate the theater audience into reexamining the existing social arrangements. In effect, as Fredric Jameson has argued, Brecht saw himself defending not subjectivism and personalism but modes of attaining a "higher" form of realism than those afforded by conventional techniques.[11]

In my own view, the practice of Brecht and the theoretical statements of Benjamin, Bloch, and Farrell, as well as the critical stance of the *Partisan Review* editors, have established a Marxist tradition that assigns a "relative autonomy" to literary forms and conventions. That is, even though from a Marxist perspective certain forms, genres, conventions, and devices may become associated with specific classes or stages of development on a historic scale (for example, the romance with feudalism, the novel with bourgeois society), artists have repeatedly demonstrated that they can appropriate all sorts of genres and devices for diverse ends.

Among Marxist writers, modernist strategies have been used most frequently to dissociate the reader from the conventional (i.e., bourgeois) perception of reality and to use symbol and myth to suggest an alternative view of history, morality, and social relations. The literary tendency featured in this book is not important for any self-identification as "modernist" (a term hardly used at the time), but for its willingness to incorporate any and all literary strategies as mechanisms to enhance craft and achieve a harmonious relation with political ideas. Wheelwright's "Skulls as Drums" is superior in its assimilation of political ideas to imaginative modes not because it is modernist, but because the author forged his craft from every resource that seemed appropriate, unencumbered by the strictures of any proletarian school or self-proclaimed radical formula as to technique, priorities, and purposes.

Consequently, this is one area in which neither Wheelwright nor Mangan is fully representative of the American literary left of their day. Like Farrell and Brecht, both belong to a minority tradition of the 1930s. Moreover, never having been attracted to the Communist party, they did not have to face bureaucrats authorized to limit their literary opinions. But even though they were free of this obstacle, the fundamental problems they faced were the same as all other committed artists during the depression: How does one justify writing poetry when political action is the predominant need? How does one communicate revolutionary ideas through myth, symbol, and the emotions? How does one find time to write between political duties and the necessity of earning a living? How does one address an audience of workers through a literary tradition and language derived from the elite classes?

This last question deserves special attention. Wheelwright and Mangan's ambiguous literary training disarmed as much as armed them for their socialist objectives in the 1930s: despite protests, they were, after all, educated in the school of Eliot, a frustrating mélange of unabashed elitism and literary excellence. Wheelwright and Mangan achieved poetic consciousness through a devotion to culture that recalls Matthew Arnold. They desired to revitalize the literary traditions studied at Harvard but absent from the working class. Their false starts, contradictions, and failures in the 1930s must be understood in the context of this drama within a drama as they sought to make their way back to the "uneducated" classes through literary means that seemed inherently inappropriate.

Here it is important to briefly identify my critical method. As Terry Eagleton points out, criticism is an actively constructing discourse and there is no way to prevent it from intruding and possibly misrepresenting the text, despite its intention to aid in the reader's appreciation of a work. This book was not written to justify any particular theory of what constitutes literature or literary production. But it does recognize the imaginative literature under discussion as a special category of cultural practice requiring special methods of analysis, even though these methods are not divorced from adjacent areas of cultural practice and even though their object is not the revelation of abstract and universal literary essences. My approach to Marxism can be called that of "critical assimilation" in the sense that I aspire to integrate useful elements from as many schools of analysis as possible into the Marxist framework of treating literature within the historical setting of the appropriate class relationships. Otherwise, this book gives priority to three special concerns: intellectual biography (the origin and evolution of the ideas of the writers), literary formalism (the devices used in their poetry), and ideology (not only the political views to which the writers subscribed, but also the ways in which the form and content of their writing interacted with the dominant ideas of their time).

The chapters following this Introduction argue that Wheelwright responded to the problematic of revolutionary art by adjusting and reworking modernist techniques. His imaginative work never lost its difficulty, but his symbols and myths were constructed on increasingly accessible ground—American history, New England culture, Marxist classics, popular figures from Greek, Roman, and Christian mythology—and he dramatized issues relevant to the lives of ordinary Americans during the depression. His clarity of perception and ingenuity in delineating political symbols make him a distinctive voice, one whose oeuvre (four volumes of poetry and miscellaneous essays) requires a more prominent place in American literature than it now occupies. It is my contention that Wheelwright went farther than any other American socialist poet of his time in developing an imaginative otherworld through which he could attempt to intervene in the political and moral life of the 1930s.

The succeeding chapters will also reveal that Mangan failed to reconcile experimental poetry with his Marxist views; he fractured his artistic sensibility so that his sporadic literary production after the mid-1930s veered sharply between impenetrable personal symbolism and traditional realism. However, it will be argued in the Conclusion that this failure occurred in a way that is significant to the understanding of the revolutionary imagination.

In this book the shape of the poets' careers matters more than any particular "masterpieces" or "triumphs." More often than dramatic successes, we will see only ambitions, conflicts, and mixed successes as the poets attempt to reconcile Marxist materialism with religion, cultural elitism with working-class loyalties, middle-class bohemianism with revolutionary discipline, and political ideology with surrealism and the New England literary tradition. Each writer, in his own way, tried to accomplish some large part of that reconciliation; in both cases, the infusion of revolutionary Marxist politics into an imagination heightened by modernism produced representative yet distinctive figures of their generation, figures who command attention.

PART I

THE LAPSE OF URIEL, 1897–1931

As Uriel spoke with piercing eye,
A shudder ran around the sky;
The stern old war-gods shook their heads,
The seraphs frowned from myrtle-beds.

Ralph Waldo Emerson, "Uriel"

I. THE HARVARD POETS

English poetry from the late eighteenth century to the present repeatedly demonstrates the attractiveness of rebellious philosophical and political views to dedicated poets from privileged social classes. The exemplars of this pattern among radical poets are Percy Bysshe Shelley and Lord Byron, who came from wealthy backgrounds yet devoted their lives to the advancement of revolutionary ideals. William Morris extended their tradition into the era of modern working-class movements when he founded the Socialist League in 1884.

The romantic rebellion of such Englishmen was echoed in the United States by Ralph Waldo Emerson's poem "Uriel," which relates the lapse of a celestial deity. Named for Milton's archangel of the sun in *Paradise Lost*, Uriel is cast from his eminent position in the heavens by older and more complacent fellow deities who denounce his philosophical statements as heresy. Even though the philosophy espoused by Uriel is transcendentalist and not socialist, the situation Emerson depicts resembles the lives of John Wheelwright and Sherry Mangan in three respects.

First, there is Uriel's intransigence. Uriel is not simply a truthseeking dissident shunted aside by those with a vested interest in the status quo; he is also a member of an elite group and jeopardizes his privileges by a resolute devotion to principle from which he never wavers. The obstinate character of Uriel's lapse, duplicated by Wheelwright and Mangan, makes for a sharp thematic difference between this book and other works in American literary radicalism, most of which tell of a rebellion soon followed by frustration and reconciliation. In particular, the biographical material presented in *The Revolutionary Imagination* stresses trajectories other than the 1930s pattern of revolt described in Daniel Aaron's *Writers on the Left*, which typically concludes in apostasy and demoralization. The story of John Wheelwright ends with a salutary synthesis of political commitment and literary achievement. Although certain ideological tensions remained incompletely resolved, his Marxist years were ones of intense productivity terminated only by his premature death. Kenneth Rexroth later wrote: "Dead in his prime like so many other American poets, he [Wheelwright] was not, like most of them, already burned out. No one has ever taken the place of this dynamic, inexhaustible and lovable mind and completely original talent."[1]

The decision of Sherry Mangan to put his creative writing aside for ten years and devote his life almost exclusively to revolutionary politics illustrates still another variant. Mangan's biography fuses diverse elements of classical tragedy. The protagonist, a man of exceptional ability, adheres to a political course at odds with his time and place. Partly undone by his own character flaws, he is relentlessly hunted down by "furies," which, in Mangan's case, have a biological and social basis in his sacrifice of health and economic security for a life in the service of his revolutionary ideals.

The second feature of Uriel akin to the poets in this book is the rebel deity's affinity for dissident philosophical ideas. Both poets—Wheelwright, from a Boston Brahmin background, and Mangan, the son of middle-class Irish immigrants—were formed and transformed by consecutive immersions in two new movements of thought that allured the most advanced of the interwar generation of writers. First, as Harvard poets and periodic exiles in Europe, they integrated innovative modernist ideas with their classical educations. Then, when the Great Depression upset their former conceptions of the world, they assimilated the revolutionary socialist politics that seemed plausible to many intellectuals during the 1930s. The result was that both poets blended aristocratic cultural training and modernist tastes with working-class political loyalties. Like Shelley, Byron, Morris, and Emerson's Uriel, they were "class traitors," rebels who turned against the privileged groups from which they came.

The third and most important feature of Uriel suggestive of the two poets is the likely Harvard setting of the drama, which is probably a fictionalized version of Emerson's conflicts with officials of the Harvard Divinity School. Wheelwright and Mangan's undergraduate years at Harvard played the decisive part in the formation of their lifelong literary attitudes. To understand the impact of the 1930s on their literary imaginations, it is necessary to first present an overview of their poetic characteristics in the early part of their careers, before the infusion of revolutionary Marxist ideas. This chapter will establish that Wheelwright and Mangan emerged from the 1920s as competent and promising poets with singular voices, yet belonged to a common school.

For more than four centuries Harvard had produced a constant stream of important American poets, from Michael Wigglesworth to T. S. Eliot. It was this environment that brought Wheelwright and Mangan to early maturity as writers. More important, their sojourns at Harvard coincided with the appearance of the Harvard Poetry Society, a group of precocious figures that included E. E. Cummings, Robert Hillyer, Stewart Mitchell, S. Foster Damon, John Dos Passos, and Malcolm Cowley. The group's work appeared in the two anthologies *Eight Harvard Poets* (1917) and *Eight More Harvard Poets* (1923).

Dudley Fitts, a member of the Harvard Poetry Society in the 1920s, recalled in 1958 that Wheelwright and Mangan were the quintessential voices of the movement, "the hope of our time."[2] Fitts wrote Mangan in praise of his surrealist story "Reminiscence from a Hilltop" (published in the fall 1957 *Black Mountain Review*), remarking that its "âpre tone" and "polite snarl" harkened back to the Harvard period: "It is you, not I (as *Time* said), who write the true neo-baroque: the really gutted convolutions of style, the cantankerous good stuff, that found a consummate flowering in Jack Wheelwright's poetry and, more morbidly, in your own [novel] *Cinderella Married*."[3]

In essence, the movement of Harvard poets was part of a broader upheaval in American cultural life associated with two events. One was the revolt against conventional literature spurred on by imagism, futurism, vorticism, and similar schools that began just before World War I. The other was the widespread disillusionment with inherited American values and, indeed, with the nature of the modern world itself that was dominant in the post–World War I years. What makes it possible to talk of Harvard poets as a distinct movement, however, is that these cultural and social upheavals were refracted through very specific features of the Harvard environment, features produced by a combination of the institution's history, its regional ties, and the social characteristics of its students and faculty.

The Harvard poets of Wheelwright and Mangan's day were sensitive to the institution's cultural legacy that extended back to the seventeenth century; but they were also receptive to the bohemianism of Greenwich Village and the cultural movements of "decadent" Europe. Malcolm Cowley, a friend and classmate of Wheelwright's, described the Harvard Poetry Society's cultural ambience just before the entrance of the United States into World War I as an attempt "to create in Cambridge, Massachusetts, an after-image of Oxford in the 1890s." The young poets admired the *Yellow Book*, Casanova's memoirs and *Les Liaisons Dangereuses* (read in French), and *Petronius* (read in Latin). At teatime in their rooms or at punch in the office of the *Harvard Monthly*, they drank

> seidels of straight gin topped with a maraschino cherry; they discussed the harmonies of Pater, the rhythms of Aubrey Beardsley and, growing louder, the voluptuousness of the Church, the essential virtue of prostitution. They had crucifixes in their bedrooms, and ticket stubs from last Saturday night's burlesque at the Old Howard. They wrote, too; dozens of them were prematurely decayed poets, each with his invocation to Antinoüs, his mournful description of Venetian lagoons, his sonnets to a chorus girl in which he addressed her as "little painted poem of God."[4]

An awareness of tradition combined with a penchant for rebelliousness was the pattern characteristic of the Harvard poets. Certain faculty members commanded much respect among the literati—especially Le-

Baron Russell Briggs (who taught both Wheelright and Mangan, and to whom *Eight More Harvard Poets* was dedicated), Charles Townsend Copeland, and Barrett Wendell—but hostility toward the institution itself was at times unbounded. John Dos Passos wrote after his graduation that "until Widener [Library] is blown up and A. Lawrence Lowell [president of Harvard] assassinated and the business school destroyed and its site sowed with salt—no good will come out of Cambridge."[5]

Many of the Harvard students were scions of old New England families, and this gave their outlook certain regional similarities. Yet their privileged financial status permitted them to spend summers in Paris and Italy, where they adopted the latest continental vogues. They were children of the elite with great expectations for the lives they would lead after graduation. Even though literary styles varied—ranging from that of Hillyer, an opponent of experimental verse, to Cummings, one of its major proponents—their writing abounded in allusive humor and intellectual fun, which were a response to the specific world of a Harvard education. Often witty and urbane, in letters and conversation as well as poetry, they bore a certain resemblance to the Scriblerian Club and the coterie of Dr. Johnson. Several had a flair for showmanship and the ability to create a personal legend. However, as they matured, two distinct attitudes developed among them concerning the relationship of art to intellect. Poets such as Fitts and Damon retained a close proximity to the classical heritage and other traditions, whereas Cummings and Dos Passos became increasingly anti-intellectual and presented the view that too many weighty books suffocate spontaneity and corrupt the ability to live and love fully.

Wheelwright and Mangan were among the classicists and intellectuals. *Time* magazine wrote that Wheelwright's poems were like the "antics of an annunciatory angel dancing on top of a Harvard education." Horace Gregory believed that Wheelwright wrote poetry "with ideas and not words," and Austin Warren judged that "things and ideas alike are real for Sherry Mangan." In 1976 Kenneth Rexroth stated that "both men were incomparably better informed of a far greater range of life than any modern poets."[6] As a consequence, their poems were frequently recondite, and, despite derogatory remarks from both about T. S. Eliot, they were much influenced by him early on. Their writings, like Eliot's, were studded with learned references. Wheelwright's books all contained notes (Wheelwright calls them "Arguments") analogous to those at the end of *The Waste Land*; bits of Greek and other foreign languages were interspersed in Mangan's anthology *No Apology for Poetrie*. When Wheelwright's "Anathema. Maranatha!" arrived at the *Modern Quarterly* office, V. F. Calverton replied that he would be delighted to publish the poem, and then added, "What the hell does it mean, anyway?" It begins with an echo of Blake's "The Sick Rose,"

O for that rose of Bolshevism which holds
memory of its own budding,—and not this;—
this drooping prophecy of wormed potpourri . . .[7]

and ends with a stormy New England landscape at twilight:

The tempest's cribbed abundance bursts its bin;
plum trees drop worm-soft fruit and ratted bark.
Thunder begins the night. In three days, it may clear.
The stars will bud.[8]

Wheelwright's explanation was that " 'Anathema. Maranatha!,' which
means 'Let him be damned. The Lord will come!,' deals with Malkuth
[one of the ten emanations of God in the Cabala] as Stalinism . . . and
gives the materialist solution to the spiritual problems of evil.'"[9]

In a similar episode, Mangan protested to *Poetry*'s Morton Zabel the
suggestion that a submission of his might be too obscure for publication:
"I've been studying 'Revenant' very carefully and believe I *have* said
what I meant." Mangan explained that the poem, about the imagined
return of a suicide husband, "was an attempt . . . to intensify a purely
mental experience by a trick of objectification: by imaginatively carrying
successive mental attitudes to the extreme of appropriate action." He
conceded that the most problematic area was the third stanza, which
concludes as follows:

The wind pauses for me to mount it, leaving
the now thrice dead cadaver, and to ride ride ride
to any death. Yet should I cherish your white frail skull
so tenderly   .   .   .   so tenderly.[10]

Sherry glossed these lines as follows: "The wind, now impossible to
distinguish as past memory, other life, simple madness, or all three,
seems the only escape. The trinity, of which one person is already dead, I
kill from the mind in the duplex incarnation, and mount the wind to
wherever it may lead, only so be it away. The poem then ends on a note
of tender regret whose somewhat macabre expression is, considering the
sort of *Spanish Tragedy* condition of the principal actors, only appro-
priate."[11] No record remains as to whether Zabel was more enlightened
or confused by this "clarification," but he relented and "Revenant"
appeared in the January 1933 issue.

The difficulty of much of Wheelwright and Mangan's writing, which
suggests the aggressive obscurity that characterizes much modernist po-
etry, was not always intentional. In their formative years they addressed
themselves exclusively to an audience of similarly erudite writers and
scholars, and so they were naturally "obscure." Mangan believed that the
serious student of poetry ought to have a reading knowledge of French

and Latin, and be willing, when necessary, to use a dictionary to translate Greek and German. When he was criticized by William Carlos Williams for writing antiquated poetry, he told Ezra Pound that "the fault lies . . . in my education. . . . it had never occurred to me that 'forsooth' was not a current word among educated people."

Mangan passionately admired Lorenzo Valla, the fifteenth-century Italian humanist who was chosen by Pope Nicholas V to translate Herodotus and Thucydides into Latin. He preferred Lucretius to Vergil "because the former fortunately died before he could take all the life out of his hexameters." He thought Dudley Fitts a kindred spirit because "he knows how to write a line of poetry . . . as Dante wrote it, Cavalcanti, and even (God desert him and give him back to us) Eliot."[12] He envied the Elizabethan writers because he believed that they were creating language as they wrote, and he approved of Gerard Manley Hopkins for trying to reproduce this achievement.

The controversy of the ancients versus the moderns was never a problem to Mangan because he naturally assumed that the poetic mind should range over all periods with a minimum of effort. Sometimes he wrote imitations of Greek or Latin poets to refresh a classical joke; or he might present a double parody, a poem with satiric references to his own day that also might burlesque or respond to something from the classical tradition. " 'Positively the Last Appearance on Any Stage' " is simply an updated version of Michael Drayton's sonnet, "Come Let Us Kiss and Part," with its title taken from a contemporary advertising slogan. The first stanza reads:

> When the irrevocable words are spoken,
> and last untruths in bitter pride are said,
> when the irreparable ties are broken,
> and memory of promised faith is fled,
> when anguished vanity makes either blurt
> the ultimate speech that may cause love most pain,
> when, after irremediable hurt
> we turn apart to go, nor meet again—[13]

The poem is characteristic of the competent, low-key performance Mangan achieved in the academic styles he favored—epigrammatic quatrains, John Donne-like sonnets, and long narrative arguments in a Florentine diction—all studded with ornamental tags from various national literatures in the original tongues. Mangan was more lively when studiously innovative. "Makes: Maker: Makes" is reminiscent of the experiments of Cummings and Gertrude Stein:

> Sensate
> that I sensate
> that I sensate that;

or moves
that moves me
that that moves me;

that I am,
that that is,
that I am I,
that that is that;

that is is is.

That that moves
unorderedly moves
sensate fear
that I be that

I therefore
poet order moving.[14]

This is a conscious experiment in the self-referentiality of language in which the grammar has become the content. Its epistemological theme is revealed as the reader is forced to consider how words are combined to make sense and is reminded that the original meaning of poet is "maker." Mangan demonstrates how the pronoun "that" contains the duality separating the poet's consciousness from the external object, and he also speculates about the motivation for writing poetry as a means of harmonizing oneself with a frightening external world.

"Makes: Maker: Makes" is an abstract poem; rather, it calls attention to the linguistic assumptions by which poetry makes statements. But Mangan's perspective is not that of aestheticism; the poem is not presented as a self-sufficient substitute for other forms of knowledge or as the supreme repository of wisdom. To him, poetry is a mode of expression that can confirm or complement philosophical or psychological knowledge. Furthermore, the mechanism by which he provides illumination in this instance is not the emotive power of language; it is through the control exhibited by linguistic manipulation, a theme of the poem itself and the prime characteristic of his art. Yet this control—his metrical and linguistic precision, his mastery of classical forms and confidence in experimentation—could deceive a reader about the nature of the man whose poetic sensibility was being expressed. To Mangan, art may have presented itself as a form of discipline, but the emotional needs served by that discipline were contrary. The following poem, "Walk Do Not Run," which personifies Thanatos as a cagey little German gentleman, appears at first to be dominated by the bouncing musicality of its metrical structure. The confident jovial voice of the narrator, animated by whimsicality and wit, is very much like Mangan's in social discourse:

In my mind lives a small clever gentleman
—ah there, Mr. Schmidt! Listening, Mr. Schmidt?
When I count from one to one hundred
Mr. Schmidt waits patiently, and between
sixty-two and sixty-three Mr.
Schmidt murmurs: "Seventy-one."
Ho ho, Mr. Schmidt! Not yet, Mr. Schmidt.

Still, it's a pleasure having you. Try
some more prolans? a nicely grilled sweetbread?
Might I suggest some Lagrima Prostatae Spumante 1930?
But I shouldn't recommend the cervelle brulée: it's
full of adrenalin today. But, my dear sir,
pray make yourself comfortable: my house is yours.

A way out.[15]

Once more, we have a highly cerebral poem; the character Schmidt
represents an abstract idea, a death instinct or the part of the psyche
fixed on the aging process. The poem operates almost allegorically for
the events depicted refer to another structure of ideas as the narrator
seeks to outwit Mr. Schmidt, to reverse Schmidt's direction by feeding
him foods concocted from fertility-producing parts of the body. He offers
Schmidt prolans (hormones that induce sperm productivity), a sweet-
bread (which R. P. Blackmur, who selected the poem for a spread in the
New Republic, substituted for the original "testicle") and a drink de-
rived from the prostate (the gland that produces a secretion necessary for
sperm motility).

Until the fourth line of the second stanza, the tone of the dramatic
monologue remains elegant and tactful; at this point, when the narrator
discourages Schmidt from eating the "cervelle brulée" (scorched brains),
a turbulence beneath the surface is disclosed. He tells Schmidt that the
brain is "full of adrenalin today," indicating that the narrator is emo-
tionally wrought and anxiety-ridden over his relation to Schmidt. The
good humor that captivated us at first has only been a mask, the narra-
tor's means of controlling his fear. After encouraging Schmidt to make
himself comfortable, the narrator pauses, and then, to himself, cries for
"a way out," an exit from the situation.

The poem's title, "Walk Do Not Run," articulates Mangan's strategy
for coping with his emotional life. The humoring of Schmidt, the genial
voice and control, is only a maneuver to stall for time while searching for
"a way out." Beneath the surface texture of the poem is the suppressed
fear of failing powers, the seriousness of which we get a glimpse in the
suicidal connotation of "cervelle brulée" ("se bruler la cervelle" is an
idiomatic French expression meaning "to blow out one's brains"). "Walk
Do Not Run" is difficult, but not aggressively obscure; its complexity re-

sides not so much in symbolism, but in allusiveness—to food, anatomy, anthropology (the primitive practice of eating parts of the bodies of humans and animals that one wishes to strengthen in oneself), and, ironically, the mask worn by the narrator himself.

Like Mangan, John Wheelwright alternated among classical forms, startling experiments, and occasional direct statements and descriptions. He was also immersed in philosophic inquiry, which sometimes produced obscure and obdurate theological symbolism. Like Mangan in "Walk Do Not Run," Wheelwright was most successful when he was difficult but not obscure, allusive but not precious. A poem embodying these qualities is Wheelwright's forceful lyrical sonnet "Father":

> An East Wind asperges Boston with Lynn's sulphurous brine.
> Under the bridge of turrets my father built,—from turning sign
> of CHEVROLET, out-topping our gilt State House dome
> to burning sign of CARTER'S INK,—drip multitudes
> of checker-board shadows. Inverted turreted reflections
> sleeting over axle-grease billows, through all directions
> cross-cut parliamentary gulls, who toss like gourds.
>
>> Speak. Speak to me again, as fresh saddle leather
>> (Speak; talk again) to a hunter smells of heather.
>> Come home. Wire a wire of warning without words.
>> Come home and talk to me again, my first friend. Father,
>> come home, dead man, who made your mind my home.[16]

As in Mangan's best work, Wheelwright forges new images while retaining a faint metaphysical strain. However, Wheelwright is distinctive in the concrete, emotive language in which he recreates the natural and urban landscape of New England. The poem vividly fuses Boston's architecture and commerce as well as its rural and coastal environs in its depiction of nature, the state, and art marred by commercialism. The wind tries to perform a holy rite with seawater soiled by industrial waste; the State House dome is blotted out by billboards; and the bridge built by the poet's father reflects into oily waves dotted by gulls searching for garbage. In the second stanza, the poet longs for some intuitively received sustenance from his father. Despite liberties taken with the conventional sonnet (there are twelve lines here, not fourteen; the rhyme scheme is an eccentric *aabcdde eeceb*), the form and content are felicitous: the billboard slogans are smoothly integrated into the text, and the message to the father metrically imitates the simple diction of a telegram.

Wheelwright retained his New England perspective even when depicting Venice in his poem "Canal Street." He claimed to use a Henry Wadsworth Longfellow sonnet as his model, and borrowed his closing line from James Russell Lowell:

> Venice, whose streets are wavering reflections
> of leaning palaces and strips of sky,—
> Byzantine water-lily where the Winged
> Lion nested; your seed-pod domes have scattered
> seeds of dome-capped towers over our cities
> constructed of steel flames, whose streets are shade.
> (Each tower is a web, spun by a spider
> efficient, diligent) now through our caves of trade
> aromas blow of pollen dust (choking,
> exuberant) from your malicious dead:
> our human Principalities and Powers
> Your Named and Nameless who are mixt with Fate.[17]

In this instance, Wheelwright's regional sources of inspiration add a distinctive flavor to his poetry, but do not intrude upon his versatility of thought. "Canal Street," whose title reminds us that the streets of Venice are actually canals, but also puns on a well-known commercial street in New York City, contrasts the Renaissance architecture of Venice (the emblem of which is the Winged Lion of St. Mark's Church) with its modern mutation, the steel towers of industrial society (in Wheelwright's view, the work of diligent spiders). The poet ruminates on how the pollen of Venetian art might have fertilized an infinite number of architectural possibilities instead of these monstrosities. He alternately chokes on and is exhilarated by the "pollen dust" of artistic inspiration. But he is also somewhat ironical about the dead of Venice, who left an achievement that torments him through its implicit criticism of his own society. The final lines show the poet trapped between the dehumanizing forces in mass society and the modern state ("our human Principalities and Powers") and the dead leaders as well as common people of Venice ("Your Named and Nameless who are mixt with Fate").

Since Wheelwright was a product of and yet rebelled against Brahmin New England, his relation to that culture is complex. By comparison, E. E. Cummings, who wrote on some of the same themes as Wheelwright, might occasionally seem simplistic and devoid of critical faculties. In "the Cambridge ladies who live in furnished souls," Cummings is content merely to mock those who live in the afterglow of the aristocratic traditions. He begins:

> the Cambridge ladies who live in furnished souls
> are unbeautiful and have comfortable minds
> (also, with the church's protestant blessings
> daughters, unscented shapeless spirited)
> they believe in Christ and Longfellow, both dead.[18]

Wheelwright was capable of writing such bitter lines about Brahmin society as "I, who wasted all my early youth / by talking about God to

older women"; but more frequently he painted nostalgic pictures of
Boston's libraries, cathedrals, and statues.[19] In "D'Autre Temps" he even
compares the irretrievable upper-class traditions favorably to the in-
creasingly dehumanized cultural values of his own time:

My mother—Bessie—tells the story;
after their precise lipping of coffee and liquor
ladies and gentlemen in Old Boston
as the gas jets all blinked low
(glancing up, opening their eyes wide
each at the middle of his-or-hers vis-à-vis visage)
simultaneously would concur
that there was yet time to descend
to drive promptly to the play
for in the Boston Museum the great chandelier
had jumped into glory;

or, was it in the Grand Opera House
or Papanti's dance hall with the spring floor
is it a tale of Old New York
or, perhaps, Philadelphia? Or yet Charleston—
In any event,
this ill-remembered bit of misinformation
speaks of a time to me, of an America
not yet quite insensitive to all scale in life—

CONTESTANTS CROAK FROM BLOODGUSH
AFTER 6 DAY BICYCLE RACE IN
MADISON SQUARE GARDEN

which is (it is to be observed) directly
across from the S.P.C.A.[20]

"D'Autre Temps" testifies to the uneven quality of many of Wheel-
wright's verses. The poem is peculiar from several conventional angles
of approach. Wheelwright stretches into eleven lines an "ill-remembered
bit of misinformation" about a gathering of Brahmins who simulta-
neously decide to step out for an evening. Furthermore, the unbalanced
stanzas, eccentric punctuation, and capitalized headlines immediately
identify the verse as modernist, yet the "message" celebrates a culture
against which modernism rebelled. Wheelwright proffers no explanation
for this intriguing dilemma. There are also other literary quirks: the
obviously unsuccessful linguistic witticism of "vis-à-vis visage," the
corny allusion to Eliot's "Prufrock" ("there was yet time to descend"),
and the awkwardness of the closing stanza.
    Still, there are phrases in the poem that haunt: "precise lipping of cof-
fee and liquor," "the gas jets all blinked low," and "the great chandelier /

had jumped into glory." The startling personal notes at the beginning and end of the poem ("My mother—Bessie" and "speaks of a time to me") indicate how cultural memory is maintained, passed from mother to son. And certain dimensions of the form and content are apt: the long elaboration of the bit of misinformation corresponds to the theme of enjoying past times less spectacular than violent bicycle marathons in Madison Square Garden; and the uncertainty about the specificity or veracity of the episode remembered reflects the poet's longing for a general atmosphere and not a particular situation. Above all, the idiosyncrasies are not simply idiosyncrasies; they are distinctly Wheelwright's own. As a mind and personality, Wheelwright was always engaging, even in the minor moments of his poetic achievement. As young men, he and Mangan were highly individualized leaves on the growing tree of literary modernism; their poems are provocative because of the ways in which they textualized singular variations of shared cultural values.

The Harvard Poetry Society's schooling in aristocratic and modernist literatures, the effects of which have been demonstrated, was the first bond between Wheelwright and Mangan; the second was formed in the 1930s, when Wheelwright led Mangan to the left wing of the Socialist party and then to Trotskyism. Furthermore, the poets were friends for the greater part of two decades. Brought up in the Boston area, they circulated at Harvard in overlapping literary and social groups. In the 1930s they were the mainstays of a select coterie of New England poets called "The Bards." Mangan designed Wheelwright's first two books of poetry, and they collaborated on a radical cultural project called "Vanguard Verse." Both came from families with literary traditions and connections, and they shared an admiration for French literature while responding to the new movement of surrealism with the same balance of appreciation and criticism. They were also alike in their religious upbringings and strongly idealistic fathers. Each poet shed theology in an individual way, but Marxism served a similar function for both: it permitted them to preserve and act upon the sense of moral duty inculcated in their youth; at the same time, it allowed them to rebel vehemently against the hypocrisies of institutional religion and the conventional values endorsed by their families.

Yet there are significant differences between the two poets that ought to be recognized at the outset. Unlike Mangan, Wheelwright may some day be accorded the status of a significant poet in American literature. He was seven years older than Mangan, his ties to the Boston aristocracy were strong and important to him, and his heterodox religious faith lasted nearly to the end of his life. Furthermore, a modest annuity from the Wheelwright family left him free from the necessity of work, so that he was able to devote all his time to activities as bard, agitator, and Boston personality. On the other hand, Mangan is securely fixed as a peripheral figure, a literary personality. The brilliance in letters evidenced before he was thirty was later deflected by emotional turmoil and his prolific journalistic and political writing. Thereafter, it was manifest on relatively few occasions. As an Irish Catholic from the industrial town of Lynn, Massachusetts, Mangan felt himself an outsider at Harvard and in other milieus in which Wheelwright was perfectly at home.

Nevertheless, Wheelwright and Mangan are ultimately comparable because of the manner in which they blended classical and modernist poetic taste with revolutionary politics. Leon Trotsky, whom they both admired and considered the foremost political thinker of their day, wrote incisively about the potential bond that exists between the social radical and the rebel artist. Its source is the refusal to accommodate the oppressive features of the status quo. Trotsky defined art as "an expression of man's need for a harmonious and complete life . . . his need for those major benefits of which a society of classes has deprived him." Consequently, "a protest against reality, either conscious or unconscious, active or passive, optimistic or pessimistic, always forms part of a really creative piece of work."[21]

In his call for an international federation of revolutionary artists, issued jointly in 1938 with the French surrealist André Breton and the Mexican muralist Diego Rivera, Trotsky argued that, given the world political crisis, authentic culture could only be preserved, extended, and elevated by an alliance of artists with the forces of socialist revolution. John Wheelwright and Sherry Mangan, who joined the organization, were differentiated from all other Harvard and New England poets of their time through the way in which they came to personify Trotsky's conception of the bond between the dissident artist and the political heretic.

The process of Wheelwright and Mangan's radicalization was distinct from better-known instances when an established figure, often called a "fellow traveler," was won over to the cause of Communism for sentimental, utopian, or episodic reasons. Both Wheelwright and Mangan entered the 1930s as militant cultural iconoclasts, having already declared war on conventional society in the name of art. Unlike contemporaries who returned from abroad in the late 1920s to find work in publishing houses and journals, neither Wheelwright nor Mangan was temperamentally suited for a conventional career. In the early 1930s they still believed that self-motivated creative activity should be the center of their lives, and in poems and reviews they railed at those forces, ideas, and individuals that posed a threat to the autonomy and integrity of the writer. Later they made an important adjustment in the ambience of the Great Depression: they decided that art alone was an inadequate instrument for the transformation of society and allied themselves with the working-class movement. In these successive stages of artistic and political rebellion, they remained pledged to a higher order of values than they believed existed in the society around them.

It was argued earlier that the obstinate character of Wheelwright and Mangan's political stance was a distinctive mark. In fact, these twentieth-century Harvard poets are set off from many radicalized writers in their generation much as the poet Emerson came to be distinguished from his creation "Uriel." Starting with his 1832 resignation from his Boston pastorate, Emerson became the storm center of a revolt against the older and more conservative members of Boston's religious establishment. This, in turn, helped to generate the transcendentalist rebellion of burgeoning New England intellectuals against a social order marked by hypocrisy, marketplace values, and tolerance for slavery. As has often been pointed out, however, Emerson's stance toward the expanding industrial capitalist system was riven by contradiction. He alternately served as its critic and its celebrator. Even though he professed to "obey the voice at eye obeyed at prime," the quondam rebel became increasingly complacent as he aged. At the time of his death in 1882, he was honored as a doyen of American letters by academia and the state.[22]

The Uriel in Emerson's poem, however, achieves no such reconciliation. After he is exiled into a cloud, it seems as if a "forgetting wind" has erased all memory of his rebellion. Nevertheless, "truth speaking things" periodically return to shame and unnerve the persecutors while the heretic remains intransigent.[23] John Wheelwright and Sherry Mangan incarnated Uriel's spirit in the 1930s. They refused to make adjustments to purely academic or Bohemian literary lives; nor did they assume an armchair radicalism for the purpose of soothing their consciences. Wheelwright and Mangan joined a revolutionary organization as a step toward remaking the social order so that the mass of humanity could benefit from the culture they so valued. Even when the apostasies from Marxism of many literati began in the wake of the Moscow trials— becoming a veritable stampede at the advent of the 1939 Hitler-Stalin pact—both poets became only more ardent in affirming their revolutionary opposition to capitalism as well as Stalinism.

Mangan remained steadfast in his convictions and committed to activism until his death in 1961. Although Wheelwright was struck by a car and killed at the age of forty-three, evidence shows that his rebellion would have continued in some form if he had lived longer. In this regard, both poets defy the pattern of reabsorption exemplified by Emerson. Their break with the prevailing abhorrent values was resolute and irreversible, and their tradition harmonizes with the lapse of Uriel. Of course, both poets had their human frailties and idiosyncrasies, as well as literary failings, but this study is not intended to be hagiographical.

The chapters that follow are designed to give appropriate emphasis to the most important aspects of each poet's life and work. For Wheelwright, more space is devoted to family history and literary analysis; for Mangan, more attention is given to the crises that interrupted his literary productivity and to the precise nature of his political engagements.

In 1909 Van Wyck Brooks's *Wine of the Puritans* advanced the view that the Puritan legacy was a blight on American culture. In so doing, Brooks initiated a tradition of twentieth-century polemics against the New England heritage. During the next decades, most of the assaults in criticism, fiction, satire, and poetry were launched specifically against the pretensions of the privileged classes of Boston. For instance, in 1936 George Santayana published *The Last Puritan*, a novel challenging the most cherished values of the Boston Brahmins. A year later, *The Late George Apley*, John P. Marquand's gentle satire on the same subject, won the Pulitzer prize.

The authors of these and other works often showed ambivalent signs of attraction to and revulsion against the object of their criticism or ridicule. In a 1935 biography of Amy Lowell, the New England scholar S. Foster Damon cited a combination of smugness and idealism as the source of mixed feelings generated in such critics by "the Hub," as the city of Boston was called by the social elite whom Cleveland Amory labeled "the Proper Bostonians": "Its character was predetermined by its founders, whom history caused to be of one spiritual type and one purpose. The purpose was to establish the perfect community, the 'City of Saints'; and through all the changes that have come about, the place has never lost its idealism, with its accompanying conviction that Boston is really better than any other city in the world or at least in the New World."[1]

Many twentieth-century radical writers have also tried to grapple with the cultural legacy of New England, with differing focuses and purposes. For example, to many left-wing intellectuals who have lived in New England, such heresiarchs as Anne Hutchinson, Henry David Thoreau, and Wendell Phillips provide a vital legacy in the search for a connection between their current commitments and the achievements of their regional predecessors.

Some of these recent New England rebels, like the pacifist poet Robert Lowell, have been direct descendants of old Puritan families; others, like the Christian socialist scholar F. O. Matthiessen, have felt a consanguinity of temperament with the regional culture. The one twentieth-century figure who was especially successful in integrating the New England rebel heritage with twentieth-century radicalism was John Brooks Wheelwright. He was a modernist poet, architectural historian, heterodox Anglican, and highly unconventional Boston Brahmin who devoted the last eight years of his life to revolutionary socialism. A source of his poetic distinction was the enrichment of his imagination by regional themes. Like Lowell, Wheelwright was a direct heir of the earliest colonizers and felt impelled to view his actions in the light of his family history, especially in regard to the idealism of his father, a socially committed and profoundly creative Boston architect. And like Matthiessen, Wheelwright sought to retrieve a vital portion of pre–Civil War New England culture for sustaining contemporary movements for social transformation—first and foremost, the iconoclastic humanitarian visions of the rebel divines, the young Emerson, and the other "enthusiasts" for which the nineteenth-century culture of the region is noted.

Wheelwright's enchanting personal qualities—a quirky but piercing power of perception, a wit that shuttled between the mirthful and sardonic, zealous devotion to principle lightly covered by a veil of capriciousness—are embedded in a literary achievement much admired by a small band of poets and scholars of his generation who pledged themselves to keeping his memory alive. Austin Warren eulogized him in the concluding chapter of *New England Saints*: "Wheelwright was a saint; he was also a poet whose books will one day take their rightful place in American poetry and scripture." Dudley Fitts praised Wheelwright's "consummate craftsmanship" and wrote that "every line of John Wheelwright's verse confirms his position among the few perfectionists writing English poetry today." Comparing Wheelwright with other left-wing poets of the 1930s, Matthew Josephson judged that "it is Wheelwright's political poetry of that epoch that documents the Depression and New Deal for us better than any of his contemporaries' verses."

In a letter of tribute sent to the *Boston Transcript* soon after Wheelwright's accidental death, the New England antiquarian Mark DeWolfe Howe indicated the stature that Wheelwright had attained as a symbol of social conscience who fused word and deed: "The eyes of other men of intelligence born into his Boston tradition have had sufficient penetration to see the decay in that tradition and the squalor of those at whose expense it was maintained. Few in his place have been able to couple their cynical awareness of the tradition's decay with confidence that the pitiably squalid might someday inherit a better world right here in Boston."[2]

Wheelwright was endowed with physical properties as oddly fascinating as his character. He had a tall spindly frame topped by an extraordinarily large head graced with silky blond hair. His forehead was high, his eyes small and light, his nose prominent and aquiline with a narrow bridge, and his neck very long. James Bradley Thayer, a friend who, for lack of accommodation, was forced to spend the night in the same bed as Wheelwright, remarked in astonishment at the sight of his countenance so close: "God certainly wasted a lot of material when he made your face!"

In the 1920s, when Wheelwright adhered to what might be called an anarchopatrician point of view, he strolled around Boston with a heavy hickory walking stick and huge fedora. He wore shiny pointed shoes and tight-waisted suits custom-made in Italy. A. Hyatt Mayor remembered his "devastating flat Haarvard accent" and likened him to "a yellow-crested cockatoo with a voice just as strident." Lincoln Kirstein recalled that there was a physical charm to Jack's fastidious dandyism and that he always smelled of a good, distinctive cologne. His appearance and demeanor on certain occasions suggested to some a throwback to what Boston aristocrats had presumably looked like thirty or forty years earlier; but there was also a hint of Dada in his outlandish manner, for he seemed to be a walking caricature of his own moribund class.[3]

A decrease in Wheelwright's annuity in the 1930s forced modifications in his style, and his new socialist activities—picketing, demonstrating, soapboxing, running for office—influenced the perception of his oddities of dress, manner, and speech. Horace Gregory and Marya Zaturenska thought that "John Wheelwright in appearance and manner was a pre-revolutionary Bostonian of radical convictions."[4] The legends were known even across the Atlantic. Muriel Rukeyser recalled that when she first met T. S. Eliot in 1936, he immediately told an anecdote about Jack Wheelwright: Jack would address socialist rallies in a bowler hat and formal evening clothes covered by a luxurious raccoon coat, which had been the fashion in his Harvard days.[5]

The spread of such stories and anecdotes, which swirled around Wheelwright throughout his life, led Mark DeWolfe Howe to close his Boston Transcript tribute on a note of apprehension: "It was, perhaps, inevitable that legends should grow up around such a person as Wheelwright, that his individuality should be labeled eccentricity, and that the legends and the label should together serve their usual function of disqualifying the man from serious attention. Those who were satisfied in his lifetime by the formulas with which they dismissed him will, of course, remember nothing more than their formulas, but those who knew him for what he was will for many years to come find his loss irreparable." Matthew Josephson added that those close to Wheelwright recognized that "his affectations of dress or manner were only of the surface, a comedy that he liked to carry on. The man within was forthright and had a strength and courage for life on his own terms."[6]

During the 1930s, Wheelwright showed that internal fortitude and resolution. Temperamentally he was, of course, an original, an "improper Bostonian" in the tradition of Mrs. Jack Gardner and Amy Lowell. But beneath the erratic behavior and incongruous physical appearance was a serious student of Marxist politics who would quote the lesser-known

parts of the *Communist Manifesto* from memory, ponder the philosophi-
cal contributions of Joseph Dietzgen and Karl Kautsky, write endless
criticisms of platforms and programs, and compose complicated poems
on Engels's *Anti-Dühring* and Trotsky's *Literature and Revolution*. At
the same time, he maintained his interest in biblical apocrypha and lost
gospels, romantic architecture in the United States, theories of prosody
and versification, and minutiae of New England history.

Through his examination of the major political events of the 1930s—
the coming to power of Hitler, the popular front policies of the Commu-
nist movement, the civil war in Spain, the Moscow trials—Wheelwright
systematically evolved from militant socialism to Leninism, and finally
to Trotskyism. Although some who knew Wheelwright considered these
views just another of his "eccentricities," the depth of his convictions
emerges from the record of his abundant activities, published essays,
poetry, recollections of his political associates, and correspondence.

What bridge did Wheelwright find to connect the New England rebel
tradition of his ancestors with the class struggle commitment of the
Bolsheviks? And how did he cross from one to the other? The answers to
these questions are lodged in the evolution of his thought as he tried to
reconcile the meaning of his father's melancholia and suicide, his need
for a religious faith that was antagonistic toward orthodox denomina-
tional doctrine, his Brahmin sense of cultural duty, and his irrepressible
passion for social justice. The soil in which many of these preoccupations
took root was Wheelwright's intense pride in and consciousness about
his family history.

Edmund March ("Ned") Wheelwright (1854–1912), the Boston archi-
tect and father of the poet John Brooks ("Jack") Wheelwright, was ninth
in descent from the Reverend John Wheelwright, a leader of the Anti-
nomian rebellion in Massachusetts Bay Colony in the 1630s. Although
somewhat younger than Henry Adams, to whom he became related by
marriage, Ned's outlook was formed in the same mold. According to his
lifelong friend Barrett Wendell, a Harvard English professor famous for
his Tory prejudices, Ned "was stirred from boyhood by a motive which,
nobly cherished, has throughout time made human hearts constantly
brave—a loyal pride of race. He sprang from one of the boldest worthies
of our first New England generations; and he meant, all his life, to be
as nearly worthy as he could be of the tradition thus committed to his
charge."[7]

As a Harvard undergraduate, Ned Wheelwright emerged as one of
the leaders of a group of iconoclasts who "revolted against the tone of
thought which they termed 'Philistine' and 'Chromo-civilized.' "[8] Barrett
Wendell, a student of James Russell Lowell, also belonged to this circle.
Under the initiative of John Tyler Wheelwright—Ned's older brother,
who likewise was a member of the class of 1876—they founded the Har-

vard *Lampoon*. Wendell created the fictional character Hollis Allworthy, the embodiment of these world-weary, clever elitists, and Ned Wheelwright drew the original cover of the *Lampoon*, which depicts St. George impaling the dragon with a pen.[9]

Even in this milieu of eccentrics, Ned's personality was so uncommon that his friends began to substitute the expression "wheelratic" for "quixotic." He was intensely emotional and especially enthusiastic about exposing shams of all sorts. But knowing that his more practical-minded classmates considered him a "damn fool," he periodically fell into despair.[10] Still, Wheelwright's architectural work left an ineradicable mark on Boston, both when he was city architect (1891–95) and when in private practice. Gifted with a wide imagination, he blended elements of Georgian and Italian schools with colonial styles and integrated spectacular detail with basic simplicity.

After Harvard, Ned studied at the Massachusetts Institute of Technology, then served as a draftsman in architectural firms in Boston, New York City, and Albany. He also passed several years abroad that included enrollment at the École des Beaux Arts in Paris. In 1882 he began his own practice, and for much of the time until his death, he shared a partnership with his friend Parkman Haven. In John Wheelwright's sonnet, "Father," he refers to the architect as the "dead man who made your mind my home." Although this phrase, a model of poised delicacy, could be meant to draw attention to some of the similarities between the architectural modes of the father and the poetic modes of the son, it literally reminds readers that the son inhabited a city that in large part had been designed by the architectural projections of the father's mind.

Besides numerous private homes, Wheelwright's Boston projects included many of the school houses that later became standard models; the Huntington Avenue Museum; many buildings of the Boston City Hospital; Horticultural Hall at Harvard; the New England Conservatory of Music; a significant part of the Boston Opera House; the pier house at City Point; the Longfellow Bridge; the Cambridge Bridge; and the subway entrances of granite and bronze at the Park Street corner of Boston Common. The humorous Harvard *Lampoon* building, a satirical castle designed by Wheelwright in 1909, was his last finished structure. Barrett Wendell described it as "sturdily honest as the founder who designed it, yet laughing at every turn with freakish gayety and beauty."[11]

Ned Wheelwright was also a writer and scholar. With his brother John, who later became a prominent Boston lawyer serving as assistant corporation counsel for the city, Ned wrote the major part of "Rollo's Adventures in Cambridge," a clever parody much relished by Harvard men of their day. Ned's writings on architectural subjects include *School Architecture: A General Treatise for the Use of Architects and Others* (1901). As a family historian, his most comprehensive work is "A Frontier

Family," originally a paper delivered at the 21 March 1894 meeting of the Colonial Society of Massachusetts, of which Wheelwright was an elected resident member. The study treats the activities of his most famous ancestor, the Reverend John Wheelwright, in great detail. However, he places a much greater emphasis on the minister's role as a pioneer and founder of New England settlements such as Exeter, New Hampshire, and Wells, Maine, than on the part he played in the Antinomian rebellion.

The study also covers the activities of Ned Wheelwright's other direct ancestors, such as the Reverend Wheelwright's son, Colonel Samuel Wheelwright (1635–1700), and his grandson, Colonel John Wheelwright (1664–1745), both of whom held prominent positions in Wells, Maine. Fourth in descent was Jeremiah Wheelwright (1698–1768), who was a lieutenant in the Louisburg expedition. His son, Abraham Wheelwright (1761–1852) served in the Continental army and later as a privateer officer. The study stops with Abraham Wheelwright; it does not include Ned's immediately preceding ancestors, such as his father, George William Wheelwright (1813–79), the founder of a paper company. Ned also partly completed a biography of Esther Wheelwright (granddaughter of the Reverend John Wheelwright), who was held hostage for five years by the Abnaki tribe and later became mother superior of Ursuline nuns in Quebec.[12]

Ned Wheelwright's sense of duty was not limited to his historical and cultural activities. It also resulted in periodic forays into political activism; he was, for instance, a friend and admirer of John Jay Chapman. In many respects he was the classic Mugwump—a reformer of high social position and conservative economic views who was equally contemptuous of corrupt city bosses and demagogues that misled the poor and who wielded influence mainly among the literate upper classes. Barrett Wendell recalled that Wheelwright was anxious to show "how civic work was done for the common good." The obituary in the *Boston Transcript* commented that, during his five-year term as city architect, Wheelwright "had rather an unhappy time, owing to his frequent encounters with political influence in the course of his work for the city. At that time he charged that the power of confirmation vested in the Board of Aldermen resulted in a detriment to the best achievements."[13]

While Ned Wheelwright was at one with Wendell in his devotion to classical art, Harvard, and the New England tradition, his cultural conservatism was contradicted by his emotionalism, his attraction to idealistic political crusading, and his strong belief in justice for the common people. Years after Ned's death, Jack examined some of the letters his father had sent to Wendell; later, Jack wrote the following to Wendell: "[I like his] calmly telling you that you only pretend to like privilege. He loved you and he hated privilege. The two couldn't go together and that was all there was to it."[14] Yet the inconsistent Brahmin also held membership in the most elite social groups in his town: the Somerset Club (famed for its policy of not having members undergo the vulgarity of signing checks), the Union Club, and the Brookline Country Club.

There is evidence that Ned had some difficulty in finding a suitable wife. As a young man just out of Harvard, he wrote to Wendell about his concern that he must be prepared in the future to "support a Mrs. E. M. Wheelwright not in affluence but decently." As his classmates got married, he remained a bachelor. Several years later, at the news that Wendell and a few other college friends had recently become fathers, Ned wrote about how each of the children would probably become good friends, "and I, a snuffy old bachelor, will be known by them as that eccentric old friend of the father of each."[15] Then, at the age of thirty-three, Ned announced his engagement to Elizabeth Boott ("Bessie") Brooks, a woman with suitably unusual characteristics for him. Whereas the Wheelwright family had an uncertain relation to the upper echelons of Boston society, the Brookses were at the pinnacle of the aristocracy, as can be seen in a brief summary of the family tree.

The first American Brooks, Thomas Brooks, arrived from Suffolk, England in 1631. His third generation descendant, Samuel Brooks, married Sarah Boylston (of the Zabdiel Boylston family). Their grandson, the Reverend Edward Brooks (1733–81), married Abigail Brown, descendant of John Cotton. In 1767 Peter Chardon Brooks was born, and both of his daughters by Ann Gorham extended the Brooks family connections in even more prestigious directions: one was wed to Charles Francis Adams, Sr. (the father of Henry, Brooks, and Charles Francis Adams, Jr.) and the other married the famed New England orator Edward Everett. Peter Chardon Brooks became known as the richest man in New England. After his time, the Brooks family was identified with Medford, a suburb of Boston, where the Brookses enjoyed a magnificent estate consisting of a large house and elaborately landscaped grounds with lawns, pools, statuary, and gardens.[16]

Peter Chardon Brooks died in 1849. His son, Edward Brooks (1824–78), married Elizabeth Boott (1799–1865), whose family owned the Boott textile mills. Their son, Francis Brooks (1824–78), married Louise Winsor, an orphan who had been brought up by an aunt on Beacon Hill; they raised a family of six that included Jack's mother, Bessie. Another daughter, Louise, was known to the poet as "Aunt Dolly," and she became a writer of verse with a wide circle of friends active in various cultural pursuits.

The union of the Wheelwrights and Brookses joined what Austin Warren called the "two strains in the New England character: the Yankee trader and the Yankee Saint (often a combination of scholar, priest and poet)."[17] Ned Wheelwright was the descendant of a famous divine, Bessie

Brooks the proud great-granddaughter of Peter Chardon Brooks, wealthiest of the colonial merchant princes. Furthermore, the Wheelwright and Brooks families were connected with many other famous New England lineages. In the home of Bessie and Ned there hung family portraits of two governors of Massachusetts and generals from both the Revolution and the Civil War. This blended heritage of saints, traders, political and military leaders, pioneers, and Brahmins profoundly shaped the mind and the art of the poet John Wheelwright.

Jack's mother, Bessie Brooks, fell through the ice into the "Frog Pond" on Boston Common one cold winter day when she was a small child; as a result, she permanently lost her hearing. She was treated and taught to read lips by Alexander Graham Bell, who was at that time running a school for the deaf in Boston.[18] Her proficiency in lipreading startled everyone and stories about her prowess abounded. In one incident, she deceived a friend's houseguest from England into believing that her hearing was normal; another time, Bessie astounded a dinner guest by her ability to determine the regional accent of a speaker by his facial gestures alone.[19]

Bessie Brooks also compensated for her handicap with a wide reading and aristocratic bearing. From the beginning of her maturity, she was a striking figure, although her eccentricities became more pronounced as she aged. Jack's boyhood friend, Oliver Prescott, Jr., remembers her as a "large, majestic, formidable woman, who moved like a ship under full sail. She terrified me. Her total loss of hearing had affected her voice which was loud, brusk, harsh, and somewhat inarticulate."[20]

Characteristic of Bessie's public demeanor was an incident that occurred when she and Jack's older sister Louise (named for the Aunt Louise called "Dolly") were returning from a European vacation. Bessie suddenly announced to her daughter that she was not going to declare any of the substantial purchases she had made abroad. Louise, aghast, expostulated with her that such a course would be harmful: she would be detected and punished. But Bessie was adamant. When the customs inspector straightaway found the dutiable items in her luggage and started to reprimand her for failing to declare them, Bessie drew herself up to her full height, assumed a regal bearing, and haughtily asked: "Young man, do you know who I am?" After a dramatic pause, she continued: "I am Bessie Brooks of Medford!" The customs inspector's official demeanor instantly crumpled and he exclaimed, "Good heavens! It was your father [an attorney] who saved me from prison!" and forthwith let Bessie and her luggage pass through, scot-free. Jack Wheelwright, in telling this story, always claimed that his mother would never admit that her encounter with this particular inspector was a miraculously lucky coincidence; to the end she insisted that she would have fared as well with any of the customs personnel, once they had learned of her association with the Medford Brookses. Despite his mirth at the absurdity of such behavior, the mystique of the Brooks family was rendered so vivid to Jack by his mother that, as a teenager, he went to court to have his middle name changed from "Tyler" to "Brooks."[21]

Bessie would have been a difficult and demanding companion for any man; but Ned was emotionally high-strung and tended to become too engrossed in his projects. Long-term stress took its toll in 1910 while he was in the middle of building his masterpiece, the $2 million bridge at Hartford, Connecticut. Overwork precipitated a breakdown that was analyzed as melancholia—extreme depression accompanied by hallucinations and delusions. He was secretly committed to a sanitarium in Thompsonville, Connecticut, where his condition deteriorated over a two-year period. Cut off from his friends and family, Ned was unable to answer letters, even those from Wendell, with more than a few stumbling sentences. Wendell later wrote that "dear old Ned . . . had fallen into infirmity from which there was no hope of recovery." He feared that "the mere bodily shell might long survive," but on 14 August 1912 Ned Wheelwright committed suicide.[22]

The suicide had a traumatic impact on his son Jack, who was then a student at St. George's preparatory school in Rhode Island. Jack had always been close to his father and he later wrote that he dated the beginning of his intellectual life "from 1902, my fifth year, when my father read me *Midsummer Night's Dream* and *The Tempest*."[23] Possibly the two-year separation from his father is reflected in the pleading lines of the sonnet "Father":

> Come home. Wire a wire of warning without words.
> Come home and talk to me again, my first friend.[24]

Jack became extremely dependent on the Anglican religious leaders at St. George's, a sister and brother named Emily and John Diman. Then he underwent a mystical religious conversion that he later described as "an experience like St. Paul's or one of those in Mauriac."[25] Like Robert Lowell thirty years later, he repudiated Unitarianism in favor of a more conservative and traditional faith. Whereas Lowell became a Roman Catholic, Wheelwright chose Anglicanism and declared his wish to become a priest.

In later years Jack criticized Unitarianism as a debased form of religion: "As once and for all King's Chapel [the birthplace of Unitarianism] had freed the Brahmins from the fear of damnation, so the Brahmins supposed that they themselves were saved."[26] Jack identified his father's fate with his having succumbed to a nihilism associated with the belief, very much like that of Henry Adams, that the cultural values he held so dear were being destroyed by the dissipation of forces in the chaos of the modern world. Jack certainly believed that his father's Unitarianism had been too weak a bulwark against engulfment by this nihilistic vision. In Jack's eyes, Ned became a tragic figure plagued by a discontinuity between his spoken beliefs and the possibilities for participating in society, that is, between word and deed.

That Jack came to this assessment is indicated in an autobiographical poem first published in 1940: "A Small Prig in a Big Square." He describes a scene in which he, his father, and his elder brother March are returning from Unitarian services. Jack expresses his hope that someday the world will be clean and beautiful like "a nice Boys' Outing Class in Franklin Park" in Boston. Expecting his father to agree, Jack is startled by the response:

> You do, do you? Well then, you are mistaken.
> The world cannot slide backwards, like a toy electric train.
> Something's going to break; but the clergymen won't break it.
> There'll be more common people (more religion, maybe)
> more distribution, more production, and more recreation;
> but there will be damned less Idealism.
> Get down to earth. I'm glad of any change.
> But I shan't live to see a change that matters.[27]

In the closing three lines, Jack associates his father's nihilistic vision with a premonition of premature death. He contrasts his own stunned reaction with that of his less sensitive brother:

> Dizzier, numb-er, I wondered, when *would* Pa die,—
> he smiling at me like that; and to you, my laughing
> brother, March. You, who were not an intellectual.[28]

From a young age, Jack Wheelwright had been precocious and highly unusual. In physical appearance he had many features of his mother, especially her prominent nose. (Jack referred to this as the "Boott nose" and said that it came from an ancestor named "Wright Boott.") But Jack was intellectually and emotionally closer to his father, with all the qualities that had earned the elder Wheelwright the sobriquet "wheelratic." Jack's classmate, Oliver Prescott, Jr., recalls that at prep school Jack was intellectual and imaginative, with a strong aesthetic sense and deep personal religious emotions: "He was utterly independent and unselfconscious. His world was his own, through which the experiences of the outer world passed like moving pictures—influencing him, of course, in many ways—but never altering the fundamental integrity of his unique point of view."[29] Jack was often in the company of his father during his pre–boarding school years. Together they shared an appreciation of the wit and fantasy of Lewis Carroll and Edward Lear. Jack's fascination with these writers would continue throughout his life, becoming a component of his own artistic sensibility.

Benjamin Kittridge, Jr., a friend who was two forms behind him at St. George's, noticed the difference between Jack and the other boys as soon as he arrived. Jack had an "eccentricity that verged on madness," which Kittridge thought might be shared by some other members of the Wheelwright family. As a group, they seemed to him somehow misplaced in the twentieth-century world and he suspected, not unjustifiably, that the inner life of the Wheelwright family was a tragic melodrama.[30] As she aged, Bessie Wheelwright became increasingly preposterous in her aristocratic pretensions. Jack's older sister Louise, after a late marriage to S. Foster Damon, fell mentally ill with delusions and other infirmities that required long-term confinement. Then there was the older brother, Edmund March Wheelwright, Jr., known as "March," whose inability to carry on the family traditions brought embarrassment to both his mother and Jack.

March was born on 28 April 1891 and was educated at Middlesex School, Noble School, and Greenough School. Although he had cut a rather dashing figure at Harvard when he attended as a member of the class of 1914, he was forced to leave after two years because of academic failure. When World War I broke out, March enlisted. While in the service, he married Ruth Nickerson, whose social status Bessie regarded as being too low for her son. When March returned from the war, he tried to cut himself off from the rest of the family, and there were stories about his eating dinner with the servants in the Wheelwright kitchen. In a letter to Barrett Wendell, Bessie remarked that she had been grieving deeply over March's "many failures" and had "suffered keenly." She then added in his defense that "he does not come from hardworking perse-vering stock on my side, [and] he takes after my people. His ancestors were for the last five generations not working people." Eventually March went to work in the cotton mills at an ordinary job, but after three years he switched and entered the brokerage business in Boston. Finally, plagued by alcoholism, he simply retired around 1936 at the age of forty-five, and, with financial support from his mother, engaged in farming at Medfield, Massachusetts, until his death in 1946.[31]

While Bessie was absorbed in March's difficult transition to manhood, Jack pursued an erratic career as a student at St. George's. Indeed, it is hard to imagine how he could have been accepted into Harvard College, except by virtue of family connections. The grades submitted from St. George's to Harvard were "B–" in English, "D–" in French, "D" in algebra, and "C" in physics.[32] On the other hand, Jack's school activities were exceptional, especially in his senior year when he was president of the dramatic association, chairman of the governing committee of the St. George's Society, and editor-in-chief of the *Dragon*, the literary maga-zine. He was also a member of the civics club; with his debating partner Prescott, he spoke frequently on current political events. Prescott, Kittridge, and Jack participated in the production of the school play, W. S. Gilbert's *Foggarty's Fairy*, in which Jack played Miss De Vere, a determined husband hunter.[33]

Perhaps the poor grades were counteracted by Jack's personal rapport with the institution's teaching and religious staff, especially the charismatic brother and sister who were the founders of St. George's. Emily Diman was a beautiful woman and John Diman had an extraordinary presence—his massive beard gave him a physical appearance that suggested to the young boys a combination of Zeus and the Prophet Isaiah. Together they set the tone and behavior for the Episcopal institution, which was organized on the traditional English model and formal to the point that everyone wore a dark suit each day to dinner.[34] John Diman told Bessie that Jack "was one of the best pupils in the school and quite the most interesting one."[35] And Jack rapidly formed attachments to older men affiliated with the school: Joseph Coletti, the sculptor who did the decorations for the chapel, and several theologians who prepared him for the Anglican communion while he was there—James S. O. Huntington, Spence Burton, and Frederic Fitts.[36]

To the literary magazine *Dragon*, Jack contributed sixteen poems and four prose pieces. Most of these are nature poems that combine traditional romantic attitudes with classical references typical of juvenilia. Several exhibit a tendency to refer to the internal drama in his life by poetic symbols and indirection, and the impact of his father's suicide is refracted through themes and imagery of death. Two of the poems, "Things Other than the World's" and "To the Moon," have as their subject a mourner. Two explicitly religious poems, "To Myself" and "A Lament," argue the need for a belief in God as a necessary means of achieving stability for the tired, mournful, and floundering soul.[37]

To admire and seek to emulate a man whose life crumbled in a tragic finale is indeed a complex fate. The suicide of the father was an enduring source of anxiety to the son. On Jack's bureau was a photograph of Ned; on the mantle stood two bronze Empire candlesticks that his father had prepared for the frontals of the Cambridge bridge. In normal discourse Jack rarely mentioned the circumstances of death. Usually he talked with pride about his father's architectural achievements, or made a point of mentioning that his father won prominence and popularity in the most exclusive Boston circles through his brilliance and forceful personality independent of the Brahmins' routine acceptance of him by virtue of his marriage to the well-born Bessie Brooks. But the suicide was the impetus for Jack's religious conversion and tribulations, and Ned's attitudes were sometimes reproduced in Jack's cultural and political values. In Jack's poetry, the enigma of Ned Wheelwright was an indirect theme and pervasive presence. Jack's decision to attend Harvard further solidified the son's emotional ties to his dead father.

When he arrived in Cambridge in 1916, he was full of ambitions that were more than just literary. Bessie Wheelwright wrote Barrett Wendell in the summer about Jack's intention to matriculate in September and asked Wendell to serve as his adviser: "He is such a charming companion —and such an exquisite little man, he goes to one's heart. I hope, Barrett, you are not too busy to give Jack some of your time, for we know no other who could fill your place."[38] Wendell, however, responded that recent illness precluded his becoming Jack's adviser. (Wendell retired in June 1917 and died on 8 February 1921.) Soon after, Jack sent Wendell a series of questions about the appropriate courses to be taken during the first year. He expressed his desire to learn several languages because he wanted "to go to Europe as soon as possible after Peace is restored to study the junk heaps war will leave." He also explained that fine arts and government were his preferred nonlanguage courses: "Government will provide a proper vantage ground from which to study Europe after the war. My interest in Fine Arts is, of course, natural."[39] Eventually he declared his major to be medieval and Renaissance literature. His adviser was the theologian George Foot Moore, who gave him special permission to take courses at the Divinity School.

Despite his enthusiasm for learning, Jack received "D's" in his two favorite subjects, fine arts and government, for his first year at Harvard. In comparative literature, English, and history he received "C's," and there was little improvement in the years that followed. He was almost always under one sort of probation or another from the administration, and the bulk of the material in his file at the Harvard registrar's office is composed of complaints about missed examinations and appointments. On 8 June 1920, Jack officially withdrew from Harvard. He made an attempt to recoup at summer school and another effort in the fall of 1920, but a memo dated 14 November 1920 from H. A. Yeomans to Dean J. H. Roper states that the "administrative Board voted yesterday to require John Brooks Wheelwright to withdraw."

A biographical memoir by his literary friend Matthew Josephson explains the event that precipitated the expulsion. Students in Jack's chemistry class were in the habit of copying each other's notebooks secretly. Jack, as a form of protest, decided to copy one in the open—in front of the instructor's eyes. He was then warned not to miss any more class sessions. Nevertheless, he soon managed to do so and sent a note to the dean on 26 October 1920, asking for an excuse. The note stated that he was absent from chemistry class because of illness brought on by a movie: "Acute nausia [sic] because 'Way Down East' excited me. I was sick one hour." The "nausia" note apparently infuriated the dean and over the years the legend spread that Jack was the only person who had ever been expelled from Harvard for misspelling a word.[40]

Yet this humorous anecdote about Jack actually masked a serious crisis, for much personal and family grief was caused by his inability to graduate. Bessie withdrew her pledge to send him to Oxford for advanced studies. Furthermore, the unfortunate episode was only a climax to a whole series of unhappy events at Harvard, the most troubling of which was the way he permitted himself to become disoriented by World War I. For the rest of his life, he sought to compensate for his failure to live up to his pacifist principles when the time of crisis had actually occurred.

On the day World War I began, it happened that Jack, still a prep school student, was in Germany on a walking tour in the Thuringian forest. When he returned to St. George's, he published an essay that communicated nothing more than aloofness and detachment about the mobilization of the German troops that he had witnessed. "It was whimsically sad; that is all."[41] Although the records of St. George's show that he participated in the school's military drill (as the company's quartermaster sergeant), his letters to Barrett Wendell in the summer of 1916 indicate a political neutrality bordering on a pro-German position.

He argued that Germany's violation of the neutrality of Belgium was a "bold and honest sweeping aside of an iniquitous contrivance of the craven and dishonest diplomacy of Britain." His view was that the Belgians had no genuine autonomy and that the only hope for world order was a balance of power among responsible large nations. He asserted that peace would not come from "Tribunals of Arbitration, or in any other engine of wishy-washy sentimentality and premature idealism." Rather, peace could only be achieved through the absorption of all small states and underdeveloped regions by five or six great empires that would "righteously and conscientiously live in obedience to Duty—'Stern daughter of the voice of God.'" He concluded that he would live to see Germany honored with England and Rome, and "I shall live to know that America did right when she held back from the great struggle, desiring first of all to learn on which side lay the right." He also sketched out the personal philosophy that would sustain his political outlook through the 1920s: "One thing America will learn from Germany is that just as freedom sprang from the Renaissance, so that if you build cultural aristocracy upon political democracy your structure falls. American democracy will fall, unless here, as in Germany, culture is given to the rich and poor alike."[42]

Some uncertainty surrounds his precise actions after the United States entered the war, but there is no doubt that he changed his views to the extent of seeking some sort of participation. His classmate Malcolm Cowley recalls that Jack was not against the war at that point and would have served in the army, except that he was given the equivalent of a 4-F classification. In a memoir composed with Alvin Rosenfeld, S. Foster Damon wrote that at the outset of the war Jack put aside his ideas about a possible vocation in the priesthood and enlisted in the Harvard Reserve Officer's Training Corps. This required a difficult routine of intensive training in the summer of 1917. However, the corps was not recognized by the government and the war ended before he was called into service. In another version of the episode, the poet and critic Winfield Townley Scott, who knew both Wheelwright and Damon, claimed that Damon was the instructor at bayonet drill for the corps. Scott reported the following anecdote: "After regarding the Wheelwright method with a bayonet, Damon said: 'Well, *you'll* be killed right away.' But Wheelwright was spared army service, and vice versa."[43]

Jack's own explanation of his behavior at the time appears in a letter he sent to his St. George's and Harvard classmate, Benjamin Kittridge, Jr., about 1921:

> You know how hysterical it [the war] made everyone, you had some taste of the personal dilemmas it brings before one, you know the mere physical horror and the disgusting uprightness of it, but you were spared the sensation of its spiritual horror, its revolting uprightness which you appreciate must overwhelm the pacifist. Action is the relief at such a time, but the family did not warm to the Italian Ambulance, the only opportunity which presented itself. Relief for me came through religion. But Christ does not spend all His time comforting and I was unhappy, troubled by doubts, by the times, by mere youthful weltschmerz.[44]

The letter to Kittridge also describes a number of painful personal conflicts at Harvard: the loss of some friends, some rivalries, a few instances of social ostracism. His recollections of these, along with his strong feelings about the death of his friend Ned Couch in military camp in 1917, supplied the background material for his 1938 sonnet sequence *Mirrors of Venus*. But a major source of compensation for such unhappy moments in Cambridge was the literary activity he undertook in connection with the Harvard *Lampoon* and the Harvard Poetry Society.

Working with the *Lampoon* had a special importance for Jack because he was the son of one of its founders. In fact, during the World War I period, his uncle, John Tyler Wheelwright, emerged from retirement to be listed on the board of editors along with his nephew. In 1918–19, Jack contributed at least five times, including a lengthy verse review of the Ziegfeld Follies coauthored with Horace Howard Furnace Jayne and the poetic prologue to the "Versailles Number" of the *Lampoon*.[45] He also served as literary editor of the *Advocate* and was a member of the Stylus Club. But his paramount literary preoccupation was the Harvard Poetry Society, and the culmination of that experience came with the publication of *Eight More Harvard Poets*, three years after he was expelled from the college. This volume marks his emergence as a poet and signals his first attempt to forge a world of myth and symbol with which to intervene in the moral life of his times.

3 · THE DOUBTING APOSTLE

Wheelwright's poetry assumed many of its noteworthy qualities from the intellectual training and psychological turmoil prior to and during his Harvard years. His regional loyalties were heightened by his family's traditions; his emotional responses were deepened by his father's misfortune. However, two new developments in his literary evolution occurred in the 1920s. First, his contributions to *Eight More Harvard Poets* (1923) demonstrated to a small layer of the literary intelligentsia that he was a poet of estimable skill. Second, his five long mythic poems of the middle and late 1920s indicate a susceptibility to overly personal and hermetic modes of expression.

The Harvard poems in the first group exhibit a stringent lucidity that would always be characteristic of his finest writing; but the group of religiomythic poems, despite its failures, is more characteristic of the dominant temper of modernism in the 1920s. Eliot, Pound, Crane, Joyce, and others were never unconcerned with the public world; their tendency was to aestheticize their social views, transforming political realities into private languages, myths, and symbolic paradigms that were intellectually more manageable for them. Whereas Eliot's use in *The Waste Land* of rites and rituals from anthropological studies like *The Golden Bough* struck a major chord among his contemporaries, Wheelwright's religiomythic poems seem to have been a diversion to byroads of esoteric symbolism. To a reader of non-Christian sensibility, their allegorical structures seem oddly flat and cumbersome, their tone overly portentous, and their allusions too demanding, even though the themes are public, not private. Channeling his imaginative energies into such efforts absorbed him in the 1920s, but he only dabbled at them episodically in the Great Depression. Wheelwright's deliberate restriction of his imaginative scope may well have been symptomatic of a narcissism that he sought to exorcise through his art. This chapter will begin with an examination of the craft in Wheelwright's Harvard poems; it will also explore the contradictions in his personal life that engendered his subsequent digression to arcane theology, as well as the shifting factors at the end of the decade that produced a new relation to modernism in the 1930s.

The official editors of *Eight More Harvard Poets* were Jack Wheelwright's friends Robert Hillyer and S. Foster Damon, both of whom served as English instructors at Harvard. Financial backing came from his Aunt Dolly Brooks and he himself took responsibility for most of the behind-the-scenes work, including the solicitation of material and the arrangement of publicity. Under the pseudonym "Dorian Abbot," he wrote a preface to the volume that presented a detailed history of poetic activity at Harvard since the 1876 publication of the first book of student verse. In this preface he characterized the 1917 predecessor volume, *Eight Harvard Poets* (featuring work by Damon, Hillyer, Dos Passos, Cummings, Cuthbert Wright, Stewart Mitchell, Dudley Poore, and William Norris), as being "in the full flood of modernist and Georgian fashion."[1]

In Jack's favorite review of the new collection, Hart Crane pursued a similar method in differentiating among the eight Harvard poets in the new group. In Crane's view, Norman Cabot, Grant Code, Jack Merton, Joel Rogers, R. Cameron Rogers, and Royall Snow could be categorized as "Georgians" because they used traditional forms to depict familiar sights and sounds of country life. But Crane sensed that Wheelwright and Malcolm Cowley stood apart from the others; he furthermore declared Wheelwright to be the more dynamic.[2]

That Wheelwright's work, even at the age of twenty-five, was distinctive in craft and freshness of perception was recognizable to others besides Crane. In the *New York Herald-Tribune*, Milton Raison wrote that "there is only one poet in the book who has a real glint of genius. He is John Brooks Wheelwright. . . . There is no classical deliberation in his verse. It is all inspired, cynical, earnest, twisted and everything poetry should be." A review by the novelist Hervey Allen, who at that time was teaching in Charleston, argued that Wheelwright's poems contained "more of thought" than the rest of the book put together: "One catches now and then in his poems that noise from beyond our outer atmosphere which scars the ears and visualizes him as that portent of modern times, 'the wise young man' whose grasp of facts is just a bit disconcerting to elders who still keep a little of the Victorian rose color in the upper portion of their bifocal lorgnettes."[3]

Almost all the reviewers of *Eight More Harvard Poets* took notice of Wheelwright, but not always with such admiration. The critic Harold Acton described him as a "disillusioned aesthete and a poseur" whose "gestures are diverting although occasionally he deserves a slapping." Another charged him with "blasphemy" and "sensationalism" for certain passages in "Rococo Crucifix":[4]

> Guarded by bursts of glory, golden rays,—
> Christ, when I see thee hanging there alone
> In ivory upon an ebon throne;
> Like Pan, pard-girded, chapleted with bays;
> I kiss thy mouth, I see thee in a haze,
> But not of tears, of heartbreak there is none . . .

Is it, oh, Sufferer, my heart is stone?
Am I, in truth, the Judas who betrays?

To hang in shame above a gory knoll,
To die of scorn upon a splintered pole,—
This was not beautiful, I know, for thee . . .
Would I have whispered upon Calvary,
"An interesting silhouette, there, see!"
While God groaned in the dark night of his soul?[5]

What the critic failed to see is the utter sincerity of the poem: it is a critique of certain religious attitudes, but from a wholly religious point of view. The first half of the sonnet describes a crucifix so beautiful that the poet is moved to kiss it. But this act causes the poet to wonder how such feelings are possible in light of the event that the crucifix symbolizes, the tortured death of Christ on the cross. Because he has experienced sensual beauty in the first stanza from such ugliness and pain, he starts to doubt his motives and to suspect that he might be a Judas. Philosophically, "Rococo Crucifix" is intended to contradict the famous equation of truth and beauty in John Keats's "Ode on a Grecian Urn," for the truth of Christ's suffering was not at all beautiful.[6] At the same time, the poet never renounces faith in God; rather, he affirms his faith in Christ by critically scrutinizing his love of religious ornamentation. The title may be "Rococo Crucifix," but the style, abundant in conceits and unusual similes, is pure baroque.

What differentiated Jack's verse, starting at the time of these Harvard poems, is not simply such unexpected use of theological themes. In "Dr. Rimmer's Hamilton on Commonwealth Avenue and Arlington Street," a poem about a famous sculpture in Boston, he brings his uncommon perception to bear on regional materials:

Granite unsharded by the fires of revolt,
granite refined to the subtlety of a porcelain goddess of mercy—
common sense Hamilton!
Under the elms' sex-partite vaulting
opposing the agitation of Washington on horseback
stands Hamilton,—

He has the stodgy dignity of a tobacco Indian
with his pompous calf stuck out after the Bourbon manner;
but his shoulders, pressing forward with the elemental impulse
of a figurehead upon a Yankee clipper
(the *Invincible*, you know, that rounds the Horn in no time)
shows us Hamilton, the genius of the Yankee
Ship of State.

> The sculptor, Rimmer,
> as he chipped in a crisp mastery the medallion on the pedestal,
> thought, no doubt, of Thorvaldsen;
> but his nostrils smarted with the native fragrance of ships' carving,
> with the nostalgic smells of China hanging over the warm wharves
>   of Salem
> as he pounded the *esprit* with a mallet and a chisel
> into the laboured, bare achievement of the staunch little spine
> of Federalist Hamilton, the arrogant bastard under a prophetic
>   mantle—
> Hamilton,
> the untroubled wisdom that speaks behind the mask of Washington,
> Hamilton, voice of Sovereignty.[7]

The middle stanza especially is remarkable for its clarity, exactness, and concreteness of detail; yet the poem is not pure description for it conveys a feeling of harsh, unresolved political complexity that mitigates the dominant aestheticism of its perspective. Behind the precise delineations of the statue and its setting is a pattern of historic references that, even at this early date, loosely affiliate Wheelwright's technique to a social mode of thought that would find wider expression in the depression. The sculptor Rimmer aspires to the neoclassical modes of Thorvaldsen; because he works in the atmosphere of Boston's commercial seaport, however, his Hamilton assumes the characteristics of a figurehead from a Yankee clipper. Hamilton's biography is limned by direct and oblique references to his illegitimate birth ("the arrogant bastard"), his ambitious rise to power ("the *Invincible* you know, that rounds the Horn in no time"), his aspiration to strengthen the powers of the federal government ("the genius of the Yankee / Ship of State"), and his opposition to the French Revolution ("Granite unsharded by fires of revolt").

The prototype for such a poem can more likely be found in the work of Amy Lowell than in that of Eliot, Pound, or the expatriate poets who were gaining a following at the time. Lowell, in fact, was a friend of his Aunt Dolly and he took advantage of the connection to introduce her to young writers such as Matthew Josephson, Kenneth Burke, John Dos Passos, Damon, and Cowley.[8] Eliot, by contrast, seems to have been the object of Jack's scorn, although his dubious criticisms of Eliot may also have been motivated by jealousy at the success of a rival Harvard poet and Anglican convert. For example, he insists in an unpublished memoir written in the early 1930s that Eliot's poems are "nothing but craft" because he borrowed diverse materials that he grafted onto his own writings. Damon, he claims, had shown him "line for line" the origins of Eliot's verses, after which they "melted into vacuity." Eliot's oeuvre, he argues, is based on passages lifted from literature for literary effect: "In most cases it said that somebody else had said something like what Eliot wanted to say. The method of citation was faulty, whether it was a citation from other authors, or citation of the lives of Sweeney and Mrs. Porter whom I did not know, whom I was not curious to know, and whom, I thought, Eliot didn't know either."⁹

Wheelwright's criticism may obliquely refer to Eliot's famous argument for the "extinction of personality" in his 1917 essay, "Tradition and the Individual Talent." Wheelwright's claim that Eliot failed to properly digest and transform his literary sources can easily be refuted, but the nature of his complaint provides useful insight into Wheelwright's own endeavor. Indeed, in reading Wheelwright's verse, one is continuously teased by the suggestion of possible models and influences that are almost instantaneously subverted. "Rococo Crucifix" at first suggests the outrageous aestheticism of Walter Pater and George Moore, but this element is rapidly neutralized by the poem's emotional intensity. The clarity of "Dr. Rimmer's Hamilton" may invoke Amy Lowell's imagism for a moment; in this instance, however, busy, involuted sentences eliminate the possibility of any "economy of language." Emersonian themes are activated by a number of poems, but rarely does Wheelwright achieve Emerson's structural elegance. If Blake, Milton, or someone from the surrealist school is invoked in one poem, the influence is quickly called into question by another poem, remarkably different in form and content. So Wheelwright's poetry is very much like Eliot's in that it reaches out and touches many poets, echoing all sorts of things; and there is no doubt that whatever Wheelwright visibly borrows from others undergoes tortuous transformation. Whether or not it is true that tradition is ultimately victorious in Eliot, it is evident that Wheelwright usually subordinates tradition to the eccentricities of his personality.

Harvard poems such as "Dr. Rimmer's Hamilton," striking in ideas as well as craft, caused Hart Crane to single out Wheelwright's remarkable ability to fuse "ideas with such subjective intensity" that poetry of an extremely "rare quality" in the United States was the result. As early as 1923, Crane recognized his contemporary's generous intellectual and emotional endowment and the brilliant stringency of which his technique was sometimes capable. But he did not live long enough to provide an assessment of the growth of Wheelwright's imaginative power as it fixed with zealous devotion on the two great passions of his life: first, heterodox Christianity in his immediate post-Harvard years; second, socialist politics in the 1930s. The first of these emerged as a resolution to the internal disharmonies that he experienced during the 1920s.

Throughout that decade, he walked a tightrope between the two poles of his personality. The values that divided him bore a distinct resemblance to the contradictory elements that plagued his father: a conservative "loyal pride of race" and a radical responsiveness to injustice combined with a zest for living. Jack saw himself as a guardian of the finest cultural traditions of his ancestors and sought to sustain his Brahmin loyalties in their purest form through his ardent Anglican religious faith. Yet a natural enthusiasm for life and a burning desire for justice frequently propelled him toward rebellious positions.

This apparent schism between conservative values and radical responses makes Wheelwright's behavior during the 1920s seem like a chronicle of contradictions. He expressed his genuine sympathy for the overthrow of czarism in Russia by naming his living quarters, a sort of cooperative for Harvard aesthetes, "The Soviet," and purchasing stationery so engraved.[10] He became outraged when the Harvard *Lampoon* published an anti-Semitic attack on his teacher, Harold Laski, who had defended the 1919 police strike, but in private letters and even some unpublished essays he did not hesitate to criticize alleged characteristics of the "Jewish race."[11]

When the Italian anarchists Sacco and Vanzetti were sentenced to death in Boston, he seethed at what he felt to be the legal lynching and wrote part of "Come Over and Help Us," his most acrimonious poem about the hypocrisy of the proper Bostonians. But he also laughed at his friend Malcolm Cowley for eulogizing the anarchists as the "dago Christs." Wheelwright regarded the working class as part of the "philistine" element in society and resented their idealization. The issue to him was that justice had not been done, and he felt that writers had a responsibility to get angry about the case, for "justice is the chief concern of the professional classes."[12]

Jack's uncommon view was evidenced elsewhere. Even though his erratic behavior as a Harvard student might suggest a lack of respect for the institution, his love and admiration for Barrett Wendell, its most notorious archconservative, was unaffected. Around 1920 he wrote: "I cannot tell you how much your friendliness means to me, who lack the valuable influence of older men. You are a link with Papa." After Wendell's death, Jack spoke favorably of him in both the *Freeman* and in the preface to *Eight More Harvard Poets*.[13]

Socially, Jack participated in the teas and cultural events of the highest circles of Boston society; yet he periodically precipitated an uproar. He appeared at a fancy dress ball at the Copley Plaza in "his own far-from-fresh pajamas and dressing gown, carrying his battered toothbrush, with an old-fashioned bathroom chain around his neck, complete with wooden handle."[14]

Through frequent trips to New York and several sojourns in Europe, Jack developed close associations with expatriate and modernist writers, especially those who appeared in *Broom* and *Secession*, but he never shared their widespread disenchantment with the possibilities of American literature nor did he assimilate some of their antisocial and apolitical attitudes. Lewis Mumford recalls Jack as a vehement, self-assured, and somewhat condescending participant in intellectual gatherings in a

MacDougal Street restaurant in the Village; these involved Van Wyck Brooks, the Irish-American critic Ernest Boyd, and Walter Fuller, managing editor of the *Freeman*. But he preferred to go carousing in Village speakeasies with Malcolm Cowley, Kenneth Burke, Hart Crane, Allen Tate, and E. E. Cummings. Somewhere along the way, his New York friends gave him the nickname "Wheels." One day S. Foster Damon took him to the Village home of William Slater Brown, a young writer and close friend of Cummings. Jack stayed overnight and then came back for several long visits. When he brought Brown and his wife Susan to meet his mother in Cambridge, Bessie was quite relieved to see that at least some of Jack's New York friends spoke English well, had good manners, and were decently dressed.

Jack's own behavior occasionally took inspiration from Dadaists and surrealists like Tristan Tzara and Louis Aragon whom he encountered in Europe. Matthew Josephson first met Jack during the Christmas week of 1922 while visiting Malcolm and Peggy Cowley in Giverny, France. At that time Jack volunteered to finance and edit several issues of *Secession*, a European-based little magazine that Josephson had founded along with Gorham B. Munson. Jack and Josephson immediately went to work on *Secession* number four, astounding Munson by cutting ninety-seven out of one hundred lines from a poem they disliked by Richard Ashton. Then, in early 1923, Jack edited numbers five and six by himself in Florence. Not only did he prove himself remarkably weak in proofreading (especially spelling), but he "revised" (in effect, butchered) Hart Crane's poem "To Faustus and Helen." When he returned to New York, Munson was fuming; but Crane, with an understanding gesture that Jack never forgot, accepted his apology gracefully and forgave him. In 1925 Jack and Josephson, along with Cowley, Burke, and Brown, continued their literary antics by publishing one issue of *Aesthete 1925*, a satire of H. L. Mencken's *American Mercury*, which had recently been lampooning the avant-garde.[15] Yet when he came to write the poem most symptomatic of this bohemian expatriate phase, "North Atlantic Passage" (1924), it was a pretentious, grave, and anguished religiophilosophical allegory reflecting none of the levity of such episodes. The contradiction between moral temperament and avant-garde sensibility was as yet unresolved. Poetic symbolism became the ground on which a reconciliation would be attempted.

Although "North Atlantic Passage" is usually noted for its surrealist technique, it is in part an attack on those poets who adulate surrealism, dadaism, or other art forms divorced from an acceptable philosophic substance. He posits that the basic "enigma" in life is that of "the One and the Many," the relationship of the individual to the rest of humankind. In the poem he refutes various ways that others have proposed to resolve this relationship, solutions that rise and dissolve like waves in the tex-

ture of the verse. The poem follows a spiritual movement that seems to
be Wheelwright's own. The reader is taken through a first stage, when a
solution is sought in the study of past history and philosophic specula-
tion. Next the answer is sought in hedonism ("enjoying the distractions
of the present show"). This effort results in a crisis, because the indi-
vidual sacrifices self-consciousness and becomes a "part of what he
sees." He therefore is "dissolved into the external world" and feels "an
enigma to himself." As a result, a search for God begins: "It is then that
he turns toward Authority to bring him assurance."

Yet the search for authority is insufficient to resolve the contradiction
created when the poet first sacrifices his inner self to achieve harmony
with his environment. Wheelwright concludes that the proper relation
to "external Authority" (God and church) can only be achieved after "in-
ternal Authority" (conscience) is acquired. Wheelwright ends the poem
with a gnostic call to abandon all external forms of aid. The reader is left
with the image of a figure stumbling away from a physical environment
—suggestive of the interior of a church—in the direction of the mys-
terious jewel of human essence:

> We must find the needle in the Camel's Haystack
> so put out the light.
> —Lead us on there, by deadened surfaces
> over faded, imitation marble
> past our incessant reflection, in cracked mirrors
> under dusky, wax-dripping chandeliers
> dustily swaying, to and fro
> a-glow with crescent, broken crystal.
>   Lead us from opalescent
>   rainbows, through rainbows
>   to black opal—[16]

The final lines render the movement of the poem unexpectedly circular,
for the words "opal-black" and "rainbows" appear in the opening stanza
as well.

The poem is distinguished by gothic imagery, but the technique is
more precisely the polyphonic prose that Amy Lowell made famous in
her book *Can Grande's Castle* (1918), in which she intermixed long
flowing cadences of oratorical prose with rhymed and unrhymed free
verse, traditional lyrics, and dramatic dialogues.[17] "North Atlantic Pas-
sage" also invites comparison with *The Waste Land*. Both attack the
mindless sensualism of the modern world and reject poetry as insuffi-
cient epistemology. Yet what Eliot depicts as a dismal human condition
almost impossible to eradicate, Wheelwright views as a perceptual prob-
lem. His poem expresses more forthrightly than Eliot's the view that a
resolute struggle will lead to a clarification and understanding of sorts.

Technically, "North Atlantic Passage" is distinguished from *The Waste Land* in that Wheelwright's allegory is all-pervasive, never blending into realism of any sort. Whereas Eliot integrates episodes from daily life into his myth, Wheelwright restricts himself to symbolic acts and images. These coalesce around the theme of "lead us not into imitation" as the poet, searching for the "black opal" of his soul, confronts a sea tumultuous with fake jewels, monsters emblematic of his own psychic agony, and characters and scenery from myth and fiction. The title "North Atlantic Passage" confirms that Wheelwright's expatriate adventures precipitated the crisis analyzed in the poem, a crisis, he concludes, that can only be resolved by turning inward as a prerequisite to outward action of a more effective type. The poem has a preparatory character, but prophesies that the imagination will be the arena for the interaction of contradictory moral and emotional impulses.

Meanwhile, Jack was developing political views as sharply idiosyncratic as his other attitudes. In the pages of the *Freeman*, he analyzed the ideas of Thomas Hobbes and announced a more-or-less conservative anarchist philosophy. On the one hand, he distrusted the authoritarian nature of the state and argued against the "Thomas Hobbeses among us" who cry for "Law and Order! Authority and Force!" in times of strikes and other disorders. He believed that "men of gentle courage" ought to point out to them that "unless you are wrong, the nihilists are right; unless law and order exist by reason of something stronger than authority and force—convenience for instance—they could not exist at all."

On the other hand, Jack despised theories of popular rule. He denounced as a "subterfuge" the doctrine of sovereignty of the people, which he believed to be a special problem in the United States: "Since the days of Andrew Jackson that doctrine has meant the sovereignty of demagogues. Its real import is tyrannical."[18] Opposed to what he thought was the inherent despotism of the state and equally skeptical of the ability of the masses to govern themselves, Wheelwright's main hope for humanity centered on his belief in the revival of poets as a priestly cast who could provide ethical guidance. In a sense, this view was "Emersonian." But Jack's personal life, with his proclivity to respond intensely to the social environment around him, hardly resembled that of the insulated sage of Concord. An unpublished journal Jack kept during his period of residence in Italy shows a surprising openness to the fascist political movement of Mussolini. It also chronicles adventures in whorehouses and hints at homosexual experiments, all undertaken from the conviction that "it is not enough to read the *Satyricon*; one must do everything and leave no cherished and unacted impulses about for one to stumble over later."[19]

Yet a personal catastrophe of a rather common sort cut short these bold Italian adventures into the unfamiliar. While he was abroad, the woman he had been courting at home left him for another suitor; for all the sexual libertinism recorded in his Italian notebook, he still hoped to make "a good marriage." In a painful letter, he bared his emotions: "I hope I shall never again deserve such punishment as you have given me, for everyone deserves what comes to him in this life. . . . Why you saw fit to do it I do not understand, but it is also characteristic of life that I was out late at a ball last night and am hardly fit to receive such news as you have made for me. . . . You say he is on the spot. I admit I am in Florence. No, I shall never be a Johnny-on-the-spot and shall be late to my own funeral, as I am now at what might have been my engagement."[20] Jack's excruciating feelings were later transformed into a set of poems called "Slow Curtain" and "Quick Curtain," in which the ending of the affair is viewed from two different perspectives. The first poem describes an actor and actress who have written their own script for a play they intend to perform, which will end in a love scene. But despite the high quality of the play, the performers become paralyzed and fail to carry out the final action—a kiss. The second poem presents imagery that objectifies their emotional agony—floating walls and the sensation of being marionettes with tangled strings—but this time the suffering leads to knowledge:

> Light pierced the leaves and flecked the mirrors;
> clear and clearer, and more clear
> the sun swam through the lessening rain.
> We had grown wise in all things before love.[21]

In Florence Jack expanded his range of cultural experiences by association with Bernard Berenson, Mabel Dodge, and Muriel Draper. When he returned to Boston, he attended architectural school at Massachusetts Institute of Technology, like his father, and wrote in letters about the importance of a poet having some alternative means of support. However, his career in architecture was irregular from the beginning. Without a bachelor's degree, he had to matriculate as a special student. Then, despite his seriousness about the subject, Jack's projects turned out to be baffling to all, including his teachers. Elroy Webber, a fellow architectural student at the time, remembers Jack's fascination with Victoriana, then quite unfashionable. The two took long walks together through Boston's decaying brownstone districts, the south and north ends, State Street, and the downtown wharves. He guided another friend, *Hound and Horn* editor A. Hyatt Mayor, around Providence, analyzing facades with an acuteness that affected Mayor's perception of architecture ever afterwards.[22]

Since Jack could not get licensed, he eventually set up an architectural practice with Zareh Sourian, but he did little actual work.[23] He turned instead to the arduous project of trying to reconcile his need for a faith in

Christ with a life that any church would have denounced as profane. ("You offend the Lord Christ less than I do," he wrote the critic Newton Arvin some years later, when Arvin was pro-Communist and a militant atheist).[24] Like his father, Jack was still plagued by a feeling of discontinuity between word and deed. His religion sustained his cultural values in the face of what he believed to be a decadent society. For his own unruly behavior, however, he had no consistent philosophical justification, other than the claim that it was a means for his "class" (the professionals) to awaken the rulers of society, on whom they were dependent for survival, to instances of hypocrisy and immorality.

After "North Atlantic Passage," a new and more sustained attempt at achieving internal authority and a reconciliation of word and deed came in the form of a series of long poems about Thomas, the "Doubting Apostle." Wheelwright referred to this effort, as well as his 1938 sonnet sequence Mirrors of Venus, as a "novel."[25] This was in part a response to the new conceptions of the novel genre stimulated by the literary experiments of the 1920s. But calling these works novels was also a way of emphasizing that the two groups of poems depicted character development. And the main character in each of these works was actually Wheelwright himself, represented by various personae.

The Doubting Thomas poems were anticipated by the long poem "Forty Days," which was published in Hound and Horn in 1929. This is an intricate work based on the agrapha (sayings of Jesus not in the Gospels) and the New Testament narrative of what occurred in the forty days between Christ's rising from the grave and his ascension into heaven. Events are presented through the mind of Thomas, who had doubts about Christ's immortality until he was permitted to touch His wounds. At the end of the poem, Thomas and the other apostles are dispersed throughout the world. But the structure of "Forty Days" makes the poem recalcitrant to all but the most sympathetic readers. A series of aphorisms is presented in reverse order, while the normal movement of time is simultaneously indicated by passages noting the activity of animals and plants and the progress of the sun. Furthermore, questions and answers are interpolated in reverse order, consequences of events are told before their causes. This, he believed, would induce the reader to experience related ideas in logical isolation.

Unfortunately, the complexity of this formal apparatus is duplicated in most of his religious writings and presents a serious obstacle to the contemporary reader, whose enthusiasm for obscure and recondite theological arguments and games is significantly less than Wheelwright's. Of course, in the basic conception of these poems it is evident that Christian legends provided a rich fund of symbols with which to express a certain category of emotional anxieties and philosophic convictions; yet it is not surprising that this initial attempt to establish a systematized imaginative world was displaced and almost abandoned under the impact of the new conditions of the 1930s. The poetic myth of Doubting Thomas that eventually followed "Forty Days" was incapable of providing an adequate imaginative response to the changed situation, if only because it required the kind of reader whose thoughts are totally removed from the issues of daily life and international politics.

However, a bond to Wheelwright's future radicalism is implicit in the poem's theme, if not in its form and sensibility. Associated with his poetic stance in both the 1920s and the 1930s was his view that poetry should play a leading role in curing a sick culture and society and that it should provide moral guidance through exhortation to an alternative mode of life. In "Forty Days," he celebrates Thomas's act of doubting and concludes two things: that "doubt . . . [is] the arena of Faith" and that Christians should "defy clergy."[26] The main event of the poem, Thomas's acceptance of Christ as God, is a manifest instance of doubt preceding action; and, as Wheelwright states in the "Argument" of the poem, the goal of action is to counter the heresy of quietism that he regards as the scourge of modern Christianity: "Many uncanonical sayings of Jesus preserved by the [Church] Fathers' refutation of false constructions long put upon them are consistent with Gospel sayings; and this uncanonical wisdom, in the author's ear, recovers for systematic Christianity moral qualities which Quietists now leave to Sceptics. The author takes for the basis of his prosodic statement of faith, these germs of act, seeds to split rock."[27] In other words, the official clergy is presenting a false Christianity—a version of quietism, which is the minimization of personal action on the grounds that God is the prime active agent. This is tantamount to a counterrevolutionary doctrine that true Christians must defy. In the following section of Wheelwright's "Argument" to the poem, his indictment of contemporary Christianity bears some resemblance to Blake's theology in its transmutation of values:

> No mere inertia causes the Church to try saints and authoritatively mistake God for the Devil, but an active hostility whose weapons of war condemn life by formulas which sanctify death. The living Crucified's discourse to the recalcitrant Church precipitated into act; first on his own part, then by contagion among his fellow men; is in its aim without concern for any worldly consequence. The Word in its passage through society assails the Father of Lies and False Witness by forces which are allied only loosely with earthly revolution, but which lead those who hear to inexorable rebellion against injustice. It is at once a ground for Faith and Doubt that decent behavior or opinion is not distinguishable from sedition, even as what is taken for stale dogma turns out to be fresh truth.[28]

Following "Forty Days" came Wheelwright's Thomas poems; the bulk of this cycle was completed in three sections: "Twilight" in August 1929, "Evening" in August 1930, and "Morning" in August 1933. They were not published in that order, however, and revisions of "Evening" were being undertaken as late as 1935. (At that time he wrote to Morton Zabel that "I guess I have worked on it ["Evening"] for nigh ten years.")[29] Fragments of a fourth component of the novel survive, and a shorter poem called "The Dark Before Day" is connected with the Thomas cycle.

In intent, the development of the Thomas legend into a full-scale myth is a typical expression of the modernist yearning for a personally meaningful order in a perplexing age. His motto, like Blake's, was: "I must create a system or be enslaved by another man's." Still, as some of Blake's own later works might suggest, an imagination potentially expansive enough to embrace revolutionary political thought can, under some circumstances, divert moral energy to building mythic systems that become an act of self-justifying aestheticism. In their personal intensity of form, allusion, and language, Wheelwright's religious poems exemplify what Fredric Jameson identifies as the major variant of the modernist experience: "strategies of inwardness, which set out to re-appropriate an alienated universe by transforming it into personal styles and private languages: such wills to style have seemed in retrospect to reconfirm the very privatization and fragmentation of social life against which they meant to protest." Yet Jameson adds the corollary that the strategies of inwardness not only reflected the fragmentation of an alienated social life, "but also attempted to overcome that reification by exploration of new Utopian and libidinal experiences."[30] Wheelwright's mode of exploration reflects the fractured character of his emotions and intellect. The Thomas poems speak directly to issues of widespread importance in his day: the need to distinguish between morality and sexual repression and the importance of courageous political action based on a scientific understanding of social ills. But these messages are buried in a language almost incomprehensible to all but himself.

His fullest description of the research that went into the Thomas "novel" is contained in a letter sent to *Hound and Horn* editor Lincoln Kirstein in 1930:

> It may interest you to know that in order to go on with Thomas, which will be an epic, my dear, an epic, I have read a lot of early Christian literature making critical notes as I go. The Book of Acts is . . . the most composite and contains a lot of material which belongs to St. Thomas of the Edessans rather than to the Saints Peter and Paul of the Roman Church. I find this deliriously exciting tho' you might wonder why—a most fascinating sort of detective

story. It will do wonders for the long poem and put it on a firmer basis than the mere episodic. Of course, much of this critical work must have been done before. But I have no library of reference, so I must dig it out myself. Later I can compare my results with those of accredited scholars. G. F. Moore, if he lives, will help me. After all there is nothing like doing the work oneself.[31]

What distinguishes the Thomas poems from "Forty Days," then, is primarily their source in Wheelwright's study of the apocrypha, lost gospels, and other religious materials excluded from the Old and New Testaments because of their questionable authorship and potentially heretical intent.[32] The basic method used by Wheelwright is to "correct" the legend of Thomas by retelling it or paraphrasing it and introducing various changes. Central to understanding these alterations are the implications of Wheelwright's discovery that "Thomas is the word for twin, Didymos. . . . This Apostle was called the brother of the Lord, and . . . like Iscariot and Simon the Anti-Christ, his name was Judas."[33] This situation of multiple identities allowed him to feel justified in taking some of the ideas usually associated with the apostle and attributing them to anti-Christian figures, at times even making Thomas act as both Christ and Christ's betrayer.

Wheelwright's most innovative change from the original Thomas legend was to introduce the viewpoint that sexual chastity is a false and dangerous perversion of Christian thought, a view not only held by Blake, but also evident in D. H. Lawrence's *The Man Who Died*. "Twilight" and "Morning" are dominated by this issue. Of the former, he said: "It begs those who doubt their spirit not to wither their bodies."[34] The crucial "correction" to the original Thomas legend occurs in a scene after Thomas presides over the wedding of a couple in India. In the original, Thomas departs and is replaced by Jesus disguised as Thomas, who delivers a homily on chastity and convinces the couple to abstain from intercourse. In Wheelwright's version, it is Simon-Bar-Judas, the anti-Christ, who disguises himself as Thomas and delivers the message.

In "Morning," the woman Teckla (whose name comes from the apocryphal Acts of Paul and Thecla) has repressed her sexuality in the name of spiritualism. Jack's conception of Teckla was explained in a letter to Harriet Monroe, founder of *Poetry*:

> The Sacrament troubles a communicant, Teckla, who is not in a state of grace for, as she tells in her confession, she practised chastity while having no vocation to leave the world. This enmeshed her in sexual fear and spiritual sloth, and intellectual lust.
> Thomas heals her. In wedding her to the Acolyte, he learns how sex is an image of duality, which joins in the union of the created with the Creator.[35]

Unlike Thomas in "Twilight," the Thomas in "Morning" takes action and plays the role of healer, openly preaching sex as a sacred act in the following words: "O, Bed more holy than the Holy Board."[36]

These first two units of the Thomas poems thematically harmonize with "Forty Days" in that Wheelwright's enemy remains quietism. In "Twilight," for example, the bride and bridegroom's decision to abstain from intercourse symbolizes their intent to abstain from participation in life altogether. Simon-Bar-Judas, pretending to be Christ, urges them to sexual abstention so that they will be all virtue and no act:

"And this know—that if you refuse this thing
You become double Temples
to Virtue unweakened by Act."[37]

Consequently, Wheelwright described the poem as "a dramatic narrative of pragmatic repression."[38]

The third unit of the Thomas poems, "Evening," is more than just a continuation; the original content of the legend underwent a veritable transformation and the final result augurs Wheelwright's future political development in unambiguous terms. He told Harriet Monroe that "Evening" deals "through Christian mythology with the objective and passive decay of society"; in a letter to Morton Zabel, he described it as "at once religious and political."[39] In the original Thomas legend, the section from which "Evening" is derived tells how a satanic dragon slays a young man out of jealousy after witnessing the young man having sexual intercourse with a woman on the road. Thomas, arriving on the scene immediately afterward, demands that the dragon suck his poisonous venom back out of the victim. The young man is thus revived and the dragon is destroyed when it reabsorbs the poison.

In Wheelwright's version, Thomas (called "Didymus") is traveling in a chariot, accompanied by a mysterious driver. They come across the body of a black youth who has been stoned and poisoned. (Ironically, the poem is dedicated to the Afro-American tenor Roland Hays, who was a frequent visitor at the salon of Jack's Aunt Dolly Brooks; more than ten years later, in 1944, Hays was beaten by a gang of whites in the South, an incident that motivated Langston Hughes to write the poem "Roland Hays Beaten.") When Didymus begins to ask a giant worm with many heads about the murder, a "Self-Righteous" head and a "Well-Padded" head accuse the black youth of atheism and sexual libertinism. When Didymus refuses to believe them, they reveal that the real crime of the black youth is that he was a political agitator: "The lad was given to a more perilous practice, even,—and among lemon-pickers stirred [discord]."

In the dialogue that follows, the driver discloses himself to be Christ and lectures about the importance of naming all things, good and evil. Of the many-headed worm, he then says:

> "But your evil name, I cannot find
> though you be called Leviathan.
> Evils work evils being falsely named;
> I cannot name your evil."[40]

Didymus next debates various voices, which represent, in the fashion of a morality play, Prudence, Mercy, Clemency, Justice, Law, Cant, Self-Reliance, Rugged Individual, Nihilist, Semantic, Skeptic, and others. When Didymus hesitates to take the action necessary to liberate the black youth from the worm's poison, Christ the driver entreats him:

> "Command!
> Didymus, Didymus,
> without command
> Destruction will not end."[41]

The object of the poem is to announce that the upholders of morality must embark on a campaign of naming the true enemies of humanity more specifically as a preparation for action. Thomas has evolved from a confused prophet, to a spiritual healer, to a revolutionary activist.

"Evening" epitomizes the crosscurrents underlying Wheelwright's philosophical quest. The poem tries to defend secular political positions by summoning a "purified" Christian tradition, thus reconciling religious training and radical values. Yet this attempt to develop his own religiopolitical system would not be realized, nor would it bring him satisfaction; his poetic activity was deeply ruptured by divergent impulses. Overbred to eccentricity, Jack's personal vision was knotty and hermetic. Poems such as "Morning" failed to reach an audience because their symbols were unable to affect the reader on any level but that of their own arcane meanings, and the meanings remained too private. If Wheelwright's religiomythic poems deepened his symbolic vision, they narrowed it as well.

The Thomas project was ultimately aborted. Before the "novel" was completed, the Great Depression intervened and new factors began to shape Jack's development. It is also possible that the new social atmosphere in the United States made his recondite theological explorations less attractive to the journals that he anticipated would serve as an outlet. When Harriet Monroe rejected "Morning" for *Poetry* on the grounds that it was hopelessly obscure, Jack protested futilely: "The audience for 'Morning' is limited only by dizzy prejudice against religion. I wish you had said where it is unclear to you, as I am surprised it is not all clear." In a second letter Jack insisted that he hated "the obscurity of amateur scholarship as much as I love the poetry of general ideas." He declared that he would be at a loss if he thought the poem were a mystification:

"It cannot be, for any expression of opinion, long lived with, finds its answer in public acceptance once the path is cleared. Won't you clear the path for Thomas and Teckla?"[42]

Another deterrent to completing the Thomas poems came from changes in the external environment. It gave birth to more appropriate symbols as his ideas about society were altered. The concept of an individual moral quest, represented by Doubting Thomas, became less tenable as his thoughts turned to the need for collective action. Hitherto, he had believed that "socialism would come to this country through business taking over the government," but after 1929 he began to witness a widespread social dislocation to which only the radical labor movement seemed to have clear answers.[43]

As late as 1930, Wheelwright was still excoriating the decline into which American society had fallen, without being able to specify his own choice of an alternative. A particular object of his frustration was the deterioration of the Puritan tradition in which he had been bred. In a review of books by and about Thomas Sargeant Perry, the New England scholar, Jack railed against the spiritual decadence of Perry and his type, "who shaped and twisted, clipped and trained the espaliered tree under whose thinning shade I live, and from whose branches still falls my native food." But all Wheelwright could offer as an antidote was an ambiguous warning to the nation that "unless it ground its roots much deeper than at present into the dark, moist narrow deeps which cleave the underlying strata of the rock beneath all rock, it will fall into supercilious, if self-tormented relapse of the creative spirit."[44]

Wheelwright's new literary outlook was still several years away, but his changing perspectives were evidenced in a poetic obituary published in *Hound and Horn* in 1931, where he settled accounts with the suicide and aesthetic ideas of Harry Crosby. Crosby and Wheelwright shared important similarities in their moneyed Brahmin background, their Episcopalian schooling, their overlapping periods at Harvard, their visionary poetry, and their susceptibility to depression. But they represented two contrasting responses of alienated writers belonging to the New England upper classes in a world in which their cultured family traditions had become superfluous. Crosby might be seen as carrying out the Henry Adams perspective to its logical conclusion. He broke in disgust from State Street, but saw no alternative social class with which to identify. Instead of forging a new social identity for himself as an artist, he immersed himself in artistic activity that became increasingly divorced from the real world. ("Crosby tried to live art rather than . . . to live for art," Wheelwright later wrote.)[45] Wheelwright's poem was addressed "To Wise Men on the Death of a Fool." He made it clear, however, that even though he deplored Crosby's philosophy, he sympathized with his rebellion:

> State Street, maintain your silence.
> His mad impiety is holier than your sane
> Infidel doubt . . .[46]

Still, Wheelwright's only alternative course for the wise men, to save them from both the conservatism of State Street and the madness of Crosby, was the vision of classical culture with which he closes:

> Magnanimous in bronze, straddling a stallion
> Over the Roman capital, diffusing
> A green benediction, rides serene Aurelius.[47]

The "green benediction" of the aged bronze statue on the Piazza del Campidoglio suggests that a spiritual sustenance emanates from the heights of cultural achievement attained by the influential equestrian monument of the stoic Roman emperor.[48] However, this was the last gasp of Wheelwright's pure aestheticism.

The first sign of a distinctly new development in his attitudes came in the same year (1931), when he learned of the personal investigation of the conditions in the Harlan county coal fields, an activity carried out by the Theodore Dreiser delegation and sponsored by the Communist-organized National Committee for the Defense of Political Prisoners. No doubt the intervention of these other writers influenced him, especially that of Dreiser, whom he had met in Greenwich Village, and Jack's college friend Dos Passos. Wheelwright instinctively identified with them as members of his professional "class"; he was impressed when they joined word and deed by exposing at first hand the persecution of the miners, using the authority of their national reputation as writers. He wrote to Allen Tate in defense of the delegation's action: "People of our class are members of a distinct class, the professional class; it is the only class whose interests are the same as the interests of society as a whole. In fact, society is the creation of this class. By 'society' I here mean culture, as the continentals use the term."[49] Wheelwright now began to entertain the possibility that his "class" should detach itself from its State Street tormentors and seek a fresh alliance with workers and farmers. He was also reviewing family papers on the Reverend John Wheelwright and was trying to determine his significance in the context of New England radicalism.[50]

Jolted by the Great Depression, he resolved the contradiction between word and deed in a new way during the spring of 1932. He joined the Socialist party of Massachusetts and, in a letter to the *New Republic*, expressed his opinion that "the radical labor movement is the most important single influence for the progress of humankind today."[51] If writers identified with this new progressive class, they had a vehicle for sustaining and advancing cultural achievements. Wheelwright had now begun to see that the New England cultural tradition had run its course as the unhappy ally of State Street, that the preservation of the values so cherished by his father depended upon the forging of a new alliance of the professional strata and the proletariat.

Although an entire generation of American writers became politically radicalized in the 1930s, only a handful persevered in their revolutionary socialist convictions through the Second World War and Cold War years. One of the most significant and extraordinary of these was Sherry Mangan, a passionate and scholarly classicist from Harvard who made a small but distinct mark on American literature in the late 1920s and early 1930s as a poet, novelist, short-story writer, critic, editor, and book designer.

According to Sherry's first wife, in his original political temperament "he was a High Tory, as from a former Johnsonian age."[1] He was awakened to other values under the impact of the Great Depression, and became a revolutionary adhering to the views of Leon Trotsky. By the end of the 1930s, he had remade his life. After working for several years as a printer in Norwood, Massachusetts, he exiled himself to Western Europe and Latin America. For ten years he was employed as a journalist for Henry Luce's *Time-Life-Fortune* complex, an occupation that he used on his own to facilitate his work in promoting the ideas and activities of the Trotskyist Fourth International. After a break with the Luce organization, Sherry eked out his living from a series of translating, editing, and rewriting jobs, and from occasional sales of his own stories and articles.

In the days of his literary association with aesthetes and exiles, Sherry was known as a sybarite with a charming personality. When interviewed in 1976, the poet and translator Robert Fitzgerald vividly recalled Sherry's unique, powerful presence. He described the Sherry of the early 1930s as very big—squarely and heavily built, though not of great height—but extremely animated in discussion with his shock of reddish blond hair and amused face. Others remembered him as a lover of good food and drink, a gourmet who sought the best of everything. He especially favored shellfish, curries, steaks, chateaubriands, and cream; his self-indulgence in these and in alcohol was so remarkable that Tessa Gilbert, a painter friend, designed a bookplate for him with the legend, "Everything in Excess."[2] He lived beyond his means, appearing rich and hospitable. Moreover, he was a master of witty and rarefied conversation. Large, jolly, and avuncular, he always seemed older than he was, encouraging the aspiring young, dabbling in psychology, and giving wise advice to others in long calligraphic letters.[3]

Although these personality traits were never totally erased, they were displaced by a new center to his being after Sherry's politicization. The life of this onetime litterateur followed a course strikingly different from that of his quondam circle of literary friends in Boston and Paris. While many of these went on to teaching posts and found varying degrees of fame in the world of culture and scholarship, Sherry's path diverged because of the intensity and endurance of his Marxist political commitment. He assumed a role of increasing importance in the organization of the Fourth International and struggled with the conflicting claims of his literary imagination and the stern requirements of Bolshevik discipline for the rest of his life.

The instability of his personal and financial situation eventually took its toll on his physical and emotional well-being. When, in the 1950s, he attempted to research firsthand a novel on the struggles of Bolivian tin miners, the exertion left his second wife dead of a heart attack and his own health shattered. The last eight years of his life were spent in poverty, physical suffering, and loneliness.

Although Sherry never abandoned his adopted vocation as a poet, his zealous devotion to revolutionary ideals deflected him from the promising literary career that had once seemed within his grasp. During his journalistic and political assignments in Western Europe and Latin America, Sherry's intransigent dedication to Trotskyism eventually isolated him from the mainstream of American writing altogether. But in his dual devotion to poetry and revolutionary socialism, Sherry sought to rise above the misfortunes that plagued his life and find individual fulfillment of a special sort. Had he lived a few years longer, he might have found an audience or at least some kindred spirits in the new generation of students and intellectuals who awakened to left-wing political activity in the 1960s. As it was, he was found dead in a rented room in Rome in 1961—alone, destitute, forgotten, not quite fifty-seven years old.

On the surface, everything in Sherry's youth and family background prepared him not for revolution but for a conventional life in some profession—law, academia, or medicine. Born in 1904 in Lynn, Massachusetts, John Joseph Sherry Mangan was the son of a respected pediatrician. (The Mangan family followed the tradition of incorporating the mother's maiden name, Sherry—a modernized form of MacSheiragh—into the son's name. Relatives and childhood friends referred to Sherry as "John" throughout his life, although he ceased using this in the mid-1920s.) Sherry's grandfather, Owen Peter Mangan, was an impoverished Irish immigrant. When Owen was nine, his father died and his stepfather threw him out of the house. To survive, Owen bound himself out to a farmer. At the age of sixteen, he went to Preston, England, where he worked as a policeman and married Mary Smith. They had three children: John Joseph Mangan (Sherry's father), James Clarence Mangan (named for the poet), and Mary Mangan.

In 1869 Owen took his family to the United States and opened a dry goods store in Fall River, Massachusetts, where seven more children were born. Then he moved to Lynn, where he worked for the Metropolitan Life Insurance Company. An autodidact, Owen Mangan taught himself the classics, learned much of Shakespeare by heart, played the violin, and read Dickens and Scott to his grandchildren. A straight and stately man, he was over six feet tall, could touch his toes at seventy-five, and lived into his eighties. His oldest son, John Joseph Mangan, was short and balded early; but he compensated for physical shortcomings by an extraordinary career in medicine and letters.

Sherry's father received his B.A. degree in 1883 from Holy Cross, the Jesuit school in Worcester, Massachusetts. Shortly afterwards, the school awarded him a master's degree in recognition of a verse translation of the *Alkestis* of Euripides. Following several years of business life, he entered the Boston College of Physicians and Surgeons (now Tufts Medical School), from which he received his first M.D., and established his practice in Lynn. While maintaining a growing practice, he attended Harvard Medical School, from which he received a second M.D. in 1904. Then came further study at the universities and clinics of Vienna and Berlin, as well as membership on the staffs of the Children's Hospital of Boston and the Lynn Hospital, where he established the children's clinic.

Dr. Mangan was also a constant contributor to periodicals. Just after the turn of the century, he wrote two monographs about the history of Lynn: *The Life of the Reverend Jeremiah Sheppard, Third Minister of Lynn* and *A History of the Lynn Newspapers*. A few years before the First World War, he began to specialize in the Reformation period. Dissatisfied with all extant works about the Dutch scholar Desiderius Erasmus, he started working on a definitive biography. The two-volume study occupied him for thirteen years; he took a number of research trips abroad, on which his son Sherry accompanied him.[4]

On the Mangan side of the family, there was a possible ancestral connection to the Irish poet James Clarence Mangan (1803–49). The details of Clarence Mangan's personal life are so obscure that no positive link has been established; however, Sherry's grandfather Owen claimed that he was a relative.[5] Sherry and Dr. Mangan, as well as other members of the family, were quite proud of their supposed connection with the famous writer who was the boyhood hero of Yeats and Joyce and whose life had provided inspiration for Joyce's *Portrait of the Artist as a Young Man*.

Furthermore, a number of parallels can be found in the lives of Sherry and Clarence Mangan that suggest some degree of conscious or unconscious imitation. Both poets initiated their careers with translations, excelled at puns and wordplay, liked to use pseudonyms, experimented with rhythms, and frequently assumed a Byronic pose and attitude of

weltschmerz. Both were noted as raconteurs and celebrated for their wit;
both endured repeated personal tragedies, including the early deaths
of the women to whom they were most devoted; both had emotional,
beguiling personalities and grew more articulate under the influence
of alcohol, with which both had problems; both became involved in
radical politics (Clarence Mangan supported the Young Ireland move-
ment); both died alone, relatively young (Clarence Mangan was forty-
six), and under impoverished and difficult circumstances, leaving no
wife or children behind.[6]

As an only child, Sherry was much doted on by his parents, especially
his mother. Mary Mangan was a devout woman who, after suffering
numerous miscarriages, began making pilgrimages to Sainte Anne de
Beaupré in Canada to pray for a child.[7] Sherry bore the greatest physical
resemblance to her side of the family, especially to her father, Patrick
Sherry, a redhaired shoe manufacturer who had the shoulders of an ox, a
wicked wit, and a penchant for drink. (Two of the political pseudonyms
Sherry used after the 1930s, Patrick O'Daniel and Terence Phelan, can be
traced to Patrick Sherry and his wife Mary Phelan Sherry. A third pseudo-
nym was Owen, after his paternal grandfather.) Patrick Sherry was a well-
known personality in Lynn. Outspoken on political matters, he vented
his sarcasm not only on capitalism, monarchies, and the British rule of
Ireland (against which he called for armed insurrection), but also on the
organized labor movement. Throughout his life he was embroiled with
the Knights of Labor and the Lasters' Protective Union. But his popu-
larity with the people of Lynn was unaffected; when Patrick Sherry died
in 1915 at the age of eighty-one, one of the largest funeral processions
ever seen in the city was organized.[8]

Sherry graduated from the Shepard Grammar School in 1917. His
parents' decision to send him to a public school rather than the nearby
St. Mary's School, which was run by nuns and Christian brothers, sug-
gests a liberal attitude toward his Catholic rearing. Religious beliefs were
short-lived in Sherry, for he lost his faith in his early teens, although he
did not announce himself an atheist until his early twenties. During his
high school years, his mother sent him off on Sunday mornings to mass
with his missal, but instead of going to church, he visited his friends
Charles and Richard Haywood, leaving for home when he saw the people
returning from Mass.[9]

In 1921 he graduated from Lynn Classical High School where he had
taken the classical course, a liberal arts curriculum emphasizing Latin
and Greek. He received a degree with a distinction in classics and his
highest marks were in Latin, ancient history, English, and plane geome-
try.[10] He was ranked in the top ten of a class of one hundred and earned a
reputation as a brilliant student who was also a smart aleck and trouble-
maker. In the middle of his senior year, Sherry and his closest friends, the

Haywood brothers, were expelled for distributing a satirical flyer that
Sherry had printed on a small foot-driven press he operated in his cellar.[11]
He was junior editor of the Lynn Classical High *Gazette*, a quarterly
magazine to which he contributed a number of stories and sketches.
Several of them reveal a pronounced fascination with wealth and power,
as well as a longing for dangerous adventures in exotic lands.[12]

A precocious, energetic, athletic, and sensitive child, Sherry thrived in
the cold New England weather, enjoying an intimate relationship with
his father. Fascinated by model trains, stamp collections, and adventure
stories, he spent hours classifying his books library-style, was orderly to
the point of compulsion, and was obsessed with charts and lists. Some-
times he drew up infinitely detailed schedules for the employment of his
time, dividing them into fifteen-minute sections, with any vacant one
labeled "Think"; but still he managed to spend uncounted hours reading
bad "problem novels." In an unpublished autobiographical story, an
adolescent Sherry cries out: "I want to see everything, do everything,
live everything, leave my mark on the world."[13]

His father was a strong moral presence in his life. When school was
canceled because of snow, Dr. Mangan insisted that Sherry not play out-
doors because children of less fortunate families were unable to do so for
lack of good shoes. Sometimes in the morning Sherry would open wide
his window to the cold and conduct a dressing ritual. He imagined him-
self to be a poor newsboy who was required to sell a certain number of
papers before he could purchase and put on his shirt, shoes, and pants.

Sherry was a brilliant child, far beyond his years intellectually and so
far beyond his contemporaries in school that it made him more or less a
loner. His friends could not compete with him and he was often bored
with them. At the age of twelve, he could speak and translate Latin
fluently; he even assisted his father in the Vatican library, where they
examined the writings of Erasmus. At Lynn Classical High, which at that
time compared favorably with the best private schools, Sherry was the
star pupil of Luther Atwood, a teacher of Latin whose approach was re-
ported to be more that of a college professor than a high school instructor.
Latin was Sherry's first love among languages, but eventually he became
fluent in French and Spanish. He also knew Greek (he carried around an
enormously heavy typewriter that had Greek letters on it), Italian, and
German, and studied Sanskrit. In later years he discovered that he could
function as a simultaneous translator as well as any professional.

Although strong and in good health, Sherry was not permitted to par-
ticipate in sports by order of Dr. Mangan, who feared for the safety of his
only child. Dr. Mangan did permit swimming, however, and Sherry ex-
celled at this until his father learned that he was going extraordinary
distances in dangerous waters and ordered him to desist altogether.
Sherry did not resent this protectiveness; he thrived on the attention

and security afforded by his family. Sunday evenings were a special joy. Twelve to fifteen relatives would gather together to present plays, sing Gilbert and Sullivan light operas, and perform concerts with violin and piano.[14] Sherry cherished his parents and family life. When he was mature, he never expressed any bitterness or resentment about his childhood—only against the world that belied the hopes that animated his youth.

At Harvard Sherry felt the object of some prejudice because he was an Irish Catholic from the industrial town of Lynn, only one generation removed from the plebeian classes. But his devotion to literature brought him acceptance in the Harvard Poetry Society. He served as its president and became friendly with former Harvard aesthetes: Jack Wheelwright, S. Foster Damon, Robert Hillyer, and Grant Code. He roomed with the translator Ralph Manheim, and through the Liberal Club (a cultural center) he cemented lifelong friendships with Virgil Thomson, the painter Maurice Grosser, and the documentary filmmaker Henwar Rodakiewicz.[15]

Mangan's Harvard poems, read at Harvard Poetry Society meetings and published in the *Advocate*, thematically mix a romantic exaltation of love and nature with fin-de-siècle world-weariness and cynicism about sex and the human condition. These poems formally combine free verse and classical structures such as Greek Sapphics and Alcaics. In language they alternate between classical allusions and fresh phrases that are sometimes colloquial and even crude. Pound, Eliot, Horace, and Lucretius are evident influences; sometimes Mangan emulates Cummings through his depiction of an idealistic young man facing the boring hypocrisies of conventional society. These are often personified by older balding men and sexless women or by academics blind to the true possibilities of the active life because they are busy lecturing about it. Harvard receives satirical jibes in "Professor Angel" (drafted in 1924 but not published until 1935) and in an unfinished diatribe called "Harvard Seen Through Green Spectacles." Only one poem shows an explicit tie to Irish culture, "The Passing of Shaughnessy," which appeared in the Harvard *Advocate*. Mangan contemplates the fate of a heroic, admired and feared Irishman who is known for his romantic exploits throughout the world until one day, for inexplicable reasons, he marries an Irish woman:

Shaughnessy the Periegete
had stood unmoved, preoccupied,
the while mercurial lightning,
missing him, had ripped
the bag that held
the blundering thunder till
it poured

its rude sonorous flood
across the sky
the Asian sky.

And yet, on one insistent night
this man so feared, made restive
by the populous stars (forgetting quite
Samina, Na-Fuy, Zema, Jeanne,
so easily accomplished) that
he flung his fortunes legally into
the arms of Miss Marion L. Murphy.

Heigh ho! All to ephemeral audacity
betrayed to latch key, and the furnace fire!

To us still drinking rum in Singapore,
to us still reading Greek in Singapore,
he is a memory and a mystery.[16]

Mangan thought well enough of "Shaughnessy" to publish a revised version ten years later in his collected poems, but he classified it as "juvenilia." Despite melodramatic excesses, it reveals at once his descriptive strength, his ability to carefully select a word to suggest a precise mood. The opening image of Shaughnessy in the sky, with the mercurial lightning and the ripped bag, subtly mythologizes him as a cousin of Hermes and Aeolus. The "populous stars," suggesting eternity, have mysteriously unnerved him even though physical danger (the pouring thunder may refer to the cannons of World War I) could not. Shaughnessy forsakes his international gallery of lovers, each name reflecting one of the different lands to which he has wandered, for the security of a simple Irish lass. His disciples—sketched as hard-drinking young classical scholars who have followed him to the East—are amazed and frightened at the ephemerality of his rebellion. They fear that they, too, may succumb to the conventional lives from which they have fled. "Shaughnessy" is the first, although the gentlest, of several pieces Mangan would write about sellouts.

The poem discloses an obvious craft, a talent for depicting atmosphere and moment—in this case, the restless feelings of his milieu of Harvard poet-rebels. Unlike the work of Wheelwright at the same age, "Shaughnessy" lacks the power of an autonomous vision. The poem profiles figures and demarcates a mood; its derivative character extends even to the borrowing of a technique (the listing of symbolic female names) from a key passage in Eliot's *Waste Land*. "Shaughnessy" is sensitively disturbing; compared to "Rococo Crucifix" and "Dr. Rimmer's Hamilton," however, the cumulative effect of its lines is thin, lacking Wheelwright's metaphysical complexity. It is devoid of metaphor as well.

Sherry's years in Cambridge combined some academic brilliance with a few rebellious pranks. An avid participant in the heavy drinking pursued by Harvard undergraduates of the 1920s, he was also part of a group that experimented with hallucinogenic drugs. In his autobiography *Virgil Thomson* (1966), the Missouri-born composer mentions that he first learned about peyote at the end of his World War I service from a minister and that he introduced the drug to S. Foster Damon and others at Harvard. Sherry developed his own system of obtaining mescal caps by mail from New Mexico for the peyote parties in his room in Weld Hall. Ground up and taken in a glass of water, the caps were a very bitter brew; after the students had drunk it, they put their heads out the window to be certain that it would stay down. At one of these parties the toilet seat in Sherry's bathroom was mysteriously burned and the current wisecrack was that someone in his hallucinations must have thought he was a comet.[17]

Flamboyant in appearance and behavior, he wore a bright red necktie as a belt and was hardly deferential in the presence of even the most respected professors. Once he caused a minor scandal by loudly sucking an enormous dill pickle in Dean Brigg's advanced writing class.[18] At the end of his junior year, he was suddenly expelled, technically for a failed course in Homer. Afterwards Sherry reported that "a would-be witty dean said it was for 'miscellaneous worthlessness.'" His version of the episode was that he had refused to attend classes "after the professor utilized the pretext of his reference to Praxiteles to utter some particularly insupportable asininities about Jo Davidson's bust of Gertrude Stein." Instead, he devoted four months to writing a long essay called "Forty-Five New and Ingenious Methods of Suicide." This was followed by an incident in which his dormitory was accidentally set on fire. Not long after came the expulsion.[19]

He managed to be readmitted for the fall term under three kinds of probation. Although his grades were unevenly ranged from "C" to "A" in almost every subject, he ultimately developed a good relationship with Briggs, who, along with Professors C. N. Jackson and E. K. Rand, provided him with letters of recommendation.[20] In the spring of 1925, he graduated cum laude in classics and sailed at once for France.

Sherry was accompanied by his friend Virgil Thomson. They lived near each other in Paris and Sherry studied music with Thomson, occasionally assisting him as secretary. Thomson, in turn, played the role of guide and counsellor. Sherry introduced various girl friends to his Nestor, who passed judgment on their suitability, and Thomson brought Sherry into the household of Gertrude Stein and Alice B. Toklas. He also introduced Sherry to the expatriate writer Robert McAlmon and the French surrealist Georges Hugnet. When Maurice Grosser arrived in Paris, he joined the group and spent part of the next year painting a portrait of Sherry in the nude.

His first publishing successes in Paris, a poem and three translations from the Greek in *Commonweal*, encouraged him to form the concept of himself as poet that lasted throughout his life. In a letter to his father he announced that his real vocation was his writing: "I can imagine giving up any other interest, but never that. It's what the psychologists call my 'life-life,' and I've got to stick with it, come what may, or fail in my own eyes."[21] But he also learned from his Paris experiences that he could not make sufficient money to live on by writing alone. When he was informed of the acceptance of his father's two-volume *Erasmus* for publication, he terminated his European sojourn to assist in proofreading and distributing the book. "Literature seems simply not to pay me," he wrote home. "I admit I am very discouraged as regards matters financial; and beginning to agree with Tommie [Virgil Thomson] that the two necessities of an artist are intent and a reasonable income."[22]

On 30 March 1926 Sherry sailed third class on the *Leviathan* for New York. Arriving in Lynn, he devoted himself to helping Dr. Mangan assemble the final version of *Erasmus*. The months when they worked together on the editing of the book was a period that Sherry would remember with particular nostalgia as "the time that—after the usual mutually wrongheaded disputes apparently inevitable for the growing up of the young and their rendering themselves independent of their parents —we met again as adults, and . . . loved and admired each other, and worked wonderfully well together." During the laborious process of reverifying the translations of Erasmus's letters, Sherry and his father got in the habit of exchanging notes, and finally remarks, in Latin. More than thirty years later, Sherry recalled "with melancholy laughter how we used to denounce each other's theory of translation: on the basis of mine (the result of my Harvard upbringing), he ironically addressed me as 'Herr Professor Doktor Umlaut.'" Sherry, in return, described Dr. Mangan's translations (the result of his Holy Cross education) as "variations on a theme by Erasmus." "But what affection and comprehension there were in those good-natured disputes in the midst of scholarly industry," Sherry reminisced. Although the work was dedicated to Dr. Mangan's own father, Owen Peter Mangan, the preface concluded by giving thanks "to my son, Mr. John Sherry Mangan, who has so long and faithfully assisted me in the arduous task of preparing the work for the press, and who in addition has aided me by his original researches and confirmed my judgment by his own."[23]

Erasmus received rather mixed reviews, and privately Sherry confessed to Ezra Pound that he had doubts about its quality. As the work of an erudite but devout Catholic, it was praised by the religious and traditionalist publications, but the liberal journals *New Republic* and *Nation* scoffed at its orthodoxy and lack of originality. Nevertheless, more than a dozen years of hard work came to an end. In the glow of success, father and son were in the midst of planning a second work on the English

Reformation when misfortune came. Just prior to the summer 1928 commencement of the College of the Holy Cross, where Dr. Mangan was to be awarded an honorary doctorate of letters, he suffered a disabling stroke. A somber Sherry took his father's place in the commencement ceremonies, and he pledged that, although he had planned to return to Paris, he would now stay close to home to care for his father during his final years.[24]

In the period following his work on *Erasmus*, Sherry attempted a career as an independent printer. Since the time Sherry was a teenager, Dr. Mangan had encouraged his son to learn a trade in case of hard times, and over the years he had acquired a good deal of printing skill and equipment. At the start of 1927, he announced the founding of the Lone Gull Press in a flyer that demonstrated Lutetia and Lutetia Italic types and was printed on Alexandra Japan antique paper. This brochure explained the choice of the name Lone Gull as follows:

> Gulls in coveys, two dozen at once, noisily bickering over a herring that one has caught. A clamorous crowd all very much alike.
> Higher in the air, planing along, a single gull, flying alone, hunting alone. Unique in itself.
> Gulls and printers. The name has not been carelessly chosen.[25]

One of the first items published by Sherry was a small book of poems by Janet Lewis called *The Wheel in Midsummer*. Arrangements were made by Yvor Winters, the poet's husband.[26] That same year, in February 1927, Sherry began the publication of the important little magazine *larus: The Celestial Visitor.*

A larus is a large cosmopolitan gull, and the purpose of the new magazine was defined in a second brochure. This stated that the journal would be uncompromising in its goal of publishing anything written of high quality and that poetry would be centrally featured, not "merely used to fill up the awkward space at the end of the page." The format and quality of production were to mirror the craftsmanship of the writing: "It will be printed by hand throughout, in the Lutetia face, lately cut by Johann Enschede-en-Zonen of Harlem for a forthcoming folio edition of LaFontaine . . . on Warren's Oldstyle Book." Since the contents were to be of "a permanent nature," Sherry also prepared a specially numbered limited edition, on hand-made paper, "for bibliophiles and collectors." In summary, he affirmed that "*larus* will not be a popular magazine; it is for the very few, and they of the highest order."[27]

Only five issues of *larus* made their appearance, the first in February 1927 and the last, a combination of three numbers, in June 1928. The central editors were Mangan for the United States and Virgil Thomson from France. The associate editor was Oliver Jenkins, who permitted *larus* to absorb his own *Tempo*, a short-lived magazine of poetry that had come out irregularly between 1921 and 1923 from Danvers, Massachusetts. The journalist Waverly Root served as *larus*'s New York City representative. The Mangan family home at 12 Baker Street in Lynn functioned as the main editorial offices, but *larus* was printed in a garage at 36 Munroe Street in Lynn, an area known as the "Sherry Block" because the main building was once the site of Patrick Sherry's shoe factory.[28]

The first *larus* editorial was one of a series that argued for the separation of art from social and worldly concerns. He wrote that the function of a magazine properly lies "at a variable point between the extremes best represented by a one-sided telephone conversation and a grand literary *garden-partouze* (or, in a notable case, by inversion, a cozy indignation meeting). As the extreme first, it were ridiculous, if not touching; as the second, obscene. Yet let it lie closer to the first." Sherry's editorial policy reflected this outlook, for he announced that he would refuse to rewrite contributions and would adhere to the printer's maxim: "Follow the copy—even if it goes out the window."[29]

In three subsequent editorials entitled "*Ars Gloria Artis* versus the Cuttlefish," parts 1, 2, and 3, Mangan defended the artist's right to complete privacy and scorned literature produced to meet popular taste. In *The Little Magazine*, Frederick J. Hoffman politically assessed these editorials in generous terms: "As a poet, Mangan wishes to have his work evaluated honestly. This position is not antidemocratic or antisocial; rather, it recognizes the difficulties of the creative artist and wishes to protect him from enervating popular attention."[30] Sherry's anger at what he saw as the tendency of many writers to become instruments of profit-making business interests was a genuine concern, but when he surveyed those little magazines with which he felt the most affinity, he chose Wyndham Lewis's *The Enemy* as the most outstanding.

He lauded Lewis's "penetrating analysis of our time," even though Lewis's cultural elitism was linked to authoritarian and reactionary political views.[31] But such cultural affinities with the far right did not lead Mangan to protofascism, a category delineated by Nicos Poulanzas that Fredric Jameson applies to Lewis. Unlike Lewis, Mangan's perspective derived from aesthetic values, not consciously political ones. He simply believed that "art is the expression of something within rather than an attempt to entertain something without."[32] Although he did not regard the desire to reach an audience as a corrupting force in and of itself, he did feel that it was a non sequitur for the artist to therefore aim at millions of readers. His stance, like Wheelwright's, can best be understood as "petty bourgeois" in the sense that Jameson delineates the social basis and political outlook of this strata: "Neither proletarian nor classical bourgeoisie, let alone big business," this segment of society valorizes "those purely intellectual skills—science, education, bureaucratic services—which might lend it [petty-bourgeois ideology] a non-class-based legitimation."[33]

While both Mangan and Wheelwright exalted culture as humanity's best hope, Sherry's aestheticism was more circumspect. He viewed art as a special arena of knowledge, one that might be compatible with philosophy and psychology, but would not replace them. Such a rational notion of literature's function did not lead him to a consideration of questions of political power in the 1920s, as did Wheelwright's strident cultural elitism, which might more accurately be termed a mystic calling fed by religious yearnings and emotional traumas of his youth. In the 1920s these seemed ineradicable in Wheelwright, even though they contradicted his worldly tastes and radical sympathies; so he sought to make his poetry a ground of reconciliation as well as prophecy. In the 1920s Wheelwright used his writing to preach, lead, and heal; the complexity of his metaphors, the intricacies of his symbolic system, are proof that he possessed a fertile poetic vision. Mangan, in contrast, wanted only to learn and experience; poetic craft became the discipline by which he sought to preserve and dissect thoughts, emotions, observations, and imaginings. Wheelwright and Mangan, the visionary and the craftsman, shared in the characteristics of each other; but the imaginative faculties of Wheelwright were more advanced at an earlier age because of the eccentricity of his temperament and the ordeals of family tragedy and religious conversion.

The high intentions of Mangan's *larus* were achieved, but its existence was brief. Contributors were primarily from two circles. The first was comprised of friends and acquaintances of Sherry: George Anthony Palmer (who wrote under the name George Anthony or the initials "gap"), Norman Lewis Dodge, R. P. Blackmur, Cuthbert Wright, Yvor Winters, Ralph Manheim, Joshua Epstein, and Dr. Mangan. The second consisted of friends and acquaintances of Virgil Thomson, into whose circle Sherry had been introduced: Gertrude Stein, Mary Butts, Robert McAlmon, and Bernard Fäy. In addition, a number of notable poets like Hart Crane, Harry Crosby, Conrad Aiken, and Lindley Williams Hubbell had an independent relation to the magazine.

Sherry lived in Lynn during the *larus* period, but his behavior was that of a misplaced Parisian bohemian. Reminiscing nostalgically about the antics of Jean Cocteau, Louis Aragon, and Tristan Tzara, he frequently kept the company of two of his most eccentric Harvard friends: Tony Palmer, a man of courtly intelligence whose early poems were filled with bitterness and despair; and Norman Dodge, a shy, self-effacing scholarly genius who spent more than forty years editing the rare book catalogue for Goodspeed's bookshop in Boston. To discuss literary matters with another friend, Joshua Epstein, a medical student who later became a lyrical representational painter, Sherry drove nine miles to Salem or picked up Epstein en route to visit a girl friend in Rockport, Massachusetts. Now and then he saw his high school classmates, Charles and Richard Haywood, and delighted in telling them outrageous stories of his Paris exploits—drinking marathons with Robert McAlmon that resulted in barroom brawls, French prostitutes and sexual liaisons with numerous young women. ("Thank God I'm still a virgin under my left arm," was a remark that Sherry attributed to one of his best friends in Paris.) He disparaged all things American in comparison with their French analogues and was an outspoken misogynist, hinting that he had been involved in homosexual episodes.

Accompanied by his collie Brian Boru, named for the eleventh-century king of Ireland, Sherry was frequently seen chasing fire engines in the town of Lynn. On visits to Cambridge and Boston, he continued the heavy drinking begun at Harvard and further experimented with peyote. One adventure involved Robert Keller, a close friend of Sherry's who later became a popular song writer. Keller "took a knife and pressed the point against someone's throat and made threats [but] they all knew there was nothing to be afraid of." Sherry told Richard Haywood that part of his unreserved admiration for Virgil Thomson was that "Thomson insisted always on being in complete control of himself and would not dream of going to a length with the drug or with alcohol where he could not instantly act as one completely sober."[34]

In letters to Thomson, written from Lynn, Sherry extolled the virtues of living an unconventional life:

> There were many young men with Erasmus in his youth, no
> whit his inferiors in promise. They were sagacious, these fellows:
> they got themselves snug little jobs as secretaries to town councils
> or tutors to royal children; they arranged their incomes just right,
> hired pleasant rooms, owed no man a penny, no woman fealty, and
> sat down to be great in a sensible way. My friend, they are so dead
> that it takes days and days of searching in Widener [Library] to find
> out their very names. Erasmus, feeble of soul though he was, lives.
> He was not wise; he was not honest and independent; he owed
> money and fealty right and left; he never, to my knowledge, earned
> a tithe of the money he spent so lavishly.[35]

Sherry then announced that he needed a patron and located a woman who gave him several hundred dollars to help *larus*. But so many debts had accrued that the magazine was forced to terminate in the spring of 1928; that fall he enrolled in Sanskrit courses at the Harvard Graduate School of Arts and Sciences. There he found his academic work disrupted by worry over his continued financial instability and also by a growing attachment to Kate Foster, an art student from the London Slade School whom he had met in Paris. He withdrew from Harvard before the end of the term.

Then Sherry's dream of finding a patron on a more permanent basis seemed to be realized. He was hired as a tutor for the wealthy Garland family of Boston at fifty dollars a week, plus all expenses and occasional trips to Bermuda. His experiences of life among the rich with the Garlands formed the background for his 1932 novel, *Cinderella Married or How They Lived Happily Ever After: A Divertissement*, published by A. & C. Boni. A first novel, *Marke Byrne*, was written around 1926; it was never published and the manuscript has been lost.

A huge estate had been left to the widowed Mary Garland and her eleven children (six of them adopted). The oldest son, Charles Garland, was a philosophical anarchist who tried to refuse his inheritance, an act deemed illegal under Massachusetts law. Consequently he established the Garland Fund, which gave money to radical projects, like the *New Masses* magazine. He also set up a free-spirited colony at Buzzards Bay on Cape Cod. One of Sherry's friends from the Liberal Club at Harvard, Henwar Rodakiewicz, frequented the colony while a student and eventually married Mary Garland, thirty years his senior.

Sherry was tutor to the children of Mary Morris, who was divorced from Charles Garland. Within a short time he became romantically involved with the wife of one of the other Garlands, a woman whose husband later committed suicide by slitting his throat. A shopgirl who married into wealth, she became the model for Ella in *Cinderella Married* —a working-class woman who marries into the royalty of a mythical Mediterranean island. Loosely based on Sherry's own affair in Buzzards Bay and on vacation with the family in the Bermudas, the plot of *Cinderella Married* traces Princess Ella's frustrations with her sexually impotent husband, Prince Lucious, and her adulterous solution to the problem.[36]

At the time he wrote *Cinderella Married*, Mangan was immersed in the works of Ronald Firbank and his own short novel emulated this model too closely. Often linked to the decadent movement of the 1890s, Firbank actually wrote in the post–World War I era and responded to some of the same cultural issues that Mangan did. Firbank's books are replete with the same precious, contrived, bored, and lethargic characters as *Cinderella Married*, although Mangan drew additional inspiration from Evelyn Waugh's "bright young people" of the 1920s, who were depicted in *Vile Bodies*. Mangan's view was that Firbank's highly mannered art masked a serious content; he wrote in a review several years later that he sharply differentiated "an artist like Ronald Firbank from a merely amusing writer like Evelyn Waugh."[37]

Like Firbank's work, *Cinderella Married* was ultimately aimed at and could only be appreciated by a small coterie responsive to the satiric portraits and the witty allusions with which the pages are studded. In the following passage, a minor character describes some of the guests who are present at the castle of Prince Lucious and Princess Ella:

—Well, there are several distinguished foreigners. One is Grant Frothingham, an American writer of children's books, the *Sadist Boys* series, beautifully published in a limited edition by the Minutes Press of Paris. *The Sadist Boys in a Vienna Sanitorium* and *The Sadist Boys with Lord Barrister Cowley* are generally held in higher esteem than *The Sadist Boys on the Mexican Border*, which is, however, most interesting to Europeans. He is also the author of the scurrilous Latin *Hymn of the Virgins to Lady Etiquetta*, rewritten from Catullus, beginning with the line *Dianae sumus in fide.* She nearly brought an action of libel over that. Oddly enough, he's a bore personally. And the eccentric Englishman, Lord Raspberry, is here. His yacht just anchored this afternoon.[38]

As in Firbank's work, the setting of Mangan's novel is not intended to be realistic and the text is mostly gossipy conversation. The dreamlike atmosphere of Mangan's book is only occasionally offset by episodic references to patently real things. For example, Mangan himself appears in *Cinderella Married* as a character; he is referred to as a titled author because he has written the titles for numerous unpublished works. He is also said to be currently engaged in writing a novel called *Life Among the Highly.* (The title is a play on *Uncle Tom's Cabin*, which was subtitled "Life Among the Lowly.") At the end of the book we are told that Mangan has become the manager of a literary press "which, in reaction against 'The Minutes Press,' 'The Golden Hedgehog,' 'The Kellemequotte Types,' and similar names, he had insisted on having called 'The Great Eastern Steam Printing Company,' [and] was chucklingly preparing for the publication of Marajuana de Duomente's satire, *Violetdust of Stardreams; or, How to Be a Distinguished Female Poet in Eight Easy Lessons.*"[39]

Mangan, however, departed from Firbank in his attitude toward his subject matter. Firbank saw comedy in the decadent ennui he portrayed, whereas Mangan's view of the world-weary elite is more reminiscent of F. Scott Fitzgerald. Like Fitzgerald, Mangan despised and satirized the rich, but he was also immersed in their world and fascinated by it. Mangan's own background had brought him close enough to taste the lifestyle of the elite, yet prevented him from a secure participation in it.[40]

Mangan professed doubts about the quality of *Cinderella Married* from the moment it began to materialize on paper, but it is possible that he felt ambivalent toward the work because of the grisly suicide of the man who was the inspiration for Lucious. (In the early 1930s there are explicit references to this incident in Sherry's poem "Revenant" and in a prose monologue called "The Epistle to Adeimantos"; the last stanza of his poem "Xanthocyanopia" begins: "Whereat my mind cutting its throat on the gillette blade.") He dallied in his revision of it for publication and referred to it in letters as "my youthful error."[41] In the book's

"Epistle Dedicatory" to Charles Arthur Lynch, a fellow classicist from Harvard who became a professor at Brown University, he draws attention to his subtitle, *Divertissement*, and refers to the novel as a "frivolous and tenuous" booklet "undertaken as a relief from constipate preoccupation with a poem."[42] In his liner notes for the book jacket he wrote: "To prevent any confusion among critics as to the principal influences on my work, I state here and now that the literary model of *Cinderella Married* is Daisy Ashford's *Young Visitors*" (a book purportedly written by a six-year-old). Mangan might have intended these words as part of his Firbankian motif in order to mask a deeper purpose behind a superficial facade; but, if such a purpose existed, it was missed by even Mangan's closest friends. The reviews were few but favorable, and emphasized Mangan's witty style. The *New York Herald-Tribune Books* judged that "There is no doubt about Mr. Mangan's cleverness. He is complete with quips, cranks and wreathed smiles, with winks, innuendoes and ambiguities. If you poured some extract of James Branch Cabell into bottled essence of Anita Loos, shook them up together and, at the last moment, added a drop or two of Hemingway, you could approximate the Mangan punch. You should be warned, however, that too much of this refreshment can put you under the table."[43]

Mangan's other main attempt at fiction in the late 1920s was a series of stories about Lynn, Massachusetts. Some of these were published individually in the *Atlantic Monthly*, *London Mercury*, *Esquire*, and *Housatonic*, but his intent was to bring them together in a single book, which he eventually decided to call "Barclay Street." "Barclay Street" was actually Baker Street, where Mangan and his family then lived, and the story titles were going to be house numbers in the final version. Viewed against Mangan's other work, the stories in this group are surprisingly conventional in form and content. "Thirteen" records the simple story of a young musician who experiences firsthand the loneliness of the unknown artist when even his friends and neighbors fail to show up at his concert performance because of a mere rainstorm. "The Coat," about a poverty-stricken couple, uses psychological realism to depict a distraught husband goading his wife into adultery. "The Alligator and the Building Blocks" is a sentimental narrative about an eleven-year-old child's first encounter with responsibility.[44]

The "Barclay Street" stories are more in the tradition of Anton Chekhov than anything in American letters in the 1920s. Mangan even referred to himself as an "Irish Chekhov."[45] However, also among his published short fiction of the early 1930s are four pieces that fall between surrealism and prose poetry: "By Reversal Salute to Those Who By Reversal Salute" (1930); "Enter in Grey; Or, Breton en Bretagne" (1930); "Nox: Not Being a History" (1931); and "Spot Dance" (1932). French experimental thought and technique are especially evident in "Enter in Grey," an obscure story about an enigmatic figure on a beach. It contains a number of symbolic references to the French neo-Thomist philosopher Jacques Maritain and exemplifies Sherry's use of literature to depict mental states.

The bilingual piece commences with a nameless narrator, perhaps Mangan, who is visiting a rocky coast in the company of a man of glass. The coast is probably Brittany (a stronghold of Catholic traditionalism) and the man may represent André Breton (whose doctrines dissolve the barriers between the worlds of dream and reality), thus accounting for the story's title. Together they observe the peculiar activities of an unidentified man in grey in the water and on the sand. The narrator is transfixed by his sensation that the figure has incredible powers of observation and regimentation. Suddenly the man of glass identifies the man in grey: "C'est Saint Thomas d'Aquin." The narrator then thinks: "The man in grey is built, like all the rest, on a premise that a severer honesty cannot accept, yet the functioning, even on this basis, is such that youth . . . cannot but envy of the grey man motionless on the rocky shore his imperturbable calm, his perfect observation, his absolute judgment."[46] The story confirms that, in contrast to Wheelwright, who emerged from the 1920s a visionary poet whose ideological suppositions would undergo a further modification by social reality, Mangan remained a high-powered craftsman who was still searching for a system of thought. He was so certain that the correct philosophical order would answer the needs of his literary discipline that he failed to anticipate the possibility that such a system might frustrate or displace rather than vivify his imaginative powers.

Despite personal and financial limitations imposed upon Sherry in the years in which his father's illness dragged on (Dr. Mangan finally died in March 1935), the late 1920s and the early 1930s were the most productive periods of his literary career. He was widely published in the leading literary magazines: *Poetry, New Review, New Republic, Morada, Front, The Forge,* and the *Sewanee Review.* He also corresponded regularly with the expatriates Ezra Pound and Samuel Putnam and enjoyed the friendships of many other writers scattered from Boston to Paris. Fame had not yet arrived, but in 1930 it still loomed as a possibility. The life of a professional writer was an objective for which Sherry seemed trained and for which he yearned with the unspoiled eagerness of youth.

PART II

THE REBEL POETS, 1931–1940

If there is any period one would desire
to be born in, is it not the age of Revolution;
when the old and new stand side by side
and admit of being compared;
when the energies of all men are searched by
fear and by hope;
when the historic glories can be compensated by
the rich possibilities of the new era?
This time, like all times, is a very good one,
if we but knew what to do with it.

This passage from Emerson's "American Scholar"
was used as the motto for Vanguard Verse,
edited by John Wheelwright, Sherry Mangan,
and Kenneth Porter, 1934–37.

In 1928 Jack Wheelwright wrote to Matthew Josephson's wife, Hannah, that socialism bored him "because I am a poet." Furthermore, he said that he doubted the possibility of reconciling freedom with majority rule or justice with equality. He described himself as a conservative "in Disraeli's sense of the word": "I believe in conserving capital, property and culture. The only way to conserve these things is to deliver their fate from the hands of the pawnbrokers, gamblers, and peddlers. I think the professional people can deliver them into the hands of the common people."[1] But by 1933 he had reassessed his conception of what "conservative" meant: "In order to be conservative one must be radical." He also had a new understanding of the process of social change: "And if one is to be radical one turns to the working class, not so much for lack of a better choice . . . but by the pressure of one's own ideas."[2]

The social upheavals of the early 1930s propelled so many intellectuals toward the left that it was not unthinkable for even a person as original in thought and personality as Jack Wheelwright to become captivated by revolutionary politics; what is more exceptional about his evolution is that he was never allured by the Communist party. From the start of his socialist phase, he sought to generate an anti-Stalinist Marxism, actively countering the Communist party's role as the center of American radicalism with a special appeal for young literati. As he wrote at the time, "For the professionals, Communism in this country is 'the latest thing from Paris,' an exotic thrill."[3]

The literary intellectuals closest to him in the 1920s, either by personal association or by temperament, parted company politically at the start of the depression. Some kept at arm's length from any active commitment—S. Foster Damon and R. P. Blackmur, for example. Others constituted a group that Wheelwright described as aspiring to create a "humane wing" of the Communist party, notably Matthew Josephson, Malcolm Cowley, Kenneth Burke, Horace Gregory, and Newton Arvin.[4]

Among the main currents of radical intellectual thought in the 1930s, Wheelwright's affinity was with the anti-Stalinist left rooted in New York City. In politics this unorganized group held that the Communist party was not implementing policies that served the objective needs of a working-class revolution in the United States, but was primarily devoted to serving the needs of Stalin's bureaucracy in the USSR; in literature it sought to liberate Marxist criticism from abuse by leftists who would evaluate writing by political criteria. This movement was led by figures like James T. Farrell, whose *Note on Literary Criticism* Jack much admired. After 1937 the main literary organ of the anti-Stalinist left became *Partisan Review*, a journal that he supported. Yet Wheelwright anticipated the development of the New York grouping by several years. Moreover, while most of the New York figures stood aloof from organizations, he sought to act upon his Leninist convictions by assisting in the construction of a revolutionary political party in the capacities for which he felt most suited. This chapter will begin by reviewing the development of his political thought as it evolved from social democracy to Trotskyism in 1936; it will then examine the manner in which politics influenced his cultural activities and interacted with the eccentricities of his personal and religious life.

Some of Jack's attitudes toward the Communist party were already formed before he joined the organized socialist movement in 1932. In his 1928 correspondence with Hannah Josephson, he rejected her claim that the only choice for intellectuals was between Communism and fascism. He abhorred fascism, he said, because he had seen its reality and was repelled; also, he had come to the opinion that any rule by the upper classes in the United States would be intolerable. This was because capitalism had driven the most valuable social elements (namely, poets and professionals) out of the upper classes. He believed that the "best" people were already as good as disenfranchised politically and culturally.

But he was profoundly dismayed by the poor quality of ideas produced by the American Communist party: "They grind out the dialectic just as the papal court grinds out its dialectic. I never cared for canned food." Even if one were to imagine the American working class becoming a force for change, a notion that Jack still doubted in 1928, capitalist exploitation had left the American worker in no condition to construct a better world, and the existing Communist party was unfit to lead the proletariat forward. He viewed the working class in the United States as debased, undisciplined, stupid, materialistic, and uncultured: "I admit that this is one of the very strong arguments against capitalism . . . [but] I think there is a peril in this unlikely American communist revolution which is not present in Europe, where the lower classes have a culture, an idealism, sense and discipline."

Though his membership in the American Socialist party was four years away at the time of this correspondence, he did criticize Hannah and Matthew Josephson, Kenneth Burke, and Malcolm Cowley for their orientation toward the Communists rather than the Socialists. He accused them of trying to "capture a cause" and polish it up, rather than constructing a genuinely honest and effective movement of their own. Jack then stated that his alternative was the development of "a party of professional minds dedicated to the cause of national culture and the happiness of the common lot, in complete [solidarity] with the oppressed class of labor, personally clean from greed and personal ambition, apostates from the religion of Mammon." In essence this would be a socialist party, but "the image of Fabian socialism, of victory by retreat, does not please me. I think General Grant had an idea of steam-roller victory, of gradual and unretreating advance. Some such image as that would suit me."[5]

How did Jack justify his membership in a working-class party, the Socialist party, if he believed that the American workers were debased, undisciplined, materialist, and uncultured? Part of the explanation is that in spite of such talk and in spite of his tendency to be rather sharp with servants and waiters, he much enjoyed the company of individual workers and could treat them with great respect. To a literary acquaintance close to the Communist party he wrote in 1933 that "I don't believe that any of you, with the possible exception of Malcolm [Cowley], knows or feels about the working class as much as I do."[6]

He sometimes mentioned that he had worked in a cotton mill in Taunton, Massachusetts, for six weeks in the summer of 1915 because his family wanted him "to know where their money came from." On that occasion he found that "the working people were pleasant to me and one another."[7] But the working class in large groups frightened him: "The instincts which are hostile to themselves seem then to get the upper hand."[8] Consequently, when he became attracted to the Socialist party, he devoted himself to the cultural and intellectual enrichment of the working-class movement. Between 1928 and 1933 his goal changed from simply creating a "party of professional minds," which would deliver socialism to the masses, to advocating the formation of a cadre of professional minds functioning within and assisting the development of a working-class party.

The prerequisite for this change on his part was the surge of optimism he experienced when he saw the American working class begin to rear its head as a fighting force in the early 1930s. In 1932 he wrote a fellow left-wing writer that he anticipated an astonishing change in the working class in the near future: "They have not yet found capitalism intolerable, and when they do they will adopt Socialist ideas. Those members of the white collar classes who have these ideas and who have imparted them to others will be authorities along with members of the working class who do the same thing." Jack saw vast areas of work that needed to be undertaken by those socialists who possessed intellectual skills. Their immediate function was to "enrich socialist ideas," but there were all sorts of theories and scientific discoveries that had to be assessed from a socialist view: "Pluralistic politics, electromagnetic materialism, the psychology of the unconscious, and how the machine may affect the labor theory of value are all unsettled."[9]

However, Wheelwright's conviction was that professionals could not be reliable allies of the proletariat until they broke all ties with the ruling class. In particular, it was crucial to recognize that declaring oneself for the defense of "culture" against the mismanagement and corruption of the capitalist order was only a preliminary and inadequate step. In a book review juxtaposing the poetry of Auden and Spender to the more limited work of Richard Aldington, Wheelwright explained how the former two used aesthetic means to reorient cultural practice:

> They [Auden and Spender] oppose the good of capitalist culture to the evils of capitalist society. When they are split open we see that they are split across as well. Intuitively they approach the realization that makers of culture, as opposed to its existing patrons, are in all countries thrown together with the makers of wealth into opposition against the owners of wealth. The poetry of Spender and Auden purposefully and emotionally push this intuition towards logical and passionate ends in letters while our whole disintegrated culture reintegrates within split individuals into the collective forces of revolution and counter-revolution. But Aldington rests at a stage before this process. That is why his poetry splits into fully truthful but not fully conscious records set down in sombre numbers.[10]

This two-stage process mirrored his own evolution. He believed that he had never had political bonds with the upper classes, but before the depression he had felt a strong "cultural allegiance." Now he saw that the determinants of social reality were not literary ideas but class forces: "The aesthetic struggle within the upper class which was once vital to me is now dead. The victory of modern art is won, and I find myself perfectly indifferent to the fact." If he lived to see the victory of socialism, he concluded that he would not be indifferent. Furthermore, whatever cultural sag might accompany the first stage of socialism, he was certain that he would prefer it to the present "capitalist degeneration."[11]

Prior to 1936 the focus of Jack's activities in the Socialist party was on literary and cultural activities. He tried participating in the Communist-led John Reed Club at Harvard for a while, but was expelled as a "disorganizer."[12] He then initiated several other radical cultural organizations. For a time he corresponded with Jack Conroy, leader of the national Rebel Poets organization. Wheelwright then established a Poetry Forum of Cambridge, which was briefly allied with Conroy's group. He also became a leading figure in the Rebel Arts Society, a nationwide cultural affiliate of the Socialist party. He formed a group called The Friends of the Rebel Arts Society in Boston as well.

When the Rebel Arts Society launched the magazine *Arise* in 1934, Jack was a director of the publication, then served as its poetry editor while frequently contributing. At *Arise* editorial board meetings, he met the artist Fairfield Porter, who was politically attracted to the American followers of Leon Trotsky, and the socialist writer Bruno Fischer. Porter wrote him about the political activities of the Trotskyists, especially their intended fusion with A. J. Muste's American Workers party, an independent revolutionary organization.

Jack organized the distribution of literature and educational material for the Boston Central branch of the Socialist party; by 1936 he was state literature agent. This assignment involved setting an exemplary record of selling materials, keeping track of sales and finances, and having a personal familiarity with all the literature items. He also mailed out circulars to the Massachusetts branches of the party in which he gave advice on sales techniques and offered opinions on educational policy, including the view that "every Socialist should read the *Communist Manifesto* every two months."[13]

He taught classes for the party and gave public speeches at large meetings and at impromptu gatherings on soapboxes. When James Laughlin was a Harvard student, he occasionally used to drive Jack out to working-class suburbs for such activities. Once he picked up Jack at a dinner party attended by well-dressed Boston Brahmins. Jack came to the car in fancy dinner clothes with his raccoon coat, carrying a soapbox. They drove to a corner in Roxbury, and Jack got out of the car, put down his box, and started to orate. Crowds of curious people soon gathered, attracted mainly by his marvelous Brahmin accent and involved vocabulary.[14]

He also ran for office, picketed, demonstrated, and was arrested for violating injunctions. He participated in the Unemployed Leagues, the National Committee for the Defense of Political Prisoners (an affiliate of the Communist-run International Labor Defense), and the American Committee for the World Congress against War. He took the lead in organizing a Cambridge local of the Socialist party. Personal relationships were formed with A. J. Muste, director of the Brookwood Labor College, and Oscar Ameringer, editor of the Socialist newspaper *American Guardian*.

From the beginning of his membership in the Socialist party, Jack considered himself to the left of the rest of the organization and had a greater openness to bolshevism. He was kept aware of the existence and activities of the Trotskyist movement through friends such as Fairfield Porter, Quincy Howe, A. J. Muste, and Cuthbert Daniel. In various ways, all of these had contact with the American followers of Trotsky, called the Communist League of America up until 1935 and after that (when they fused with Muste's American Workers party) the Workers party. In the early 1930s, the aspect of Trotsky's doctrine that most influenced Jack was the analysis Trotsky offered of the events in Germany leading to the Nazi conquest of power in 1933. In particular, Trotsky had vigorously campaigned for an authentic united front of Communists, Socialists, and trade unionists against Hitler, but his warnings were ignored. At that time the Communist parties of the world regarded the Social Democrats as nothing but "social fascists." The reformist Socialists, in turn, were too timid to organize a militant resistance to fascism.

Jack came to believe that a united front among Socialists, Communists, and all other working-class parties was the best policy for the United States as well. Consequently, he carried out a program of joining Communist-dominated organizations and fighting for joint Communist-Socialist actions even when he did not have proper authorization from his own party. This controversial behavior brought Jack into repeated conflicts with Alfred Baker Lewis, a wealthy socialist who lived in Cambridge and served as state secretary of the party.[15]

By 1934 the Socialist party had developed a distinct left wing comprised of two currents called Militants and Progressives. Jack's views were clearly in this camp. In February 1934 he submitted to a Socialist party discussion a document calling for the party to adhere to a more revolutionary line and urging it to distinguish its proposals more incisively from those of the Democrats and Republicans. He also criticized the party for a poor theoretical understanding of bourgeois democracy, arguing that democracy is not a working-class weapon, "but a partial victory, won by working class weapons. Unless political democracy grows into industrial democracy, it will die. It can be defended only by working class victory." Warning of the danger of fascism in the United States, he believed he saw a potential for its growth among "white collar demagogues and in the N. I. R. A. itself." He believed that the Soviet Union should be characterized as the "world's only workers' and farmers' republic" and that it should be defended by the Socialist party against the encroachment of capitalist nations. In a section of his document subheaded "The Road to Power" and in other sections outlining the connection between legal and illegal actions and the use of class struggle to subvert interimperialist war, he demonstrated that the main influences in his political thought were the ideas of Lenin and the Russian Bolsheviks.[16]

Some of Jack's political views in the 1932–34 period were dramatized in verse in his "Masque with Clowns," which was initiated in collaboration with a playwright named William Blake whom he met in Provincetown. If performed, the masque would have resembled a Brecht play; the characters are symbolically defamiliarized for didactic purposes. The masque describes a national election campaign that Jack likens to a circus. The oppression of farmers and workers during the depression is indicated by the setting, the corner of Milk and Mill streets, both of which are cluttered with signs reading "No Help Wanted" and "Help Not Needed." Each existing political party is then satirized. The Democrats and Republicans are shown to be twins; the Socialist party is mocked as dainty, middle class, and politically watered down. Then comes a parade of the Communist party, various expelled factions of the party, Industrial Workers of the World, anarchists, fascists, and others. In the ten years that pass, the economic depression worsens. Only at the end of the decade is hope revived; this new hope is symbolized by a giant tractor and dynamo which appear on the stage shooting three arrows. (Three arrows was the insignia of the left-wing Socialist party of Austria, which was distinguished from other Socialist parties by its 1934 armed resistance against the reactionary Dollfuss regime.) The three arrows destroy the oppressors of humanity, paving the way for the creation of a new society. The narrator concludes:

> *Three Arrows* wing, *Three Arrows* sing, *Three Arrows*
> *Three Arrows, Three Arrows, Arrows;* Farmers and Millers
> clad in star-spark-feathered shafts
> with fore-arms flexed salute the GIANT ARCHERS.
> But the MAN makes no salute, except to strike
> his handcuffs on the monstrous MACHINES;
> his handcuffs spring!
> Unhinged, TRACTOR and DYNAMO
> disclose ANOTHER WOMAN and ANOTHER MAN.[17]

"Masque With Clowns" indicates the distance Wheelwright had traveled from his early modernist principles. A masque is a traditional literary form that is frequently political in content; instead of being court entertainment, Wheelwright's masque is addressed to the working class. He attempts to amaze and estrange the public at the same time: to allow the recognition of the subject, but to render it unfamiliar. An important part of this strategy is to achieve a comic response by connecting alienation effects with politics in the hope that he can jar the audience free of bourgeois illusions. "Masque with Clowns," along with a mass recitation called "Footsteps," demonstrates how Wheelwright incorporated characteristic depression material into his literary practice: political parties, unemployed workers, labor lawyers, machinery, Bolsheviks, slum children, strikes, and breadlines. Furthermore, the masque is "occasional"— it expresses his sympathy with the Militant and Progressive factions of the Socialist party in their struggle against the conservative Old Guard. When the Old Guard split from the organization in 1936, he was delighted to be rid of an irritating obstacle.

In the spring of 1936, when Norman Thomas persuaded the American Trotskyists to officially disband their own organization and enter the Socialist party as individuals, Jack began to find new allies. His strongest political ties to Trotskyism ensued through his friendship with Dr. Antoinette Konikow, a pioneering birth-control advocate and early disciple of Trotsky; Larry Trainor, a young Irish-American worker whose father was a Boston policeman blacklisted as a result of the 1919 police strike; and John Philip Hall, an advent Christian from Lynn and later a labor historian.[18]

However, Jack was not an instant convert to Trotskyism. While certain personal sympathies for Trotsky had existed for years, he hitherto regarded the American disciples of Trotsky as too sectarian to be effective. Even when the Trotskyists issued their official platform inside the Socialist party, in the form of the "*Appeal* Program" (named for their Socialist party organ, *Socialist Appeal*), he qualified his support with a series of criticisms contained in a letter sent to the Trotskyists:

> Revolutionary Socialism yes. But Scientific Socialism. This involves the Leninist use of reforms. Distinguish between reformers ("reform, ah, reform it utterly,—" *Hamlet*) and reformists. The program is free of infantile leftism, but the recruits are not. . . .
>
> In regard to pacifism, how come there is no mention of the idiotic "socialist" opposition to popular military training, a most admirable institution? Let us encourage it while redoubling our anti-war strikes and resistance to militaristic propaganda and perversion of the soul.
>
> It is wild sectarianism to hold every other party to be our enemy. We'll never make friends with that in our hearts. Keep your shirt on! Don't waste time weakening and destroying. Hold to a *positive* aim against all and with all. Only so can polemic and fraction accomplish the Revolution.[19]

In the course of the internal struggles convulsing the Socialist party, he managed to sign the program of a native faction, that of the Clarity caucus, at the same time he endorsed the *Appeal* program; but by 1937 his views had become firmly Trotskyist.

Coexisting with Jack Wheelwright the Socialist party activist was Jack Wheelwright the poet and architect, who seemed to have time and energy for an entirely separate life. He served as vice-president of the New England Poetry Society (for which he wrote the official history), as the director of the Shirley Eustace House Association, and as a craftsman of the Boston Society of Arts and Crafts. He occasionally remodeled homes as part of his architectural work. With John Ames he designed the house of his friend Robert Hillyer.

Of the stories in circulation among Jack's friends were several about the facility with which he could compose his poems. Malcolm Cowley remembers an incident in 1919 when Jack was arrested for reckless driving in a Model T Ford. He was taken to Brighton jail across the Charles River from Harvard. Cowley, who was a passenger in the car, stayed in the cell with him overnight because he had nowhere else to go. Jack had trouble sleeping so he composed a poem called "Fantasia in Brighton Jail," which was published in the Harvard *Advocate*.[20] The publisher Edward Weeks recalls a dinner that he and Ferris Greenslet, editor of the Houghton Mifflin Company, arranged in honor of T. S. Eliot at the St. Botolph Club in 1932. Jack was there and ducked into the library, where he composed on the spot a poem that was read to the audience.[21] However, Mary Marshall, who typed many poems and articles for Jack, is certain that in most cases he worked on his poems over a long period of time and put them through countless revisions. But she does recall that when she asked him why he always dedicated his poems to friends and acquaintances, he jokingly answered that this was done in order to insure the sale of a certain number of books.[22]

In early 1933 he wrote to Van Wyck Brooks that he was working on a host of literary projects: a memoir of the 1920s (inspired by Malcolm Cowley's *Exile's Return*), a history of American architecture, a volume of satirical verse about America, research into the history of American religion, and numerous poems and reviews.[23] The latter were published most frequently in *Poetry*, the *New Republic*, and *Hound and Horn*. He also placed articles in the *New England Quarterly* and in V. F. Calverton's *Modern Monthly*. An essay was included in a satirical anthology called *Whither, Whither or After Sex, What?*, along with contributions by James Thurber, E. B. White, Edmund Wilson, and E. E. Cummings.[24]

In more than a dozen reviews for *Poetry* between 1930 and 1939, Jack established himself as an opinionated interpreter of the course of American letters. A constant preoccupation was the impasse to which the imitators of T. S. Eliot and Gertrude Stein had come; he insisted on the inferior quality of work by seemingly diverse poets such as Walter Lowenfels, Laura Riding, and Leonard Bacon. Often he interjected a socialist perspective into his critical comments. He contrasted Archibald MacLeish's view of war in *Air Raid* to his own belief that "international war is civil war against the working class." He criticized Stephen Leacock for confusions in his thought because, "like Shaw, he is unable to grasp on any tangible resolution of capitalist contradictions." He characterized Robert Frost as "the laureate of the New Deal." He concluded that Ernest Walsh's poetry failed because of his fixation on abstract notions of "love," because "without hierarchical reference to other things, the literature of love is nihilistic. Social revolution exacts fresh relationships from passion."[25] For the *New Republic* he wrote on a broader canvas. His book reviews, appearing once or twice a year until mid-1937, concerned New England history, religion, the architectural work of Frank Lloyd Wright, the paintings of Thomas Eakins, and the poetry and prose of Robert Hillyer, Lincoln Kirstein, and R. P. Blackmur.[26]

Jack's closest literary association through the first half of the 1930s was with *Hound and Horn*, which was initiated in Cambridge by Lincoln

Kirstein and others in 1927. His contributions included not only reviews and poems, but also longer studies of American art and architecture. In sympathetic essays on Lewis Mumford's *Brown Decades*, on the massive collection of monographs called Masterpieces of Architecture in the United States, and on Charles Moore's *Life and Times of Charles Follen McKim*, he probed the social significance of art and architecture throughout the changing pattern of American history. In an illustrated study entitled "Remington and Winslow Homer," he argued that the Civil War was a cultural watershed, after which the central cultural issues in the United States shifted away from the interaction "between man and the world of nature" and toward "man and the world of his own making." Consequently, for Jack's own generation of artists, "the subject matter is the class struggle."[27]

In the spring of 1932, Granville Hicks, a critic who was increasingly identified with the Communist party, reviewed Lincoln Kirstein's novel *Flesh Is Heir* in the *New Republic*. In passing, Hicks described Kirstein's *Hound and Horn* as the organ of leisure-class writers aspiring to create a leisure-class culture. Kirstein, along with A. Hyatt Mayor and Bernard Bandler, challenged Hicks on this matter in a letter to the editor, and the exchange of views ran over several issues. Kirstein and his associates defended themselves largely by the argument that cultural exploration had an inherent value even when detached from social activism. Consequently, even though they considered themselves experts in cultural matters, they had not yet developed, nor had they yet heard about, a sufficiently convincing plan for social transformation. In addition, they decried the use of the term "leisure class" in connection with *Hound and Horn* on the grounds that most writers did not come from such a background.

Jack Wheelwright, however, did not sign their letter. He submitted his own protest against Hicks called "Scorn Not the Nobly Born." He began by pointing out that twice in the pages of the *New Republic* Hicks had accused the regular contributors to *Hound and Horn* of being members of the leisure class. "The editors of the *Hound and Horn*, in taking up that challenge, have exonerated those of their contributors who are not members of the leisure class. This leaves me to exonerate myself, as I am a member of that class." Jack's response was also quite different from those by Kirstein and the other editors because of its friendly tone. He politely pointed out to Hicks that the leisure class had contributed a disproportionately large number of leaders to radical and revolutionary movements, as well as geniuses in the field of art. If an essay in *Hound and Horn* had some particular weakness, he said, there was no particular reason to correlate this with the author's class background. But Jack did admit that *Hound and Horn* differed from the *New Republic* in its predominant method of criticism. The *New Republic* tended to favor the sociological approach, whereas *Hound and Horn* leaned toward the technical. As for himself, Jack wrote that "social progress is impeded more than it is furthered by critics who substitute sociological prophecy for the discernment of the next immediate technical advance in the arts and science."[28]

Jack Wheelwright did come from the leisure class and he remained in it in the sense that he was not obliged to work full-time for a living. However, the fortunes of the Wheelwright family had steadily declined since the death of Ned Wheelwright. After World War I, both Jack and his brother March wished to join the Somerset Club, but Bessie Wheelwright ruled that the family funds were insufficient. In the 1920s Jack was allowed an annuity large enough to permit some travel abroad with accommodations in the best hotels, and he frequently lent money to friends like Malcolm Cowley. But when the depression began, he wrote Van Wyck Brooks that he lacked the funds to travel in the way that he used to; in 1933 he wrote Cowley that his allowance had been severely cut. After that time, Jack lived at home with his mother at 415 Beacon Street in Boston, manipulating his monthly allowance by borrowing from friends and obtaining advances for his publications.

Living together, Bessie and Jack were evenly matched in their uncommon behavior and odd appearance. Sometimes Bessie would leave town for the summer, precipitating a crisis because she ordered all of the water in the house shut off. Jack was thus obliged to appear suddenly at the residences of his friends, asking if he might take a bath. A love-hate relationship existed between the financially dependent son and the overbearing mother. Bessie could be tightfisted with money and Jack complained that she kept him in a state bordering on penury. But when Jack once grew a lush, droopy mustache that added considerably to his bearing, he shaved it off without hesitation when he learned that it caused his mother difficulty in reading his lips.[29]

Jack took full advantage of the humorous side of his public image as a revolutionary activist living in a house decorated with Chinese vases and screens from a family trading empire, and who attended his Socialist Party meetings dressed in a tuxedo. He once showed up on a breadline wearing his raccoon coat. A policeman approached and asked, "What are you doing here?" "I'm a poet," he explained. On another occasion he was queried as to why he dressed so elegantly for working-class rallies and demonstrations. "It's only the honor that is due them," was his response. His most notorious soapbox oration was an agitational speech in which he explained the operations of the capitalist system by pointing to himself as an example of how certain members of society lived on unearned increment.[30] Gus Tyler, a leader of the left wing of the Socialist party in the 1930s, once organized a street corner meeting in an industrial section of Boston with Jack scheduled as a speaker. Arriving late and in a fluster,

Jack explained that he could only orate briefly because "mother is giving a tea." He mounted the platform with some difficulty because his walking stick kept getting in the way. After dabbing his brow with a dainty handkerchief, he began: "We, of the proletariat. . . ."[31]

A bohemian side of Jack was evidenced in the summer of 1933 when he stayed at the Damon house in Rhode Island. Damon's wife, Jack's sister Louise, was away for the summer. Wade Vliet, a poet outspoken in his homosexual views, moved in with Jack and Foster. Jack grew a ferrous beard so that he resembled the golden-haired, blue-eyed chromo of the "Aryan Christ" found in some evangelical Sunday schools. One day he interrupted Frank Merchant, a Brown University student who was in the house typing the manuscript of Jack's book Rock and Shell, insisting that they must go for a walk at once and marching out of the house in a bedraggled raincoat. Before long, he and Merchant ended up in a rough section of town in which groups of men and youth, out of work because of the depression, were hanging around with nothing to do. Beards were not acceptable then. Merchant and Jack were suddenly surrounded by a group of tough-looking characters who jeered at Jack's appearance. Merchant recalls that Jack persisted in "speaking to them sensibly, mostly asking why he shouldn't have the right to look as he wanted to. His retreat was both delayed and dignified, although I felt we were always on the point of having stones or trash thrown at us. Jack never turned a hair."[32]

Even when he was clean-shaven and dapper in his appearance, his antics still persisted. In the spring of 1933 he arrived at the artists' colony of Yaddo in Saratoga Springs, New York. When he was introduced to the dignified director of the institute, Elizabeth Ames, she was startled by the fact that he was barefoot. "We Wheelwrights always go barefoot in the country," Jack explained. Later Miss Ames discovered that he had the habit of bringing strange objects into the tub with him when he bathed—bananas and her prized statuettes, for example—and he was asked to leave.[33]

At times Jack could be quite arrogant and rude; but he could also incite a room full of people to gales of laughter. A favorite trick was to suddenly duck beneath the carpet in a room during a formal gathering and crawl from one end to the other. He performed this once while Allen Tate was giving a poetry reading at Harvard, but Tate managed to pay no attention.[34] Professor Samuel French Morse remembers that when Jack came to Dartmouth College to give a poetry reading, he scandalized some of the faculty by bringing his whiskey bottle to the platform.[35]

Although insufficient data exists to permit a psychoanalytic interpretation, the compulsiveness of Jack's iconoclastic behavior demands some sort of psychological probing. Muriel Rukeyser thought that behind the gaiety of his public antics she caught glimpses of the ill fortune that had befallen his family.[36] Not only was he imprisoned by the memory of his father's suicide and the economic dependency on his eccentric mother, but his brother March suffered from alcoholism and his sister Louise was institutionalized in a psychiatric hospital. In 1934–35 melancholia became so intense that some of his friends feared that the son might follow in the steps of his father.[37]

Yet the source of his anxiety may have been less a fear of insanity than the displacement of sexual frustration. Elroy Webber remembers that the precise sexual orientation of the mature bachelor son "was a constant mystery" to his friends: "He didn't speak much of girls nor did he seem to know many." Yet Webber also recalls a party at which Jack was accused of making improper advances toward a female guest in a coat closet.[38] Matthew Josephson and Malcolm Cowley thought there were homosexual liaisons, while other friends imagined Jack so immersed in spiritual tribulations that he eschewed or repressed sexuality altogether.[39]

Polly Thayer Starr, who knew Jack well, believes that he grew increasingly lonely in his thirties and "would have welcomed the permanent commitment of marriage."[40] For a while he was seen in the company of Christina Sedgwick Marquand, the first wife of the novelist J. P. Marquand, but they drifted apart. Howard Nemerov recalls that Jack "once tried timidly to kiss me" and conjectures that he was probably "a touch homoerotic rather than homosexual, and equally timid with women."[41] Jack's only explicit statement about his sexual views in later life is in a letter he sent to Kenneth Patchen after reading a draft version of *The Journal of Albion Moonlight*. He bitterly attacks "those who split the monism of love into the dismal triad of heterosexuality, bisexuality, and homosexuality."[42]

Some of Wheelwright's poetry exhibits the classical pattern—described by Freud in many places, including his study of Leonardo da Vinci—in which sexual longings are sublimated into creative work. Homoerotic imagery is evident in the sonnet sequence *Mirrors of Venus* and sexual themes are explicitly manifest in the Doubting Thomas "novel." Elsewhere Wheelwright's complex allusions, symbols, and systems embody tensions that may be correlated to sexual energies.

Complementing his mysterious sexuality was the split in his daily life wherein he retained social and personal ties to the upper class while simultaneously joining a political movement seeking to overthrow that class. One explanation is that Jack's Brahmin bolshevism served a dual function: atonement for guilt and the substitution of world socialism for Christian salvation. But this hardly explains the way he used the contradictions of his life-style for aesthetic effect, as a theatrical gesture similar to the times he played the "fool" by crawling under rugs. By talking proletarian revolution in Brahmin salons and wearing a tuxedo to socialist rallies, he defied in person, as he did in poetry, the conventional expectations of both classes. Jack's ambiguous sexuality is bound up in this split as well, with personality traits that his society regarded as masculine given over to bolshevism, while feminine traits remained domiciled with mother on Beacon Street.

Jack may have actively cultivated this split in his daily life for literary purposes. Unconventional living or possession of a personality that is highly responsive to nature and the emotions may assist in priming a poet's sensibilities for his work. Although Marx and Engels did not subscribe to the view that the authentic artist must be neurotic, they did seem to believe that a special temperament was characteristic of most poets. In a letter to Joseph Weydemeyer, Marx pointed out that the literary sensibilities of Ferdinand Freiligrath demanded special treatment and warned that "you must not forget the difference between a 'poet' and a 'critic.'" Marx is also reported to have made the following remark to his wife when she criticized the political vagaries of Heinrich Heine: "Poets . . . [are] queer kittle-cattle, not to be judged by the ordinary, or even the extraordinary standards of conduct."[43]

A similar emphasis on the eccentric element in the temperament of the authentic writer was communicated by the American literary radical Harvey Swados, who wrote the following in his 1962 book of essays, *A Radical's America*: "Although I am a political man, I am a novelist, not a politician, and shall never join any party nor run for mayor of any place. If he is not inconsistent, the novelist is nothing. This is also why . . . I have resisted all efforts to make of me a systematic thinker."[44]

Although there is no evidence of a correlation between erratic thinking and artistic quality, there is a connection between Wheelwright's ability to fertilize his poetic imagination in his Marxist-activist phase and his many personal eccentricities, some of which were rooted not only in personal traumas and sexual unhappiness, but also in his deep regional ties and the associated religious heterodoxies. One can see analogous patterns of eccentricity in some other successful Marxist poets: Neruda, for example, had profound regional ties and a semimystical attitude toward nature; Brecht and the surrealists André Breton and Benjamin Péret were devotees of their unique aesthetic theories to the point that their personal behavior took on an odd dimension. In contrast, later chapters will demonstrate the alternative evolution of Sherry Mangan: the more he immersed himself in purely rationalistic thought and activity—first in his studies of linguistics and science in the early 1930s, then in his aspiration to play a politically important role in the Trotskyist movement—the more difficult it became for him to sustain his imaginative world.

Two elements were necessary for Wheelwright to channel his fractured mode of being into art. First, there was the complex apparatus of symbols, allusions, and myth that he would never relinquish, even under pressure to make his poetry more accessible in the 1930s. Such mechanisms are an understandable response to a disconcerting external reality. If one cannot prevent the death of a father or express one's true sexuality in the outside world, one can at least compensate by controlling the inner world of the imagination through an intricate art and theatrical personality.

Second, a dynamic center is required to effectively use this apparatus to achieve appropriate effects in art and behavior. Wheelwright indicated as much in a book review of R. P. Blackmur's poetry. In part, the review was the continuation of a quarrel with Blackmur over poetic technique. In an essay for *Poetry* on Wheelwright's *Rock and Shell*, Blackmur had pointed to certain irregularities in Wheelwright's technique of versification; Jack responded at once with a personal letter to editor Morton Zabel: "Those of my disorders which he [Blackmur] enumerates are the result not of carelessness, but of years of care. . . . all cadences are justified, or not, simply by their sounds."[45] When the opportunity arose to review Blackmur's *From Jordan's Delight* for the *New Republic*, he criticized his friend for a weakness that he thought typical of many poets from the same modernist school as himself—the tendency to elevate technique over myth. In words that might have applied to Sherry Mangan as well, Wheelwright concluded:

> Yet no myth takes firm hold on Blackmur. If he continues as a minor poet, it will be because—although with tones of authority he supplicates at the threshold of ideas—he uses philosophy only for poetic purposes, and is not made victim to any major obsession that compels one to use poetry for philosophic purpose. . . . Verse need not be philosophic to be poetry, but if it comes near, it must meet or surpass; for prosody is a science of managed association which has more profound powers than the charms of texture that preoccupy the priesthood of "pure poetry."
> Blackmur is preoccupied with "pure poetry." . . . Gentle and pacific, Blackmur, like all the alert who are not fired by revolutionary myth (and like many who want to be so fired) is nihilist.[46]

The argument is not simply for a greater intellectual content in Blackmur's poetry, it is for a heavier dose of the unconscious and, more significantly, for the virtue of obsession. One's art must be organized around the eruption of a powerful idea, a brilliant force that bursts aggressively into the ossified world of bourgeois culture. Wheelwright's language, "fired by revolutionary myth," sounds religious, but the religion of his youth was no longer capable of satisfying this need.

In fact, in his voluminous correspondence, texts of speeches, notes for debates, drafts of documents, and other materials that survive from his Socialist party activities, there are virtually no references made to his

Christian beliefs. Certainly he was not a "Christian Socialist" or a radical in the "Social Gospel" tradition. The views he espoused in all his surviving political statements were scientific socialist, and Marx and Lenin were indubitably his main inspirers. Yet it is also true that his theological convictions were not kept a secret, and some of his friends thought that his belief in God contradicted his political perspective. In the summer of 1932, Newton Arvin wrote him that religion and communism were utterly irreconcilable. Jack retorted sharply that he refused to discuss religion "with one who is not interested in it, or thinks he is not. The Holy Spirit will tend to you just as it tends to me."[47]

With those who were interested in discussing religion, he was as voluble as he was on the topics of Marxism, architecture, and poetry. Fairfield Porter remembered that Jack used to explain that "if I weren't a Christian, I would certainly never be a socialist." Porter also believed that Jack conceived of modern socialism as a consistent development from seventeenth-century American radicalism; he cited one occasion when Jack defended "the Communists to me by saying that they were the modern Puritans."[48]

Jack retained his connections with St. John's Church in Roxbury, although Mary Marshall remembers that he was fond of saying that "religion is good bunk, but a bum racket."[49] When Polly Thayer Starr painted Jack's portrait in 1932, it showed him looking into a mirror at an image of himself dressed in the robes of a subdeacon. To Van Wyck Brooks he wrote that same summer: "I trouble my head not at all with the laws and doctrines of theology. But I listen to my own heart and feed it and exercise it by daily life (so far as I can) and by being a faithful, though intermittent worshipper in church. I do not permit the church to shut me away from contemporary life."[50]

The mirror image of Polly Starr's painting is more appropriate for Jack's dual world of religion and politics in the 1920s than in the 1930s. By the time of his 1932 decision to join the Socialist party, his behavior had become so modified that even his highly personal version of Christian faith remained a contradiction. Either religion or Marxism would have to go. Increasingly the evidence was that it would be the former, for in Marxism Wheelwright now had what he believed to be a clearcut antidote to the nihilism that had overwhelmed his father and threatened to wash away or debase the culture he valued. Socialism provided a set of values that pointed to precise action and served as the "obsession" needed to inspire creativity: "Social rebellion is the most vital phase of poetry today," he argued in *Poetry* in 1933.[51] In "Meet Six Nihilists," a review for the Socialist cultural organ *Arise*, he analyzed the work of eleven poets. Five of these he deemed to be unworthy of discussion; the other six—Archibald MacLeish, James Agee, Lincoln Kirstein, Theodore

Spencer, Robert Fitzgerald, and James Neugass—he took to task for lacking "effective philosophic equipment" that could transform their technical achievements in versification into genuine steps forward for American poetry.[52]

A study of the socialist classics led Jack to see the Bolshevik leaders as the symbol of continuity in culture. They represented the assimilation of past achievements into a program for the future. They stood as the contemporary expression of the Promethean tradition that Jack celebrated in his poem "Titanic Litany":

> Prometheus!
> Prototypal Christ, pre-crucified
> pushing the invisible
> advance upon our pushes upon chaos.
> Discoverer and inventor, never let 'em say:
> "Human nature cannot change." Institutor of fire's Sacrament
> and outward forms of conscious inner will;
> Prometheus!
> Forethought of freedom (freedom
> for her and him; concrete, in that and this)
> Titan, tortured by the tyrant vulture
> whom Vulcan riveted as firmly as machines
> can rivet laborers to capital;
> Prometheus!
> O, let it never be said that the human of nature cannot
> change. Saul changed to Paul. All saints change
> man's nature, as men change nature's change.
> Show us in our own acts that we hear our supplication.
> Never a saint is revered who was not reviled
> as a rebel. Every rebel, in so far prophet
> breeds holy doubt and skeptic faith in deeds'
> Melchizedekian Succession.
> While boom the double guns of Act and Word,
> mutating fire swims through the protestant
> blood of Christ, erect above your shadowed rock
> Prometheus!
> Our supine Crucifixion.[53]

"Titanic Litany" bears the dedication "For Leon Trotsky," and the characterization of him as a forethinker with his energy and will directed to the future was apt.[54] However, Wheelwright's rhetorical stance in the poem is ambiguous. He begins by making the association—presumably outrageous to bourgeois ears—of Trotsky with the best-known member of the Titan race, who is depicted as a Christ figure (the tying of Prometheus to a rock is said to be a "supine" version of the crucifixion). But Wheelwright's epic lines border on the mock-heroic. Just as one is beginning to wonder whether Wheelwright has lost perspective and regressed from the twentieth century altogether, he inserts the colloquialism in the fifth line, "never let 'em say." Thus he breaks the heroic pose with a wink at the reader, then immediately reverts to it for the rest of the poem.

In contrast, the content is lucid. Wheelwright is celebrating the materialist act of transforming human nature by praxis—conscious intervention in the material world. Yet both Prometheus and Trotsky are also associated with a prophetic tradition; the reference to the tribes of Melchizedek is a reference to the origins of the Christian priesthood. Here religion is reduced exclusively to the realm of moral inspiration; the realm of action is guided by an understanding of the laws of the material universe for which the Marxism of Trotsky is more appropriate. Elsewhere he described Trotsky as "a man whose accomplishments are equivalent to those of a Calvin, Cromwell and Clarendon," as one who "worthily occupies the post of champion of civilization against barbarism."[55] The exiled organizer and historian of the Russian Revolution personified the harmonious unification of word and deed for the entire Marxist phase of Jack's life.

From the perspective of his ultimate evolution, it is clear that Wheelwright was always a misfit in the Socialist party. He was an uncompromising figure in a party of compromise. But it is doubtful that the Communist party would have tolerated him; the Socialist party, however, in addition to providing more leeway, appeared to him at that time to be less morally tainted than the Stalinists. Wheelwright's movement from heterodox religion to Socialism to Trotskyism cannot be dismissed as a bizarre episode, nor can it be evaded by the formula that E. P. Thompson uses to explain William Morris's complex relation to scientific socialism: "[Morris] was an original thinker whose work was complementary to Marxism."[56] Throughout the 1930s, Wheelwright's Marxism steadily encroached upon his theology. His poetry, which he sought to make a ground of reconciliation, became, in fact, a ground of contradiction.

Yet contradiction is not inherently harmful to art and may even be a spur to imaginative feats; Wheelwright's literary strengths and weaknesses in the 1930s do not correlate to the degrees of Marxism and religion manifest in his work. Rather, aesthetic value is more directly dependent upon the vitality of his vision and its expression through craft. His three published books of poetry in that decade, though they contain work originating from different moments in his life, provide evidence that the Great Depression era inspired fresh attempts at creating myths and imaginative worlds that elevated his art to a higher plane. The first of these, *Rock and Shell*, presents a "Wheelwright world" of New England culture that radicals must excoriate and revitalize. The second, *Mirrors of Venus*, was an experimental novel in sonnet form; its felicity of theme and structure succeeded, where the Doubting Thomas poems had failed, in the aesthetically brilliant dramatization of a spiritual quest.

The poet who seeks to commit his art to the political movements of his time must invariably broaden his audience by forging more public forms of expression. Poetry that is subjectively revolutionary but objectively elitist creates an impasse for the artist who aspires to move from the position of observer to that of participant. Yet Wheelwright, like Eliot, thought that poetry in the modern age must be difficult; and his association with *Hound and Horn* suggests a consanguinity of temperament with the New Critics, who arose precisely to defend a difficult poetry. Since Wheelwright was incapable of abandoning his characteristic modes of expression for pragmatic purposes, he sought to resolve this dilemma in the 1930s by appropriating the themes, symbols, and allegorical potential of traditions more accessible to the public than the esoteric theological allusions of the Doubting Thomas "novel." The imaginative world through which he sought to influence a new audience was derived from New England cultural traditions. This usable past was frequently of the Puritan epoch, a time of political turmoil and self-examination when members of the educated class (the ministry) stepped into the arena of social strife to "purify" those institutions of church and state that had succumbed to worldly corruption.

Long after the institutions fostering the Calvinist perspective had withered away, certain habits of mind persisted in the region and created a strong intellectual tradition that sustained the memory of the regional past among many layers of the population. Its poetic manifestations vary in the twentieth century, but in one way or another this tradition touched other writers in the Boston area, including S. Foster Damon, Austin Warren, R. P. Blackmur, Howard Blake, Robert Fitzgerald, George Anthony Palmer, and Robert Lowell. Wheelwright's first collection, *Rock and Shell* (1933), maps out his imaginative reconstruction of this regional legacy. In addition to numerous historical references, there are three elements of Puritan New England culture that decisively shape its structure and themes: spiritual autobiography (a literary form in which divines and others describe the phases of their conversions and spiritual ordeals); Ramist logic (a doctrine of contraries used in Puritan thought in which ideas are distinguished by setting them against their opposites); and the jeremiad (a sermon that excoriates the evils of contemporary society).

The "Argument" that Jack prepared for his last and posthumously published book, *Dusk to Dusk*, provides information that confirms this analysis. There he writes: "All *Rock and Shell* is religious; its successors are no less heretical; none demands great knowledge of Christian apologetics; the use all make of concepts is not personal but traditional."[1] This statement is augmented by an outline demonstrating that *Rock and Shell* is not an anthology but a sequence. It follows the same movement as the Doubting Thomas poems: behind the poetry is a mind that evolves outwardly from self-absorption and quietism. Furthermore, the development in *Rock and Shell* seems to move by a progression of opposites: doubt is counterposed to faith, soul to void, pretty pictures to ugly thoughts, infidelity to faith, decadence to decorum, action to feeling.[2] The entire sequence then culminates in an unambiguously public poem called "Gestures to the Dead," in which Wheelwright rewrites a philosophical poem from his Harvard days, interpolating sarcastic observations about the political hypocrisies of his society.

The concluding lines of this long poem plainly exhibit several features of Wheelwright's attempt to forge a more public poetry:

> Booth evaded the fame he sought, by speaking
> justly of Lincoln, *sic semper tyrannis*.
> It was banal enough to be immortal.
> You, Judas, sacrificed for our Messiah.
> You, Brutus, needful for our Caesar cult.
> Yours is the signal deed of all our history
> for pure liberty, for freedom, not reform.
> Some men fight Fate with its own fatal weapons,
> and ever believe they kill themselves for the life
> of the things they kill, as Lincoln died for the Union.
>
> Others who fail find that no path lies open
> but the bridle-path of remaining dignified.
> It took Robert E. Lee three days to become a "traitor,"
> and he rode to his gray end, a college president.
> When men of action fail, and failing, ask
> sanctuary of thinkers, destiny rests.
> There is nothing more to say. Can Tate and I
> stand against the black drift of storm
>
> forever changeless, against a changing sky?[3]

Using the Civil War as a parable of the present social crisis, Wheelwright argues that John Wilkes Booth may have been sincere in his belief that the death of Lincoln would liberate humanity; but by acting within the terms of conventional individualism, he accomplished nothing except the creation of a martyr. Likewise, Robert E. Lee's dignified withdrawal from political life was equally meaningless. What is required for the solution of social malaise ("the black drift of storm") is the development of new approaches that respond to the transformations wrought by history ("a changing sky").

New in the poem is the strident hectoring voice, aggressively inter-preting American history for the reader. But this lecturing is hardly doc-trinaire, for the allusiveness and condensation of modernism remain to complicate matters. In addition to the voice, the poem is more public because the parabolic references are to familiar figures from history (Lincoln, Lee, Booth), or to well-known figures from religion and litera-ture (Judas and Brutus). Thus the work is accessible to anyone with a dictionary or a history book. A third feature is the precise use to which the modernist technique of aggressive defamiliarization is put: Wheel-wright enlists the reader's attention with his startling, if not outrageous, depiction of Lincoln as tyrant and Judas. After exploding our normal perception of the historic event, however, he aspires to reconstitute our view of historical change in a new way: the poem argues for a rejection of all forms of political individualism, from terrorism to aloofness, as in-struments of social regeneration. This argument, of course, appears in complex form; it is accessible, but not without the reader contributing some degree of reflection. This corresponds to Wheelwright's problem-atic view of individualism itself, as indicated in a letter he wrote to Van Wyck Brooks at that time:

> Individualism is the finest flower of America. Its time of flow-ering has passed. Its seed time even has passed. A corporate sense is needed in this time. Let [William Ellery] Channing sweetly and lovingly be laid to rest with gentle words and acts of sweetest gratitude and over him let the monument read to the effect that "he spoke for his time for single souls. Now let souls join. But in joining never forget that each must essentially remain himself. That ultimately his most valuable office is to differ. The choice before us is to join in action. Grave perils are in that choice. We must join, the finest spirits among us will teach a corporate lesson. Be ready to stand alone, but now join in will and purpose."[4]

The Great Depression wrought several noticeable changes in the form and function of Wheelwright's poetry: first, the more frequent use of symbols, allusions, and allegory from more widely accessible resources like American history; second, the development of verse forms that could accommodate the rhetoric, syntax, and metrics of public oratory; and third, the intentional fragmentation of the reader's perceptions for the purpose of reconstituting them in a manner conducive to socialist political values.

The book's title, *Rock and Shell*, is typical of Wheelwright's use of plurisignification. As symbols, "rock" and "shell" should be approached in the manner advocated in his "General Argument" to the work: "On a symbolic poem, as on a clothes horse, many persons hang many things." Nevertheless, he continues, the value of symbols may be judged "as much by the number of meanings which cannot be put on them as by the rigidity with which they can sustain the meanings to which they are susceptible. Their words are transcendentally intended plot for any characters who obey."[5] Characteristically, Wheelwright provided a further qualifying remark on his technique in a 1938 note that appeared just before the final section of *Mirrors of Venus*:

> The four elegies with which the Preface encase the *Mirrors of Venus* might have served as title poems to *Rock and Shell* whose "General Argument" did not prevent a critic's assertion that the Author uses "rock" for "faith." This is not so. Neither the rock of Ararat, Moses' rock in the Wilderness, the rock of Golgotha, the rock which sealed the Tomb, nor the rock of Antioch (Peter's original See) are rocks of faith, whatever they may be; and Simon to whom Jesus said, "You are a rock; and on this rock I build my church," (which is to say, "You're a brick; I rely on fellows like you,") was, like his successors, deficient in faith.[6]

There are, of course, many possible sources for the symbolic use of "rock" and "shell," including the Bible, Wordsworth, and Descartes. However, the elegies to which Wheelwright draws attention in *Mirrors of Venus* provide a more cogent interpretation.

These four poems, named for the seasons, depict the life and death cycle of humanity. The final elegy, "Winter," begins: "Rocks cleft and turned to dust reveal / cleft shells to be as stone."[7] That is, rock and shell are shown to be of the same substance in the end, even though one (rock) is the product of inorganic matter and the other (shell) is the product of organic matter. The rock, then, stands for impassive and inanimate nature, while the shell is probably a symbol for the human body, which sustains the soul. This use of rock and shell may even derive from Oliver Wendell Holmes's "Chambered Nautilus." Holmes, like Walt Whitman, was a poet with whom Wheelwright conducted a dialogue. (Wheelwright's "Mossy Marbles" is an answer to Holmes's "The Voiceless.")[8]

Rock and Shell is structured as a spiritual autobiography. This type of literature evolved in New England from literary attempts to trace the progress of the conversion experience in order to assist in the discovery of one's prospects of salvation. Edmund S. Morgan wrote that the consequence of such explorations was to "establish a morphology of conversion, in which each stage could be distinguished from the next, so that a man could check his external condition by a set of temporal and recognizable signs."[9] Wheelwright's spiritual autobiography bears an ironic relation to this tradition.

When he wrote that "all *Rock and Shell* is religious," he also clarified that the religion was heretical; consequently, when he next wrote that the religious concepts in the book are "traditional," it must be understood that they originate from traditions that have been strikingly transformed. Thus, as a spiritual autobiography, *Rock and Shell* is as heretical in the direction of its movement as his religious views are in their underlying assumptions. Instead of traveling inward to a scrutiny of the self, *Rock and Shell* journeys outward to an understanding of society. Furthermore, the Ramist logic he employs in his counterposition of opposites becomes transformed into a Hegelian dialectic as contradictions become the source of progression and then of leaps and transformations. Finally, his jeremiads on the deterioration of New England society also depart from the traditional perspective. Instead of calling for a reinstatement of the tranquillity of earlier days, Wheelwright's jeremiads point forward to a revolutionary overthrow of the present social order.[10]

The only feature of his thought that he seems to have appropriated unchanged from his Puritan predecessors is his argument that faith requires doubt, a traditional belief of the Puritan divines. The surest mark of election was sometimes said to be uncertainty, as in the following Puritan text: "The faithful have not yet this assurance so perfect, but they are oft troubled with doubts and feares. . . . But they that have this false assurance are most confident, and never have any doubts." Morgan argues that the Puritan preachers were constantly transmitting the message that "in order to be sure one must be unsure . . . the surest earthly sign of a saint was his uncertainty." Since saving faith was "distinguished by doubt and subjected to continual combat with despair," it was necessary for the Puritan to be fully alert in order to recognize it; he "assisted himself by constant self-examination, frequently in writing."[11]

Rock and Shell documents Wheelwright's prolonged "conversion experience" between 1923 and 1933 (the official dates of the poems used in the book). It is dedicated to three women: his mother, a link to the New England past; his Aunt Dolly, a link to culture and the arts; and his sister Louise, a link to S. Foster Damon, her husband and Jack's literary mentor. He depicts a morphology of conversion that passes through six distinct phases, each signified by a key poem placed at the turning points. For example, he begins with a review of his evolution in the 1920s. The first phase is the rejection of both quietistic self-absorption and institutionalized religion, indicated by "North Atlantic Passage." The second is the recognition of the interrelationship of doubt and faith, indicated by "Forty Days." But the third phase signifies his leap into the world of social class and economic realities, evidenced in the poems "Paul and Virginia" and "Plantation Drouth."

On the surface, "Paul and Virginia" is a lament for the disappearance of the Brooks's family garden in West Medford, which fell victim to industrial expansion in the twentieth century.[12] Its first stanza reads:

Nephews and Nieces,—love your leaden statues.
Call them by name; call him "Paul." She is "Virginia."
He leans on his spade. Virginia fondles a leaden
fledgling in its nest. Paul fondles with his Eyes.
You need no cast in words. You know the Statues,
but not their Lawns; nor words to plant again
the shade trees, felled; ponds, filled, and built over.
Your Garden is destroyed, but there are other Gardens
yet to spare from the destroying Spoor
unseen, save in destructful Acts. Unseen
a hungered Octopus crawls under ground
as Fungus; eats the air as Orchids on all trees;
and on all waters spreads translucent Slime.
Nephews and Nieces, who would breathe sweet Air
and till rich Ground, spy out against its suction;
wither these spreading tentacles, these roots
and radicals of cancerous Greed.[13]

Once more Wheelwright assumes the voice of command, as if addressing
a public audience; this poem is probably intended for future generations
because the dedication is "For My Brother's Children." One literary
allusion may not be immediately apparent: the statues saved from the
garden to commemorate the beauty that once was are named "Paul" and
"Virginia" after the hero and heroine in Amy Lowell's poem "The Statue
in the Garden." But his depiction of a destroyed Eden is a familiar Bib-
lical reference, and the choice of the octopus to represent industrial
capitalism echoes the title of the popular novel by Frank Norris. Still,
the metaphor of the octopus crawling under ground is difficult to visual-
ize and perhaps not wholly convincing, although the idea that Wheel-
wright wishes to communicate by this is not a simple one. Capitalism
mystifies its operations and obscures its multifaceted role as a destroyer,
parasite, pollutant, and generator of human greed.

From the economic malaise of the North, Wheelwright moves south
in "Plantation Drouth." This was written when he visited the family
home of his prep school and college friend, Benjamin Kittridge, Jr., near
Charleston, South Carolina:

It has not rained.
The fields lie powdered
under smoke and clouds.
The swamps are peopled
with smouldering cedar
reflected on black, hoarded water.
The furrow in the field
behind the negro's heels
smokes, as though the plowshare stirred

embers in the earth.
As the furrow lengthens;
the rising powder fades to sky-dust
below the powdered sky.
The spongy land is parched
and draws the salt sea to it,
up all its earthly rivers.
It drinks brine, like a thirsty goat.
The river reeds are withered.
It is April in the meadows
but, in the empty rice fields
it is Winter.
The roots of the cedars drink
slow fire under the sod.
A flame seeps up the core,—
a tall tree falls.
From the bark, the white smoke bleeds.
Midway, between midnight and daybreak
the sky egg cracks across.
Goats move in sleep
Night then speaks with one dry boom.
The goats veer in their steps and stir
fire-flies from live oak trees
with their small lightnings.
One horned beast trots from the herd
more in disdain than fright
into the open, a little distance foraging.
The old devil knows
despite that bright, slow, loud antiphon
it will not rain.[14]

This grim pastoral is typical of depression literature in its imagery of economic decay and social stagnation. It contains less public rhetoric than that in "Gestures to the Dead" and "Paul and Virginia," but the voice is clear and speaks purposefully. There is economy in the exactness of its language, although no displacement or fragmentation. The atmosphere of the poem is ominously prophetic as the poet surveys the economic wasteland of the South. Diabolical allusions constitute one source of its menacing tone—the sulfurous environment of smoldering cedar and smoking fields, the goat depicted as a "horned beast."

Considering that Wheelwright was a man of religious temperament, one is struck by the overwhelming materiality of the poem. Dry powdery dust, stirred by the black worker plowing the fields, floats upward and mars the heavens; the result is the impotence of the "dry boom." Even the goat perceives the hoax; thunder will not bring rain. (The goat and

dry thunder may allude to Eliot's "Gerontion" and *The Waste Land*.)
Human beings are shown to be more dependent on earthly bread than
heavenly sustenance and become bleeding cedars with whom the swamp
is "peopled." The poem itself assumes the shape of a damaged tree, al-
though the uninterrupted series of lines also imparts a sense of the
unending monotony of economic depression.

With these designations of the national plight, Wheelwright enters the
fourth phase of *Rock and Shell*. He issues a call for revolutionary politi-
cal action in "The Huntsman":

> My cartridge belt is empty.
> I have killed no beasts.
> I have one bullet.
> Can we; with untrembled pistol
> when a serpent clasps a child;
> send the bullet through the serpent
> past the small head of the child?
> Be not disconsolate if the bullet
> pierce both child and serpent.
> A trembled pistol spares the serpent
> to kill the child.
> Throw the empty belt away.
> Take the pistol.
> Shoot.[15]

The rhetoric of command is partly subverted by the enigmatic sym-
bolism of the inexperienced hunter's dilemma, thereby creating a prob-
lematic mood. Yet once the allegorical significance of certain words is
revealed, the meaning of the poem is lucid. Six years later he glossed his
key terms in the "Argument" to another poem: "serpent—Capitalism;
child—Culture; bullet—Revolution."[16] Thus "The Huntsman" ad-
dresses the relation of culture to revolutionary action and is appropri-
ately dedicated to *Hound and Horn* editor Lincoln Kirstein. It depicts a
hunter who has only one bullet (revolution). Before him stands a serpent
(capitalism) with a child (culture) in its coils. The poet, who provides
political guidance, warns the hunter against indecisiveness out of fear
that the bullet may strike both serpent and child, because the conse-
quences of inaction are guaranteed to be fatal. "The Huntsman" provides
a useful variant on Wheelwright's strategy for making his poetry more
accessible. If the poem itself is hermetic, the gloss he eventually provides
is reductive; between extremes of complexity and simplicity, a tension is
established that affords the possibility of the poem being understood
while retaining its modernist features.

From the beginning until this fourth phase in the conversion sequence,
Rock and Shell imitates the movement of the Doubting Thomas poems:
indecision, recognition of the interrelationship of doubt and faith, nam-

ing the enemy, taking action. But Wheelwright then moves into a fifth phase by a unique turn that focuses attention on the role and responsibilities of the poet by presenting two verse obituaries: one for Harry Crosby ("To Wise Men on the Death of a Fool"), the other for Hart Crane ("Fish Food").

We have already noted (in pt. I, chap. 3) the scorn that Wheelwright held for Crosby because of his foolish waste of life. Therefore it is a significant contrast that he is gentler and more sympathetic in dealing with Crane. He obviously felt much empathy for the young homosexual poet who was driven by hatred of society and self to make a death leap into the Caribbean Sea. Furthermore, Wheelwright felt some guilt for the episode during his editorship of *Secession* when he irresponsibly rewrote one of Crane's poems. In "Fish Food" Wheelwright refers to himself as a "bad friend" for this action and reports that when he held out his hand to apologize, Crane said: "Do not talk any more. I know you meant no harm."

Nevertheless, "Fish Food" is critical of Crane's failure to fulfill the responsibilities that Wheelwright now delegated to the poet. With his familiar penchant for drawing half-humorously on the epic, he compares Crane unfavorably with Thor in the Norse fable. This legend tells of Thor's drinking ale from a flagon, thereby lowering the level of the ocean, and then budging a cat from the fireplace, thereby dislodging the earth from its accustomed location. Wheelwright defines the flagon as "the infinite of conceivable sensation" and the cat as "the universe of possible act." According to Wheelwright, Thor combined his gratification of the senses with a powerful action upon the material world and thereby achieved an admirable balance. In fact, his dislodging of the earth can be taken as a symbol of effective social action. But in Wheelwright's questionable interpretation, Crane took too little interest in the cat and devoted himself exclusively to the flagon: "He drank more than his fill, and was overwhelmed by ale fumes."[17]

Wheelwright believed that Crane, like Crosby, was justified in his revulsion against the world of fact, that as a poet he had the right to indulge his senses. But in the end he judged that Crane abused his poetic responsibilities because, in refusing to intervene in the world of fact, he instead drove his resentment "inward" against himself rather than "outward against foes no less vulnerable than himself—foes more worthy of hatred."

For all of Crane's indulging of his senses, Wheelwright thought that he lacked the true sense of sight and hearing. In the beginning of the poem Wheelwright asks:

> Did you not see the Cat
> who, when Thor lifted her, unbased the cubic ground?

You would drain the fathomless flagons to be slaked with
   vacuum—[18]

At the end of the poem, Wheelwright still seems incredulous at Crane's
obliviousness to the real world:

What was the soil whence your anger sprang, who are deaf
as the stones to the whispering flight of the Mississippi's rivers?
What did you see as you fell? What did you hear as you sank?
Did it make you drunken with hearing?[19]

Then, in words recalling those in which Crane is said to forgive Wheel-
wright for his *Secession* prank, Wheelwright forgives Crane's misuse of
the power of the poet:

I will not ask any more. You saw or heard no evil.[20]

After this rare moment of sentimental toleration, the jeremiad theme
comes to dominate the closing section of *Rock and Shell*. It is antici-
pated in "Salvation Army Girl," which appears between the poems on
Crosby and Crane, and reaches its height in the two long poems, "Come
Over and Help Us" and "Gestures to the Dead." Together, these three
poems reject conventional religion, individualism, and the culture of
Boston as instruments for solving the contemporary social crisis. The
unspoken agent of regeneration in this critique is the working class,
which Wheelwright intended to make the subject of a sequel to *Rock
and Shell* called *Salutes to the Living*.[21] This sequel was eventually
published in 1940 under the title *Political Self-Portrait*.

The "Salvation Army Girl" personifies the spirit of Protestant reform,
which had swept westward into the New World:

A Salvation Army girl stands on the western
steps of a Cathedral Church.[22]

In her the "unrest of the Lollards and Levelers bubbled up" and she de-
nounces Boston as the "western Babylon." Through an action that sug-
gests Christ's throwing the money changers out of the temple, the
Salvation Army girl provokes a riot against the church of this unholy
city. Yet the rebellion comes to naught. The mob dissolves, the church
calculates its losses, and the Salvation Army officials (General Evange-
line and Captain Miles Standish) disown any identification with the
uprising:

—The total loss had not been figured
though the clergy spent the afternoon
pounding the Cathedral adding machines.
—The Salvation Army girl, held for inciting to riot
is released on bond for psychopathic observation.

—General Evangeline feels no responsibility
and Captain Miles Standish tells our special correspondent
that he has always taken pains to get on pleasantly
with the Bishop and Trustees of the Cathedral Church
of Mary, the Star of the Sea.[23]

While Wheelwright obviously admired the fighting spirit of the Salvation Army girl, the failure of her revolt indicates disillusionment with traditional religious movements as agents of change. Her radical Protestantism is compared to Crosby's rebellion, and Wheelwright judged her to have "accomplished as little as he" because her actions were "sluiced through the unscientific channel her religious ancestors provided."[24] Technically, the challenging rhythm and direct language of the poem's opening may have afforded a shock effect for those accustomed to visualizing Salvation Army girls on street corners rather than the steps of great cathedrals; yet the stanza quoted above is talky without justification, and a series of words ("Salvation," "Evangeline," "psychopathic," "observation") creates a flabby long rhythm indicative of a loss of technical control.

"Come Over and Help Us" and "Gestures to the Dead" are animadversions against a group of faults that Wheelwright held responsible for the contemporary malaise and impotence of New England culture. The paramount heresy was self-absorption, the refusal to act upon the world, the canalization of one's energies into the dead end of spiritual self-improvement in isolation from social change. In Wheelwright's view this attitude produced a combination of hate toward the outside world and self-righteous chauvinism about one's own society. That he also blamed these attitudes for his father's inability to reconcile word and deed is suggested by his analysis of the outcome of this perspective: "These minds are faulty membranes between their persons and exterior events. They break down in active madness or they turn to callous prisons in passive solipsism."[25]

Wheelwright's working notes for "Come Over and Help Us" are contained in a notebook prepared in the late 1920s, part of which the *New England Quarterly* published in 1973. Here he presents the thesis that "New Englanders dislike more intensely than they like. It is not that they are dispassionate—anything but. They are the most passionate people in the world, but their passion is negative." Wheelwright locates the origin of this outlook in Calvinism, explaining that mental activity of this kind becomes perverted and destructive when cut off from its original sources: "The New Englander while spiritually weak is tirelessly at work hating, censoring, depreciating, discouraging, joylessly, with conviction, without relish or satisfaction or reward, seeking no end, serving no purpose, desiring no result."[26] In "Come Over and Help Us,"

these feelings are intensified by the creation of a terrifying metaphor for
this state of mind, a metaphor expressed in a seven-beat epic meter bor-
rowed from Blake with Dickinson-like symbols for punctuation and
breaks:

> The Hate in the World
> outside our World
> (Envious, malicious, vindictive) + makes our Hate gleam in the
> splendor
> Of a Castrate + who with tongue plucked out + arms, legs sawed
> off;
> Eyes and ears, pierced through; + still thinks + thinks
> By means of all his nutriment, + with intense, exacting Energy,
> terrible, consuming.[27]

The title "Come Over and Help Us" is multiply suggestive. The phrase
has a biblical origin in the Macedonian salutation to the Apostles, and
Ned Wheelwright placed it upon his pier house at City Point, Boston.
But the Puritans also used the slogan when establishing their common-
wealth; they placed it beneath a picture of a Native American Indian on
the Massachusetts Bay Colony seal. This was, of course, a false motto,
since the Indians had never asked the Puritans to come and help them,
and the Puritans were not so motivated at that time. In the poem Wheel-
wright intended to direct this motto "to the world that is not Boston."[28]
    A subtheme of "Gestures to the Dead" and "Come Over and Help Us"
is the execution of the anarchists Sacco and Vanzetti. In "Gestures to the
Dead" Wheelwright declares:

> What a pity Amy [Lowell] was not president of Harvard!
> What a pity Anarchists tried to frighten Yankees!
> Needles of law pierced the blindfolded eyes
> of Justice; and the eyes flowed in tears and blood.
> Maybe the Judge's secretary knew
> the judge believed the culprits innocent.
> But innocent of jurisprudence, innocent
> of clemency. . . .
>   stalwart Lawrence Lowell
> (the memory of deed can never fade)
> condemned two men to death because the *Transcript*
> held not in all its files their alibi,—
> a wop clam-bake at Plymouth.[29]

Once more we are confronted with an ambiguous rhetorical posture, a
strategy meant to capture the audience's attention by teasing it. The
poem begins with a mock-heroic lamentation about the Harvard presi-

dency and then embarks on a roller-coaster descent to the vulgar phrase "wop clam-bake at Plymouth." The description of Justice's eyes pierced by needles balances on the edge between the serious and the comic.

Although "Come Over and Help Us" does not mention Sacco and Vanzetti by name, Wheelwright's "Argument" to the poem states that it "embodies in part the author's response to the case of Sacco and Vanzetti during the latter year of whose trial it was composed."[30] But neither poem is actually *about* the anarchists; in a letter to Bruno Fischer, Wheelwright explained that he had responded so emotionally to the executions that he was incapable of writing directly on the subject. The concern in both poems is that the intellectual leadership of New England —personified by Harvard President A. Lawrence Lowell, who was chosen to head Governor Fuller's commission to review the trial, conviction, and sentencing of the two Italians—capitulated to the hysteria incited by the media. Wheelwright's bitterness about this never abated; in 1936, at the tricentennial celebration of Harvard, he added his name to a list of twenty-seven signatories on a pamphlet reminding Harvard alumni of the crime committed by its former president.[31]

Rock and Shell was not a money-making venture; indeed, Wheelwright had great difficulty in locating a publisher and finally worked out an arrangement with Bruce Humphries, a small Boston printer, whereby Wheelwright was obligated to sell a certain number of copies of the book in advance to subscribers. The printing was only five hundred copies. Nevertheless, *Rock and Shell* was reviewed favorably in numerous publications. Eda Lou Walton wrote in the *Nation* that "technically, Wheelwright is a most expert poet." Horace Gregory called Wheelwright "one of the few matured poets in our time," characterizing the book as "an epilogue to the tradition of New England culture." He suggested that "one has only to remember Jonathan Edwards and to read passages from Emerson, Thoreau, Oliver Wendell Holmes, to find the emotional sources of this book."

Several reviewers did complain about the difficulty of the poems; others failed to recognize the authentic political implications of Wheelwright's idiosyncratic religious stance, even though he tersely dismissed T. S. Eliot's conservatism in two lines: "Classicist, Royalist, Anglo-Catholic / long names for the four-letter word, a snob." However, most reviewers perceived his left-wing sympathies. Morton Zabel pronounced Wheelwright one of the three leading revolutionary poets in the nation, along with Horace Gregory and Norman MacLeod. Muriel Rukeyser wrote in the *New Masses* that the book "outlines the development of a poet passing from religious preoccupation to activity in the revolutionary movement"; she urged that his work not be "dismissed as confused or confusing." In his review for the journal *Poetry*, R. P. Blackmur cited the balance of diverse elements in *Rock and Shell*. Noting that Wheelwright wrote "with a kind of constant fitfulness, requiring of the reader an ability to receive a rapid and tightly bound succession of disparate observation," he concluded that the "impact of mass" is given to "what is usually fragmentary, disjunct, and irreconcilable." This resulted in "tough, squirming, gnostic verse, modified and exhilarated by New England wit and New England eccentricity, and the unique heresy of New England Anglo-Catholicism—and the whole qualified by New England political radicalism."

Having presented such a laudatory appreciation of Wheelwright's quality of mind, Blackmur waxed more critical in treating the metrics and formal arrangements of the poems. Wheelwright adhered to a theory that metrics and structure should be judged according to sound, not sight; but his ear, and his conception of how a poem should be read aloud, did not always correspond to the interpretations of other readers. In his review, Blackmur made the following complaint: "Like the sprung meter of Gerard Hopkins, the mouthful lines of Whitman, or the epic meters of Blake . . . Mr. Wheelwright's peculiar adventures in prosody cannot be justified on any ground other than the author's immediate convenience and the magnetism of eccentricity." Blackmur cited defects such as an elliptical syntax, an internal rhyme that accented a logical incoherence, and an inequivalence in the branches of a simile. Later, in a more circumspect critique of Wheelwright's meter, Blackmur concluded that "in a great deal of his work he based the length and look of his lines upon equivalence of stresses. He held lines to be in balance, to continue or complete a pattern, if the major stresses came out even. The number of unstressed syllables did not count, but their cumulative value did count; hence scansion was variable even within a poem."[32]

Wheelwright defended himself against these and similar criticisms in the final section of his "Argument" to *Political Self-Portrait*. There he insisted that ear should have priority over eye and that mind should have priority over ear. He concludes: "Verse is an engineering of sound which, when it rises to poetry, engineers meaning. Verbal music and word pictures are ancillary to the mental music of governed association."[33] In blaming the weaknesses in Wheelwright's poetry on a theory of cumulative stresses, Blackmur was perhaps too single-minded. In their *History of American Poetry*, Horace Gregory and Marya Zaturenska correctly note that Wheelwright's ear was at times sacrificed to the higher purpose of experiment and invention. They ascribe some of his weaknesses not simply to a faulty theory, but to the fact that the rhythm behind some of the experiments "had yet to achieve its maturity," doubly complicated by his tendency "to write poetry with ideas and not words."[34]

Another critic enthralled with the experimental and intellectual features of Wheelwright's verse was Sherry Mangan, whose printing skills had been put to use in preparing the book design. In a review intended for publication in England, Mangan counterposed the evolution of Wheel-wright's work to what he thought was the wrong turn taken by the sur-realists, despite the similarity in the origin of techniques: "Approaching by a quite different tangent, nor knowing the French official school, Mr. Wheelwright has individually crossed *through* surrealism, reaching a point beyond it, from the path to which, in escape, surrealism turned at its critical crossroads. For here, within the true automatism, is meshed logical symbolism: the deepmind-moving freedom is structural—a result impossible from conscious filing, but coming only from the unique mind wherein, simply, no triviality distracts." Equally important to Mangan was the way in which Wheelwright had suffused politics throughout his art so as to enrich and not restrict the operations of his imagination: "Socialism is not the mere excuse of his poetry, but—something far more important—its *prime given*. They are not socialist poems; but no one save a socialist could have written them." To Mangan the experience of reading Wheelwright's "spiritual autobiography" dislodged him from prior conceptions about the relationships between revolutionary politics and cultural regeneration. Poetry need not be the handmaiden of politics; politics might be a fit subject for poetry. He ended his review with an observation more personally relevant than he realized at the time: "In a country where 'left' is all too often synonymous with 'anti-intellectual,' he is thus an exceptional and encouraging portent."[35] The "conversion experience" from self-absorption to social action that Wheelwright re-corded in *Rock and Shell* was symptomatic of the response of a gen-eration of which Mangan would also be a part.

Rock and Shell ended with the announcement of a new public voice—deliberate, sometimes menacing and sometimes sarcastic—with which Wheelwright sought to intervene in and provide leadership for the moral and cultural life of the 1930s. Yet throughout the decade he also sus-tained and nearly perfected a private voice—lyrical and often gently ironical. The thirty-five poems that comprise *Mirrors of Venus: A Novel in Sonnets* (1938) began as a series of variations on the sonnet form, with some of the pivotal verses dating back to his Harvard days. However, *Mirrors of Venus* expresses a distinctly fresh stage in his philosophical evolution and shows the response of his imagination to the Great De-pression in a different way. After he had published *Rock and Shell*, he believed that he had attained a higher point in his poetry wherein the direction of his work would be increasingly clearer. At that time he wrote Horace Gregory that "the ground for my hope is that socialism has pulled my thoughts together. I have been plowing a hard furrow, with an incomplete plough." Previously things had struck him as "good, bad, right and wrong, true and silly. This almost corresponds to a savage man's reflexes who lacks adequate language. Now I think language has come."[36]

About a year later, in the heat of Socialist electoral activity, Wheel-wright reported to Gregory in another letter that "in spite of the campaign this year I am working on a book,—the sonnets. It is growing into something with much more to it than I ever thought it would have. And I think it is almost done." To Willard Maas, an editor with Alcestis Press, he explained that, technically, the first twenty-five sonnets in *Mirrors of Venus* "are consistent with the rest of my work, but although there is no personal philosophic inconsistency between them and the rest of my ideas they just don't seem to fit ideologically, in much the same way that furniture will sometimes not fit into a room."[37]

When *Mirrors of Venus* finally appeared, it was much admired by fellow poets, but little understood. In the *Nation* Paul Rosenfeld called it a "brainy, realistic, and reserved little book of a true poet who is also a loving friend." Kenneth Patchen wrote: "It is above all the work of a poet whose gifts are major. . . . When recorders begin the work of sorting the chaff from the wheat, the name of John Wheelwright should find its way to a great many lips." In the *New Republic* Muriel Rukeyser wrote that "John Wheelwright's sonnet sequence is brilliant and sage, full of dia-grammed exercises, inventions and variations on the sonnet, and his valid eccentric note." In the *Boston Transcript* Merrill Moore, famous for his own experiments with sonnets, judged that "complete originality is the outstanding characteristic of Wheelwright's newest book."

For a number of reviewers, however, two aspects of Wheelwright's originality caused perplexity and sometimes provoked hostility. One was his subtitle, *A Novel in Sonnets*; the other was his inclusion of diagrams for the structure of each sonnet. Harry Roskolenko wrote that "Mr. Wheelwright really has written separate sonnets, though he insists that his book is a novel"; Louis MacNeice complained that Wheelwright "spoiled his book by attaching to every poem rather pedantic or exhi-bitionistic pieces of commentary."[38]

In correspondence with Roskolenko, who was likewise a Trotskyist and a poet, Jack argued that "the preface which you find pedantic is intended to diminish the pedantic practice in writing sonnets." He then went on to defend his innovations. He insisted that he called the book a novel "because it is one, one which wisely avoids the necessity of setting down a time table of the various goings and comings of the characters or recording their every word or conversation. Certainly it has a plot and deals with the analysis of human feeling and character." He also explained that the left-hand pages containing outlines of the rhyme schemes "are meant for those who like to see how works are organized— I refer you to the excellent program of the Boston Symphony Orches-tra."[39] Since the mode of the sonnet sequence is lyric, Wheelwright's diagrams may serve to remind both the reader and himself that the effu-sion of such personal sentiments is not to be seen as mere emotionalism, but actually is to function within the disciplined structures of philosophy and poetics. The term "novel" may also be taken as a reference to the narrative basis required for the sustained allegory found in *Mirrors of Venus*.

Before extrapolating the content of ideas in this complex work, it may be useful to explore this new manifestation of the diversity and complexity of Wheelwright's technique in light of his attempted reconciliation of modernist strategies with socialist ideology. *Mirrors of Venus* affords an intriguing example of such efforts because its socialism is implicit, not explicit as in *Rock and Shell* and *Political Self-Portrait*. Wheelwright's poems of the 1930s confirm that modernism, to him, was the expansion of poetic technique to its fullest range of possibility. He could move rapidly from one strategy or pose to another within poems as well as between them. At one moment he sang a "Titanic Litany" or wrote of "flagons," as if striving for an epic vision or seeking to insert himself in the tradition of Milton or Tennyson. The next moment he exuded the melancholy sensuousness of the pre-Raphaelites or Ernest Dowson. His metrics alternate between prosaic flatness and provocative rhythms that pull dynamically back and forth.

Wheelwright's blurring of genres, eclipsing of distance, and assumption of a grandiose pose that he subtly or shockingly deflates a few lines later are the efforts of a revolutionary imagination seeking to transform the formal apparatus of literary production, not simply for aesthetic reasons, but for new relations between means and ends that accommodate the special demands of the literary-ideological problematic. If Wheelwright is uneven in his accomplishments and inconsistent in his approach, particularly in regard to the degree of difficulty his poems present, one must recall the obstacles faced by any pioneer who lacks adequate precedent.

Wheelwright called *Mirrors of Venus* a sonnet sequence, one of the most traditional forms; yet the sonnets embraced under this rubric are innovative to the point of defying the very notion of "tradition," as can be seen in "Village Hangover":

> Stuttering chirrups wake me, fluttering
> over the counterpane your cascaded
> shadow cast on dream new wine and seltz.
> The sun slipped on a sky-scraper.
> Yellow is turned ash color.
> *That's Madagascar Blues.*
> More and more, form shows by shade
> till life is lit by faded dream
> and, *Zulu Booze*
>   and, *Bugaboos*

and, *Baby shoes.*

Voodoos
       That's
              Madagas-
                     car Blues.[40]

Without knowing the precise references in this depiction of a person waking from a dream, the reader has to be struck by the rapid movement from impressionism ("The sun slipped on a skyscraper. / Yellow is turned ash color") to terms that evoke an exotic primitivism in mood ("*That's Madagascar Blues,*" "*Zulu Booze,*" and "*Voodoos*"). On one level the poem seems to be a sort of finger exercise in surrealist "voodoo poetry," strongly reminiscent of writings by Leon G. Damas and Leopold Senghor.[41] In this sense, "Village Hangover" is almost a period piece, for it looks back on the post–World War I era when many American writers, from Eugene O'Neill to Vachel Lindsay, transformed aspects of African culture into symbols of elemental mysteries.

However, an examination of the sonnet in the context of the sequence as a whole reveals that these and other key terms are synecdochical representatives of a pattern of memories and fears in the mind of the awakening poet as he struggles to suppress his sensation that a loved friend is no longer faithful: the bird that wakes him flutters over his friend's shadow because his friend had promised to wake him by a phone call; the "*Zulu Booze*" and "*Madagascar Blues*" are memories from a Harlem nightclub where the poet and his friend went the night before; "*Bugaboos*" refers to his uncertainty about the fidelity of his friend; "*Baby Shoes*" were probably hanging in the window of the taxi cab that drove the poet home from the nightclub; "*Voodoos*" refers to his disconcerting emotional response to the black telephone that never rings, associated in his mind with the Harlem nightclub where the false promise was made.

The aggressive experimentalism of "Village Hangover" strikes the reader immediately through its form and italicized key words; in contrast, "Winter" seems formalistically more traditional and perhaps even archaic because it is the conclusion of a sequence called "Spring," "Summer," "Autumn," and "Winter." Yet this is precisely the kind of traditional setting that incites Wheelwright to his most daring feats:

Rocks cleft and turned to dust reveal
cleft shells to be as stone; and cricket skulls
in powdered light give your quick, analytic mandate:
Un-think these things. Gun-roused at dusk
a cock'll bugle "Kyrie." Get the geometry of event.
When your lungs failed at war

my mother pulse of dividends revived.
Other theorems of Truth; of Beauty, other corollary!

As over water when a mill-sluice shuts
film ice twitches between inverted
tendril and frond, frond and tendril;
your rushing brain lay still.
Our bold-voluted immortality, fallen
        is only rock
—though proud in ruin, piteous in pride—
        Ned. Ned.
Snow on a dome, blown by night wind.[42]

This poem about death is appropriately entitled "Winter" and its ice imagery is pivotal. Wheelwright moves systematically from his personal symbols of rock and shell, which represent inorganic matter and the human body, to the stream of consciousness of a soldier's last thoughts before death. The soldier, Ned, appears to be struggling to attain a rational perspective on what is happening to him as he sees military commands appropriate natural processes and religious sentiments for dubious ends. Ned's death reorients the poet to a new philosophy.

Wheelwright's second stanza evinces a clarity that ought to warm the heart of any New Critic. He describes a thin layer of ice twitching as the sluice gates of a mill are shut; then, after a terrifying delay, the fourth line switches to the image of a dying human consciousness. The frozen tendrils and fronds of vegetation in the stream now become the parts of a dead brain. His repetition of the name "Ned" tolls like a death knell; the poet lyrically caresses the memory of his friend even as he lets it go. "Dome" in the closing line echoes the elaborate simile of the twitching ice and dying brain.

Although *Mirrors of Venus* is a philosophic excursion into the interiors of mind and emotion, the principles of Wheelwright's radical modernism are illustrated as creatively as they are in *Rock and Shell*, where the objective is to agitate the audience into critical political thought. In order to defend modernism and all other literary forms as potentially adequate instruments of the revolutionary imagination, Wheelwright needed to consistently demonstrate his belief that even the most traditional structures can be transcended and subverted by the appropriate vision and craft.

How did the series of individual sonnets in *Mirrors of Venus*, some of which were originally drafted before the First World War and some of which were added after 1935, come to cohere in a verse novel? Was this mere showmanship or affectation, as some of Wheelwright's critics thought? A careful study of the sequence indicates that, despite the origins of certain sonnets at different points in his life, the series is unified in expressing a single theme: it starts as a lament for the death of a friend, in the tradition of Milton's "Lycidas" and Tennyson's "In Memoriam," but evolves into a startling rejection of belief in an afterlife.

A main character operates throughout the sonnet sequence; like Judas-Thomas in the Doubting Thomas poems, it embraces dualisms and contradictions. As in the Thomas poems, this character is a Wheelwright persona, although in *Mirrors of Venus* he is simply called "Z" without explanation; the other main characters are called "X" and "Y." The sonnet sequence, however, is more accessible than the Thomas poems. The background is explicitly Wheelwright's own—the death of his architect father, World War I, boarding school and Harvard days, bohemian life in New York City, and several religious ordeals.

The opening theme of the sequence is the transitory nature of human friendship. Wheelwright juxtaposes memories of and fantasies about a friend who dies (and whose friendship thereby becomes immortalized) with a narrative about a friend who lives (but whose friendship grows estranged). The list of dedications in the sequence indicates that the friend who died was "Ned Couch." Edward Seguin Couch, a Harvard student during 1916–17, was from Cromwell, Connecticut. He was friends with S. Foster Damon, who wrote Wheelwright after Couch's death that he had visited Couch at Cromwell while writing his poem "Holy Gilde." Couch entered military service at the start of World War I and became a second lieutenant in the Fifth Provisional Officers Battalion. He was reported killed on 7 February 1918 in an accident at Ft. Leavenworth, Kansas.[43]

The list of dedications for the sonnet sequence begins with Couch's name, but ends with the following: "To Richardson King Wood, who was its inception." Wood was a Harvard student during 1921–22 and then worked for the Knopf publishing house and Time, Inc.[44] It is possible that Wood's relationship to Jack suggested the idea in the sequence for the friend who lived, but whose friendship died out. *Mirrors of Venus* has a prose introduction followed by three sonnets in blank verse. Then there are twenty-seven rhymed sonnets followed by a group of four in blank verse. The design of the book suggests a movement or transition in thought and feeling as the reader travels from section to section.

The opening sonnet, "Death at Leavenworth," is a lament for the dead Ned Couch. It emphasizes that Ned was still young and vibrant, far from old age when the physical senses normally become diminished. The poet then states his belief that Ned may have committed suicide because of his hatred of the war:

> Out there at Leavenworth that bored you;
> shy at your shoulder-strap; back among friends;
> and then Across;—"An overdose of morphine"?

That is absurd. Mere doctors could not kill
a soldier who detested war, a soldier
thus self-innoculated against death.
                    Ned. Ned.
Why after twenty years do I think you killed yourself?[45]

Wheelwright's use of "Across" to indicate Couch's death suggests that at
this point he still believes in an afterlife; and a note to the first poem
says that "trust in the Immortal Self together with trust in undying love
forms the positive theme of the whole work." However, a note to the
second sonnet states that "faith in the Immortal Self drops to the halluci-
nation of personal persistence after death"; in this sonnet Jack describes
how Ned Couch's mother keeps the memory of his childhood alive in her
imagination. Jack also describes how Ned's friends fantasize that Ned
still exists in some sort of ghostly form, as a specter who walks among
them when they sit drinking around the piano during the evening:

But, as now and again, when tipsy friends plumb deeps
of conversation unexpressed, you came
to hover over the home-brew, and then spoke
in random piano notes some fellow made
to ornament his wit.[46]

In the sonnet "Movie Show," a new theme is introduced in the se-
quence. Wheelwright wonders whether his whole conception of the
world, with people passing from one form of life to another just as pa-
trons in a movie house go outside after the show, is only an illusion. In
allusive imagery that almost defies paraphrase, he poses the question of
whether he will be taken to Eden or will merge into nothingness when
he dies:

                    will they bear you
toward gentian evening water, there to hear
a Voice that walks beneath apple trees . . . ?
                    Or, first dead friend,
is the Communion of Latter Saints to find
annihilation, immortality
and our salvation in oblivion?[47]

At this point Wheelwright has stated the countertheme of the sonnet
sequence: "a loss of faith in the Immortal Self which, together with
a loss of trust in undying friendship, will form the negative theme of
the work."[48]

The prefatory sonnets of Mirrors of Venus end with "Link," in which
Wheelwright makes several important connections. First, he observes
that if his friend Ned had lived, the friendship itself might well have
deteriorated with the passing of time:

Had you not died, our friendship might be dead
for the world it was born to died in war
and may drag on only in avatar.[49]

Yet the poet still wishes that Ned had lived, even if this would have
meant that the friendship would have been laid to rest, because:

Not only were I livelier had you lived
work-mate to lay a morbid culture's ghost;
but you yourself embalmed, beautified
in friendship's reliquary, and I shrived
in love's confessional, where love is lost
as our love would be lost, had you not died.[50]

It is not clear just how Ned Couch qualified as a "work-mate" to "lay a
morbid culture's ghost." However, it is possible that the poem is actually
establishing a new and different kind of "link" between Ned Couch, the
suspected suicide and dead friend, and Ned Wheelwright, the known
suicide and dead father of the poet. In "Movie Show," for instance, the
poet referred to Ned Couch as his "first dead friend"; nine sonnets after
"Link," he will refer to Ned Wheelwright as "my first friend." To compli-
cate matters even further, there is a third "Ned" associated with the
book: the title *Mirrors of Venus* comes from a famous painting by
Edward "Ned" Burne-Jones, the pre-Raphaelite artist. Although Ned
Couch's precise relationship to Jack remains a mystery, the close identity
that Jack felt with his father makes it seem plausible that the elder
Wheelwright was considered by the son to be a "work-mate to lay a
morbid culture's ghost."

The heart of the sonnet sequence begins with "Abel." Here the main
character (a persona for Jack Wheelwright) is designated as "Z"; later Z
will be identified with Cain. Also introduced is a friend of Z called "Y";
Y will eventually be identified with Abel because he will be victimized
by Z. The setting of the poem "Abel" is said to be a funeral for the dead
friendship between Z and Y. Because Z does not understand the transitory
nature of human friendship, he curses Y for letting the friendship die:

In the dead night we walk behind a hearse
zigzagging toward a dancing colonnade;
knee-deep, through dust of faded petals wade
past thornless flowers through thorns. Hear us converse;
"Whom do we mourn?" you ask me, half afraid.
"I mourn for you, and whom I mourn, I curse."[51]

Following this surreal vision of the "dancing colonnade" and the swift
ambiguity of "I mourn . . . I curse," a third figure called "X" is introduced
in this sonnet. X is said to be "always present with friends." He seems to
be a symbolic figure who fuses Ned Couch, Ned Wheelwright, and all

dead persons whose love has become idealized and immortalized in the imagination of the bereaved and to whom the bereaved are driven to compare earthly and transitory love and friendship. Later, in the sonnet "Adam," this fused image of X is idealized as a prelapsarian man, free from all earthly impurities:

> In him, all admirable traits appear
> and he is kindly, for he owns no fear.[52]

This idealization of X is further praised in "Sanct"; but in the sonnet "Heat and Cold" we return to the issue of the human friendship that is dying between Z and Y. Z describes a nighttime rendezvous with Y in the woods; Z fears that Y is no longer loyal to him, but dares not ask questions about Y's fidelity because he dreads the light of truth. The sonnet "Flux" contains further meditations by Z in the daytime, when he again wonders about the possibility of there being "oblivion" instead of an afterlife.

In "Sophomore," Z examines himself in a mirror and comes up with a bit of self-analysis. He recalls his loss of sexual "innocence" in a mysterious and possibly homosexual incident at boarding school, then remembers an early sensation that his peers were more "shallow" than himself. After further thought, Z wonders whether he actually despises himself or in fact narcissistically loves himself for being different:

> because, unlike his classmates, he preferred
> talk with autumnal women, ever mellow,
> or boys, with whom his well-considered word
> not always marked him as a crazy fellow?[53]

Self-doubt is pursued in the sonnets "Sophomore," "Classmates," and "Mother," all of which develop the theme that his suspicions about the fidelity of his friend Y are actually a projection of Z's doubts about his own ability to be faithful.

In "Father," there is further evidence for identifying Ned Wheelwright with the dead friend, X, who has been idealized by the mourning Z into a prelapsarian Adam: "X, who has been compared to a prophet, to Adam, to the Third Person of the Trinity, and whose good intention Z has followed with parental concern for Y's death as a friend, is addressed through the person Z's own dead father."[54]

"Rococo Crucifix," which was discussed in chapter 3, reorients the sequence to a critique of religion. By contrasting the difference between the ornamental crucifix and the act of crucifixion, Z poses the question as to whether religion itself might be a way of painting up and falsifying the true nature of human existence, suffering, and death. The following sonnet, "Holy Saturday," transfers this lesson to Z's relationship with Y. Z wonders whether further proof that he is a Judas can be found in his feelings about Y. He realizes that he "betrays" his friend Y because he expects from Y the impossible kind of fidelity that his imagination associates with his dead and idealized friend, X. In "Lens," Z recognizes that part of the reason he is so attracted to Y is because Y seems unconcerned with these kinds of disturbing questions.

The next twelve sonnets trace the vicissitudes in the relationship between the friends Z and Y in a variety of physical and emotional settings —urban and pastoral, meditative and orgiastic—so that Z's quest for a relationship with Y becomes elevated to a quest for the significance of friendship in general. However, by the time the sequence reaches the sonnets "Phallus" and "Mirror," Z has come to identify himself as "Cain" because, in expecting unearthly fidelity in Y, he has been expecting too much and thereby is a victimizer of Y (identified with Abel). Furthermore, Z increasingly realizes that his distrust of Y's fidelity is only a projection of his own unfaithful feelings. In "Keeper," the final sonnet in the main part of the sequence, Z states that "none but a God can be his brother's keeper" and that "friendship can continue only at the price of separation."[55]

This chronicle of the poet's experience with the dangers that come from false idealizations, engendered first and foremost by the illusions of religion, leads Jack to a complete repudiation of belief in an afterlife in the four elegiac sonnets that close *Mirrors of Venus*: "Spring," "Summer," "Autumn," and "Winter." In place of an afterlife, he recognizes the truth of the "oblivion" awaiting the individual soul, which he refers to as "eternal solidarity," a way in which humanity transcends egoism and blends together in nature.[56] In the first two closing sonnets, Wheelwright tries to discredit the blind optimism that he associates with the Romantic poets. He criticizes Shelley, in particular, for his belief in the immortality of the individual self, a view that Wheelwright believes is responsible for fostering a false perception of human existence.

In "Autumn," the third elegy, Wheelwright rejects the analogical proofs of immortality advanced by the Greeks and others. In "Winter," the last elegy, he concludes that the human body after death is not immortalized at all, but is merely a shell that differs only slightly from an inorganic rock. Thus he concludes that human existence is only a delicate transitory phase in the process of nature. The end of the poem is emotional in tone but stoical in perspective as Wheelwright reluctantly rejects his former idealizations of his dead friend and father:

Our bold-voluted immortality, fallen
is only rock
—though proud in ruin, piteous in pride—
Ned. Ned.
Snow on a dome, blown by the night wind.[57]

The book provided a vehicle for capturing the experience of the diminishment of his religious faith at the very moment when his mind was breaking down its resistance to Marxist materialism. In the period between the publication of *Mirrors of Venus* (1938) and his next book, *Political Self-Portrait* (1940), Jack wrote to Van Wyck Brooks that his Anglican commitment "is unaccompanied by the degree of faith which I once had. The shortcomings of the church have made my own shortcomings greater as a Christian communicant." Instead, he now found "the working class movement the inheritor of anything of value in the church, though also of most of the vices of bourgeois society which botch the church."[58]

As a philosophical allegory, *Mirrors of Venus* succeeded where the Thomas poems failed, not because Wheelwright abandoned modernist modes, but because his reorientation of imaginative energies and modernist strategies within a socialist vision provided direction and coherence. Like *Rock and Shell*, this sonnet sequence depicts a troubled mind and its mood is therefore characteristically problematic. Yet in contrast to "North Atlantic Passage," "Forty Days," and the three Thomas poems, there is a balance among form, devices, and content. In the former works, the chaos that first strikes the reader never truly abates because the myths are to some degree self-perpetuating. *Mirrors of Venus*, on the other hand, operates by a strategy of amplification; once the basic issues are defined, Wheelwright proceeds in a flexible but systematic manner by argumentation, comparison, reasoning, and accumulation. This provides a necessary foundation to the book, for there are moments of extreme condensation, displacement, and economy in individual sonnets, as well as places where Wheelwright readily eschews "realistic" description when he has the opportunity to depict a mental state. The work coheres because of its frame, and that frame is an aestheticized socialism. Wheelwright is the survivor mentioned in the "Argument," the one who "grew in faith from Immortal Selfhood to Eternal Solidarity." Although not directed toward political action as *Rock and Shell* is, *Mirrors of Venus* is indubitably intended as the emotional and imaginative testament of a socialist.

Drawing of John Wheelwright by Albert Sterner, Peru, Vermont, 1924.
By permission of Paula Sterner and Brown University Library.

John Wheelwright in the 1920s.
By permission of the Brown University Library.

John Wheelwright in his raccoon coat in the 1930s.
(Barrett Library Prints, #9364-a)
By permission of the Manuscripts Department, University of Virginia Library.

Sherry Mangan as a Harvard student in the 1920s.
By permission of the Houghton Library, Harvard University.

Sherry Mangan when he was a European war correspondent for *Time, Life,* and *Fortune* in the mid-1940s.

By permission of the Houghton Library, Harvard University.

Sherry Mangan about 1950.
By permission of the Houghton Library, Harvard University.

Despite his record of success in literary activities and the promise of more to come, the moving forces in Sherry Mangan's life were driving ineluctably toward a crisis as the Great Depression deepened. His 1931 marriage to Kate Foster (an English art student on the younger fringe of the Bloomsbury set) was faltering. The family fortune continued to dwindle as Dr. Mangan's illness dragged on. With old debts unpaid and new ones piling up, the dreaded possibility of having to work full time at a nonliterary occupation was fast becoming a reality. The growing threat to Sherry's ability to devote himself entirely to writing was the most important factor contributing to the coming impasse in his literary work. Stephen Spender recalled in the early 1950s that "from 1931 onwards" he felt "hounded by external events," so he adjusted his poetic activity accordingly.[1] For Mangan the feelings were the same, but the consequences were devastating for his anticipated literary career.

The decade began with such a flurry of literary activity that his various projects—books of fiction and poetry, editorial work, criticism—carried him forward for a number of years beyond the point at which he first knew he was in trouble. Then his search for a new poetic orientation, hitherto just one of several concerns, became transformed into a major quest. This search for a new aesthetic was part of his motivation for closely associating with *Pagany: A Native Quarterly*, a leading literary magazine of the 1930s.

Pagany was founded by Richard Johns, a fellow writer from Lynn and a former contributor to *larus*. Sherry knew Johns well and assisted the magazine with enthusiasm by turning over his mailing lists from *larus*. Between 1930 and 1933, he devoted much time and energy to soliciting contributions from friends and contacts in the United States and Europe. Shortly after his marriage to Kate in 1931, they traveled to Palma-de-Mallorca and en route enlisted a whole series of talented writers to contribute to *Pagany*.

Mangan's most memorable literary appearance in the magazine was "'A Note': On the Somewhat Premature Apotheosis of Thomas Stearns Eliot." Dedicated to his father, Dr. Mangan, the essay is a cleverly erudite rejection of what Mangan considered the negative features of Eliot's precisian criticism. Virgil Thomson pronounced it "one of the wittiest polemical pieces" that he had ever read; it was much admired by Gertrude Stein; and as late as 1976 Kenneth Rexroth wrote that it still "remains as a masterpiece."[2] The first sentence reads:

It is not without diffidence that one protests against the Eliot myth, not only because an unknown young man feels a certain lèse majesté inherent in caviling at an older and established writer, not only because Mr. Eliot, critic, is able, admirable, plausible, and above all formidable, but most especially because his critical station is in opposition to so many objectionable camps with which one is in fear a casual reader might identify any adversary that there seems scarcely to be left any tenable ground save Mr. Eliot's own.[3]

With its transposed syntax, Latinity, and foreign locutions, such a prose style is difficult to read; his message, however, is sincere and lucid. He judged Eliot a good poet, but believed he was directing the young writers who adulated him toward stale ideas and the defense of the status quo. He thought that Eliot should be relegated to the position of a historical figure, a writer who summarized and closed off an era, so that poetry of the 1930s might be free to depart in some new direction. Shortly after Mangan's essay appeared, Ezra Pound published an evaluation of *Pagany*'s first year, in which he singled out Mangan's writings: "In choosing Sherry Mangan as its critical spokesman, if he was chosen, *Pagany* could not have done better."[4]

Another memorable publication in *Pagany* was Gertrude Stein's "Poem Pritten on Pfances of Georges Hugnet." Stein originally proposed to translate Hugnet's poem "Enfances" for publication opposite the French text. But her translation assumed a life of its own, evolving into an original work that instigated a row between Stein and Hugnet. In the heat of the controversy, Stein telegrammed *Pagany* that it was "imperative" that her part of the work be published under the title "Poem Pritten on Pfances of Georges Hugnet." Mangan and Johns scratched their heads, wondering whether this was a new literary experiment or whether the telegraph operator had erred; but they obeyed her orders and the poem appeared under that title.[5]

The pride that Sherry felt from his connection with *Pagany* was indicated in a 1932 letter he sent to Johns, in which he expressed pleasure that the magazine featured young and little-known people: "Even if the sum total is not so grand as it would be if you went over to the big boys, it (a) makes *Pagany* always more interesting and unexpected, and (b) makes it fulfill a special function very valuable to the republic of letters and very decent on your part."[6] In these same years, many friends from his Harvard days identified with *Hound and Horn*, a rival publication that devoted the greater part of its efforts to a search for a new academic criticism. Most important among such friends was R. P. Blackmur, the cousin of Sherry's Harvard classmate Tony Palmer.

Blackmur never attended college, but worked at the Dunster Street Bookshop in Cambridge, where he associated with Sherry and other members of the Harvard Poetry Society. Intimate friends in the late 1920s, Sherry and Blackmur continued to be part of a close set in the early 1930s. Boston gatherings at the Ararat or Athens-Olympia restaurants or at a salon hosted by the painter Tessa Gilbert would draw Sherry and Kate Mangan, Dick and Helen Blackmur, Tony Palmer, Murray Borish (another cousin of Blackmur), and Jack Wheelwright. Austin Warren was sometimes there, as well as the painter Richard Carline, a former suitor of Kate's visiting from England. Occasionally they would all visit the Mangan home in Lynn or would vacation in a cabin kept by the Blackmurs in Maine. Their favorite activity was quarreling about literary matters; they also criticized each other's poetry and played games involving the identification of some literary work.[7]

"'A Note': On the Somewhat Premature Apotheosis of Thomas Stearns Eliot" was partly aimed at Blackmur, who at the time was presenting Eliot as a model in *Hound and Horn*. Mangan admired Blackmur as a poet, writing enthusiastically in letters about an unpublished novel Blackmur had completed. Nevertheless, frustrated by Blackmur's literary criticism, he expressed to Johns his astonishment at the "difference between his [Blackmur's] theories and his work." Mangan's objections to Eliot applied equally to Blackmur: the criticism of both elevated the critical faculty to the detriment of the creative faculty. He thought that *Hound and Horn*, led by Lincoln Kirstein, Varian Fry, Bernard Bandler, A. Hyatt Mayor, and Blackmur, was nothing less than the organized expression of this tendency. Learning that Eliot was under consideration for a faculty position at Harvard, Mangan cried in mock horror to Johns that this would produce "Blackmurs and Bandlers at every turn" and that he would soon be "smothered by Kirsteins." He pledged himself to become "the sole representative of my own private movement: the 'After-Eliot-What? Movement.'" He also sensed that *Hound and Horn* was a self-aggrandizing operation, "a shoehorn for getting into Boston society," and suspected that Blackmur was being corrupted by an all-consuming desire for success in the academic world.[8] In 1938 he satirized Blackmur in an epigram called "Matthew Arnold B____, Man of Letters," which contains the following lines:

Herein a patient methodology divulges
the anti-solipsistic proof that Henry James'
left tibia multiplied by eighteen perses equals
the floor-length of the second (the descending) shaft
of Cheops' pyramid.
                    Reviews will ring with this!—
among the sesquipedalian jargon on James, Hemingway,
and Proust.[9]

The range of Mangan's literary activities and associations was wide, and his criticism in journals attracted much attention. But he confessed to Samuel Putnam, editor of the *New Review*, that "I don't regard myself as an either sound or interesting critic"; to Ezra Pound he explained that writing criticism usually involved an emotional "blow-up which leaves me unable to work for a week afterwards."[10] First and foremost came his own poetry, which brought him a substantial reputation in a relatively short time. Whereas most of his short stories were rejected several times before finding their way into print, Sherry was usually in the situation of not having enough poetry on hand to meet all the requests he received. Many of his best poems were collected in *No Apology for Poetrie and Other Poems Written 1922-1931*, published in 1934 in Boston.

Mangan invokes Whitman in the introduction to the volume: "Do I contradict myself? / Very well, then, I contradict myself."[11] But Mangan's poetry lacks Whitman's transcendental fulsomeness; the attraction is only to Whitman's acceptance of a complex and contradictory self. Beyond this, much of the book is imitative of classical forms and derives many themes from Mangan's milieu and time of life. Like the work of the modernists Joyce, Pound, Yeats, and Eliot, Mangan's work expresses an Alexandrian fascination with myth, linguistics, eroticism, and forgotten areas of history and literature. At the same time, it is dulled by the conventional concerns of the transition from undergraduate life to manhood: frustration in love, philosophic doubting, the power of poetry, disappointment with the unheroic reality of the adult world, and the moral ambiguities of ambition and lust. Yet Mangan, with quiet workmanship, was sometimes capable of transforming such cliché topics into finished verse. He does this in "Hallelujah of Hercules in the Harem," which depicts a student having intercourse with a prostitute in his room:

> Her baloonface below my scowling books
> (the bed being shoveled beneath the case)
> puffs like the winners in the fat mens race
> as at her lovecrest she gaily unhooks
> her souls true banner from round her arse and
> waves it whooping about my mind which shies
> good horse with arching back and rolling eyes
> she drools from both mouths and one pudgy hand
> grabs the bedpost the other mine it does
> not matter to either the bedpost or
> me which still I pump into this stale whore
> energy disgust sudden the minds buzz
> warns me too late I am hold now christ bite
> less than thy complement thy slave tonight.[12]

The theme is traditional: the student discovers that the mind is ul-

timately subordinate to passion when he becomes even less than the
"complement" of the prostitute, in fact becomes her "slave." But the
bawdy realism of Mangan's lines renders the episode unusually vivid.
The prostitute "puffs" in excitement, "like the winners in the fat mens
race," while drooling "from both mouths." The poem bounces along in
decasyllables that imitate the movements on the bed as he "pumps"
energy and disgust into the woman with the "baloonface." Under the
glare of his "scowling books," his fearful mind shies from her like a
horse; but in the end intellect is shown to be inferior to sex and the
scholar becomes like Hercules in the poem's title, a mythical figure
noted for his weak mind.

Sometimes Mangan's poetry expressed the fear that his imaginative
powers might fail, an obsessive theme for romantics like Wordsworth
and Coleridge (for example, in the latter's "Dejection: An Ode"). In
"Resurgam," he disguises the theme by dressing it in Christian garb; the
"God" in the poem is Apollo, not Christ:

> Grimness in silence, Thou, my God, salute,
> hooded in purpose, motionless in growth,
> broken like hostbread to Thy worship's oath,
> intact in essence, one though convolute.
>
> My edge was turned as though my steel were lead:
> perceive the dusty mount that marks me; yet
> the very self that sinned has no regret,
> for I am most myself when I am dead.
>
> Grant me my strength again with moving pain,
> that after regrowth may mine edge be keen;
> O, come Thou in Thy singleness to glean
> my dust and find the missing vital grain.[13]

"Resurgam" simply calls for assistance in the resurrection of creative
power, although there is much Donne-like wrestling in diction and
metrics. The poet, grim in his artistic silence, cries out "salute" to his
god, explaining that he has lost his direction, even though he remains
"intact in essence." What most frightens him is that his lassitude seems
to be a natural state in which he feels most himself. "Dust" becomes a
central symbol in the poem—dust accumulates as a result of his trying
to sharpen himself when he is in a state more like lead than steel; dust
invokes the dust of death in the Bible; dust is the source in which the god
must seek out the vital grain for his resuscitation. Sherry's images here
are presented in terms of symbolic and abstract concepts; there is little
reference to external reality.

This mode of expressing problems in isolation from social reality, with the world in the poem functioning primarily as a corollary for subjective states, becomes more dominant toward the end of the volume. The title poem, "No Apology for Poetrie," is far removed from the fleshy realism of "Hallelujah of Hercules":

Sonnets are such silly flowers
to drink passion's whiskey out of

Or need we mention love? Thenafter . . .

Observation begat didacticism: we fled
the essay, currently scanning. Socrates mere
ethics; the rest as bad or worse. Sickened
as well the smell of incense. Li-Po (was it?)
with a skinful of rice-wine, sought the moon
in a garden pool. This proved no anodyne.
Rows in Vienna: Sigmund begat André—and then
the deluge. Progressively sickening, we sought
the purple swamp again, Aristotle cicerone.
Rode grandly in a cerebral intoxication
through Thomas, laying the ghost Uncertainty;
drunk, as on rice-wine, with the conclusions,
knowing how inacceptible the premises.

And stopped short, at three twenty-two p.m.,
like an apoplectic recovering from a shock,
asking the usual senseless "Where are we?"

O tightrope-walkers of the antique logic, wishfully
juggling with truth, once let the new blade, far
sharper than Occam's knife, cut through the trusted
cord, then we're exactly nowhere.

In this house at the age of eight he learned
the behavior of quicksilver and methods of masturbation.
Short errands, five cents; long ones, ten. Growing up,
he found it much the same: money and women
and the problem of certainty.
                                        As we turned
this little croquis in our hands, our eye
saw in the air between—$G_{yv} = 0$;
and we fled, terrified. Beyond this nothing?
This is the shortest line through to death?

(. . . against the pedal-point of death, the cant
'o sestet admirable felicitous
antithesis, ô phrase bien tournée. . . .')

May I not die before I wake.[14]

This is an elaborate extension of the theme of "Resurgam," an account of the artist's defeat. As in much of his early work, this poem reflects scant interest in the problem of audience and derives its form from the content. More important than far-reaching communication is Mangan's fixation on the honest reproduction of his feelings of the moment. However, he does show an ear for a new poetic speech; his mixture of modes creates a jarring effect that corresponds to the inner disharmonies recorded.

The poem is essentially intellectual autobiography. He begins by questioning the ability of traditional poetry (the sonnet) to communicate true passion and then presents an unrhymed sonnet that traces the stages of his evolution: traditional scholarship, meditation, Freudianism, surrealism, neo-Thomism. Despite the intoxicating conclusions of the last stage, he rejects it because of its unacceptable premises. At a point somewhat past the middle of his life (the simile of the "apoplectic recovering from a shock" may allude to the impact of his father's stroke), he suddenly questions his whole existence. Mangan assumes a lightly mocking tone as he quickly reviews his achievements, for which he invokes "Occam's razor" (William of Occam's axiom, "What can be done with fewer assumptions is done in vain with more"). He realizes that the issues that preoccupied his youth—money, sex, and "the problem of certainty"—are still unresolved. Recognizing that life is a struggle against the dominant tone ("the pedal point") of death, the well-turned phrases of poetry seem impotent. His last line—"May I not die before I wake," which echoes both a child's prayer and Eliot's "Till human voices wake us, and we drown"—is a plea that he might survive at least until he achieves illumination.

The poem is a paradigm of Mangan's impasse; it records a state of mind in which he feels compelled to act, but is also confused about the appropriate values by which to determine the next correct move. Since the early 1930s, new questions have entered his life and disturbed his mind; the change in his situation is so great that a new poetic world needs to be invented in order for him to experience it imaginatively, but the poet is at a loss about how to proceed. Equally disturbing is a hint of nihilism in the poet's disillusionment with intellectual solutions. This is evidenced even more strongly in the last poem in the collection, "Words to Time's Winds":

Lady Lady
little lady
gentle lady
of my heart

lady lady
gentle lady
little lady
of my heart

the rest   words only
words which let time take
leaving me you.[15]

Here the poet seems to reject words and intellectualizing altogether as a distraction from real life; the implication is that he desires not to think of the loved lady, but only to experience her. Yet the joy of the carpe diem motif—present in Cummings, as well as occasionally in Mangan's earlier work—is totally missing, and there is pathos in the final repudiation of poetic language.

In contrast to Wheelwright, who underwent and resolved his crisis of the early 1930s in social terms, Mangan's poetic images indicate that he saw his crisis only as a crisis in poetry or, at best, in philosophy. The questions he asks are essentially the same as those asked by Wheelwright, although they are not posed in a Marxist framework: Mangan is concerned with death, with the function of poetry in healing a sick culture, and with the location of a philosophy that will give him a purposeful role in society. Furthermore, he clearly sees the central problem as that of writing a new poetry for a new time. Public issues invaded and disordered the private lives of Wheelwright and Mangan. Wheelwright perceived the crisis in poetry as a social problem and addressed it in his work, but Mangan's perception was narrower, causing him to all but abandon poetry as a useful mode of action.

No Apology for Poetrie was published by Bruce Humphries in an edition of three hundred; like *Rock and Shell*, it sold for $2.50. But despite this small circulation, it was a succès d'estime. Writing in the *Saturday Review of Literature*, William Rose Benét described Mangan's anthology as "the latest book the intelligentsia like" and called it an example of "the new precocity," although Benét then proceeded to attack the writings for their world-weary and hedonistic traits.

The highest praise for Mangan's poems came in reviews by William Fitzgerald in *Anathema* and Austin Warren in *Sewanee Review*. Fitzgerald dubbed Mangan a member of the "Modern Metaphysical School" and described him as a representative voice among poets concerned about the poverty engulfing contemporary philosophy. He praised Mangan's keen "perception of the unhackneyed word, the gracious line," and pointed out Mangan's affinity to Ezra Pound in his "flippancy and ample scattering of the classic tongues throughout his verses." Like the seventeenth-century cavaliers, Fitzgerald observed, Mangan used the "unexpected quip" and the "hidden shaft of irony."[16] Austin Warren argued that Mangan fulfilled Eliot's definition of the poet as one who is "constantly amalgamating disparate experiences." He noted that Mangan, who was not only familiar with the school of Eliot and Pound, but also "quite as learned . . . as these eminent instructors, [had] gone to their *fontes et origines*." Warren also provided a personal portrait of Mangan as a man who "wears the sturdy boots of a peasant and talks an English so elegant, so manicured, so mellifluous, that officials hesitate to engage him to work under them."[17]

Mangan's work did not escape criticism, however, especially from the circle of his closest friends. Writing in the *New Frontier*, the poet Howard Blake, whom Sherry had met through Jack Wheelwright, admitted that Mangan's standing was high in comparison with his contemporaries, but his work could not be considered an original contribution when measured against the whole tradition of English literature. In particular, Blake was skeptical that Mangan had furthered the gifts bequeathed upon him by Pound and Eliot, the two greatest influences on all poets of his generation. Furthermore, though he praised Mangan for his "delicate, precious, nice use of words" and the eloquence and elegance of his whole endeavor, he charged that Mangan lacked the metaphorical gift, leaving his ideas "too infrequently fused with images, with sense perceptions."

A special concern with the lack of relevant content in Mangan's work was set forth in Jack Wheelwright's review. Writing in *Poetry*, Wheelwright argued that Mangan's work was in the main an expression of the boom times, the days gone by. Wheelwright offered the following analysis of the crisis he saw operating in the background of Mangan's work: "The trouble (and there seems to be trouble) was that an agile, clear mind withdrew from an unclear and stiffening society, not so much for safety as for adventure, into a world of Love and Letters. It is because this fantastic world is firmly grounded in fact that it shifted beneath the fancy. Mangan found his exploration more tiresome than staying at home; but he is not ready to turn his agile clarity upon the factual society which surrounds him."[18]

No hint of resolution is given in *No Apology for Poetrie*, which merely states the problem. But Sherry's correspondence with Virgil Thomson indicates that he had begun his search for an alternative at least by 1930. In the spring of that year, he wrote that "a cursory re-examination of past philosophy leaves me with the rather strange belief that it is, for all its pompously exact appearance, largely emotional and ethical." Sherry proceeded to describe his disgust with the purely emotional in literature and "with the belief that whatever happens to come out is right. . . . I find Maritain, St. Thomas, etc., fascinating, but cannot accept their premises. Eliot is weak. Humanism is a colossal joke. What remains?"[19]

Sherry tried to answer this question a year and a half later from Palma-de-Mallorca. In another letter to Thomson, he related how he was jarred into a need to consider the issue further when he read Samuel Putnam's anthology *European Caravan*. Never before had he clearly seen all contemporary European literature spread out before his eyes, and he was "shocked at its feebleness, cowardice, and lack of imagination. All escape; escape in every form: sport, dreams, religion, the unconscious, nihilism, criticism." It looked to Sherry as if it "needed a little guts; or

some unifying principle to stop the niggling and fill it with beans again."
Five possibilities suggested themselves to him: "Religion, Surrealism,
Art for Art's Sake, Communism, and Science." In passing judgment on
these five, Sherry immediately placed religion at the bottom of the list.
He thought that religion held the potential for "a violent mindless reac-
tion," that it was something the avant-garde artists ought to campaign
against. Surrealism he rated second from the bottom, for he thought that
it was also, ultimately, an escape, but not a dangerous kind of escape; he
predicted that it would soon die a natural death.

The concept of "art for art's sake" ranked near the top of the list, for he
saw himself as one who had replaced the false illusions of God and love
with devotion to Apollo (the Greek god of the arts and intellect). For
Sherry, devotion to Apollo was to be seen "not as a belief but as a con-
cept, and by poetry considered . . . as a priesthood." For this reason Sherry
rejected communism at this point because "it will have no other god be-
fore it, including art." He mentioned that he had talked with "an official
Communist poet of considerable ability, Norman MacLeod, who finds it
pretty cramping. But eventually, when communists need no longer be
shock-troops, it may work out well."

His preference, then, was the last on the list: science. He explained to
Thomson what he intended by using science to establish a unifying prin-
ciple behind his poetry: "Not 'stainless-steel skies.' Not a stupid worship
of the machine. . . . Not a trick of saying 'dreaming after your—$(a + b)^2 =
(a-b)^2$—red-hot thighs.' Nor any of that bunk." Instead, he wanted to
develop "poetry which will not need untruth to be emotive, whose prin-
cipal beauty will lie in its perfect and thrilling lucidity." He admitted
that he found religious poetry the most moving poetry to date ("Donne
on eternal damnation or some of Hopkins's devotional verse"), but he
believed that this was only because "ages upon ages have built up a
corpus of contexts around religious verse" and such a corpus had not yet
been developed in regard to scientific concepts. He stated that he was no
longer interested in poetic material that required the abandonment of
fact to make its effects. "Technique is still poetic," he acknowledged,
"and only poets will ever be able to write poetry." But he concluded that
"technique one catches like a cold; material one must study and experi-
ence. . . . it seems to me that what we need is: To stand in the draught
made by the wings of Dante, but to study Wittgenstein like hell."[20]

This plan to intellectually embark in a new direction was never real-
ized; Mangan's quest for a different road for artistic creativity was symp-
tomatic of his disorientation. This was evidenced by his efforts to write
"Salutation to Valediction," a long and profoundly pessimistic poem.
"Salutation" was first conceived in the late 1920s as the introduction to
a major verse work called "Valediction," which he described in a letter to
Virgil Thomson as a "very serious poem . . . about rhythm and death-

before-thirty." In a three-month period he had completed twenty-nine
lines, which he considered a good pace. The half-humorous idea behind
the poem was to "avoid dying by thirty by spending all the time until
thirty telling in all the gruesome detail just how one is dying. Wake up at
thirty-one still writing. Fool death."[21] However, by the time that Mangan
had actually completed the "Salutation" section of "Valediction," the
poem had been transformed into the depiction of a situation all too true.
Many years later, he described "Salutation" as an "apparently separate
poem [that] is only the preface to a long poem in completely modern
style . . . about how the modern world kills poetic talent."[22] Of the poem
itself, Sherry never produced more than notes; but a number of friends
who knew the introduction asked him to publish it separately. So he did,
first in the magazine *Anathema* and then in 1938 as a separate brochure
by Bruce Humphries in an edition of five hundred copies.

The tone of the "Salutation" section suggests that a feeling of utter
despair overwhelmed Sherry when he began to realize that he was not
going to be able to fulfill his poetic objectives. In the poem the agonized
poet pleads to Apollo for just enough song to make a confession of his
failure:

> For I have flung
> the care of sacred oath to casual wind
> and, swept into the phrensied Bacchic train,
> against Thy priesthood thoughtlessly have sinned.[23]

The poet turns against himself, blaming his failure on his own selfish-
ness, thoughtlessness, and hedonism:

> —I who have oft preferred the Phrygian strain,
> have seen with Midas's gold-blinded eyes,
> and, tempted, fallen, died—and died in vain.
> (Swift as Thy cloud-compelling father hurls
> the shrieking bolt, flay me that Marsyas,
> clap me some asses' ears upon these churls.)[24]

He compares himself to the Phrygians (who were drowned because of
their selfish behavior toward Apollo when he came among them dressed
as a beggar) and to Midas (whose stupidity led him repeatedly into trouble
and earned him asses' ears), as well as to Marsyas (a satyr horribly pun-
ished for daring to challenge the gods with his flute). Mangan's last lines
are doubly desperate; his only request is to be permitted enough song to
finish his confession of failure:

> For this is swan-song, Soter, this is last
> confession, for my prentice-time is spent,
> the hour of reckoning already past,

and as I, of unpardonable sin,
sin-struck, sincere repent, oh imminent
I see the end draw near, the night draw in.

Chrüsokitharistes, Chrüsostomos,
create, restore in me song's golden power,
that even this my shame may honor thus
the Lord of Song. O, of all songs the Breath
Breathe once more in me at this final hour:
bless this my song, and bless, with it, my death.[25]

Like Wheelwright's "modernism," that of Mangan was partly the vehicle
for resurrection of older forms. "Salutation" reverberates with the an-
guish of the seventeenth-century Metaphysical poets; phrases like "sin-
struck" and "sincere repent" imitate the sprung rhythm of Hopkins.

Toward the end of his life, in a 1957 letter to his friend Charles Hay-
wood, Sherry attempted to explain why the most important decision
of his life—his transformation from a litterateur into a revolutionary
Marxist—was not a turnabout or a reversal, but a pilgrimage undertaken
for the preservation of his original goals. He explained the important
role played by coincidence, the fact that the depression, his unfortunate
marriage to Kate, and his father's bankrupting long illness occurred
simultaneously. But the turning point came when he recognized that
social forces were going to prevent him from fulfilling his artistic aspira-
tions. He told Haywood that just at the point where he should have been
emerging from lyricism into subjects of a graver nature and greater scope,
he was going to have to "stop poetic activity and scrabble about in some
kind of money-making to keep self and wife alive." This produced recog-
nition "of the fact that our present civilization has no place for a poet
such as I was."

A significant hiatus occurred between Sherry's perception of the prob-
lem and his discovery of the proper kind of solution. For several years he
wrestled with the new realization "on a purely personal basis, and with a
fundamental embitteredness such as I think nobody suspected," until,
late in 1936, he "discovered that there was potentially another kind of
civilization in which poets might be not only permitted but encouraged
to be poets." He then proceeded to study Marxism and to assess the
course of the civil war in Spain; eventually he emerged convinced that
the socialist movement "not only could produce a really civilized world
but indeed was the only alternative to barbarism and disaster—a concep-
tion which was then purely theoretic perhaps but which has now become
atomic and terrifying."[26]

This transition to political consciousness occurred entirely after
Sherry's marriage to Kate, which was brief and stormy. They met in Paris
in 1924; between 1928 and the wedding in 1931, Sherry fretted about his

suitability for matrimony; by the end of 1933, the marriage was in deep trouble. A final attempt to save the relationship came with a trip they took to Mexico in the winter of 1933–34. South of the border, both attempted to pursue their cultural interests. Kate painted and Sherry wrote. Kate also contributed the "London Letter" to *Pagany*, and they coauthored a magazine piece about Mexico.[27] But at the end of the sojourn, relations were worse than before. When they arrived back in New England, Sherry took a job in Norwood, Massachusetts, doing a combination of book designing and some executive work for Plimpton Press. On 18 September 1934 Kate sailed to England for a vacation. There she developed a new relationship with a German named Jan Kurzke.

Sherry believed that the main reason the marriage broke up was his inability to support Kate in the manner she desired. Prior to the Mexican trip, they had been living with the Mangan family in Lynn, an environment Kate found stultifying. There had also been a particularly depressing period in which Sherry had searched for work. At one point they drove to Washington, D.C., in the hope that Sherry could get a job as a typographic designer with a new public department. They stayed for a while with Grant Code, one of the Harvard poets, but the position never materialized. Later Sherry wrote to Ezra Pound that this job hunting brought him to the point of "despair" and that only "¼ of self" was able to function. He wanted "to get into a cranny out of the storm but there aren't any crannies." He was not qualified to teach formally and the printing industry had overexpanded. He complained that "after 28 the only real problems in life are financial. By that age one has his life quite decently arranged, but alas not the world."[28]

In the period just after the separation from Kate and his first months of work in Norwood, Sherry fell into a fit of depression and began drinking more heavily than before. He came into Boston now and then to give lectures at the Wentworth Institute on the subject of typography, and he kept the company of writers he knew from the 1920s as well as several newer acquaintances. These included Austin Warren, Warren's brother-in-law Howard Blake, a Harvard student in chemical engineering named Cuthbert Daniel, and the Harvard psychologist B. F. Skinner. Sherry also befriended three young Harvard poets, James Agee, James Laughlin, and Robert Fitzgerald.

The previous year, 1933, Sherry had occasion to stay with Fitzgerald in his room at Dunster house. Together they worked on a classical translation for the Horace prize. It was submitted under Fitzgerald's name, but failed to win the hundred dollars. To Fitzgerald, Sherry seemed to be an older and more established literary figure, and he did not anticipate that Sherry might vanish from the cultural scene just a few years later. He assumed that since Sherry was such "a very rich and interesting human being," the promise shown in his early writing would be fulfilled in an important way.[29] But the novelist John Cheever, who also lived in Boston at the time, remembers Sherry as having been "a spirited, gifted, sensuous man who, to my narrow eyes, lacked any sort of direction."[30]

The most original and fascinating member of Sherry's circle of friends, however, was Jack Wheelwright. He had first met Jack in the early 1920s through the Liberal Club and Harvard Poetry Society, but it was only after 1930 that their close friendship began in earnest. In early 1933 he wrote Virgil Thomson of his fascination with his new friend and urged Thomson to get together with him as soon as possible: "Wheelwright, whom you may remember from Harvard, gets madder daily and more interesting." Later, after he had succeeded in reuniting Thomson and Wheelwright, he wrote: "I am delighted as I am surprised to hear that you like Wheelwright. . . . Of course he is difficult, but I think the divine spark flutters somewhere in that bony frame."[31] Between 1934 and 1936, Sherry was a regular in "The Bards," a small circle of New England poets centered around Jack. Among others, it included R. P. Blackmur, Tony Palmer, and Howard Blake. Some degree of identity as a regional group existed, for, after the New Republic published a selection of poetry by the "Auden Group" in England, Blackmur was authorized to choose writings for a spread of "Eight New England Poets." These poems, appearing in the 14 August 1935 issue, included those by S. Foster Damon, Dudley Fitts, Sherry Mangan, Winfield Townley Scott, Jack Wheelwright, Kimball Flaccus, Theodore Spencer, and Blackmur.

Working in Norwood, however, remained depressing, and Sherry's drinking and temper tantrums were by now quite pronounced. On 12 July 1935 Sherry was stopped by a policeman for running a traffic light; when asked his occupation, Sherry belligerently replied "poet." The policeman thought Sherry was mocking him and hauled him off to jail, where a row ensued. The police then announced that Sherry was drunk and fined him. Sherry, in turn, charged that he had been refused the right to be examined by a physician and asked his friend Charles Haywood, recently graduated from law school, to take the case. Haywood fought it all the way up to the Massachusetts Supreme Court, but lost.[32]

During one of Sherry's bouts with depression and drink, he ended up in the hospital. There he met a nurse of Swedish extraction named Marguerite Landin, whom Sherry called "Marguerita," "Margretta," or usually just plain "M." In August 1936 Sherry wrote Thomson that he had moved outside the town of Norwood and was living in a pleasant little cottage in the pines "with a little nurse who, if not the paragon of beauty, is at least the perfection of devotion—very soothing to the Kate-abandoned vanity." He reported that he drank no liquor "except wine with meals (and marvelous meals they are, too—light and delicious)" and that all this was enhanced by "lots of satisfactory love."[33] Sherry and Marguerite were eventually married in Lima, Peru, in 1941, although for unexplained reasons Sherry had their passports and all other records altered to read that the wedding occurred in Dampierre, France, in 1939. The relationship was never revealed to Sherry's parents, who, as devout Catholics, condoned neither divorce nor remarriage.

In the beginning, Sherry's association with Jack Wheelwright was not at all political. Cuthbert Daniel, at that time a Socialist party member with Jack, recalls that when the three of them would get together for a poetry reading or discussion, Sherry would laugh at their Marxist ideas.[34] However, it was not long before Jack enlisted Sherry to design his book *Rock and Shell*. After that, Sherry and Jack jointly issued a series of radical poems under the general rubric of "Vanguard Verse." These came out between 1934 and 1937 in two formats: "Poems for a Dime" and "Poems for Two Bits."

Most of the contributors to the series were little-known radical poets. Jack Wheelwright, Kenneth Patchen, and Kenneth Porter were the most frequent writers. To Horace Gregory, Jack explained that contributions "must have some connection with the class struggle, but I intend to be pink, loose, and watery in 'ideological' editorial guidance. Priggish cant makes me sick, red, pink, or black. The battle front of a writer is wider than that of a union organizer." He further explained that "our next struggle must be prepared now along with the struggle against capitalism" and that this would be "against philistine obscurantism."[35]

At first Jack was the only official editor, with Sherry listed as a printer who was "a friend of the Socialist Party." Then Kenneth Porter, a Socialist and a Christian from Kansas who was doing graduate work in history at Harvard, was added as an advisory editor; then Jack, Kenneth, and Sherry were listed as advisory editors; and finally, after Kenneth left the area to teach, Jack and Sherry were solely in charge. The issues of Vanguard Verse were studded with various quotations, including a passage from Emerson's "American Scholar." Most issues of Vanguard Verse also contained advertisements for Wheelwright's "Correspondence Course on the Form and Content of Rebel Poetry." A registration fee of one dollar and a tuition of one cent per line of verse were listed as the charges. Frequently advertised in the issues were also Jack's *Rock and Shell*, Sherry's *No Apology for Poetrie*, and Howard Blake's *Prolegomena to Any Future Poetry* (which Sherry had designed). Fairfield Porter contributed woodcuts for the cover of one of the issues, and the fourth issue of "Poems for a Dime" was devoted entirely to Jack's "Masque with Clowns."[36] Sherry translated for publication a poem by Manuel Marples Arce, who was the founder of stridentism, a Mexican movement analogous to surrealism.[37]

After two years of collaborating with Jack on Vanguard Verse, Sherry had himself become reoriented toward Marxism. Yet Sherry was not the only one who had changed. During the same two-year period, Jack evolved from a left-wing socialist into a Trotskyist, and it was only when he reached this new political orientation that he began to wield his political influence over Sherry. In December 1936 Jack gave Sherry a copy of Trotsky's *History of the Russian Revolution*. On 27 December Sherry wrote Jack that "the Trotsky is magnificent." He exclaimed that he could not put it down, was already through the first two volumes, and was neglecting everything else. He then added: "I want to talk to you about . . . whether the Socialist Party, at its present low ebb, can use any personally inactive but gladly dues-paying members." Two days later, Sherry wrote Jack again: "Shall I join the Party? Or am I of more use outside?" And on 30 December: "Thanks for proposing me on the card. Want to talk further to you before going through with it—you'll see why."[38]

Although Sherry did become a member, his relations with the Socialist party and the Trotskyist caucus were somewhat modified by a new plan he had developed: to leave the United States once and for all and live in Paris. Since the 1920s this had been Sherry's dream, and he frequently spoke of Paris in letters as "the city of light" and "my true mistress." In 1933 Sherry wrote to Thomson that he was invariably stricken with nausea after visits to New York because the city symbolized to him the worst qualities of the United States. He declared his burning desire to return to France as soon as his family obligations and financial situation made this possible. His heart was set on Paris, "where I always feel completely at home, and either naturally happy, or, if sad, sad in so agreeable a form of gentle tristesse that it is as good as being happy." Sherry also had found that he could work more successfully at his poetry there: "Miraculously, for I never seem to be working; but whatever I've done there has lasted."[39]

For many American radicals during 1936–37, the central political issue of the day was the civil war in Spain. Sherry immersed himself in a study of the complex situation, engaging in debates with the Socialists and later with Trotskyist factions. He knew Spanish, had translated poetry by Federico García Lorca for the magazine *Smoke*, had lived on Mallorca, and at times had thought of moving to Spain. Although the Communist party gave uncritical support to the Republicans, the Trotskyists criticized the Republicans for defending bourgeois property rights, repressing revolutionary tendencies among the insurgent workers, and refusing to grant independence to the Moroccans. Virgil Thomson wrote Sherry that he read the Trotskyist analysis of Spain in the journal *New International* and found it depressing. Sherry responded that he was "more depressed by the tragic defeats in Spain resultant upon not following those theories and principles." He agreed that the Trotskyists were not "'hopeful' like the Communists in the sense that calling the Negrin government 'el gobierno de la victoria' is hopeful . . . we are neither Pollyannas nor Coués." The Trotskyists, Sherry elaborated, followed Lenin's maxim, "Patiently explain." But if hope could be defined "as the belief that sound principles, class loyalty, hard work, and an unshakeable belief in the ultimate inherent honesty and intelligence of the workers of the world will win a mass following adequate to smash fascism and bring about the socialist revolution, then we are indeed 'hopeful.'"[40]

Like Jack, Sherry fell under the personal influence of Antoinette Konikow and Larry Trainor. In all-night sessions with them, pamphlets were read on the spot and discussed. In collaboration with Jack, Sherry solicited supporters for the American Committee for the Defense of Leon Trotsky during 1937. The purpose of this organization was to enable Trotsky to defend himself against the charges in the Moscow purge trials. When the Trotskyists were expelled from the Socialist party in the fall of 1937, Jack and Sherry were among those who left. Both became founding members of the new Trotskyist organization, the Socialist Workers party, which was established on New Year's Day 1938.

In January 1938, under the pseudonym Terence Phelan, Sherry began to publish articles on the situation in France in the Trotskyist newspaper *Socialist Appeal*. On 6 February 1938, under the same name, Sherry gave a public talk in Boston on the topic "What Next in France," sponsored by the Socialist Workers party. Early in June, Sherry and Marguerite departed for Paris on the S.S. *President Roosevelt* out of New York. Toward the end of the month, a letter was sent by mail from Socialist Workers party national chairman James P. Cannon to the international secretariat of the Fourth International in Paris. It identified Sherry as "a contributor to our press and an active worker" and urged that "this note will facilitate his rapprochement with the French comrades."[41]

8. FROM ANTINOMIANISM TO REVOLUTIONARY MARXISM

In the last two years of his life, Jack Wheelwright's revolutionary imagination reached a high pitch of intellectual and emotional urgency. He blended socialist political activity with poetic creativity to a degree unequaled in American literature. In polemical, political, historical, and topical poems, he forged fresh emotive images worthy of comparison with other unique poetic voices in literary history. His cultural achievements also included participation in numerous political and literary activities radiating from the American Trotskyist movement and the completion of two new books of poetry, one of them published in his lifetime. Although his religious views never fully abated, they retreated to increasingly restricted ground. Hesitant to abandon such long-held commitments, his strategy was to render religion extraneous by burying his faith beneath an elaborate Marxist structure that would eventually stand on its own.

His religious views were almost unknown to his political associates; he had no desire to proselytize and devoted his moral energies to constructing a revolutionary vanguard free of the defects he had observed in the Social Democratic and Communist parties. During the late 1930s, the latter had taken up its popular front program—a strategy of alliances with liberal capitalist forces against the far right, entailing the subordination of revolutionary agitation and even requiring some patriotic excesses. The Socialist party, in contrast, continued to become more radical; one wing considered itself unabashedly revolutionary. Several months after the Trotskyists entered the Socialist party, Jack wrote his old friend John Marshall about the pride he felt in the role that the Socialists, who were now more left wing than the Communists, were playing in the 1936 elections: "The Socialist Party stands alone. It has kept its head and is at its old work more directly and vigorously than ever. . . . I was never prouder of anything in my life than I am of the S. P. at the present time."[1] Shortly afterward, he wrote to the Trotskyist leader Max Shachtman about his optimism that the Trotskyists might win over the left wing of the Socialist party, thereby forcing the right wing to simply walk out. He offered a series of suggestions for improvement of the *Socialist Appeal*, at that time the organ of the Trotskyist caucus, and concluded: "The coming world war makes it our sacred duty to build a revolutionary party in this country."[2]

Since 1934 he had supported the Trotskyist theoretical journal *New International.* That same year, he corresponded with its business manager, Martin Abern, about the possibilities for arranging asylum for Leon Trotsky in a safe country. This correspondence led to Jack's first association with John McDonald, George Novack, and other intellectuals drawn toward Trotskyism in the early 1930s. Together they collaborated in establishing an early version of the American Committee for the Defense of Leon Trotsky.[3] Two years later, when a more viable committee emerged at the time of the 1936 Moscow trials, with John Dewey at the head of its investigatory subcommission, he was a persistent activist on its behalf, although his irascibility led to occasional disagreements with the staff on tactical matters.[4]

When *New International* was reestablished in 1938 (it was dissolved during the time that the Trotskyists entered the Socialist party), he became an enthusiastic backer, vigorously selling subscriptions and sending off a stream of recommendations to the editors. Writing to James Burnham, a professor of philosophy at New York University and a leading Trotskyist theoretician, Jack volunteered to review poetry for the journal and urged closer collaboration with Delmore Schwartz and other poets close to the Trotskyist movement. He researched an essay on Karl Kautsky and asked Ruben Gotesky, a Hegelian scholar in the Socialist Workers party, for assistance. He told Burnham that he attached much importance to working out "socialist religion, philosophy and morals or counter-religion, counter-philosophy and counter-morals."[5]

However, he found himself sharply at odds with the official position of the Trotskyist party in one episode regarding cultural orientation. In late 1937 *Partisan Review* was relaunched on an anti-Stalinist basis, issuing an editorial that called for "independence" in both art and politics. The Trotskyist newspaper *Socialist Appeal* responded editorially that independence in political matters was an unrealistic perspective. The *Socialist Appeal* editors argued that the problems earlier encountered by the *Partisan Review* editors, when they were allied with the Communist party, did not prove the impossibility of collaboration with a non-Stalinist party. But Jack, who read the *Socialist Appeal* editorial as symptomatic of a desire to submit literary activities to political supervision, sent an angry letter to the editors; when he heard a rumor that the *Socialist Appeal* might not publish it, he also sent a copy to *Partisan Review* and another to Trotsky in Mexico.[6]

Contrary to the rumor, the *Socialist Appeal* did print Jack's letter, along with a second editorial defending its policy. For several months Jack was irate about the matter; in fact, with the duplicate of his original letter sent to *Partisan Review*, he enclosed a note to editor Philip Rahv declaring that "wherever this ugly philistine authoritarianism raises its head it must be socked."[7] In an exchange of correspondence between

Jack and the Trotskyist writer George Novack, who was the author of the offending official article, Novack thanked Jack for his compliments about his essay on John Brown in the *New International*, but then questioned Jack's tactical judgment in sending a copy of his letter to the *Partisan Review* before the *Socialist Appeal* had a chance to answer it. Jack responded that it was his "loyalty to Revolutionary Socialism which had made me insure the publication of my letter by sending a copy to the *Partisan Review*." He emphasized that "I have complete confidence in the principles of our party. It has no policy toward the arts and sciences. I can help form such a policy as will agree with the stated principles."[8]

Several months later, however, Jack cooled off, admitting that he had been too hasty in his handling of the disagreement. He wrote to Max Shachtman that Antoinette Konikow and her son Willie had told him he was "very wrong to have sent the *Partisan Review* a duplicate copy. They know more of revolutionary decorum than I do, so I hasten to write that I am sorry I violated this decorum, if I did." But he still insisted that he reserved the right "to express publicly my agreement or disagreement with the party's consensus, or opinion, or the stand of its officials, or even its official line, on cultural matters, particularly on matters pertaining to my own profession, which is letters." He concluded sharply: "A scientist, doctor, or painter would do the same or else be a moral jelly fish."[9] He continued his campaign inside the party for greater attention to cultural matters and by 1940 was engaged in a correspondence with James P. Cannon, the national chairman, that seemed to point toward a resolution of differences. Cannon wrote to Wheelwright:

> I think I would go even farther than you and say that I have no interest whatever in the proletarian revolution except as a step towards socialism. I have thought for a long time that the entire communist movement in America for the last twenty years (not excluding the opposition groups) concentrated their propaganda too much simply on the side of the struggle for power and said not enough about the socialist goal of the struggle. . . .
>
> In my opinion you are entirely right in your statement that the workers must be reinspired. And only a certain emphasis on the socialist goal of the struggle can really inspire them.[10]

Jack responded:

> Your letter delighted me. I wrote what I did about the secondary interest I take in the *proletarian* revolution (as distinguished from the *socialist*) in order to get your goat or pull your leg. You have been presented to me as an anti-intellectual ogre, you see. You fooled me completely. But I hasten to tell you that from my entry into the Socialist Party (1932) and for years before, I emphasized the con-

cern with the struggle for power as the distinguishing mark of "Utopians" who mean business from those Utopians who do not.[11]

During 1939–40 a political struggle convulsed the Socialist Workers party. This was a year of widespread political demoralization and disillusionment among left intellectuals. In addition to the defeat of the Spanish revolution and the bloody consequences of the Moscow frame-up trials, World War II was beginning in Europe and the Hitler-Stalin pact disoriented those who had hitherto considered the USSR to be, despite its defects, the main bulwark against fascism. At the same time that Granville Hicks and other intellectuals resigned from the Communist party, a large minority of the Trotskyist organization, led by Max Shachtman and James Burnham and endorsed by young party members such as Irving Howe, Leslie Fiedler, Harvey Swados, Saul Bellow, and Isaac Rosenfeld, was developing the view that Trotskyists could no longer defend the Soviet Union as a social system superior to capitalism. In the spring of 1940, the minority split and formed a new organization, the Workers party.

The issue of whether the USSR still remained a "degenerated workers' state" (that is, progressive in its abolition of capitalism and its nationalizations, but reactionary in its totalitarian political superstructure) or whether it had evolved into some new form of class society (Burnham was already using the term "bureaucratic collectivism") was at the heart of the six-month debate that ensued. However, the Shachtman-Burnham opposition was ostensibly organized around the political analysis of the Soviet-Finnish war that occurred in the wake of the Hitler-Stalin pact. While vigorously denouncing the Kremlin's conduct of the war, Trotsky maintained that Stalin's main motivation was protection of an exposed flank from a possible attack by the Nazis; he called for support to the Red Army in the actual fighting. The Shachtman-Burnham opposition rejected both Finland and the USSR equally, calling for a condemnation of both governments and armies.

Jack disagreed on certain tactical matters with the party's majority, which was led by Cannon and endorsed by Trotsky, but he was convinced that the USSR remained a workers' state in spite of its horrendous aberrations. He contributed to the debate a document called "Not Soviet Patriotism, but Bolshevist Renaissance," which began: "No title of our program is more salient than the Russian. Without incontrovertible factual evidence of the expected change in the nature of the Russian economy, a change in our Russian policy plays into the hands of capitalism."[12] In a private letter to Cannon, he explained that he considered the "victory of the Majority (with a minimum loss of membership) essential to the life of the Fourth International. At the same time, I consider the Political Committee's Finnish policy (which is a type for many

future developments) quite mistaken." He also predicted that the out-
look of the Shachtman-Burnham faction would lead "ideologically to
surrender to democratic chauvinism in the USA."[13]

Jack's document represents a serious effort at a political contribution
to the Trotskyist movement, an attempt to work through the knotty
problems of revolutionary policy in his own terms. He accepted the
classical Marxist view that in a war the primary issue must be the class
character of the societies involved, and that class character is something
to be determined by sociological and economic data, not momentary
anger or moral outrage. On this basis he maintained that the Soviet inva-
sion of Finland was actually a greater threat to the survival of the USSR
as a workers' state than it was a viable defensive action, because the
aggressive Soviet invasion drove the working class of Finland, as well as
much of the rest of the world, into the arms of reactionary powers. He
predicted that the minority's more fundamental error of reclassifying the
class nature of the USSR was an ideological step toward a rapprochement
with U.S. imperialism. This prediction seems to have been confirmed by
the subsequent evolution of the minority's leaders, Shachtman, and
Burnham. Furthermore, Jack accepted Trotsky's characterization of the
minority as a middle-class intellectualist group highly susceptible to
changes in public opinion. In supporting the Cannon faction, he felt
that he was siding with the more proletarian and serious elements in
the organization.

Strict adherence to a proletarian line in politics did not transform his
personal demeanor, which was always unpredictable. He might come
late to a party meeting, yet insist on leaping into a complicated discus-
sion, most of which he had missed. Larry Trainor recalled one meeting
when Jack jumped up from his seat in the middle of a business point on
the agenda and went to the financial secretary to pay his dues. Upon
being informed that he had to wait because finances were the next point
on the agenda, he repeated his request over and over in a loud voice until
the treasurer had to relent. Nevertheless, Trainor insisted that Jack was
"not just another poet but also a student of the movement" fully familiar
with "Trotsky and Lenin—not to mention Marx, Engels, and Lux-
emburg"; hence he was accepted and respected by the working-class
members.[14]

Since Wheelwright immensely admired Trotsky—he once called him
the "world's incomparable revolutionary" alongside of which Stalin was
"a butter and eggs man"—he sent copies of his poems to the exile in
Mexico.[15] In 1939 Antoinette Konikow visited Coyoacan, later reporting
to a branch meeting of the Boston Socialist Workers party that Trotsky
"sent his thanks for the book to the comrade-author and apologized that
his command of English was insufficient for him to fully appreciate the
poetry."[16] Yet Jack's admiration was never transformed into adulation;

unlike Auden and British left intellectuals who longed for a new revolutionary hero to lead them, Wheelwright was firm in his view that the socialist movement was a collective enterprise. Shortly after Trotsky's assassination in August 1940, he wrote to Harry Roskolenko that the chief danger in Trotsky's death "is that a scholastic phase may overtake the movement, people quoting chapter and verse to prove their points with no first rate philosopher to set them right. It will be interesting to see who the next persons are who have a whole grasp of Socialism. Will they be Americans?"[17]

Jack was indefatigable in attempts to organize writers and intellectuals into revolutionary activity. He was a central figure in establishing the League for Cultural Freedom and Socialism, the American section of the International Federation of Independent Revolutionary Art that was inspired by a manifesto issued by Trotsky, André Breton, and Diego Rivera. It was initiated at a time when the Communist party still held considerable influence over radical and liberal intellectuals through its League of American Writers. Wheelwright traveled to New York City to attend meetings of the Trotskyist-influenced league, always well prepared with criticisms and proposals. Dwight Macdonald, secretary of the league, regarded Jack as overanxious to establish a chapter in Boston. In the spring of 1939, responding to a complaint that Jack had felt personally slighted at a league gathering, Macdonald wrote, "At the first meeting, there was considerable objection to your talking simply because you took up an unfair amount of time, and also, if I may say so, because you kept making the same points over and over."[18]

His literary ventures continually multiplied. He attempted to establish a new magazine, *Pulse*, with Kenneth Patchen; with Harry Roskolenko and Helen Neville, he was instrumental in the formative stages of Exile's Press; and he organized a series of poetry readings over the Boston radio station WIXAL.[19] Attempting to broaden his audience, he gave recitations of his poetry at the Workman's Circle in Ashland, Dorcester, and Worcester; at the WPA Writers Group of Lynn; at the Young People's Socialist League of Boston; at the Chelsea Labor Lyceum; and at branches of the Socialist party and Socialist Workers party. Following political meetings, it was not unusual for Jack to bring a group of his comrades back to his Beacon Street home and discuss poetry and politics until four in the morning.

When Jack's political friends complained that his poems were incomprehensible, he conceded that they might be difficult but insisted that they were not obscure. In a 1938 essay in *Partisan Review*, he pointed out that an authentic revolutionary poem might recognize "mysteries and wrestle with them, which is a different matter from willful mystification, although indistinguishable to persons who have stultified their interior resources. Poets need care little if they be called obscure by

Philistines."[20] He genuinely believed that even the most allusive of his own passages would become intelligible if the reader were truly open and responsive. If that occurred, the reader would be changed in some way. "The main point is not what noise poetry makes," he wrote at the end of *Political Self-Portrait*, "but how it makes you think and act,—what it makes of you."[21] To achieve this end, Wheelwright's *Partisan Review* article suggests that revolutionary poets should "find examples in experimental masters of all rising classes that struggled throughout the centuries for mastery."[22] Such a broad range of influences is clearly manifest in his final book, *Political Self-Portrait*, issued six months before his death. As with his earlier books, the publisher was Bruce Humphries and the price was $2.50. This time the edition numbered 750 copies, although Jack had no hope of making a profit.

Mirrors of Venus and the Doubting Thomas poems show how Wheelwright divested himself of Christianity's belief in an afterlife, as well as the ordination of some of its adherents against sensual living and participation in the world of action. Thus he was psychologically and philosophically prepared for assimilating Marxism, a process depicted in *Political Self-Portrait*. Its significantly placed first poem, "The Word is Deed," is clearly an attempt to overcome the contradictions between his religious spiritual life and his scientific socialist political life. The first two stanzas read:

> John begins like *Genesis*:
> *In the Beginning was the Word;*
> Engels misread: *Was the Deed.*
> But, before ever any Deed came
> the sound of the last of the Deed, coming
> came with the coming Word
> (which answers everything with dancing).
>
> In our Beginning our Word:
> 'Make a tool to make a tool'
> distinguished Man from Brute.
> (Men who dance know what was done.)
> Good and Evil took root
> in this, the cause of Destinies
> whence every Revolution rose and stirred.[23]

This poem, first published in *Partisan Review* two years before *Political Self-Portrait*, does not present the final stage in his evolution, but it indicates the ground on which he sought political-theological reconciliation. He argues that Engels was incorrect in *Anti-Dühring* when he changed the statement of St. John to read that the deed preceded the word. Wheelwright insists that some sort of divine inspiration set human action in motion; the dancing in the poem signifies controlled, purposeful activity

—what Marxists call praxis, except that Wheelwright considers it divinely ignited. In rhythms reminiscent of Hopkins, the poem's sixth and concluding stanza reads:

> Deeds make us. May, therefore, when our Last
> Judgment find our works be just:
> all tools, from foot rules to flutes
> praise us; and our deeds' praise find
> the Second Coming of the Word.
> (Dance, each whose nature is to dance;
> dance all, for each would dare the tune.)[24]

Thus, since both Engels and Wheelwright agree that humanity transforms itself through deeds and tools, they can share a common strategy for achieving the "Second Coming of the Word"—socialism.

Such a loose framework for combining the antithetical doctrines of Marxist materialism and Christian idealism was expedient, but could hardly endure. In his poetry, however, the temporary alliance produced striking verse that blended images and ideas both revolutionary and theological, permitting him to dress religious leaders in revolutionary garb and to sanctify communist heroes. The content of ideas was often intriguing; for example, the first two stanzas of "Resurge from Decrescence" initiate a review in poetic form of a complex theological exchange between Wheelwright and Sherry Mangan:

> M." woke to Mangan's room in Lynn, and hears
> the April roll to Long Beach from Marblehead;
> and a light truck bump; and the eggbeater
> inside its radiator churn salt air
> all the way to the brownstone Town Hall:
> "Why did Jack call Jesus the Ur-Rebel?
> I understand that Lucifer is Rebel."
>   Waves in nines scoot up the tawny shore
> through kelp, against a punge of Spring-burned
> leaves, and Mangan answers her: "Wheels said
> at the Indian Summer time of yesterday:
> 'Lucifer is arch-Rebel in the Rebellion
> of Rebels who rebel but for Dominion.' "[25]

The setting of the poem is Lynn, where Marguerite ("M") and Sherry are in the Mangan house. This first assertion contends simply that Lucifer's rebellion was inauthentic; he rebelled only to gain power ("dominion"), whereas Christ, like Prometheus, rebelled to liberate humanity from oppression. As the poem unfolds, we learn—again in maieutic form— that even though Wheelwright opposes the Catholic church, he also happens to regard Luther and Calvin as greater corrupters of the revolutionary potential of Christian doctrine than either Augustine or Dante; he recommends the ideas of Machiavelli as "a means toward a liberation from authority."[26] Wheelwright develops the argument that by traveling backwards to the wellsprings of Christian thought, one can obtain new powers of insight that will assist in understanding the revolutionary character of Christ. Structurally, references in the poem likewise travel backwards, with the number of waves on the Lynn beach decreasing from nine to six to three and the months regressing from April to February.

A second important manifestation of religion in *Political Self-Portrait* is his attempt to forge an imaginative realm out of socialist thought, experiences, and values, a sort of counterreligion complete with its own pattern of imagery and its own mythological figures. In the "Argument" to the book, he states that "if you will read the numbers through and after, if you please, each argument and poem (always reading as one reads the verses of the Bible, or for that matter, between the lines of a newspaper), what will emerge is rather more humanist than materialist, and much less of a political treatise than a self-portrait of one who has found no way of turning, with Scientific Socialism, from a mechanical to an organic view of life than to draw from moral mythology as well as from revolutionary myth."[27] In this task, Wheelwright proceeded analogously to the French syndicalist Georges Sorel, who, in *Reflections on Violence*, developed the idea of the general strike as a myth: "The *myth* in which Socialism is wholly comprised, i.e., a body of images capable of evoking instinctively all the sentiments which correspond to the different manifestations of the war undertaken by Socialism against modern society."[28] Since Wheelwright's notion of strategy and tactics was not organized around the general strike, his poetic images were aimed at clarifying the political issues of the day, subverting the ideological facades of the ruling class, and unifying the disparate mass of humanity into a collective will that could transform society.

There is a consistent pattern of symbolic figures throughout *Political Self-Portrait*, figures usually identified with real or mythological persons, or with social forces. Prometheus, for example, is linked with Trotsky; the pope, with Stalin; Vulcan, with early capitalism; Alexander the Great, with imperialism. Wheelwright's most sustained effort at the creation of a revolutionary mythology was his use of the biblical figures Seth (the third son of Adam and Eve, who was born to replace the murdered Abel) and Cain. To each of these he attributed a "city," which he said was inspired by St. Augustine's *City of God*. The forces of reaction are identified with the city of Cain, those of revolution with the city of Seth. In the poem "Cain and Seth," which is dedicated to Powers Hapgood (a Harvard graduate who became the CIO director for New England in the 1930s), Wheelwright dwells on the ambiguities and complications caused by the fact that some of the citizens of Cain secretly live in the city of Seth and vice versa. In "Seven from Four," he identifies the men of Seth with the four elements and the men of Cain with an abuse of the seven sacraments.

Many of these religiopolitical poems in *Political Self-Portrait* are colorful, clever, entertaining, and provocative; but as a body of thought they are ultimately illogical and philosophically ambiguous, for, no matter how modulated, religion is one of the primary forms of alienation that scientific socialism seeks to transcend. Whenever Wheelwright delved into this ideological contradiction in a more serious way, he reverted to the hermetic and somewhat dull formulas of his 1920s religiomythic works. But a temptation to periodically try to resolve the contradictions did remain with him throughout the decade. At one point he toyed with the idea of completing the Thomas "novel" and drafted the skeleton plot for the fourth episode. His last (unfinished) poem, "The Other," is a recondite dialogue between voices of faith and doubt; it begins with a review of the history of religion from the time of nature worship.

Wheelwright's most significant contributions to American radicalism were his literary strategies for joining poetry and political ideology and his exemplary role as a writer—a culturally independent-minded but politically disciplined catalyst within a working-class movement. His efforts to find a modus vivendi between religion and Marxism produced startling poems and effective organizational concepts for his poetry collections, but his eccentric thinking on this matter seems to confirm the ultimate incompatibility of theological idealism and historical materialism for a serious intellectual. A striking example of Wheelwright's limitations as a theorist is his consistent policy of calling putatively apolitical poetry "nihilist." In contrast to those who correlate this type of writing with the interest of the ruling class, Wheelwright's approach seems less mechanical and sectarian; yet it is indicative of a hesitancy to pursue the issue thoroughly. In my judgment, the achievement of Wheelwright in the 1930s is unfinished, and, because of underlying ideological contradictions, unfinishable. That is why his literary opus was characterized by so many new starts: New England history, masques, revolutionary myth, and Christian-Marxist dialogues. His revolutionary imagination was remarkably ingenious as it sought to triumph over contradictions that may have been ultimately unresolvable at that point in his life.

Gradually, Wheelwright abandoned his long-term Christian beliefs. At first he renounced Anglicanism and for a brief time talked of a return to the Unitarianism of his ancestors. In 1939 he wrote to Sherry Mangan in Paris that "you will be glad to know that J.C. [Jesus Christ] means less and less in my life than used to be the case. It makes me feel strange. I do not know quite how to step without him. But I see more and more of D.M. [dialectical materialism]. . . . What effect this will have on my poetry will be interesting." In the end, Wheelwright lost his old faith altogether.[29] It is impossible to conjecture in a precise manner how the change would have affected his writing if he had lived. Analogous situations are known to have occurred among other Marxist writers; for example, Walter Benjamin's "Theses on the Philosophy of History" resemble some of Wheelwright's poems in their aim of linking theological objectives with historical materialism, but Benjamin successfully dropped this motif from view in other writings. Certainly an important part of Wheelwright's achievement in the 1930s stems from his ability to textualize the contradictions of his religiopolitical outlook in an entertaining or agitational way. Yet his ties to New England culture, his impulsive temperament, his self-parodying mannerisms, and his revolutionary fervor could be manifest independently of his religious faith; *Political Self-Portrait* has many poems that evidence no religious sentiments at all.

This is especially clear in the several poems in the book that inveigh against the danger of a Second World War. The prime focus in each of these is to use poetry to provide political guidance, to urge a course of action in rebellion against a sick, exploitative society. "You-U.S.-US," dedicated to his reactionary friend William Bradley Thayer, is a satire underscoring "the chief difficulty in proletarian revolution, the subservience of the masses to war hysteria."[30] "Skulls as Drums" is an answer to the Civil War poetry of Walt Whitman, which Wheelwright felt was naive about the class nature of the conflict. His philosophic "Train Ride," dedicated to Horace Gregory, uses as its refrain a slogan attributed to Wilhelm Liebknecht: "Always the enemy is the foe at home."[31]

"You-U.S.-US" is a paradigm of radical modernism in an extreme form. Replete with the techniques of poetic jolting, clashing fragmentation, word surprises, abrupt appearances and disappearances of emotions and imaginings, the poem is also bonded to canonical modernism in its attempt to function as a moral advisor to a misguided society. Here Wheelwright extends his attempt, initiated in *Rock and Shell*, to transform his poetry into a more public instrument. He surpasses earlier efforts in the virulence of his tone and colloquialism of his language—many lines are essentially sarcastic parodies of common expressions, children's songs, and advertising slogans. Allusions and references in the poem are to familiar depression scenes (the urban and rural unemployed, industrial working conditions) or to famous political figures (Wilson and Roosevelt). Hence the political ideas are aggressively lucid.

"You-U.S.-US" opens with a depiction of the purveyors of war propaganda in macabre terms, referring to them as "Youwhos," U.S. versions of Jonathan Swift's Yahoos:

> O sing the Daisy Chain of grinning Death Heads,
> and come across, you Youwhos, who'll support War.[32]

War itself is represented as a means by which the economic exploitation of the working class is intensified:

> The tin hat of Mars
> is passing upside down. Don't let it drop!
> Empty your pockets of Coppers, filings from black molars,
> plugs and buttons, protested notes,
> Squares and Compasses, Company Scrip.[33]

In language alternating between simplicity and histrionics, the remainder of the poem argues that war creates a false sense of national unity that objectively serves the interests of the bosses, as in passages such as the following:

> Weave a Daisy Chain of "Loves me,—Loves me not"
> Richman, Poorman, Beggarman, Thief,
> Doctor, Lawyer, Indian Chief
> All Created Equal, to be Queen
> of the Maybe the President Loves me,—
> Loves me not.[34]

The main strategy in all of Wheelwright's antiwar poems is not so much to foster the socialist alternative explicitly as to assault the values that sustain the status quo. Wheelwright battles to expose the true social relations hidden behind a veil of ideology. He uses language that shows the influence of Lewis Carroll and other nonsense writers, irony exaggerated to the point of black humor, and a heavy complement of maxims that sound authoritative. These poems urge commitment and collective action as the only effective mode of opposition, a viewpoint strikingly different from the individualist pacifism found in the antiwar poems of his contemporary, E. E. Cummings.

Other poems in the volume serve to dramatize diverse political themes of concern to the revolutionary left. In "Lanterns of Time," a poem dedicated to Kenneth Patchen, Wheelwright discusses the degeneration of the Russian Revolution and the rise of Stalinist gangster rule. Putting forward the view that the main hope for proletarian revolution lay in the activation of the proletariat in the West, his analysis resembles Trotsky's ideas at the time. Yet at one point Wheelwright employs the expression "Stalin's Red Fascism," likening the bureaucratized workers' state in the Soviet Union to Nazi Germany, a superficial equation that Trotsky rejected. At the end of the poem, the Kronstadt uprising of 1921, which Lenin and Trotsky believed threatened to throw the fragile postrevolutionary society into the hands of the White Guard, becomes the symbol of a coming political upheaval that would sweep out the misrulers in the Kremlin. However, in a note at the beginning of the book, Wheelwright apologizes for the fact that some of his poetic expressions might lead the reader into a false understanding of his political outlook: "The author regrets that such references as those to Kronstadt and to 'Red Fascism' pass beyond poetic license toward political license; but is unable to find apter language."[35]

"Redemption," a poem dedicated to Austin Warren, presents ideas about Marxist aesthetics in mixed modes—lyric, polemic, colloquial. In the first sections, he defends the thesis of Trotsky's *Literature and Revolution*, that the aim of the socialist revolution is to produce a higher form of culture based on a classless society, not a "proletarian culture":

> What do you want, you who form our Army?
> More bottled mayonnaise? D'y' want hamburger?
> More beefsteak (like your boss)? More baseball bleachers?
> Shorter (but duller) jobs; longer (but duller) loafing?[36]

Although Wheelwright does not feel that revolutionary poets can force their concern with culture onto the proletariat, he warns about what might happen to the course of the proletarian revolution if the poets are not heard:

> and make sure not to board the wrong train for
>   Beulah [the future paradise];—
> (it may land you up in Englehood, New Jersey).[37]

After satirizing various schools of literary criticism, Wheelwright explains the Marxist view of the evolution of art from its origins in labor, and he looks forward to the day when class society's bifurcation of a high culture for the rich and a so-called lowbrow culture for the masses will be as obsolete as war and dinosaurs:

> (soon soon) work and play be recreate
> and (shadow souls in worlds of shadow fires)
> intellectual highbrow, lowbrow proletariat
> forgot with battleship and mastodon.[38]

Political Self-Portrait is clearly related to earlier writings in its application of Wheelwright's revolutionary imagination to New England history. By choosing his own ancestors and reconstructing select political events, Wheelwright's poems offer a concrete past as a means of uniting his readers through revolutionary myth. The pivotal figure in this historical endeavor was his own ancestor, the Reverend John Wheelwright (1592–1679), leader of the Antinomian rebellion. In 1933 he studied the surviving papers of the Reverend Mr. Wheelwright and at the outset of his Socialist activities he increasingly began to sign his published writings "John Wheelwright" instead of "John Brooks Wheelwright." Matthew Josephson recalled that "Jack liked to think of himself as a later reincarnation" of the "famous nonconformist divine."[39] Certainly Jack must have been aware that his left opposition to the Socialist move-

ment that resulted in his expulsion in 1937 paralleled the earlier Wheel-
wright's "left opposition" to the Puritan establishment that resulted in
his expulsion exactly three hundred years earlier. However, Jack's intense
identification with this first rebel leader in the colonies also bonded him
to figures who led subsequent intellectual and political revolts in the
1830s and after. This is logical because certain common characteristics
link the Antinomian revolt (1636–38), led by Anne Hutchinson and the
Reverend John Wheelwright, with the mid-nineteenth century heresies
in New England that were sparked by the transcendentalists and aboli-
tionists. They seem to constitute separate stages of a single tradition.
The historian Charles Francis Adams, who was related to the Wheel-
wrights by marriage, expressed an enduring insight when he surmised
that "the seed sown by [Reverend John] Wheelwright, in 1637, bore ac-
tive fruit in the Great New England protest, under the lead of Channing,
two centuries later."[40]

A remarkable number of similarities existed among leaders of these
waves of rebellion: the link extended from Hutchinson, Wheelwright,
and Roger Williams, to Ralph Waldo Emerson, Henry David Thoreau,
and Margaret Fuller, to Wendell Phillips and William Lloyd Garrison.
Most came from the upper strata of society, but even though they broke
with those strata on specific political issues, they often retained ties of
occupation and cultural interest. Whether through theological convic-
tion or personal temperament, they thought of themselves as members
of an "elect" who were more directly in communication with God than
those conforming to the rules of the dominant church and state.

Members of both groups aimed at conversions, preaching their doc-
trines in the militant language of religious warfare. Like the Antino-
mians, transcendentalists such as Emerson and Thoreau evolved what
were seen as religiophilosophical heresies in their desire to separate from
all organizations. As Stanley Elkins argues, "The anti-institutionalism
so characteristic of the Transcendentalists reached heights of extrava-
gance in the speeches and writings of the radical abolitionists."[41] Gar-
rison and Phillips regarded existing political parties and the United
States Constitution as tainted by sin and as institutions from which one
should withdraw.

The career of the Reverend John Wheelwright might be taken as a
prototype for such a heretical evolution. Jack Wheelwright, tenth in
direct descent, suggested as much when he referred to his "immigrant
ancestor in blood" as the "brain ancestor of all immigrants I like" in the
poem "Bread-Word Giver." The poem depicts the events of 19 January
1637, a fast day called to cool down the controversy in Boston and to
express the establishment's dismay over the political and religious up-
heavals in Germany and in England. Wheelwright appeared at the fast-
day services in Boston, and, at the invitation of John Cotton, walked to
the pulpit and delivered his extraordinary "Fast-Day Sermon."

Jack Wheelwright called his poetic tribute to his ancestor "Bread-Word Giver" because the sermon argued that the calling of a fast signified a community distanced from God by enemies who were obscuring the true relations between humanity and the Lord. When he urged the community to take up "the word of God" as a weapon to "kill" the "enemies of truth," the minister was providing "bread" to break the fast.[42] Wheelwright's poem paraphrases three paragraphs from the sermon, the very ones cited by Charles Francis Adams as the most important and the ones in which the metaphor of armed warfare was used for the intense spiritual combat the Reverend John Wheelwright had urged upon his audience. In the poet's paraphrase, "If we / fight not for fear in the night, we shall be surprised."

But this paraphrase elevates the sermon to a call for eternal struggle and vigilance—to "make our renunciation of dominion / mark not the escape but the permanent of rebellion"—by divesting it of the Christian frame of reference and the Calvinist content. While the Reverend Mr. Wheelwright speaks of the "well" (the source of communication with God) being clogged by Philistines and the "rod of iron" (which can "break" nations in "pieces") as a symbol of the "word of God," the poet simply affirms in secular terms that "the springs that we dug must be kept flowing" and redefines the iron rods as "working wills." The Reverend Mr. Wheelwright closes this passage by saying: "Therefore, in the fear of God handle the sword of the spirit, the word of God;—for it is a two-edged sword, and this sword of God cutteth men to the heart." Jack Wheelwright's poem ends: "Wherefore, handle our second / swords with awe. They are two-edged. They cut their wielders' hearts." By changing "fear" to "awe," eliminating the reference to God, and stating that the dangerous two-edged swords are meant to cut their bearers' hearts, Jack merged his own Marxist political perspective with that of his ancestral "saint, whose name and business I bear with me." Jack Wheelwright might have imagined the sword cutting through the wielders' hearts as analogous to the proletariat dissolving itself in the process of abolishing class society, a theme upon which he often dwelled in letters and documents.

The events that befell the Reverend Mr. Wheelwright after delivering the sermon are tersely presented in the opening lines of "Bread-Word Giver":

> John, founder of towns,—dweller in none;
> Wheelwright, schismatic,—schismatic from schismatics;
> friend of great men whom these great feared greatly.[43]

He was tried for his sermon, found guilty of "sedition and contempt," and sentenced to banishment. Doctrinal disagreements kept him from accepting Roger Williams's invitation to join the dissident community in Rhode Island, and his later writings reveal that he had differences with

Anne Hutchinson as well. He moved relentlessly from settlement to settlement, pioneering new towns and establishing new churches, only to encounter inevitable conflicts that drove him onward. In 1642 he humbly requested a pardon from the Boston authorities, which was granted, although he followed this apology by publishing *Mercurius Americanus* (1645), a vindication of his teachings and doctrines.

From the Antinomians to the intellectual rebels who came almost 250 years later, a tradition of radical protest against injustice and ruling class hypocrisy was forged and maintained. In his poem "In Poet's Defence," Jack Wheelwright takes note that the Civil War marked the triumph of capitalism on the continent; he then urges that revolutionary writers prevent another triumph of the "golden chain" of capitalism in the coming "second Civil War" of class strife. The "golden chain," an expression similar to one used by Orestes Brownson, refers to the servitude of the wage system that had replaced chattel slavery.[44]

Wheelwright, like many Marxists of his generation, took as his starting point the thesis presented by Charles and Mary Beard in *The Rise of American Civilization*: "The so-called Civil War was in reality the Second American Revolution and in a strict sense, the First."[45] In this perspective, the Antinomian controversy of the 1630s, the abolitionist movement led by Garrison and Phillips, and the transcendentalism of Emerson and Thoreau have to be assessed as expressions of leftward moving and more militantly democratic forces within the bourgeois revolutionary movements. But the pre–Civil War New England rebels did not question the private ownership of the means of production, although Thoreau's "Life Without Principle" and Brownson's "Laboring Classes" show an awareness of its incompatibility with thoroughgoing democracy and social equality.

In "In Poet's Defence," Jack Wheelwright juxtaposes two intricate thirteen-line stanzas:

> Rebel poets, who've given vicar aid
> to murdered agitator and starved minor,
> starve in your mind and murder in your thought
> indignant will-to-help unfused with Revolution.
> Nurture the calm of wrath. Though Labor fumble
> a second Civil War, prevent a memory
> like its first forged golden chain
> to bind white peon and black serf apart.
>   While labor power'd come too nearly free
> in the open market of free trade for jobs,
> choose from Concord conspirators their thoughts
> which still remain Sedition; forget braggarts
> after victory whose rage contrived defeat.

Not by old images of grief and joy,
nor mummied memory of the Civil War,
nor Mayflower Compact, nor by rebel oaths
which made the Thirteen States palladium
and shield and shibboleth, adjure ourselves.
   Now boom the double guns of Word and Deed
while liberal persons fall in love with ice men
and Wilson's ghost'll vampire Lenin's mummy.
Every memory of hope, every thought,
passions and nerves our stern philanthropy
with cheer, with eager patience for laborers' slow
smoldering of hate to crack down pedestals,
compact from bones and gold, of Quirinus and Mars.[46]

The first stanza focuses on the past and the second on the future, al-
though a symbolical overlapping is achieved through a complicated
pattern of repetition of the key words: "rebel," "murder," "thought,"
"labor," "gold," "mummy," "civil war," and "memory." The core of the
poem is a call for critical assimilation of the viable and authentically
revolutionary elements in the American radical tradition in order to
unite effectively word and deed. (It is significant that he dedicated the
poem "For Van Wyck Brooks," a distant cousin who was a critic and
historian of New England culture.) Wheelwright warns against a senti-
mental eulogizing that blurs the political essence in the lines "choose
from Concord conspirators their thoughts / which still remain sedition,"
and in the five lines beginning "Not by old images of grief and joy. . . ."
Wheelwright understood that, even though the New England rebels'
ardor must be emulated, their dominant figures had not been interested
in constructing an alternative social system. Rather, they attacked the
existing institutions for having betrayed them, for not living up to the
promises of the Protestant Reformation and the Revolution of 1776. At
first they urged those controlling the institutions to realize those prom-
ises; when rebuffed, they withdrew from churches and political parties
and put their trust in the "inner light," in the morally superior indi-
vidual, in various notions of an "elect."
   Throughout his life, Jack Wheelwright remained "Antinomian" in the
concept of himself as the autonomous agent of a moral vision that he
communicated through his poetry, and also in his unconventional be-
havior, which he believed helped to "purify" society of pretense and
hypocrisy, thus facilitating the advance of more enlightened political
forces. But his study of New England history and his observations of the
events of the 1930s led him to see the obsolescence of an "Antinomi-
anism" penned within the confines of the now-exhausted bourgeois-
democratic tradition; there was no point in purifying a system that had
been on a moribund course since the latter part of the previous century.

This may explain why his " Antinomian" disposition—his distrust of institutions and violation of conventional religious and social rules in the name of higher duty—did not lead him to anarchism. From Wheelwright's point of view, the political terms of the bourgeois revolution had been transcended by the Russian Revolution, which forthrightly spoke to the issue of collective economic control. Some of his remarks indicate that he thought Stalinist communism parallel to the Puritan movement in the colonies, both being wings of the revolutionary movement of the era that had lost sight of their original goals; from this perspective, Trotskyism might be said to parallel the Antinomian rebellion in the sense that it sought to revive the original objectives of the revolutionary movement.

In 1932 the alternative of Trotskyism was not clear to Wheelwright; he joined the Socialist party because he thought that it was the most fertile ground for the development of some purer form of Marxism than existed at that time in the Communist or Socialist parties. However, by the time he allied himself with the Trotskyists, his political acuity had heightened considerably; he was able to join the Trotskyists on the basis of programmatic agreement, despite his considerable dislike of some members and his opposition to certain secondary policies. A consistent element throughout this trajectory is that Wheelwright's "Antinomianism" never involved an antipathy to political organizations after 1932; to the contrary, he polemicized vigorously against anarchists as well as Council Communists like Paul Mattick. He obviously believed that intellectual and imaginative freedom need not be incompatible with self-imposed political discipline and party commitment.

All indications show that his fascination with the imaginative possibilities of New England history intensified as the decade proceeded, while his religious faith waned and his revolutionary outlook crystallized. Six months after the Hitler-Stalin pact, at a time when many radical intellectuals (Communists, Trotskyists, and others) were abandoning their former convictions, Wheelwright told Marya Zaturenska: "More and more clearly the only answer appears to be world revolution."[47] At the same moment, "Blackstone and Appleseed," a book-length epic poem that critically examined New England history, was in the formative stages.

Then in his early forties, Jack continued to live a thoroughly unconventional life. Howard Nemerov, at that time a Harvard undergraduate, recalls that late one night Jack and Kenneth Patchen suddenly burst into his room in Adams House. They had just read "Inventory and Statement," published in the *Advocate*, and decided that it had made Nemerov into a genuine poet—a fact that had to be celebrated at once with a drink.[48] Jack was also an indefatigable host. After a visit to Boston, Ruben Gotesky sent Jack a note of thanks for "the long discussion of Proust and dialectical materialism." V. F. Calverton came for several social gatherings and wrote: "I had such a goddam good time with you, John, that I just have to tell you so. I met you in New York as you remember, but seeing you this way, so much more intimately and so much more often, meant a great deal more to me. It was all very fine and I shall remember it."[49]

His final months may have been among the happiest of his life. The publication of *Political Self-Portrait* was well received, and a fourth collection called *Dusk to Dusk* was almost completed. The New Directions publishing company had made plans to issue a selection of his works, chosen and introduced by R. P. Blackmur, which promised to enhance his reputation. He prepared an application for a Guggenheim Fellowship to write a book on romantic architecture. He issued a self-advertisement brochure and received invitations to lecture and read poetry. He befriended many younger writers who came to Cambridge, such as Delmore Schwartz and Robert Lowell. On 26 February 1940, he wrote to Kenneth Porter of his pleasure at the large turnout for a reading he gave in the Harvard Poetry Room, and concluded: "I have been in the best health I have enjoyed of any winter of my life."[50]

On Sunday evening, 14 September, Jack dressed himself in a dark grey suit with a white shirt and brown shoes and socks. With his friend John Ames, a Beaux Arts architect, he went to a Massachusetts Avenue saloon for a few drinks. Toward midnight Ames said he had to leave. Jack, who could always sit up longer than anyone else and who hated to go to bed, protested, but Ames left anyway. Shortly after twelve, Jack also left the bar. About 12:20 A.M. he started to cross Massachusetts Avenue from west to east in front of number twenty-three. A Chevrolet coach driven by a man named John A. Lewis struck Jack and knocked him down. When the police arrived, they arrested Lewis for drunkenness and put Jack into an ambulance. However, he was pronounced dead on arrival at the hospital and the same ambulance drove his body directly to the morgue. No one answered at the Wheelwright's Beacon Street home —Bessie was out of town—so March Wheelwright was contacted at Medfield.[51]

The Wheelwright family arranged for a large impressive funeral to be held at St. John's Episcopal Church in Roxbury. The services were elaborate and the crowds substantial. A bouquet of red roses sent by the Boston branch of the Socialist Workers party was placed among the other flowers.

After Wheelwright's death, almost a dozen poems appeared expressing the response of other writers to his life and literary achievement. One by Frank Merchant appeared in the *Providence Journal*. It described Wheelwright's body as it was prepared for funeral services in a church with which he had refused to conform, as it was viewed by crowds of Boston Brahmins against whose privileges he had aspired to lead a revolution.

Merchant concluded his elegy with lines that anticipate the obscurity into which Wheelwright's work would fall for the next three decades:

> In the crowding street
> disagree over his death,
> over its right and wrong.
> He said unheard truths upon the Common,
> he would have had you think, and test his books;
> he has brought you out for the last time
> and you do not know him.[52]

PART III

MANGAN IN EXILE, 1938–1961

> If you tie a red ribbon to the
> leg of a seagull the other gulls
> will pick it to death. To the
> soul of Clarence Mangan was tied
> the burning ribbon of genius.
>
> W. B. Yeats, 1891

When Sherry Mangan moved to Paris in the late 1930s, he had already assumed the double identity that he would retain for the rest of his life. Prior to his departure, he wrote for the *Socialist Appeal* and delivered a Marxist lecture in Boston under the name Terence Phelan. Pseudonyms were common in the Marxist movement of his day to disguise identities from employers and the police; but to Sherry, thirsting for adventure and poised to assert his deflected artistic energies where he might, deeper psychological functions were probably served by the fashioning of a second identity.

The creation of two people—one for bourgeois society, another for the revolutionary movement—provided a strategy for survival in the repressive economic institutions of capitalist society. A pseudonym meant a secret self. It meant that his bourgeois employers would never possess him completely because ultimately his relationship with them would be insincere; the "secret" Sherry would be using them and not vice versa. At the same time, letters and autobiographical fiction provide evidence that a pseudonym afforded the opportunity to satisfy certain emotional and imaginative needs. For Sherry, the simple act of choosing a pseudonym became deliberate and ritualized. The names he selected at that time, and others chosen over the next twenty years, were carefully assembled from a gallery of Irish ancestors. In the Trotskyist movement abroad, under one of these names, the exiled Sherry strived to personify revolutionary internationalism—an ideal in the 1930s popularized by legends about the Comintern agent Mikhail Borodin and reflected in fiction by Malraux's Katov in *Man's Fate* and Hemingway's Robert Jordan in *For Whom the Bell Tolls*.

The psychology of a blocked writer who sublimates artistic energy by creating a romantic character to substitute for his frustrated self is understandable. Most people live according to fantasies of one sort or another, and Sherry's creation of a secret self, an aestheticized political identity, was objectively justified by the dangers he faced if exposed as a "subversive" in a foreign country. Still, a highly dramatized life can be unstable and the inadequacies of this one were revealed over the next few years.

When he actually became a prominent political journalist, his occupational identity was nothing less than an open secret among leaders of the Trotskyist movement. Word of his political identity eventually traveled back to his bosses, causing him to be treated with suspicion and ultimately fired. Furthermore, the bifurcation of his life into revolutionary and journalistic work may have satisfied a certain category of imaginative needs, but it left little room for the actual writing of poetry. With creative work progressively squeezed out of his life, his youthful dream of becoming a poet increasingly haunted his psyche. For a man whose demands on life are absolute, a prolonged conflict between daily existence and fundamental values can lead to demoralization and crisis. At the age of forty-four, Mangan suffered a mental breakdown. Although his desire to write returned as an instrument by which he sought to heal his divided self, the form and content of his literary work was riven by a split sensibility that alternated wildly between incomprehensible modernist experiments and a simple but elegant realism.

He attempted a literary comeback in the 1950s that was an agonizing failure, but he periodically textualized the contradictions he faced as a Marxist writer in poems and stories, several of which are highly emotive, linguistically brilliant, and of rare beauty. These writings offer unusual testimony to the resources and operations of the revolutionary imagination when it struggles under unpropitious conditions. The following chapters also use Mangan's everyday life to examine one variant of the problem of fighting for the future while surviving in the present. Radical intellectuals have many times noted the tripartite dilemma of trying to write creatively while working for a living and being politically active; C. Day-Lewis refers to this in his 1935 pamphlet *Revolution in Writing*. The following review of Mangan's activities from the late 1930s to his death in 1961 provides the first dramatization, biographical or fictional, of an acute form of this experience. It is a story supremely tragic in the young Lukács's sense of the term—the hero is driven by an ultimate passion for meaning to the extent that he is brought to the point of destruction by the apparently meaningless world that denies him.

Sherry's need to keep his two identities distinct caused complications from the day he left the United States for France in June 1938 aboard the *President Roosevelt*. He wrote to Jack Wheelwright of his difficulty in masking his true political feelings when in public: "I have laid low, per instructions, lest my utility in Paris be lessened; but M [Marguerite] has been comically worried lest I bust loose." One night at the ship's concert, a group of Abraham Lincoln Brigade members led in the singing of the *Star Spangled Banner* and Sherry refused to stand up for the anthem. "One, seeing me seated, made the wonderful remark: 'Even if you are a Marxist, get up and sing for democracy.' My blood pressure went up twenty-five points, but M's kicking of my shins was unnecessary."[1]

With the help of his friend Robert Fitzgerald, then acting head of *Time*'s art department in New York City, Sherry received his first journalistic assignment in Paris—gathering material for a *Time* cover story on Pablo Picasso. Richard de Rochemont, assigned by *Time* to supervise the reporters, correspondents, and stringers based in Paris, quickly assessed Sherry as the most intelligent person on his staff and increased his responsibilities. When Sherry wrote to Wheelwright again in the fall of 1938—to explain that he had arranged for his painter friend, John Ferren, to have the use of his car in Lynn during a visit to the United States—he mentioned that his own activities included, in addition to journalism for *Time*, "translating the entire issue of a new art magazine called *XXeme Siècle*, giving English lessons, and most of all working for the party."[2]

Political work had commenced dramatically in June 1938, when the exiled German Trotskyist Rudolph Klement, administrative secretary of the Fourth International, disappeared in what was clearly a political kidnapping. The First World Congress of the Fourth International was to be held in just a few months and Sherry was called upon to assist in overcoming the crisis. His first communications to the Socialist Workers party in the United States reported on desperate attempts to locate Klement throughout the summer; Klement's cut-up body was later found in the Seine. When Socialist Workers party leader James P. Cannon attended the founding conference of the International in September, he requested that Sherry translate world congress materials into English and prepare fortnightly dispatches on the political situation in France for the *Socialist Appeal*.[3]

But the weight of Sherry's political responsibilities intensified personal conflicts between himself and Marguerite. In late November Sherry wrote Wheelwright that Marguerite's growing insistence on the need to have a formal marriage had precipitated a near break. "It was a very shocking business, and has completely put me off, since, if she behaves so now re matrimony, it would not be long before she would be putting on a similar act re a child." Sherry felt that Marguerite was eventually "entitled to both marriage and a child, but it should be obvious to her that, under my special circumstances, what with poetic and revolutionary activity and financial limitations, all such things have to be arranged with care and advance notice, and at the convenience of my career." Furthermore, Sherry had now been named a full news correspondent for *Time*, and this brought him face to face with a new problem that would plague him for the next ten years: "Earning my living occupies all my time and energy." Sherry closed his letter with a warning about the importance of keeping his true identity a secret, a precaution doubly warranted since the assassination of Klement: "In the year ahead it is not out of the question that I may be of great service to the movement provided my anonymity is kept. Can't explain in greater detail; but request your discretion."[4]

In late January 1939, Cannon returned to Paris to help resolve conflicts among the French Trotskyists. He collaborated closely with Sherry, and by May Sherry was incorporated in a secretarial capacity into the International Secretariat, the leading body of the Fourth International.[5] When the Trotskyist attorney Albert Goldman and youth leader Nathan Gould came to Paris in mid-May, they also collaborated with Sherry. In June he moved to England for five weeks on assignment for *Time*, using the opportunity to hold meetings with leaders of the British Trotskyist movement. Then, at the 9 July 1939 meeting of the International Secretariat, he was formally designated as technical secretary of that body.[6] Stefan Lamed, a Polish exile on the International Secretariat at that time, recalls him as a quiet, courteous man, "quite different from the passionate, excitable political refugees who formed our circle in Paris at that time. We did not consider him politically well-educated (in our partisan sense) or experienced, but he was an ideal chairman."[7] In letters to the Socialist Workers party, Sherry expressed his desire to work full time for the international movement; but he reported that Albert Goldman had urged that he not relinquish his journalistic position because of the valuable resources it afforded. With his time and energy spread thin between *Time* and the Fourth International, hope that his poetry might be resuscitated in the Paris environment began to disappear.[8]

In the meantime, in lieu of his own creative work, Sherry contributed a column to *Partisan Review* under the pseudonym Sean Niall. The column was entitled "Paris Letter"; it started in the fall of 1938 and lasted until the spring of 1939. It chiefly focused on the progress of the International Federation of Independent Revolutionary Art and on the activities of left-wing writers in France. In the first installment, Sherry reported that the organization aspired to become a rallying point "for those artists who have grown more and more uncomfortable in the increasingly smelly Stalinist ambience"; he also noted that more than fifty signatures of leading artists had been obtained for the group's manifesto. Sherry criticized some of the surrealist members for trying to dominate the organization and also for refusing to hail André Gide's break with Stalinism because they objected to his literary style. Nevertheless, he quoted with enthusiasm Benjamin Péret's poem on the subject ("La conversion de Gide") and remarked that Péret's *Je ne mange pas de ce pain-là* was so extraordinary that "not even Trotsky's irritation with it as 'poésie ouvriériste' can diminish the general admiration for this volume, where sheer violence of invective reaches amazing heights." He concluded by acknowledging that most of the first-rate literary talents in France had been linked to surrealism, but now he judged the movement to have "outlived its superlatively admirable utility." Although surrealism had been anti-academy in its inception, Breton's dictatorial activities had transformed surrealism into "a massive anti-Academy Academy— an opposite pole, but a structural parallel," subverting its claim to be the definitive school for avant-garde literature.[9]

Sherry's second "Paris Letter" described the launching of *Clé*, the monthly bulletin of the International Federation of Independent Revolutionary Art. *Clé*'s first issue featured a manifesto in defense of the right to political asylum in France, as well as articles on "politico-artistic" subjects by Jean Giono, Georges Heinen, Maurice Heine, André Breton, Albert Paraz, Henri Pastoureau, and Benjamin Péret. He thought that the magazine's purely political-minded readers might "cavil somewhat at a violence of language, a personality of invective, that smack a trifle of literary ultraleftism"; but he believed those writers who had been "nauseated by the dead-level Stalinization of French liberals, the careerist degeneration of such once-brilliant writers as Aragon, and the general sickliness of the whole politico-artistic situation in France, will perhaps understand and sympathize with the desire of *Clé*'s director to have its opening blast utterly unequivocal and violently purificative."[10]

His third "Paris Letter" was largely devoted to the assessment of recent books that had appeared in Paris, but many of his comments concerned Nicholas Calas's *Foyers d'Incendie*. Calas was a Greek sympathizer of Trotskyism living in exile in Paris. Sherry had met him when he was helping Maurice Nadeau edit the first issue of *Clé*. Later, after the German occupation, Calas was one of several people for whom Sherry obtained a visa to the United States by use of his *Time* position. In *Partisan Review* Sherry described Calas as a sort of "Wyndham Lewis of the Left," who alternately rapped "the knuckles of both Marxism and psychoanalysis when the more religious of their practitioners try to extend them beyond the limits of their own fields."[11]

Sherry's "Paris Letter" columns were praised by Breton and Péret in Paris, and the *Partisan Review* editors urged him to continue his contributions. In July 1939 editor Dwight Macdonald wrote that "your revised Paris letter . . . [is] one of the best pieces of prose we've printed." A few months later he added that "you have quite a following among our readers, in case you don't know it." But Sherry abandoned the letter for lack of time, recommending that Calas take his place.[12]

Meanwhile, Sherry's stature in the Luce publishing corporation steadily improved. From articles exclusively in the art section, which sometimes contained information about personal friends such as Maurice Grosser, Gertrude Stein, and John Ferren, his range expanded to cover cinema and broader cultural issues. His cover story on Picasso appeared on 13 February 1939, and he contributed several pieces on Jean Cocteau. For the issue of 5 May 1939, he prepared a cover story on James Joyce's *Finnegan's Wake* that elicited letters of praise from Joyce himself. Characterizing the book as "a gigantic laboratory experiment with languages," Sherry concluded: "Whether Joyce is eventually convicted of assaulting the King's English with intent to kill or whether he has really added a cubit to her stature, she will never be quite the same again."[13]

After this, he was frequently assigned by *Time* to cover political news, and on 5 June 1939 he wrote the cover story on Edouard Daladier.

Under the name Terence Phelan, Sherry was simultaneously covering political events in Europe for the *Socialist Appeal*. Max Shachtman, editor of the paper, read parts of Sherry's articles aloud to editorial board meetings as exemplary Marxist journalism. The 3 March 1939 edition featured an interview Sherry had conducted with Julian Gorkin, an ex-Trotskyist who had become a leader of the Spanish Workers Party of Marxist Unification (POUM), and M. Casanova, a pseudonym for a Polish Trotskyist who participated in the Spanish civil war. Writing from Perpignan, near the Spanish frontier, Sherry prefaced the interview with a description of how the two men and other members of their organizations had been left in Barcelona by the Stalinists, deliberately "locked up in prison, at the mercy of Franco's bombers and executioners, and saved only by a daring escape that reads like the wildest adventure story."[14]

At first Sherry and Marguerite lived in the rural suburb of Dampierre, in the valley of Chevreuse. Sherry commuted each day, bicycling majestically to and from his trains. Then he moved into 17 Quai Voltaire, the same building in which Virgil Thomson lived, directly across from the Louvre. He obtained a luxurious studio flat with three high balconies from which he liked to watch the German bombings of the city. Also in the building was Theodate Johnson, a singer who was the sister of Philip Johnson, an architect known to Sherry and Jack Wheelwright. All three of them—Sherry, Thomson, and Johnson—worked for the French radio, translating texts for broadcasting into English. After a while, Thomson recalled, "Sherry . . . became something of a star, it having been discovered that his warm bass voice and perfect enunciation made him an incomparable radio speaker."[15] At times his journalistic and political work were so overwhelming that he shut himself up in isolation for as long as three days. Marguerite delivered his meals to him on trays, and his private secretary, Annette Kraeutler, picked up little notes he tossed over his balcony containing requests for information.[16]

Sherry's *Time* dispatches from Paris continued up until the Nazis marched into the city on 14 June 1940. Virtually every other American journalist had fled by then, in expectation that there would be armed resistance to the Nazis. But Sherry remained behind, ostensibly to cover the events for *Time*, but also to assist in preparing the French Trotskyists for their switch to an underground organization. In the last months before the Germans finally expelled him from the country, he arranged for a number of Trotskyists and Trotskyist sympathizers to receive credentials as *Time* researchers: the youth leader Marcel Hic, who died at Buchenwald; the actor George Vitsoris; and the novelists Victor Serge and David Rousset.[17]

On 1 July he wrote to his *Time* boss David Hulburd in New York that the entire staff had been evacuated on Sunday night, 9 June, except Del Paine and his wife, who left in Richard de Rochemont's car at dawn on the following Tuesday. He declared his amazement at the paradoxical turn things had taken since then. When he stayed in order to report the bombardment and capture of Paris, it seemed to be a very foolhardy venture; evacuation to the south seemed the part of common sense and prudence. Yet, by a strange reversal, he found that he had "run no danger, whereas I am terribly worried about what may have happened to the main staff in the terribly bombarded towns and choked roads to the south."

Although his activities in Paris became increasingly restricted by the Germans, he acted as if his status as a journalist from a noncombatant nation afforded him a great deal of latitude. One newspaper in the United States reported that "the ex-Bostonian Sherry Mangan, serving as *Time* magazine correspondent when the Nazis moved in, was constantly irritated with the crisp manner in which the German officers always answered the phone—thus: 'Capt. Schultz speaking. Heil Hitler!' Sherry finally got around that by always replying, 'Sherry Mangan speaking. Wintergreen for President!' "[18] Sherry also made a proposal—apparently rejected—to the German military command that he be permitted to fly with them on their bombing raids to England, at the same time requesting that *Time* extend his insurance coverage so that his family could receive benefits if he were shot down.

On 4 August he felt that the situation in Paris was sufficiently safe to send a communication to David Rousset, summoning him to return clandestinely to the city for party work. However, on 8 August the German police officials ordered Sherry to their offices and demanded that he leave the country within four days. The story was reported in the *New York Times* under the headline, "U.S. Writer Ordered from Paris."[19] On 12 August he and Marguerite began to make their way to Portugal. Upon arrival, he discovered that all the news reports he had filed through Berlin had never been released to *Time*. Excerpts from these were published in *Life* on 16 September with the title "Paris Under the Swastika."

Upon his return to New York City, he learned that Jack Wheelwright had just been killed in a car accident and immediately traveled to Boston to see Tony Palmer and other old friends. To Kate he wrote that Wheelwright's death "hit me so hard that I've had to freeze all thought about it. Some day soon I'll let the feeling out, and try to get it into poetry." In the weeks just after his return to the United States, Sherry also began to express, for the first time, some misgivings about the political and organizational character of the American Trotskyist movement.[20]

In his absence a split had occurred between the followers of Cannon (with whom Sherry was in political agreement) and the Shachtman-Burnham faction, which now constituted the Workers party. (See Chapter 8 for a fuller discussion of this important political dispute.) To Albert Goldman, one of the few intellectuals who stayed in the Socialist Workers party, Sherry wrote a long letter expressing his view that, although members of the Shachtman-Burnham group were behaving like irresponsible splitters, some of the tactics used by Cannon may have assisted the split dynamic. Sherry declared himself to be in favor of the party unloading itself of dilettantes and cranks, but he insisted that that was not what the 1940 split involved. "No use kidding ourselves: it was split right down the middle. The unpleasant fact is, that there are too many damn good elements in the Workers Party; and when I hear everyone around New York congratulating us on being rid of them. . . ." Still, Sherry by now was convinced of the necessity for constructing a Leninist party and vented his scorn against those whom he believed to have, in effect, walked out of the revolutionary movement: "Any party member who thinks the way to eradicate what he believes to be an evil is to run away from it instead of staying in the party and fighting it, is to my mind no Bolshevik at all but a petit-bourgeois pantywaist."[21]

On 3 December 1940, Sherry and Marguerite arrived by boat in Buenos Aires, Argentina. Time, Inc. had assigned Sherry to serve as head of the *Time-Life* bureau in Argentina and also to work as a roving correspondent for Chile, Peru, and Ecuador. But there was another reason for this move to Latin America. The American Trotskyist leader Felix Morrow wrote to an Argentine Marxist: "The fact is that Comrade Phelan [Mangan] accepted his actual employment at our request. We wanted him to take this work so that he could get to South America. I repeat, his present employment is a designation of the party."[22] Thus was initiated a period of seven years in which politics and journalism dominated his life to the extent that all literary activity and associations receded into the background.

His revolutionary political activity in Latin America during 1941 and the first part of 1942 centered on the difficult task of trying to coalesce organizations that had split apart or had developed autonomously. In the main, and for a brief period of time, he was successful. Under the name Terence Phelan, he met with leaders of the different parties and helped prepare congresses that ultimately succeeded in unifying most of the Argentine and Chilean Trotskyist movements. Mangan, in fact, can be credited as the real organizer of the leading Argentine Trotskyist party of that time, the Workers Party of the Socialist Revolution (PORS).[23]

In the course of this activity, Sherry collaborated closely with a number of young Argentine socialists who later became well-known figures in Latin American leftist circles: Jorge Abelardos Ramos, Hugo Sylvester, A. Perelman, Nahuel Moreno, and Juan Posadas. However, a negative outcome of this unification work was that Sherry became a bitter enemy of Liborio Justo, son of the former president of Argentina (General Agustín P. Justo, who held office from 1932 to 1938). Under the names Quebracho and Bernal, Justo had been running his own semi-Trotskyist organization. By the fall of 1942, all ties between Justo and the Fourth International were broken and in 1959 Justo published a book called *Leon Trotsky y Wall Street*, in which he charged that Trotsky had allied himself with U.S. imperialism during his Mexican exile. In later years Justo even spread the slander that Mangan had worked for the CIA.[24]

Sherry devoted part of his time to studying the history of Argentina; then he attempted to apply Marxist theory in order to understand the unique features of Argentina's social development and the prospects for change. According to Nahuel Moreno, a leading Argentine Trotskyist who knew Sherry in those years, Sherry wrote two documents that have some importance in the history of Argentine Trotskyism. One was a political thesis and the other was an organizational pamphlet. Moreno recollects that the political thesis overcame the dilemma in which Argentine Trotskyism had been caught, in which one side held that the principal task was national liberation, while another held that it was socialist revolution. Sherry's organizational document posited that the unification of all Trotskyist forces, combined with the publication of a common periodical, would supplant the movement's crisis and atomization.[25]

In the spring of 1941, an incident occurred that underscored the difficulties Sherry faced in trying to maintain two public identities simultaneously—Sherry Mangan, *Time-Life-Fortune* journalist, and Terence Phelan, official representative of the Fourth International. The April 1941 issue of *Fortune* magazine featured an article under Sherry's own name called "Report on Argentina." The Communist party of Argentina soon discovered that Sherry Mangan was the same person as their archenemy, Terence Phelan. Within a short time, the Communist newspaper *La Hora* produced its own translation of Sherry's article in Spanish, introducing certain changes to make it seem as if Sherry were recommending the very imperialist policies against which he was inveighing. Other Argentine newspapers picked up *La Hora*'s story and a great public animosity against Sherry began to accumulate during the several weeks before he was able to arrange for the appearance of an accurate translation of the article.[26]

In Argentina Sherry also became friends with a Jewish Austrian refugee. Because he still lives under the threat of possible political persecution, I shall refer to him by the pseudonym of Karl Goldstein. Goldstein was working in Buenos Aires as a journalist. He had been a revolutionary socialist in his youth and in 1934 had participated in armed struggle against the reactionary Dollfuss regime. In 1937 Goldstein was captured in Switzerland, where he was smuggling arms to the Spanish Republicans. After he was expelled, he eventually made his way to Latin

America. Goldstein was at the founding conference of the PORS and he and Sherry later bought guns on the black market to be used for self-defense purposes by the Trotskyists and militant workers. Goldstein believes that their activities along these lines probably helped to start left-wing guerrilla movements in Argentina, Uruguay, Bolivia, and Brazil.

Mangan and Goldstein had temperamental affinities in their heavy drinking, gambling, and woman-chasing. They also developed a journalistic association. Mangan obtained part-time work for Goldstein with *Time*, but the job was terminated by the Luce corporation almost as soon as Sherry departed for the United States. Goldstein then developed an interest in stock market and business affairs, and he began to publish a circular containing news about stock market activities. During the course of several years, he accrued enough funds from his own investments to initiate an export-import company. After the 1940s, Goldstein's political activity was less regular and he lived in numerous countries on several continents; but a strong memory of the ideals that motivated his youth remained, causing him to make periodic financial contributions to the Trotskyist movement and to carry out certain activities.

In the spring of 1942, Sherry returned to the United States with Marguerite and took a six-month leave of absence from Time, Inc. When he resumed work in New York, his assignment was to direct the Luce corporation's radio program "La Marcha del Tiempo" ("The March of Time"), which was broadcast in Latin America. Subsequently he undertook various journalistic assignments for the Luce magazines, including a feature article for *Fortune* that ran some fifteen pages in the November 1943 issue. Based on a two-month tour of the United States in which he interviewed workers in places such as Buffalo, Los Angeles, Minneapolis, Seattle, and Detroit, it was called "State of the Nation: Minority Report." In an effort to soften the impact of Mangan's Marxist approach, the editors prefaced the essay with a comment that it "derives its chief interest, in the opinion of *Fortune*'s editors, not so much from its thesis as from the corollary of that thesis: the application of European terms of political observation to American facts." The editors acknowledged that this method was "not entirely new, but in Mr. Mangan's able hands it gives American readers a useful—if startling—view of the pattern their country can present to many a man from Europe."

The thesis of Sherry's "Minority Report" was that "national unity" had not been achieved in the United States during the early war years and that an anticapitalist sentiment was growing among the working class that might explode in the near future: "The speciously triumphant and historically short-sighted rightward swing of the legislative and executive powers is more than balanced by the setting in of a massive leftward tide within U.S. labor. It is only at its turn, not its flood; but it runs only one way." Some of the workers interviewed for the article were undoubtedly Trotskyists; and one of the photographs carried a caption that was rather remarkable for *Fortune*: "Slick Walter Reuther who knows how to put himself at the head of rank-and-file revolts in order to slow them up, perfectly exemplifies the type of middle-of-the-road labor leaders who will have their brief and stormy innings in the period between the collapse of the extreme conservative bureaucrats and the rise of a revolutionary leadership in the unions."[27]

Much of Sherry's energies during the last part of 1942 and most of 1943 were devoted to publications of the Socialist Workers party. Living mostly in New York City or nearby in Connecticut, he was often at the party's headquarters. In late July 1942, Virgil Thomson visited him there and wrote a "musical portrait" of James P. Cannon.

Sherry had already made his debut in the party theoretical journal *Fourth International* in the spring of 1941 with two articles on the fall of France. The first was a historical analysis called "The End of French Democracy," explaining from a Marxist view the reason that France had fallen to the Nazis so easily. He regarded the so-called Battle of France as "a mere mopping-up operation" from the viewpoint of history. He believed that French democracy had already lost the war in three decisive battles: "Their dates: 1933, 1936, 1938. Their respective battle-grounds: Germany; Spain and France; France itself. Principal organizer of the defeats: democratic capitalism. Principal tool: Stalinism."[28]

The second installment in the series was a personal account of "How Paris Fell," which the editors quickly recognized as a classic of radical reportage. Sherry's description of the events was animated at times by a lyricism usually not found in most Marxist journalism: "Paris as it fell was tragically beautiful. Late in the afternoon of Wednesday, the 12th of June, the petroleum and gasoline reserves in all the suburban refineries were set on fire by retreating French troops. Paris was ringed with monumental and sinister columns of jet, oily smoke. These, meeting at the zenith, far above the white cumulus clouds, slowly blotted out the sun, and spread a black pall over the doomed and deserted city. The blotting out of 'the city of light' by that cloud was a sort of grim apocalypse." Sherry proceeded to transfer the analysis of his previous article—about the way in which the rulers of France had actually prepared the nation for surrender—to concrete descriptions of how social power had been transferred to the Nazis. His knowledge from books about the breakdown of czarism and the collapse of the Kerensky regime paled beside his observation of the dissolution of the French state, "a sight—and a lesson —never to be forgotten. Literary descriptions can give a theoretical understanding of the process and its significance, but it is quite a different thing to see the state structure crumbling before your very eyes." The event was an occasion to reaffirm his socialist commitment: "In an hour like this one really feels, in his own skin, the absolute rightness of the

Marxist analysis of the state as the executive committee of the ruling class, of government as an instrument of armed repression. One sees how the ruling class maintains itself by bribing a thin segment of the workers to act as mercenary police against its own class struggle; and realizes how thin that segment is."

The personal emotions elicited by the fall of France (which Sherry had to repress in his *Time-Life* journalism on the same subject) burned brilliantly at many points in his Marxist testament. In one paragraph he described a midnight visit, just hours before the arrival of the Nazi troops, to the now-abandoned Tomb of the Unknown Soldier: "The perfect symbol of the completely forgotten man, the plain ordinary guy who gets killed so that one gang of exploiters rather than another can make his widow and children work for less pay and live in more misery. At that moment neither of the gangs had any real interest in him. For a brief hour, the unknown soldier was left alone [because the guards had deserted], with only a stray foreign revolutionary standing by to honor him, with pity and vengeance in his heart."[29]

Sherry's other contributions to *Fourth International* were strictly political in character and sometimes scholarly. In the spring of 1942, while he was still in Latin America, Sherry had published two reports written in Chile and Ecuador. They were called "Washington's Offensive in Latin America" and "The Real Situation in Argentina," both summarizing the situation in Argentina and Chile and simultaneously providing an assessment of the growth and activities of the Trotskyist movement in those countries. In July 1943 from New York City, he published a full-scale analysis of the barracks revolt in Argentina on 4 June ("Behind the Argentine Coup"), which warned against the danger of United States intervention in the country.

At the beginning of 1943, Sherry initiated a series of essays in *Fourth International* on twentieth-century European politics. "A Reminder: How Hitler Came to Power" (February 1943) was one of a number of attempts made by American Trotskyists to convince those sections of the public they could reach that the German working class had been the victim and not the willing beneficiary of fascism. Sherry argued that there had been a "contemptible campaign of misrepresentation and confusion," that it was necessary "to remind the new generation of American workers how courageously their German brothers fought for fifteen years for a workers' world—fought on the barricades in 1918–19, 1921, and 1923—and were ready to fight again to smash Hitler in 1931–33, but were betrayed to the Nazi terror by the folly and treachery of their leaders."[30]

After this, Sherry published the first two parts of a proposed three-part study of the Versailles peace treaty. According to the editors of *Fourth International*, the purpose of the series was to "answer . . . the current claim that American participation in a league of nations would have saved the world." The argument of Sherry's first installment, "Woodrow Wilson and Bolshevism" (April 1943), was that the main preoccupation of the Paris Peace Conference was actually to find a means of rolling back the 1917 revolution in Russia. The second installment, "What the Peacemakers Did to Europe" (May 1943), tried to provide documentation that the Versailles conference had so thoroughly laid the foundations for the rise and triumph of fascism and the outbreak of World War II, that the participation or nonparticipation of the United States in the League of Nations "would have made no significant difference."[31]

During late 1942 and early 1943, Sherry also collaborated with Frank Lovell, a Trotskyist seaman who wrote under the name Frederick Lang, in the preparation of a book called *Maritime: A Historical Sketch and Workers Program*. The book presented documentary material on the role of the United States government in the maritime industry from its earliest days and also analyzed the different groupings in the leadership of the maritime unions. Lovell had undertaken the initial research and gathering of materials, but had to leave New York City when the work was less than half done. Sherry then took on the task of condensing, rewriting, and editing the various sections, adding new facts, and designing the book itself.[32] The finished work was praised within the party as an example of the proper relationship between a skilled intellectual and a working-class organization. Sherry's book design also elevated the standards of the party's publishing work.[33] Consequently, Sherry was assigned to work on a new book about unions in the auto industry. But these plans were interrupted by his decision to take a new journalism assignment in the fall of 1943 in London, as the head of *Life* magazine for all of Europe.

A combination of factors propelled Sherry toward this new job. Most importantly, the International Secretariat of the Fourth International (located in New York City during the war) saw that there were important tasks that Sherry could carry out in such a position. On 15 July 1943 Sherry wrote to Karl Goldstein (still in Argentina) that Jean van Heijenoort, international secretary of the Fourth International and later a philosophy professor at Brandeis University, had "ordered" him to take the position.[34] But Sherry was also having difficulty in finding a satisfactory role for himself in the Socialist Workers party.[35] The doubts Sherry had felt about James P. Cannon's organizational methods at the time of the faction fight with Max Shachtman had not disappeared. Suspicions were nourished by Sherry's association with Felix Morrow, a leading intellectual in the party who was in the process of assembling his own oppositional group with Jean van Heijenoort and Albert Goldman.[36] They believed that Cannon's policies were hardening the Socialist Workers party into a narrow sect. These initial criticisms would later evolve into a repudiation of Marxism altogether; but at this early stage Sherry was drawn to Morrow because he also had a desire to loosen up the atmosphere within the organization.[37]

Sherry arrived in London in mid-November 1943 and at once began the work of unifying Trotskyist groups just as he had done in Argentina in 1941. The British Trotskyists had first organized themselves in 1932, but as early as the following year they had begun a process of splitting that continued into the 1940s. Sherry's efforts were temporarily successful and a fusion of several groups took place in March 1944. A new Trotskyist organization called the Revolutionary Communist party was formed. Shortly afterwards, however, Sherry was absorbed in a new problem when a number of Trotskyists were arrested for strike support activity. In the northeastern part of England, the government had begun a conscription program to overcome the shortage of mine workers. The government demanded that young workers who had begun the engineering apprenticeship program break off their apprenticeships and go into the mines. This was met with great anger by the apprentices, many of whom had made sacrifices in order to get into the apprenticeship program. The Trotskyists supported the resistance activity of the apprentices and several members of the Revolutionary Communist party were arrested in April 1944. The newly formed party was then thrown into a crisis about how to handle the case and a number of members resigned because of demoralization and also because of fear of further political repression. The trial of the British Trotskyists occurred in June. Several members were sentenced to prison, but were eventually released on appeal.

In the midst of these and other activities in London, Sherry met Pierre Frank, a French Trotskyist leader and one of Trotsky's former secretaries. Impressed by Sherry's ability to assimilate his new environment, Frank thought him "the least 'Americanocentric'" of all the Americans he knew. Marguerite also remarked on this trait, once bragging that Sherry "could land in a strange country, penniless, knowing nobody, not even speaking the language, and in three months be established in comfort."[38] In London Sherry did live well—a fact used against him by some of his political enemies. He gained quite a bit of weight and in his war correspondent's outfit looked like Henry VIII in an American uniform.[39] When Sam Gordon, an American Trotskyist who had attempted to unify the British parties at an earlier date, visited him at the Dorchester Hotel, they had drinks and dinner in Sherry's room, where he maintained a wardrobe full of extra food, drink, beef from the Argentine embassy, and Irish whiskey. At the end of the meal, Sherry invited Gordon to come up to the roof to watch the air raids. When Gordon asked if there was any danger, Sherry assured him that the Dorchester could not possibly be a target because "every fifth columnist in London is staying here."[40]

Unfortunately, other aspects of Sherry's life did not go as smoothly as his political work in London, which resulted in the unification of several Trotskyist groups. The first problem was his inability to make arrangements for Marguerite to accompany him. In their weekly correspondence across the Atlantic, Marguerite continually pressed Sherry to make greater efforts to get her a passport, but he insisted that the various bureaucracies refused to make an exception for her to travel under wartime conditions. From all evidence, Sherry was sincere in his desire to be united with Marguerite. Even though their relationship had been stormy, sometimes coming to the point of dissolution during the period in Latin America, he wrote to her that things had improved so much in the last few months spent in New York City that "the old deep love and companionship, and the desire to have you always with me" had been restored.[41] They had even attempted to have a child; although Marguerite had undergone an abortion a few years earlier, it now turned out that Sherry's sperm had become subfertile.

From Sherry's point of view, Marguerite's attitude toward political activity had changed for the better during their first months of separation. Previously she refused to have anything to do with the Socialist Workers party or any other political group. During his stay in England, however, she began to visit the party offices regularly and to assist with the newspaper as well as with the work of the Civil Rights Defense Committee. This committee was formed to defend eighteen Trotskyists and teamster militants who had been sentenced to prison under the Smith Act.

His letters to Marguerite occasionally remarked on his sexual activities. "Still faithful, by the way, in case you're interested, but don't insist on your being if it's too hard," he wrote to her in late January 1944. Several months later, however, he reported that he had stopped going to prostitutes and had found a regular girl friend. When Marguerite objected, Sherry seemed surprised that she was upset over his having a regular girl instead of floating about. "Don't make me sorry I told you. Let me once and for all and very solemnly reassure you about us. I love you very deeply; you are my permanent companion; I want you with me; I am going to get you with me. The present business is very gentle and tender but purely stoppage. It is in no sense a replacement of you; the minute you are en route, it automatically stops."[42]

Sherry's conflicts with the Luce corporation began on the day he arrived and his ultimate expulsion from Time, Inc. had its origins in the bad relations that developed in England because of his political views. Sherry's relations with Henry Luce himself had always been contradictory; the corporation's founder disliked Sherry's Marxist interpretations of history, but at the same time expressed amazement at his ability to predict world events.[43] In London, however, *Time*'s key operative, Walter Graebner, began a campaign to isolate and discredit Sherry. After a proposal to be dropped behind enemy lines to cover incipient revolu-

tionary uprisings was rejected, Sherry gave up his position as director of
the *Life* bureau to become a simple reporter for *Time* again. But despite
strong praise from *Time*'s editor-in-chief T. S. Matthews ("your flying
bomb story is one of the best reporting jobs these editorial eyes ever
beheld"), Graebner began to censor Sherry's articles on the grounds that
they were too pro-socialist.[44] The final outrage occurred after the Nor-
mandy campaign began in June 1944. Sherry was denied permission to
accompany the troops to witness the Liberation.[45] He finally returned to
Paris in late September 1944, but Marguerite was still unable to join him
at their old 17 Quai Voltaire residence until the spring of 1945.[46]

Sherry's anger at Time, Inc. was counterbalanced by near euphoria
upon taking up his political activity once more on the continent. He was
exhilarated by the prospect of seeing old friends and immediately made
contact with the remnants of the Trotskyist organizations. He lent his
services to tracking down various persons and learning of their fates
under the occupation.[47] He was the first to discover that David Rousset,
one of the Trotskyists captured while doing propaganda work among
German troops, had not died at Buchenwald, but was still alive. Sherry
also helped organize and participated in the first reunified congress of the
French section of the Fourth International in early November.[48] He deliv-
ered a report on the activities of non-European Trotskyist groups during
the war, and this was later published in the French Trotskyists' theoreti-
cal magazine, along with a translation of one of his earlier articles criti-
cizing the Versailles treaty. Sherry was also incorporated into the Euro-
pean Secretariat of the Fourth International, a body sustained during the
war period through the efforts of Trotskyists Michel Pablo, Marcel Hic,
and Abram Leon.[49] Of these, Pablo was the only one who survived; he
was much admired for his underground work against the Nazis. Hic died
after imprisonment at Buchenwald and Leon was killed at Auschwitz.

Sherry had first met Pablo through George Vitsoris, a Greek Trotskyist
who was a successful actor in France during the prewar years and who
later belonged to a circle including Jean-Louis Barrault, Roger Blin, the
actress Simone Signoret, and the poet Jacques Prévert. Vitsoris intro-
duced Sherry to Pablo on the eve of the occupation, although Pablo had
been one of the Greek delegates to the 1938 founding congress of the
Fourth International. From 1944 until the late 1950s, Pablo was a close
personal friend and political mentor.[50]

One day in 1945, George Weissman, who had known Sherry when he
was a Trotskyist student at Harvard in the 1930s, showed up at the
Time, Inc. office. After some initial chitchat, Sherry brought him into a
back room and introduced him to the French actor Roger Blin, whom he
described as "part of the Trotskyist fraction in cinema." Later Sherry
talked of his enthusiasm for *Les Enfants du Paradis*, a film in which

some of the theater figures influenced by Trotskyism participated. He also spoke of his friendship with Iris Barry, who instituted the first film library in the world at the Museum of Modern Art.

When Weissman was about to depart for the United States, Sherry asked if he could have the guns that Weissman, like other American G.I.'s, had collected to bring home as souvenirs. One of these was a tiny Belgian pistol that Sherry asked to have for his personal use. It was about the size of a cigarette lighter and fired miniature bullets. Weissman had decided that the pistol was inappropriate to use as a weapon and intended it to be a gag gift for his wife. It had no safety features; since it was a repeater, it was dangerous to use because, if dropped, it might go off and keep on shooting. But Weissman was aware that a number of figures in the leadership of the Fourth International had been assassinated by Stalinists and others, so he willingly turned the gun over to Sherry.[51]

Sherry's initial assignments for the Fourth International (he was known as Owen during the 1940s) involved the supervision of the movement's work in Spain and the maintenance of communication with Trotskyists in Latin America. At a later point he served as treasurer of the Fourth International and also as the liaison between leaders of the International and the leadership of the French party. Sherry, in fact, was a member of the French party and took Pierre Frank's place on the central committee and political bureau until Frank could return from England. Beyond this, Sherry used the mobility afforded by his journalistic position to establish contact with other Trotskyist groups in Europe (the Austrians, for example, whom he visited in early 1945) and to solidify their relations with the International. He also assisted in healing the never-ending splits. As he had done before the war, he continued to hire Trotskyists as his research assistants when it was appropriate. In the postwar years, the main assistant was the Belgian Trotskyist Ernest Mandel.[52]

In March of 1946 there occurred an episode that significantly endangered Sherry's relationship to Time, Inc. and his ability to continue using his journalistic position as a cover for political work. At that time a gathering of Trotskyists was held in Paris in preparation for an international congress. The French Trotskyist party was still underground, because, among other reasons, the Stalinists were at the height of their influence and the Trotskyists feared that they might try to frame them on charges of "collaboration" with the Nazis.

Consequently, the participants in the precongress gathering met secretly in a first-floor room in a cafe near the Porte St. Denis in Paris. On the second or third day after the meeting began, the door suddenly burst open and men armed with machine guns entered. At first it was assumed that they were Stalinists, but when Pablo began to protest, it was discovered that they were French security police. In the meantime, Sherry had gathered up all the papers and documents from the meeting, stuffed them into his large briefcase, and insisted that the papers could not be touched because they were his personal journalistic property.

The police then rounded up all the participants, including two Americans, George Breitman and Sam Gordon, and loaded them into a police van. As they drove to the station, Breitman noticed that Sherry was smoking continually and dropping ashes outside the window every few moments. Later he learned that Sherry had been dropping the bullets to his tiny Belgian pistol along with the ashes, and finally the pistol itself. He had been afraid that the gun might start going off if he dropped it onto the road while it was still loaded. At the station Sherry managed to get himself released and Breitman was sent back to his military unit. The other Trotskyists continued their conference during the night in their cell block and were released the next day.[53]

The following summer, during July and August of 1946, Sherry and Pablo traveled to Greece. The aim of the journey was to attend the unification congress of the Greek Trotskyists. Sherry, Pablo, and Marguerite journeyed in a litte Greek boat that cautiously wove its way to Piraeus through waters of the Mediterranean that were sown with mines from the war. Because he was a war correspondent, Sherry had the right to wear the uniform of an American military officer. Pablo accompanied him in the post of secretary to avoid difficulties with the police, for Greece was then in a state of civil war.

The congress of unification was held on a barren mountain near Athens. Guards were placed to watch the approaches because the Trotskyists feared the incursions of the police, who were at that time hunting for subversives. At the end of the conference, Sherry discovered that no planes were available for their departure. Consequently, he used his authority as a war correspondent to commandeer a military plane, and the three of them flew to Rome. There they checked into the fanciest hotel in the city, ostensibly for journalistic purposes. Despite a shortage of rooms, Sherry gave orders that Pablo's quarters had to be kept vacant during his absence, even when he was away from the city on "research assignments," which were, in reality, gatherings with Trotskyist groups in various parts of Italy.[54]

From this time until the spring of 1948, Sherry was immersed in intense and continuous political work. Charles Curtiss, an ex-Trotskyist who took assignments in Mexico in the 1930s and 1940s, recalls that Sherry was "a prodigious worker who gave painstaking attention to detail." Yet his attitude was always "kind and generous" and his manner "unassuming."[55] Pierre Frank also remembers that whatever personal conflicts may have troubled Sherry, they could not be detected under the equanimity with which he carried out his political duties. He functioned with "exemplary regularity" and with a temperament that sometimes seemed "serene."[56] Sherry was frequently employed as either a chairman or a simultaneous translator at gatherings. He composed the organizational statutes for the Fourth International. For a period he was assigned to assist in relations between the bureau (working committee) of the International and the French Trotskyists, and he met several times each week with Jacques Privas of the French party's central committee. His articles appeared frequently in French in the theoretical organ of the International and in discussion documents. In all his rushing back and forth between political and journalistic duties, he still found time to sustain a fairly active social life.

In her letters, Alice B. Toklas records a number of social engagements with Sherry in 1947. She and Gertrude Stein had known Sherry in the 1920s; now she commented that he was "no longer a beautiful young poet but quite a gross middle-aged newspaper man but with a very fine head."[57] A more regular companion of Sherry in Paris was Joel Carmichael, son of the prominent American Zionist Louis Lipsky and later a successful author and editor.

Carmichael recalls that Sherry was "a first-class journalist," but bereft of the caution necessary to conceal his true political viewpoint from his employer. "Everybody must have known about it, because he didn't conceal his opinions or his organizational connections, so it must have gotten back to *Time* in the ordinary course of events." He recollects that Sherry used to like to get drunk and talk politics, but his attitude was very "pious" and he did not like to argue. "He would simply reaffirm his faith. That would be the sum total of the argument, because finally he would simply say that things were absolutely bound to come out the way he predicted and that was it and there's nothing further to be said about it. And then he would raise his voice and talk about a 'tidal wave changing everything.'" Carmichael also sensed that Sherry suffered from sexual conflicts: one moment he exhibited characteristics that Carmichael intuited to be bisexual or homosexual; the next moment he acted "terrifically macho. He looked a bit like Hemingway, and he was a burly chap, and very handsome. So he would get drunk and pound the table and bellow and stamp around. . . . But at the same time he was quite charming."[58]

Ever since the journalistic friction in England in early 1944, when Sherry felt that he lacked the full backing of his company, he began to suspect that his association with the Luce corporation would come to an unpleasant conclusion. The story about his arrest at the gathering of French Trotskyists kept coming up, and in another incident he reportedly lost his temper and "baited" Averill Harriman at a press conference. In the spring of 1946, shortly after his mother died, Sherry found that his job worries were affecting him more seriously than he had anticipated. He wrote Charles Haywood about "driving my machine hard." A few weeks before, he had thought he was becoming "slightly hysterical and it looked as if I'd either have a breakdown or be forced back to alcoholism or something. But by being slightly tough about refusing work, I have pulled up again."[59]

In October 1945 Sherry was transferred from *Time* to *Fortune*; his title was general European correspondent, but his salary was cut by a third.[60] In November 1946 and again in July 1947, he visited New York to consult about his deteriorating status. But the best arrangement he could work out was the promise of a hundred dollars each for a monthly letter for *Fortune*, and several special assignments at a thousand dollars each.[61] He was never able to obtain an "official" statement of the reasons why he was knocked out of Time, Inc., but there is evidence that it was a combination of jealousy and political suspicion.[62] John Hersey, his former co-worker, regards Sherry's dismissal as part of the general purge of liberals and radicals (Hersey himself, Theodore H. White, and Charles Wertenbaker) that took place in the 1944–45 period when Whittaker Chambers was foreign news editor.[63]

In February 1948, just after he returned from a stay in Nice, Sherry suffered a mental breakdown. Several months later he wrote to Charles Haywood that he had lost forty-five pounds "and the end does not seem in sight." A period of almost total insomnia had convinced him to enter the American hospital for four days of enforced rest and examination. He then sent a letter off to Coenraad van Emde Boas, the Freudian psychoanalyst in Amsterdam, asking for an appointment. "As soon as I have run up to see him," he wrote Haywood, "we'll have all the materials for a judgment. But in any case, I have thrown up all jobs and duties here." He speculated that he might leave Europe, take "the short course at the Mergenthaler Linotype School and then . . . disappear into a furnished room somewhere in the vastness of Brooklyn for six months or so."[64]

On 13 May 1948 he wrote to Haywood of a change in plans. "I went there [Amsterdam] to get a diagnosis from a Vienna witch-doctor to see whether I should go to a spetz in New York and lie on his couch for two years in the intervals of linotyping. He opined, after a bit, that it was not necessary to take the entire car to pieces in this way and rebuild it, but that a tune-up would suffice." Sherry explained that he and the psychoanalyst had spent nine full days in session, the equivalent of three months of treatment. "Very exhausting. But, on a pragmatic basis, successful." Sherry said that he was weak but well, and now believed that his breakdown was "self-provoked on pretexts which concealed quite different and more serious things, and hence have abandoned the Brooklyn project, which was only a very elaborate form of running away from a difficult situation, which could be solved on the contrary only by being faced."

Sherry said that his first step would be to get back to work and to straighten out his gravely compromised finances. "This interim report can only be hopeful, not triumphant."[65] So ended a decade in which Sherry had almost fully suppressed his creative side. It was now time for him to return to the other half of his life's work—literature—and to attempt to realize the goals that he had envisioned in his youth.

Sherry's psychoanalysis in Amsterdam with van Emde Boas was as painful as it was educational; for the rest of his life he was disturbed by the insights he had gained into his character and by the causes of his emotional crisis. His personality became suffused with melancholy undertones. Writing to Marguerite from Amsterdam, where, accompanied by Mina Curtiss, he was receiving treatment, Sherry reported that "Mina had warned me that when I lifted the lid off the subconscious I would be horrified: I would find it a place of dirty diapers, self-assertive howling, and infantile greed." His initial response was desperate misery because he could not see a way out. "I am such a practiced liar, self-deceiver, ham actor, etc., that it is impossible for me to make any statement at all which is not loaded with charm, plausibility, escapism, cowardice (probably including the present one)."[1]

On 5 May 1948 he reported to Marguerite that he was about to have a session devoted to his drinking and money problems. He anticipated that he would still be in a fairly shaky state upon his return, "but clear in the head at last." He thought that he would never be able to tell Marguerite some of the details, "but one thing I must say right now—your greeting of the announcement of a 'new life' with a whoop of 'hold your hats!' was the profoundest psychological observation anyone's ever made of me. The trick is to stop these attempts to make myself into something I'm not, and to use what I *am* to its full and efficient effect."[2] When he wrote Marguerite again four days later, he reported that he and van Emde Boas had struck a slight snag that required working out for a few more days. It concerned his Rorschach test.

To van Emde Boas's visible surprise and Sherry's own discomfiture, the test showed him to be almost totally devoid of imagination, creative powers, and initiative, except in latent or potential form. Van Emde Boas found Sherry's capacity for imagination on the test to be at a remarkably lower level than their conversations had indicated during treatment. The conclusion they reached was not that those qualities had been lacking in Sherry, but that they had been rigorously suppressed:

> This ties in with the guilt I have felt toward the little friends [an expression Sherry used in correspondence when referring to the Fourth International] because of living in both worlds: we have already recognized that I have tried to compensate for living more richly and comfortably than they do by refusing to take pleasure in

my broader cultural opportunities, the one exception being *oral* satisfaction (food and drink) which had to replace poetry, art, music, entertainment, and all sensibility. It has to do with my messianic delusion that I am God Almighty, and if I can't write poetry, then poetry and the other arts are of no importance or simply don't exist.[3]

Elaborating about the nature of his "God complex" in a letter to Mina Curtiss, he interpreted the fragment of a dream he had just had, in which for the first time he was able to recognize clearly a dissociation of himself in two people. "You and I were walking up a terraced street . . . to visit a great man. He was very impressive, though so well-equilibrated and calm that he was not particularly exciting intellectually." When he began to wonder who this man was, "it suddenly struck me as clear as a lightning flash that it was myself as I should like to be. One might almost say that my Id escorted you up a hill to see my Super-ego."[4] Mina Curtiss answered Sherry a week later, explaining that she had discussed his problems with a psychiatrist in New York. This psychiatrist, who had analyzed seven former Catholics, assured Curtiss of the soundness of her conviction that the church was the most critical factor in Sherry's neuroses.[5]

Sherry's sense that he would one day play an important historical role had also been reflected in his practice of saving copies of his own letters. He explained to Curtiss that he had done this because of his belief that he might one day be the subject of a biographical memoir. "At that time I was certain that I would end up the equivalent, not of Lenin or Trotsky, certainly, but at least of Zinoviev or Sverdlov [general secretary of the Bolshevik party prior to Stalin]. These are surely proper subjects for biography: not in the mere facts of their personal lives, but in their political accomplishments."[6] Sherry now turned his thoughts to an earlier goal, the idea of "leaving scars on the earth" through some sort of literary achievement, but this time the literary achievement would serve the needs of his political convictions as well.

Sherry did not consider his journalistic writing to be part of his real "life's work." He wrote Curtiss ruefully about the ten years he had devoted to crushing his own literary sensibilities in his service to Time, Inc. He admitted that he liked compliments on the technical smoothness of accomplishments in this field, but "I tell you that there is not one word I have written in it worth the powder to blow it off to hell. I am not even ashamed of it; it's just zero; it doesn't exist. It means exactly as much as a stick I whittled while waiting for an interurban bus. And it has touched me just as little."[7]

He expressed surprise that Curtiss had thought he took pride in his journalistic work. To the contrary, after the turmoil of the depression had caused him to give up the state of mind and sensibility necessary to write poetry, he believed that journalism had proceeded to "debauch" his literary gifts. "I had lived for years in the naive belief that everybody took me for a tragic case, whereas everybody took me for a satisfied hack. The old Irish danger of falling into the profession of the charming failure crept up on me from a totally unsuspecting quarter."[8] Curtiss suggested that Sherry redeem his talents with an autobiographical novel in a Joycean mode.[9] Sherry responded that he would attempt to surpass Hemingway's *For Whom the Bell Tolls* or Malraux's *Man's Fate* if he ever undertook a novel. But he was "afraid that a really good political novel about the revolution (I do not deny that there may be good ones about bourgeois politics) will have to be written by a professional revolutionary; and I equally fear that, until after the revolution, they will either be too busy with the tasks thereof, or in keeping alive with bourgeois work, or devoid of the necessary literary and artistic talent."[10]

For Sherry, the primary problem at the moment was "keeping alive with bourgeois work," because the opportunities available to him in journalistic circles had continued to decline as the Cold War political atmosphere intensified. His periodic contributions to *Fortune* came to an end after he submitted an article on a south Italian farm worker; it was butchered to unrecognizability by the editors. Sherry's association with *Commentary*, which was facilitated at first because of his friendship with Clement Greenberg, followed a similar trajectory.

From 1947 to 1950, *Commentary* magazine published a series of feature articles by Mangan on French topics, for which he was paid two hundred dollars each. "The Outlook for France's Jews: The National Crisis Threatens Their Security" (November 1947) reviewed the whole history of French Jewry from the mid-eighteenth century to the German occupation, arguing the classical Marxist view that "anti-Semitism is the bastard child of economic crisis." Thus, Mangan concluded, the fate of French Jews at the present time was linked to the outcome of the new social struggles that had erupted over the recent "bread crisis," as well as the character of the political movements vying for power as a consequence of the inability of the Fourth Republic to solve France's long-term economic problems.[11] "France: Is de Gaulle Fascist?" (January 1948) pursued a similar method of historical review in order to update and freshly present more or less traditional Marxist and Trotskyist concepts. Mangan began by analyzing the political evolution of de Gaulle, as well as the social conditions that make possible the rise of a Fascist movement. Despite the presence of many of these conditions in France, Mangan concluded that de Gaulle's Rassemblement du Peuple Français (RPF) was not an authentic Fascist party. "The word fascism," he argued, "largely as a result of being hysterically employed for the last twelve years as an *omnium-gatherum* term of abuse by the Communists and their friends, is not clearly understood in the United States." He distinguished fascism from other forms of reaction by its need for a genuine plebeian mass base, a pseudorevolutionary program, and by its objective of total extirpation of any and all independent labor organizations. He thought that a more appropriate comparison for de Gaulle was, not the National Socialist Hitler, but the straight nationalist Hugenberg or, in France, the law-and-order reactionary de la Rocque, of the Croix de Feu.[12]

The first of Mangan's articles to provoke controversy with other contributors to the magazine was "Is Europe's Middle Class Finished? The Political Future of the 'Third Force'" (August 1948). In a harsh appraisal, Mangan surveyed the past political practice and present political alternatives of the French middle class, then came up with a pessimistic prognosis: "Caught hopelessly in the present pragmatic choice between Stalinism and anti-Stalinism, too 'realistic' to flesh the thin bones of the genuinely revolutionary-socialist movement, the most honest and radical of the middle-class intellectuals can find no other solution than to quit the political field entirely.... The pathetic Sartre, all whose brilliance, not unlike Eliot's before him, is devoted to demonstrating that nothing means much of anything, is perhaps today the doomed and questioning European middle class's most representative symbol."[13] Writing from England, George Lichtheim accused Mangan of sectarianism for his statement that "Social Democracy has no longer very much to do with socialism." From Princeton, Irving Howe (still a member of Max Shachtman's Workers party) called Mangan's characterization of RDR (the Rassemblement Démocratique Révolutionnaire, a coalition that Howe's group supported) as advancing on the road to political retreat a "malicious" act; he also used his inside knowledge of Mangan's real identity to expose him as a Trotskyist: "Perhaps his [Mangan's] reference to the RDR can be understood more readily when one knows that he still clings to the notion that Russia is a 'degenerated' workers state to be defended from 'attack.' The RDR has, happily, rejected this absurdity, which may explain why his article, while eloquent enough in denouncing Stalinism, says nothing about the role of the Russian state in European politics."[14] In the political atmosphere of 1948, Howe's identification of Sherry's political tendency in Commentary was, regardless of intentions, a blow to Sherry, especially since Howe's summary of the Trotskyist view of the USSR failed to accurately communicate Sherry's real opposition to the political rule of Stalinism, a cause for which a good number of his associates had given their lives.

Only a few months later, Sherry found his relationship with Commentary in deep trouble. He had been commissioned to write a report on two self-proclaimed "peace" conferences held in Paris in April 1949. One was the Stalinist-dominated World Congress of the Partisans of Peace, the other was the pro–United States International Day of Resistance to Dictatorship and War. Sherry submitted an essay criticizing both events;

he called it "Which Peace Do You Mean? Paris's Rival Peace Camps Whoop It Up for the Rival War Camps." He then discovered that *Commentary* editor Elliot Cohen had revised it with unacceptable changes. The new version could not be published and an argument ensued over whether he would be paid for his work. Greenberg wrote Sherry frankly that the editors objected to the article because it was not sufficiently partisan on the side of the second conference: "Of course *Commentary* is on the side of Hook, Farrell and Co. [who were by this time hard-line Cold Warriors]." He reminded Sherry that this meant a distinctly different perspective from "your own commitment to a certain variety of Bolshevism."[15]

While the peace conference article never appeared, an essay called "The French Intellectual Merry-Go-Round" was published in the June 1949 issue. Here Mangan discussed the politics of the RDR in more detail and with somewhat more sympathy than he had in the earlier piece, calling it "a curious well-meaning mixture" that could be "the groping and naive forerunner" of a revolutionary tendency. But he mostly poked fun at Malraux and other intellectuals who had undergone remarkable political turnabouts in recent years.[16]

Then, in February 1950, Mangan published a piece quite removed from contemporary political controversies; it was entitled "The French Turn to Psychoanalysis: Freud Breaches Reason's Citadel." With characteristic confidence in his knowledge of French history and culture, Mangan compared different theories about why France, "with the highest reputation for hospitality to advanced ideas and the greatest tolerance concerning sexual matters," should have originally been hostile to psychoanalysis. "French psychoanalysts today are overwhelmed by patients; and the existing analysts are worked to a frazzle trying to cope with the flood of medical students and practical physicians wanting to undergo training analysis prior to becoming analysts themselves." How was it possible that the nation "which used merrily to quote that 'the chains of marriage are so heavy that it takes three to bear them' now seems to need a fourth in the person of a psychoanalyst"?

Exploring the reasons for France's historic resistance to the new discipline, Mangan concluded that it was due to a combination of factors, including France's own early prestige in psychological study in the nineteenth century (which had been an influence on Freud), the intense nationalism of early twentieth-century France, the French pride in language that resisted Freudian terminology, the association of Freudianism with surrealism (which hardly communicated the rationalist and materialist elements in Freudianism), and the importance of Catholicism in France. But Mangan attributed the most significance to France's national temperament—its tolerance for sexual freedom (including a widespread acceptance of infantile masturbation) and individualistic behavior—which thus reduced the anxiety that produces many neuroses. "It is possible in Paris to wander past the cafés on a Sunday afternoon in Indian chief's regalia, complete with war paint, with hardly a glance from the terrace sitters," he insisted. "More importantly, tics, phobias, hypochondrias, compulsive rituals, perversions, manic excitations, depressive glumnesses all pass, if not unnoticed, at least uninterfered with. Anyone has a right, the French feel, to his moods, his *manies*, and his eccentricities." Mangan contrasted this to the situation in the United States, where there is constant anxiety about the social acceptability of one's own behavior. "The French think this is a huge joke, and adore the inverted greeting they attribute to one New York analyst meeting another on Park Avenue: 'You're fine, thanks. How am I?' "

Yet this liberal French ambience had not changed; so what had caused the new acceptance of Freudianism? Mangan based his answer, in part, on recent writings by Franz Alexander. Alexander had argued that sexual repression was no longer the basis of many contemporary neuroses; rather, the ground had more recently shifted to something to which France was less immune: "emotional insecurity, a conflict between competitive ambition and stress upon individual accomplishment, and a deep longing for dependence and security." Mangan concluded that neuroses and character disorders centered around fears, aggressions, frustrations, and, above all, insecurity that had been brought about by drastic new changes in France. Those changes were a consequence of the repeated social crises of the 1930s that had finally resulted in the German occupation, the inflation and chaos that came with the Liberation, and the present situation with France as a potential battlefield between the United States and Russia. With a quote from Otto Fenichal, he explained from a materialist point of view why the new French turn to psychoanalysis was the product of a political conjecture: "For though the deep original conflicts predisposing to the central neuroses of today lie as ever in the oral, anal, and genital stages of infancy, the inciting external factors that aggravate them to the point of full neurotic breakdown are visibly sociological and economic."[17] Mangan might have cited himself as a case in point.

About this time, Sherry wrote to Joshua Epstein—his friend from the *larus* days who had now become an eye surgeon in New York City—that even though the *Reporter* magazine had offered him "a fairly free hand," he was giving up journalism altogether. "After the other experiences I know it doesn't mean anything: in the current situation objectivity has the chance of a pinch of dried shit in a cyclone."[18] He intended to pack up his possessions and return to the United States to look for a new occupation. From his political responsibilities he was more or less on a leave of absence, and Marguerite was devoted to taking care of him full-time. She occasionally did some hospital work, and for several years after the war she was very active as a European representative of the American Committee for European Workers Relief, an organization initiated by American Trotskyists to ship food, medicine, and clothing to Europe for the aid of leftists just out of concentration camps or otherwise in dire need.[19]

Just at this low point in Sherry's life, Karl Goldstein, whom he had befriended in Argentina nine years earlier, suddenly turned up. Goldstein had become a successful businessman and presented Sherry with a dream offer: he would provide Sherry with full support for a year at three hundred dollars a month while he went to Bolivia to write a novel about the tin miners there. Sherry jumped at the opportunity and spent August 1949 getting ready by sketching out some poems and stories. But in September Goldstein asked Sherry to come to Zurich for a while, before he left. Goldstein had a company there, a fabulously complicated mess that was driving him crazy. He wanted Sherry, partly as a favor and partly as a speculation, to take over its administration and see if he could save Goldstein's investment therein, which was in the neighborhood of forty thousand dollars. Sherry would receive a third if he succeeded, and Goldstein would have peace of mind while he was trying to do so.

The winter of 1949–50 was hell for Sherry: up at 5:30 A. M., to the office at 6:30 A. M., sandwiches at his desk, home for dinner at 8:30 P. M. —including Sundays and Christmas. His nights were divided between insomnia and nightmares. At one point he was almost killed in a car accident while racing to an appointment on a rainy day. By the time he got the bookkeeping straightened out, it was evident that there was nothing to be done: the company was essentially insolvent when he had taken it over. Finally, in mid-February, Sherry had to petition it into bankruptcy and get out of Switzerland with creditors and the police only two steps behind him. Meanwhile, Goldstein had overextended his capital in other investments and had to withdraw his offer of the Bolivian venture, leaving Sherry mired in debt. In a letter to Tony Palmer, Sherry poured out the sad ending to the tale. His morale, which had sunk "lower than whaleshit," was momentarily revived by a check for five hundred dollars from a good friend who knew how Sherry loved to gamble. The accompanying letter said: "Turn this into two or three thousand in your usual style, and you'll feel better." But that was naturally the moment that the tables took their revenge for "that incredible winning streak I had from 1945 to 1949: the dough went, not like gambling, but like a hemorrhage. In ten days, despite a few wins, we were cleaned, and crawled back from Villefranche to Paris, more dead than alive."[20]

Sherry was doubly frustrated because he had already mentally begun to write the Bolivian novel. Now he was forced to look for a new job in Europe just so he could earn sufficient money to allow him to carry out the earlier plan of moving to Brooklyn. He wrote Joshua Epstein that

"I'm 46 now, and if I don't get back to my own real work [writing] pretty soon, it's going to be too late." He thought that an honorable earning of one's living is "all very admirable; but I should hate to go down at the end as a newspaperman and scriptwriter without having had at least one go at my own writing on a subject that deeply moves me."[21] He explained that it would be necessary to be on the spot in Bolivia in order to complete the novel, because he was writing a very specific novel about a very specific subject, "which I can't properly do without seeing on the spot what I suppose it to be like, and either confirming or utterly changing my preconceptions." Future novels might include one about the Spanish civil war in Barcelona and another "about Boston, Lynn, Salem, and way points."[22] But if he had the chance now, he desperately desired to put into a novel "the heroic and to date ever defeated struggles of the Bolivian tin-miners." His awareness that Bolivia might burst into civil war at any moment heightened his enthusiasm for being on the scene in the manner of Malraux, whose firsthand experiences in Indochina and China had formed the background to *Man's Fate* and *The Conquerors*.[23]

Epstein responded to Sherry's melancholy letters about his financial situation with a check for three hundred dollars to facilitate the move to Brooklyn. Simultaneously, Sherry found temporary work as a scriptwriter for "The March of Time" newsreels, and he began to ask himself whether the Bolivian plan might somehow be salvaged. The first task was to clean up his French debts, which he did by producing a script for "The March of Time" called "French France." He had never done a film script before, but his amateur efforts pleased the directors, who hired Sherry on a regular basis. So, during the summer of 1950, Sherry sweated away on "March of Time" scripts and made a little money on the side with other movie work. One of these involved preparation of English subtitles for a film called *God Needs Men*; another involved adapting, scoring, and narrating a documentary on Balzac, which won Sherry the first annual Woodstock International Film Festival Award in 1951 for the best English commentary to a documentary film in 1950.[24] In the meantime, Sherry reorganized the Bolivian venture by spreading out a $300-a-month subsidy from three people who had confidence in his ability to produce an important work of literature: Karl Goldstein, Joshua Epstein, and Mina Curtiss. The money was given to Sherry on a monthly basis and was considered a loan to be repaid out of any royalties from the book or out of Sherry's salary in future years if the project should fail.

Sherry and Marguerite sailed for Bolivia in late December 1950 and arrived in early January. From the city of Cochabamba he wrote to Charles Haywood that he was devouring histories of Bolivia and meeting union leaders from the mining regions, which he planned to visit immediately thereafter. "I am happy as I have not been for twenty years, and all work is effortless." But to Goldstein he reported that "M . . . slower than I in adapting to the altitude . . . collapsed under the strain of working at this altitude."[25] Tony Palmer wrote in April and asked for a report on Sherry's activities, saying that among his old friends he had become a "mythical figure," one that was "midway between Falstaff and Don Quixote." Sherry answered by reporting that his new home was in the "agreeable town of Cochabamba," which was 8,300 feet high; however, the mining centers where he went for research were between thirteen thousand and fifteen thousand feet. He and Marguerite dwelled in a "little three-room rose-bowered cottage (the roses are geraniums), with quite a good maid, living very comfortably at $300 a month." But since he had found that Bolivia was "worse than Mexico for arranging anything," he had passed the time needed to arrange visits to the miners and their company-town villages writing some short prose pieces and poems.[26] Several of these will be discussed in the Conclusion to this book.

The novel began to take shape under the title "The Mountain of Death," but, although he struggled with it for the rest of his life, the effort was ultimately aborted; he only completed about half the writing, and much of this was in unpublishable draft form. Mangan's intention was to depict the growing political consciousness of Pablo, a young Bolivian tin miner of the Quechua Indians. Pablo is propelled into the leadership of a strike and begins to associate with left-wing political figures resembling Guillermo Lora, a well-known Bolivian Trotskyist, and Juan Lechin, a leader of the Movimiento Nacionalista Revolucionario (MNR). Yet Mangan erred in his decision to have each chapter in the book seen through the eyes of whichever character was most central at the time. He later told Catherine Carver of Viking Press that "concern with individuals at all was a mistake."[27] The real subject of "The Mountain of Death" was not individuals, but events, masses, and forces; not psychology, but history. If he wanted to write in a realist mode, he probably should have gone back to the classical auctorial point of view, which permits description, explanation, and pure narrative, and also allows individuals to take their places within the scale of a larger frame. What matters in a subject of the sort Mangan aspired to depict was not what some particular character felt or thought about it, but the great historical sweep in which he or she is caught up.

Because of this initial error, Sherry's approach to realism in the book backfired. Even though the characters were studied and reproduced from real life, they would strike most readers as lifeless or dull or both. In his aspiration to be true to objective reality, he overdocumented and underdramatized. Nevertheless, in the surviving chapters, he did not idealize the Indian miners. They are naturalistically presented: dull as posts, brutal as animals, inarticulate as children. They swing from unfounded enthusiasm to discouraged apathy to unreasoning rage; they choose critical moments to get sodden on chicha; they murder hostages with sadistic savagery. The publishers in New York and London who later rejected Mangan's outline of "The Mountain of Death" as a morality play or tract could not have done so on the grounds that Mangan had the miners representing the forces of Good or Idealism or Sweetness-and-Light; the political point of the book was simply that their cause was unquestionably just and that they stood, in their stumbling and distorted way, for the progress of humanity.

During his early months in the mountains of Bolivia, Sherry completed "Breath," a realistic story that featured an oxygen tent, a likely reflection of the environment. Although Sherry regarded it as a serious artistic endeavor, he was forced to sell it to *Argosy*, where it appeared in somewhat altered form in the summer of 1952.[28] By May of 1951, Sherry had produced another story, "A Costume for Carnival," which eventually appeared in the *Arizona Quarterly* in 1958. This piece was an explicitly political tale: it followed the fortunes of a dress suit worn by a pseudo-revolutionary, a suit ending up as a child's costume for a carnival celebration. It was based upon a story told to Mangan by an activist in the Bolivian MNR named Prado Vargas. Although Vargas contributed nothing to the writing of the piece, Mangan listed him as coauthor under the name Rogerio Prado.[29] Later that month, Mangan completed an unpublished children's book entitled "That Strange Red Hen."[30]

In addition to several surrealist stories and poems (which will be discussed in the Conclusion), the most successful piece of the Bolivian period was the posthumously published "Snow," a literary expression of Sherry's fixation on memories of childhood happiness and his belief that patterns exhibited in youth are decisive in character formation. Throughout the spring of 1951, Sherry felt his literary powers surge through him as they had not done for years. In late June he wrote Virgil Thomson passionately that "there isn't so enormously much time left us to say what we have to say, and one begins to wonder if there aren't some non-essentials that can be lopped off to give us greater leisure and single-mindedness for it."[31] Apparently Sherry felt that the success of his first few months in Bolivia signaled the possibility that he might actually be able to achieve a literary comeback and develop a reputation. He could then earn an income from sales that would permit him to write fiction and poetry full-time for the rest of his life. Under the impetus of this new optimism, Sherry began to conceive and write "Snow," which he described in a letter to Charles Haywood dated 28 June 1951:

> I am up to my ears in a new piece called "Snow" which is I don't know what, either a long short story or a novelette, but because not only of length but also of subject is I fear not particularly saleable. But it moves me profoundly. It starts on the top of the Arlberg pass

in a blizzard, and ends up on the northern short cut up from the Voralberg to Germany, but it is really all about my childhood in Lynn, Mass., and way points and above all what snow has meant to me. In one sense, Charlie, it is the kind of "put-the-bucket-under-the-faucet-and-let-it-out" technique that you have often recommended to me; in another, it's a very fancy Greek tragedy, with the hero punished for hübris and inattention. What I think is the most moving scene takes place on Lynn Common just after dawn to a seven-year-old boy. It's the most autobiographical piece I've ever written, I think; but whether my tears in writing it get enough into the story so that the ordinary reader will be moved is another question.[32]

Sherry worked on "Snow" during the summer of 1951, doing a major revision in the fall and a minor one in the spring of 1952. Because of its length, more than fifty pages, the manuscript received only limited circulation and was never published in his lifetime. Sherry was also pessimistic about "Snow" getting into print because it had strong political implications. He described the essential point to Charles Haywood: "You can work for a Bolshevik movement for fifteen years and still not be a real Bolshevik."[33] But a large section of the piece consists of nostalgic reminiscences of his own childhood and young manhood; the atmosphere of these materials closely approximates Alain-Fournier's Le Grand Meaulnes, a classic of the modern French cult of adolescence of which Sherry often spoke with enthusiasm.

The setting of "Snow" is Western Europe in the post—World War II era. Michael Farrell, an Irish American writer who has decided to devote his life to the Trotskyist movement, has just completed a political mission in Vienna. Severely weakened by the Fascist powers during the war, the remnants of Trotsky's Fourth International are seeking to regroup and reestablish themselves in order to continue their struggle for socialism. But now, in addition to facing repression from the victorious capitalist nations, the Trotskyists in Western Europe also fear violence at the hands of the Soviet troops and police apparatus, which are present in certain zones as part of the army of occupation. Farrell himself carries a snub-nosed automatic in the glove compartment of his car. That evening, just after it has begun to snow, Farrell reaches the entrance to the Arlberg Pass. There he recklessly ignores the cries of guards, who order him to halt because of dangerous snow conditions. Later, after parking his car in the Austrian town of Bludenz, Farrell notices the tracks it has made in the snow; these tracks unlock the sluice gates of memory about his New England boyhood. During his dinner at the Goldener Adler Inn he indulges nostalgically in a sequence of vivid recollections. These involve members of his family, his first sexual infatuation, and, most importantly, the day he spends recreating the routes of the local railway system by making paths in the snow on the common of the town.

Following these and other reminiscences, a political ally arrives and informs Farrell of an unexpected mission in Germany. Departing for this mission, Farrell permits his mind to wander, overestimates his control of the car, and finds himself careening toward death:

> "Snow!" he roared, as if incredulous at some unimaginable betrayal. "Snow!"
>
> And the snow was waiting. Two hundred and thirty feet below, where slides had mounded, wind had drifted, and new falls blanketed, it lay deep, soft, and white, as yet unmarked by any human track.[34]

For the epigraph to "Snow," Sherry intended to use a passage from Malraux's *Man's Fate*: "Before I die, I want to leave marks on the surface of the earth." This motif appears three times in the manuscript. It first appears when the tire marks remind Farrell of the railroad he designed in the snow on the common of his home town in Massachusetts. The second reference occurs when he is a teenager wearing his first pair of long pants; he cries to his friend Walter, "I want to build everything, make anything, leave my mark on the world." The final ironic reference occurs in the closing section quoted above.

Snow is a conventional image in the New England literature on which Sherry had been raised. Whittier's "Snow-Bound," Emerson's "Snow-Storm," Longfellow's "Snow-Flakes," and Frost's "Stopping by Woods on a Snowy Evening" all use snow to probe themes of death and artistic creation. In building his fantasy railroad on the virgin snow of the common, young Farrell carries out the work of all artists who strive to recreate the world on the blank canvas or page. In the course of this work, Farrell finds his greatest pleasure in the bridges of communication he builds to his father and a passing workman. Nevertheless, Mangan transforms the snow into an ambiguous and disturbing symbol at the close of the manuscript. The marks Farrell had hoped to make on the world through art and daring acts are in fact made by his accidental death on the snow-blanketed mountainside—a death caused in part by his inability to divest himself of his youthful egoistic dreams. Writing this narrative in a self-imposed exile from his native land, Mangan dramatized in Farrell's reveries his own nostalgia for a world more perfect than the one he inherited as an adult. The intensity of his feeling is manifest in the careful articulation of his childhood landscape.

His confidence restored by "Snow," Sherry admitted in a letter to Haywood that several times he had entertained the notion that he might not be a writer at all, but a "self-deceived ham." One time was just after his short psychoanalytic therapy in Amsterdam, another time was immediately after his arrival in Bolivia. But he decided this was not so for two reasons. One was "a kind of fierce inner certainty that is difficult to explain and even if explicable would prove nothing except a sort of hübris." The other was the fact that even when working "with one-tenth of my powers, half my taste, and none of my principles, I have made a fair living at one kind of literary hacking or another—on that pragmatic basis, it is hard for me to believe that when I work at full power I am just a ham." It seemed to Sherry far more reasonable that he was at least a competent and talented writer totally out of touch with the audiences whom he accidentally contacted. "Beyond that I won't go: history will take care of it. I express myself as well as I can; for that expression to become communication there is necessarily a correlation of circumstances which has as yet rarely occurred." Sherry realized that it might never occur fully, and in that case: "I shall go down to obscurity. All right: I shall go down to obscurity, in my own way, trying as hard as I can."[35]

Nevertheless, the fact that so many of Sherry's stories and poems were slow in finding publishers brought about moments of deep discouragement. In response to a question from Haywood about the audiences for whom Sherry was writing, he answered that he wrote his stories for anyone who wanted to read them. "It appears that the experts, i.e. the editors, think that nobody wants to. Very well. All I can think to do in answer to that is to archivize them carefully enough so that when somebody does want to read them, they will not have disappeared."[36] And in a letter to Haywood the following month, he reaffirmed his resolve that he should become again, as he was once, "a specially sensitive machine for the concentration and transmission of human emotions in words."

According to Sherry, each generation had many of these machines—of various levels of sensibility, technical competence, and, most variable of all, degree of contemporaneity. He pointed out that there are brilliant expositors of hopelessness and the collapse of culture, from Eliot to Bernanos to many United States novelists; that there are equally brilliant practitioners of the technique of clinical case histories (James T. Farrell was the example he cited). But "there seems to me to be very few—Malraux is the only example that comes to mind—who, like myself, have half their thought in the future, both its immediate horrors and its ultimate hope." From this he concluded that he had a responsibility. "Sure, writing is 'a grand and glorious *pleasure*,' as you say. I always find it so." Sherry knew of literally nothing else in the world—"love or glory or danger or whatever"—that could compare with the feeling one has, after all the travail, all the ups and downs of composition, when finishing a writing job that meets one's standards and is as good as one can make it. "It's certainly not a 'chore'; if it's a 'duty,' it's a joyful one; but it is, I think, a 'mission.' If one believes, rightly or wrongly, that a complex of circumstances has given one a certain gift which is rare, then one feels a certain sense of responsibility that that gift not be wasted." Sherry concluded his argument by stating that his conscience would never have let him stand the last ten years of not producing imaginative literature had he not sincerely believed that the Trotskyist movement was then so shorthanded that everybody from auto workers to poets had to pitch in and give a hand, and as nearly as possible a full-time one. But now he believed that the Fourth International was "over the hump" and could spare him. "So I can pick up my life where I dropped it about 1936, and try to catch up those years as fast as possible and move on to new and I hope more important uses of whatever I've got as feeling and writing machinery."[37]

This did not mean, however, that Sherry had entirely abandoned his political commitments and responsibilities. Even en route to Bolivia, he had carried out some political missions in Argentina. Then, from the time of his arrival in Bolivia, he tried to establish contact with Guillermo Lora, a leader of the Bolivian Trotskyists who had been jailed by the government. He wrote to Karl Goldstein in March 1951 that with much difficulty and work he managed to see Lora in jail for two hours. "He impresses me as first-rate, better than any others I have seen so far. From what I have learned to date about the regime, I urged that they [the Trotskyists] enter into immediate negotiations with the Minister of the Interior and Justice to swap: he is to agree to accept exile in return for release from prison."[38] Lora, however, managed to escape from prison on his own. At Sherry's urging, Goldstein arranged for him to have free passage out of Latin America in the capacity of an employee for Goldstein's international travel agency. With further encouragement from Sherry and Pablo, Goldstein also arranged passages for other Latin American Trotskyists who wanted to attend congresses of the Fourth International in Europe.

However, most of Sherry's political contacts with Bolivian Trotskyists were connected with the research for "The Mountain of Death." On 25 April 1951 Sherry wrote to Goldstein that he was away from the sixteenth to the twenty-first at the Patiño mines at Catavi and elsewhere. "It was a most interesting trip from every point of view except that of talking to miners. It was, for that, so 'personally conducted' that I got only one afternoon free, and then addresses provided by the little friends turned out to be all wrong, of course." At the Hochschild and Aramayo mining centers, where the union had not been smashed, he hoped that this aspect would be easier. In the meantime, while negotiating for these other trips, Sherry proposed to read all the newspaper files he could locate for the critical events, "because memories of ex-miners are vivid about personal details but very weak on dates and facts."[39]

In June 1951 Sherry reported to Virgil Thomson that the only trouble he was having at the moment was the slowness with which he was able to research "The Mountain of Death." He stated that he had a long and useful visit to the mines; that he was pretty well along in a study of the newspaper archives; and that he had all he needed of atmosphere and scenery. But he did not have, and was having a difficult time obtaining, the detailed human reminiscences and descriptions of the miners who went through the events that were intended to be the plot of the book. "Everything takes ages to arrange, people never keep appointments, they promise and never perform. And in the few cases where I've nailed somebody, he has turned out to be inarticulate, frightened, and suspicious."[40] Sherry pledged to keep hammering away at it, but he now realized that it was going to take pretty near the whole year to assemble the material and plan the book, with no time left for writing it.

In the fall of 1951, Sherry returned to France for several months in order to sell his car and pack up his voluminous archives and other possessions in case it was decided to make a total and permanent move out of the country. In the winter, back in Bolivia, he fell ill with a serious urinary tract infection, and then Marguerite was bitten by a dog. The dog was shot by its owner before it could be observed. Even though laboratory tests showed that it was not rabid, Sherry and Marguerite felt nervous enough to decide that she take twenty-one daily shots of antirabies vaccine in the belly.

Two months later, Sherry reported to Haywood that "when health and friends permit, I disappear into the files of *Los Tiempos* here and soak myself in their records." He started with January 1941, had reached October 1948, and intended to go up to February 1951. "It will be a very different book from the one I came to write: far less one-sided in favor of the mine-workers, but also far more objective and rich, I hope."[41]

Then, on 12 October 1952, Sherry came back from feeding his hens and found Marguerite collapsed on the bed—no pulse, a weak heartbeat of thirty-eight, icy cold and covered with a chill sweat. For two days she fluctuated between life and death. The doctor diagnosed that she had suffered a coronary thrombosis of the occlusion type. But then the prognosis turned favorable, and the doctor predicted that Marguerite would recover if she had several weeks in the hospital, a month at home in bed, and three to four months of semi-invalidism. In April Sherry wrote to Goldstein that her condition had deteriorated instead of improving. "She began to seem like a ship breaking up on a reef. She got some kind of bowel obstruction, developed abcesses on six teeth, and got worse and worse with the edema. The mercury injections which reduced the edema caused severe enteritis and colitis." Sherry and the doctor hardly knew what to tackle first. Slowly, bit by bit, they began pulling her around, but she was still miserable and mostly bedridden. The worst symptom became a psychosomatic one. "Her fear of death is such, now that she has been so close to it, that she is afraid of sleep." Although she was desperate with exhaustion and sleepiness, the minute she dropped off she woke up again with terrible nightmares. She often spent the night in a state between sleeping and waking; Sherry reported that "she raves deliriously and sings, all in a loud voice."[42]

Marguerite finally died on 11 May 1953. Her second attack of coronary thrombosis was instantly fatal. It was particularly unexpected because she had been improving rapidly in the previous ten days. Sherry had finally found the type of medicine that would clear up the enteritis and colitis, which had made medication difficult. The edema was yielding rapidly to diuretics, and the massive doses of digitalis were bringing the pulse down toward normal and curing the enlargement of her heart. Marguerite had just time to call Sherry's name, and then she died as he put his arms around her. He had the impression that her last moments were without pain or fear. He wrote to Haywood that "many people found her an odd sort of wife for me. But I found her as brave and gay and devoted a companion as any man could ask. We had nineteen years together, with ups and downs, joys and disappointments, but always with love and merriment. I know I can and must go on alone, but right now I don't quite see how."

During Marguerite's fits of hysterical fear, Sherry swore that he would never leave her in Bolivia, no matter what. Now he learned that the laws of the country required that her body be buried. He thus arranged for an elaborate funeral with an empty coffin, and then had her body cremated in secret. He transported the ashes around with him in a tin for several years. But after a while the tin began to make a strange rattling sound because of the metallic component, so he scattered the remains shortly after he returned to France in 1956. In the meantime, the fate of his book had not been settled. He wrote Haywood that "Unless I find myself so emotionally knocked to pieces that I just can't work at all, I propose to go on and finish the book by September. Perhaps I'm sentimental, but it seems to me that I have an added reason now: M hated Bolivia, and stayed only because of the work, so that to abandon it now would make nonsense of that sacrifice."[43]

In the half year leading up to the death of Marguerite, Sherry's financial resources were drastically depleted. Because of Marguerite's seven months of invalidism, Sherry had long overstayed his year in Bolivia and had to delay work on "The Mountain of Death." Medical expenses for Marguerite were substantial, but Sherry was unable to find time to produce and sell any short stories or journalism. (The last was a feature article on anti-Semitism in Bolivia that appeared in *Commentary* in August 1952.) Then he learned that Karl Goldstein's business speculations had taken another turn for the worse and that Goldstein would no longer be able to keep up his payments.

Sherry insisted to Virgil Thomson that it was necessary for him to be present in Bolivia as long as possible, because "The Mountain of Death" "concerns places, people, and events which I did not personally experience; thus every chapter turns up a dozen little points on which I have to consult experts or eyewitnesses."[1] Yet he confided to Goldstein that it was becoming more and more difficult to stay because he was having "awful periods of loneliness" and was "perpetually bursting into weeping." Only by sheer willpower was he forcing himself to concentrate "on the main job" in order to keep "the words flowing." His outline of the book was nearing the end, but he had difficulty in judging the quality of what he was doing. "To me, as it comes out, it reads rather pedestrian; but maybe it's all right. The essence seems to me to be to get the story down, and the decorating with any flowers of style that may be necessary can come later."[2]

As usual, several friends responded to Sherry's pleas for loans in order to see him through this last difficult phase. In addition to his usual resources, Richard de Rochemont sent him a check and Mina Curtiss named him the first recipient of the Chapelbrook Fellowship, a Guggenheim type of foundation that she arranged by placing her taxes in trusteeship. But as the summer months passed, Sherry's desperate melancholia failed to lift and his goal became simply to produce a complete outline of the novel, which would be fleshed out at a later date under more felicitous circumstances. In early September, Sherry traveled once more to the mountainside mines at Catavi, in order to gain further descriptive and technical information, and while he was working he suffered a bad attack of altitude sickness. Pains began in his heart and his legs started to swell. When he visited a doctor, he sadly informed Sherry that he was

following in Marguerite's footsteps with a degenerative dilation of the
heart and should go to bed at once and stay motionless. "It was typical of
Bolivia to try to kill me in the last days before I escaped," Sherry
commented in a letter.[3]

Instead of taking up bed-rest, Sherry rallied himself to one great final
exertion and packed all his things so that he could travel back to the
United States via Chile. He arrived in New York City on 18 October
1953, intending to stay with Virgil Thomson at the Chelsea Hotel; but
his friends quickly recognized how serious his illness had grown. They
persuaded him to go to Beth Israel Hospital in Boston, where Sherry
could receive treatment at reduced rates because of a contribution that
Mina Curtiss's family had made to a new nurses' home.

At Beth Israel, Dr. Edward Meilman, a specialist in high blood pressure,
diagnosed Sherry as suffering from malignant hypertension and exten-
sive diverticulosis. According to his prognosis, the hypertension was
terminal; the only solution was to get Sherry into shape so that, with
mild medication and dietary restrictions, he could live a few more years
without too great discomfort. But Sherry managed to make a spectacu-
lar recovery. "I shall make the AMA Journal like our old friend Mrs.
Quincy Howe," he wrote to Thomson.[4] Meilman predicted that if he
lived a semi-invalid life for a maximum of six months, he could last
twenty-five years.

Several weeks later, Sherry returned to New York City and took a
room at the Chelsea. (He wrote to his Harvard friend Norman Dodge that
"my room . . . turned out . . . from the enquiries of my Negro maid as to
whether I was also not a poet, a Celt, and a drunk, to have been just
precedently that of one Dylan Thomas, carried out therefrom feet first.")[5]
Sherry immediately began a new short story based on the incident in
Bolivia when Marguerite had been bitten by a dog. The story explained
the reasons why she had undergone the painful treatment of rabies shots.
It appeared in *Harpers* in the summer of 1956 with the title, "A Question
of Principle." In the story an American engineer in Bolivia named Pat
Callahan—partly modeled on Sherry, but also on his old friend Cuthbert
Daniel—discovers that his wife Maggie has been bitten by a dog that was
subsequently shot by its owner. Although a medical examination of the
dog's brain shows that it was not infected with rabies, the Callahans
eventually make the decision to have Maggie undergo the series of
abdominal shots "just in case"—more out of superstition and fear than
conviction. Sherry wrote Charles Haywood that he was touched by his
immediate recognition of the tribute to Marguerite, "one stone in a
mosaic monument I hope to have time to raise to her." He further
clarified the point of the story, that "love is more important than even
scientific principle. This is of course against my theoretic beliefs but is
an honest testimony from my experience. His [Callahan's] own life he

could risk for a principle, but not a life so precious and necessary to him as hers."[6]

Convalescing in New York City, Sherry found himself in the company of old friends who introduced him into intellectual circles that had some connections with those he had touched peripherally in the 1930s. He struck up an acquaintance once more with Mary McCarthy and met Saul Bellow for the first time. Around the turn of the year, his friend Joshua Epstein brought him to a salon hosted by Hannah Arendt. There he met Rose Feitelson, a New York intellectual who worked closely with Arendt and assisted with most of her early books. Feitelson was the daughter of a middle-class Jewish family; she earned degrees from Barnard and Columbia before doing graduate work at the Sorbonne. Sherry wrote Haywood that he had fallen in love: "The 'girl I've met' is 39, beautiful, ten times as intelligent as I, but unfortunately a sort of social democrat with anarchist tendencies. Love at first sight, and moving with the speed of light, but whether we can ever reach a political modus vivendi, I doubt. She thinks we can, and we're trying."[7] A month later Sherry added that he and Rose were still in love and would "marry in April or May if she can stand me that long. She would be taking an awful load but mostly she has confidence that she could bear me without tailspinning into hysteria or melancholy."[8]

As suddenly as they were drawn together, they began to drift apart. In March Sherry desperately sought out any kind of work that was available in order to make himself a more stable prospect for marriage. He wrote Haywood that "her parents will slam the door in her face, she believes, if she takes up with a penniless bum like me."[9] Yet all his employment inquiries led nowhere. He told Goldstein that he even humbled himself to the point of visiting the offices of *Time* and *Fortune* "to see if—on my not very difficult conditions (no informing or denouncing, no propaganda, either for their or my ideas, but just clear reporting of what happened last week)—they could use me again in Paris, New Delhi, or Buenos Aires."[10] But all doors continued to be shut against him, so he struggled along on what remained of his Chapelbrook Fellowship and on money from some occasional odd jobs. One of these, a translation of Apollinaire's *Mamelles de Tirésias* for the Angel Records album of the musical setting by Francis Poulenc, was described by New York opera director Dorle J. Soria as a "brilliant" piece of work.[11]

Sherry sadly reported to Haywood that, "as the arbitrary date [of the marriage] approaches, Rose begins to see clearer and clearer what nature of beast she has by the tail, and is backing down."[12] To Goldstein he complained that for the first time in his life he had been feeling "suicidally withdrawn." He was uncertain about getting his passport renewed because of his political associations and was continually scrounging for piecework jobs to eke out enough money to survive. "I cannot, for health reasons . . . do a full-time job. I am alive, but every time I try to use my energy as I used to, I am knocked out, and have, with a bitterness that you can well imagine, to resume semi-invalidism."[13]

Complicating Sherry's frustrations about his inability to find work and his deteriorating romance with Rose were his fears about the possibility of atomic warfare (a subject to which he referred often in his poetry, fiction, and letters) and a bitter faction fight in the Fourth International. The fight had resulted in the formation of two rival organizations: the International Secretariat, led by Pablo, and the International Committee, led by Cannon's Socialist Workers party. The political issues involved in the dispute were complex. Essentially, the European Trotskyists under Pablo's influence (with whom Sherry was allied) had concluded that world Stalinism was moving into a period of tremendous crisis and that a new set of strategies and tactics was in order, including, in some cases, entry into mass Social Democratic and Communist parties. On the other hand, the Trotskyist groups allied with the Socialist Workers party argued that Pablo's analysis was in reality a capitulation to Stalinism that would lead to the liquidation of the Trotskyist movement as an independent revolutionary current. The immediate cause of the split was the expulsion of most of the members of the French Trotskyist group for refusing to implement the new orientation.

In New York Sherry paid a visit to Bert Cochran, leader of a group of former Socialist Workers party members who were thought to be sympathetic to Pablo's ideas, but he found Cochran totally uninterested in having international affiliations or even in talking about the matter.[14] To Haywood Sherry poured out his feelings of intense depression because, "after spending the better part of ten years in working for the formation, consolidation, and growth of the Fourth International . . . it is in a state of split and of danger, if not of dissolution, of practical impotence."[15]

All these factors combined in driving Sherry into a prolonged depression, and he recorded his experiences in an unpublished story called "Blackness of a White Night." In the closing pages of the manuscript, he explores his feelings about suicide:

> Financially, the way job-hunting was going, he'd soon end up a public charge: the only available jobs were in advertising, publicity, public relations, or in government propaganda agencies, and he'd put an honest bullet through his brain before he'd descend that low; or as a messenger, and he doubted he could even walk as much as the job would require. Politically, not only was the country in the grip of the worst reaction in history, but, what was far worse, did not seem even to want to fight it. . . .
>
> He was utterly and permanently alone, in that aloneness where ultimately all choices are made. He had had enough; he was finally defeated; he wanted out.
>
> But could he? His library and archives scattered in five places over

three continents; debts of honor that eventually must somehow be paid; not enough money on hand even to bury him; unfinished work; uncompleted promises. It would be a frightful mess, an intolerable nuisance to his friends, and he felt none of that retaliatory kind of bitterness that would have rendered such a thought pleasurable. He had not the right even to die. His despair deepened to utter desolation. . . .

There, in the medicine cabinet, was peace. He would not have to get up in staggering weakness the next morning to face the savorless burlesque of living, the empty treadmill of the day, the hopelessness of the future. His longing for death deepened till it became like a longing for a mother's breast, for a loved one's body.

The desire so mastered him that, like a sleepwalker, he got up. But the action itself brought back full consciousness, and the realization that it would be impermissible to escape until he had somehow managed to bring some order into his chaotic affairs. He sank to the bed's edge again, thinking miserably: I cannot, it would be dishonorable.[16]

Around this time Sherry prepared his will, which left instructions that "my body be cremated and that my ashes be cast upon the waters of the River Seine from the lower Quai Voltaire after the setting of the sun."[17]

By the fall of 1954 Sherry was convinced that there was no future for him in New York City. The love affair had been waning steadily and Virgil Thomson persuaded Sherry that he was no longer employable in journalism. Thomson had picked up some insight into Cold War hiring policies from his own job as music critic for the *Herald-Tribune*. According to Thomson, the *Herald-Tribune* had a principle of defending anyone already employed against "investigation"; but when hiring new people, it avoided taking on anyone whose political past might embarrass them. Thomson believed that this was probably the case on every newspaper in New York. He therefore suggested that Sherry chuck the whole idea of finding a "respectable" ordinary job, and, by hook or crook, return to his "real work," creative writing. Sherry wrote to Haywood that he and Thomson "had a talk about my odd situation, and his position seems to be that if the devil doesn't want my soul even if I am willing to sell it, then the hell with the devil—get back to work."[18]

By letter Sherry investigated places where he could live for less than the $350 a month necessary for survival in New York. He finally concluded that he could get by in Spain, near Malaga—and have the help of a maid—for only $150 a month. Sherry believed that he could raise the money by launching a new career as an independent editor or by serving as a translator for a group of clients. So in mid-October he undertook his last major literary job in New York to help raise funds for the move. It was the assignment of revising and preparing for rehearsal his own translation of the Varesco libretto for Mozart's *Idomeneo, Rè di Creta,* which the Juilliard Opera Company scheduled for performance on Mozart's birthday. *Idomeneo* premiered on 27 January 1955 at the Juilliard concert hall on Claremont Avenue; it continued for five performances. Sherry sailed out of New York on 17 February.

When Sherry wrote Tony Palmer that he now lived at "Calle del Poeta Salvador Rueda 48, Santa Fe de Los Boliches cerca de Fuengirola, Malaga, Spain," Palmer responded that, "as usual, you pick a place with a magnificently imposing address." Sherry then expressed his delight that the street was named after the Spanish poet Salvador Rueda and that "Los Boliches is the name for a certain kind of very illegal fishing-net, and indicates that the original inhabitants of this village were by the way of being rascals, which also seems to me highly suitable."[19]

To Goldstein he reported that his health was relatively stabilized, though he still tired easily. He described his life as "austere, sober, industrious, and lonely" and said that he was "reduced to borrowing against the poor remains of M's jewelry" shortly after he arrived.[20] In order to make his monthly budget, Sherry had promises of work from *Adventure* magazine (edited by Alden Norton, a childhood friend from Lynn) for $75 a month, Angel Records for $35 a month, and Intercultural Publications (edited by James Laughlin) for $200 a quarter.[21] By March, however, Angel Records had given him only $15 worth of work and *Adventure* came through with nothing at all. Worry about financial catastrophe, combined with his inability to work more than four hours a day, interfered with his completion of "The Mountain of Death." In May he confessed to Goldstein: "If I don't succeed, I don't know what I'll do: I have suffered so many defeats since 1948 that one more would be pretty near unbearable."[22]

This melancholy underside of Sherry's temperament during the Spanish period escaped the notice of some of the American artists and tourists who came to live in Santa Fe de Los Boliches or in nearby towns. The filmmaker Gunther von Fritsch recalled Sherry's "great sense of humor about himself" and his pleasure in telling anecdotes. One concerned a maid who gave birth after four months of employment and accused Sherry of being the father; another involved his being mistaken for Hermann Goering as he walked into an official building in Berlin a few years before.[23]

On the other hand, Pearl Kazin did recognize a tragic side to Sherry's situation. Saul Bellow had directed her to Sherry for assistance in settling in Spain. She knew that Sherry "had lived high on the hog when he worked for *Time* before and during the war" and believed that "he could never accustom himself to the fact that after he left *Time* he could acquire neither the money nor the perks that he had once taken so completely for granted." Furthermore, she believed that, by the time he came to Spain, he had become extremely embittered about his lack of

both literary esteem and general connection with the New York intel-
ligentsia. "He expressed great contempt for them and their world. . . .
things had gone so badly, the promise had fizzled out so thoroughly, and
he tried so hard to convince himself and his friends that he really *was* a
great writer, that someday the world would indeed see this, etc." She also
thought there was a certain pathos in the way that Sherry played up his
resemblance to Hemingway, "not only physically but as men of the
world, of radical politics, as womanizers and high-living heroes."[24]

Nevertheless, Sherry's writing in Spain was steadily productive even if
there were no significant breakthroughs. In June of 1955 he temporarily
stopped taking reserpine, his medication for high blood pressure, and
discovered that his "morale and energy" began "spurting upward at a
prodigious rate." He began to wonder if the "melancholia that drove me
nearly to suicide in New York" was largely produced by the medicine.[25]
Most of his free time was devoted to "The Mountain of Death," but he
also worked away on a number of poems that were published in *Western
Review*, *Arizona Quarterly*, and *Essence*. One of these, "Thoughts on
Approaching Fifty," had originally been drafted in Bolivia. It poignantly
expressed the motivations for his perseverance in literary work at this
late date, with public recognition so unlikely. The poem stated in part:

> I should be content if occasionally two lovers, reaching a
> certain line, raise their eyes from the book, and look at
> each other; or even perhaps put the book down; or
>
> if, two older men talking, one remembers a sentence and the other
>   nods,
> "Yes, that was well said," and they reflect a moment; or
>
> if a worker one night reading slaps the page and says: "Now there
>   was one
> that didn't moan about his soul, one who wouldn't run with the paid
>   pack,
> one who saw clear through to us and now."[26]

A general plan for his literary projects began to form in Sherry's mind.
He would first devote several months to revising "The Mountain of
Death"; then he would spend another few months reworking the stories
around the "Barclay Street" theme into a collection by that title; after
that he would complete a new collection of poetry; and finally, "if I have
not previously died or been caught by the boys in white with the butter-
fly nets," he would complete a half-finished anthology of his surrealist
pieces under the title "Alphabet in Disorder." "After which, I shall be free
to look around me, and either 1) find again a paying job, 2) start a new
book, or 3) blow my alleged brains out. If I get the four books done, I
don't care much which."[27]

Nevertheless, when rejection after rejection came in response to the partial manuscript of "The Mountain of Death," Sherry exploded in tantrums of frustration. He wrote to Haywood that it was the "apogee of the comic: that I, who cannot sell more than one piece a year of my own writing, should be earning my living by tidying up other people's is just too ridiculous. What a world!" He once thought that what he had to give humanity was "a quality like Chekhov's of pity-and-terror reduced to tenderness and satire; but it turns out that all they want out of me is spelling, punctuation, and the knack of turning out good narrative-hook leads. Excuse me while I go out and vomit on my rose bushes."[28]

The delicate balance achieved in Santa Fe de los Boliches was steadily undermined by the tenuous financial arrangements on which it was based and by the failure of Sherry's clients to come up with all the work they had promised. At one point Sherry served as the Spanish agent for picture stories for the horror-and-gore magazines that were replacing the old pulps; on another occasion he was the ghostwriter for the bullfighter César Girón, whose views about death and wounds were published in *Argosy* magazine.[29] At the end of the year, Sherry wrote to Palmer that financially it had been "the godamdest cliffhanger you ever saw." He said that "The Perils of Pauline" and "The Escapades of Elaine" were nothing compared to "The Money-Troubles of Mangan." But each time he had been "tied to the log and pushed into the sawmill, some job . . . arrived to save me in the nick of time."[30] In a letter to Haywood about the condition of his will, Sherry predicted that "I am sure of only one thing: I shall die in poverty, and good friends will have to rally around for the expense of disposing of the corpse."[31]

The situation in Santa Fe de Los Boliches hit rock bottom for Sherry by December of 1956. He was evicted from his house and what little cash he had was stolen by the maid. When a letter arrived from his old Harvard roommate Ralph Manheim, offering him a job translating Valéry if he could move to Paris, Sherry departed at once and settled in a small hotel.[32]

The Paris environment initially had a resuscitating effect on Sherry. With his literary interests rekindled by the Valéry project, he reread all of Shakespeare and Baudelaire, and cultivated a taste for the work of Michael Leiris. He asked Tony Palmer why he had ever left Paris: "It is only here that I am myself, that I am treated as myself, that I function as myself. And, lonely though I am, I still love about the place its quality of smelling of love the way that New York smells of money and Los Boliches smelled of poverty."[33] Such optimism did not correspond to Sherry's objective circumstances and was bound to be short-lived.

A more accurate indication of the state of Sherry's mind in the 1956–57 period is revealed in a letter he sent to Tony Palmer when he learned that Palmer's wife Marjorie had died and left him in a state of lonely despair similar to what Sherry had gone through in Bolivia:

Marjorie and Marguerita were cut out of the same stock, they were of that nowadays rarer and rarer race of women who are companions rather than rivals, partners rather than enemies, who, if they find men who are worth it, live their lives through love and become part of a team which without them would long since have careened off into some ditch. Gallant, courageous, unselfish—you took the words out of my mouth—and blessed furthermore with a sense of reality and a sense of humor that made them buoys in a stormy sea. I was thinking with wry laughter just before dinner that this is enough to make a man want to believe in heaven, just to be able to imagine the two of them meeting there with hoots of joy and sitting down to their rum-and-coca-colas to engage in hilarious and scandalous reminiscences about the complexities of running such an impossible pair as you and me and what fun they had doing it.[34]

This letter reflects Sherry's growing recognition that Marguerite's death had actually brought the best part of his life to a close. The modest literary and journalistic triumphs, the wide circle of social and cultural associations, the domestic stability and harmony he had once known were all decidedly behind him. His four remaining years would be a struggle against the current in a strange world in which he had no place as an artist and a literary personality. The only familiar terrain, the only line of continuity from past to present to future, was his commitment to socialism, which now reemerged as the stable center of his existence.

Political responsibilities dominated the final phase of Sherry's life, from the spring of 1956 to the spring of 1961. The central event causing his return to revolutionary activity on a full-time basis, after a hiatus of nearly eight years, was the appearance of a wave of oppositional movements inside the Soviet bloc countries. Sherry believed that the character of these struggles, which aimed at democratizing the political structure as opposed to returning the economic relations to capitalism, confirmed the earlier Trotskyist analysis and prognosis for the Soviet Union. In the early 1930s, Trotsky and his disciples viewed the Stalin regime as a contradictory hybrid between a postcapitalist economic order and a bureaucratic political system; they predicted that the system would eventually explode in a mass "political revolution" (as distinguished from a "social revolution") very much like the ones that Sherry saw beginning in Eastern Europe.

The oppositional movements actually began with an uprising of East German workers in 1953. A year later, in New York City, Sherry had debated their character and significance with Hannah Arendt. According to Sherry, Arendt held that the 1953 Berlin events were nothing but a "Stalinist provocation"; that the USSR would continue on as it had under Stalin, without significant modifications; and that the view of change coming because of mass pressure from below was "pure wishful thinking, with no connection with *Realpolitik*."[35] Sherry, to the contrary, felt that his political perspective was vindicated and that he was living in a whole new era of possibilities for revolutionary activity when, on 28 June 1956, the workers of Poznan, Poland, went out on a general strike that grew into an uprising, then students and intellectuals in Hungary began a series of demonstrations on 22 October 1956 that also touched off a major revolt. When he was in Paris in the early months of 1956, Sherry studied *Le Monde* each day for news and details of the events that were precipitating the Polish and Hungarian upheavals. In May he wrote to Joshua Epstein that he might have to abandon writing and "get back into it." This course seemed more acceptable to him now because "the tide has turned and I am positively zooming up from the discouragement I felt in the year of 1954 in New York (the worst, I think, since 1939): I may not last to see it, but at last history's back on the rails again."[36]

Sherry even saw a special political significance in the appearance of one of his Bolivian stories in the summer 1956 issue of *Arizona Quarterly*. Entitled "Impeccable Is Perhaps Too Strong a Word," the story depicted the reprehensible role of a Latin American liberal whose reformist politics leads him into a situation of betraying mine workers during a prerevolutionary situation. He wrote to Epstein that he was glad to hear that he liked the story. "I hope that will hold the cowardly liberals a while till I can think of a way to hit them again from my Bolshevik point of view, the bastards." With "deStalinization on the gallop," he wished he had time to characterize "these obedient time-servers in another story with the implication that they won't get out of it this easy, or indeed by any way short of a Leninist political revolution to throw them out into the dust-bin of history and bring the real revolutionaries back."[37]

Throughout the rest of 1956, Sherry's health remained stable, although there were several bouts with pneumonia. Further examinations confirmed that Sherry had a damaged kidney (a result of the 1952 infection in Bolivia), which, when inflamed, triggered off potentially quite serious cardiovascular problems. Financially, Sherry continued translating and editing for his various clients, and received additional pay for the Valéry translation in progress. In March 1957, however, he was asked to carry out an assignment for the Fourth International in the United States during April and May. His main responsibility was to attempt to open negotiations for a possible reunification of the International Committee, led by the Socialist Workers party, and the International Secretariat, based in Paris. In addition, he was to consult the Trotsky papers at Harvard University and try to gain permission to publish the correspondence between Trotsky and Lenin that existed in the closed section of the archives at the Houghton Library.

With free passage arranged by Karl Goldstein's travel agency, Sherry arrived in New York City on 29 March 1957. He took a small room at the Chelsea Hotel, where he cooked off a burner with utensils borrowed from Virgil Thomson. Soon he learned that Natalia Trotsky had also arrived in the United States without passport or visa by special permission of the State Department. The American Trotskyists feared that she might be pressured or misled into testifying before one of the U.S. government witch-hunt committees.[38]

A few days later, Sherry was able to visit with Trotsky's widow for an hour and a half at the home of George Weissman. He transmitted the information that Pierre Frank had recently obtained from a man who had shared a cell with her son Serge in the Soviet Union; however, he was careful not to mention that this was shortly before Serge was executed. When he turned to the subject of the special circumstances under which she had come to the United States, he was pleasantly surprised to hear her say that *"reflection faite,* she was going to refuse to appear before any investigating committee whatsoever." Sherry wrote to Pablo that "she is simply breaking her side of the agreement in a characteristically feminine manner."[39]

The trip to Harvard was far less successful. The librarians appeared to be rude and uncooperative, Sherry's temper flared, and he was stricken by his kidney ailment, which forced him to rush back to New York for hospitalization under the care of Dr. Meilman. When he was once more able to resume negotiations with the American Trotskyists, he found himself confronted with repeated insinuations that he was not "sufficiently official" to represent the International Secretariat in unity negotiations.[40]

It soon became clear to Sherry that nothing significant could be accomplished in New York without first flying to California to meet with James P. Cannon, who was living in Los Angeles. He wrote to Pablo that this was an encounter that he regarded with trepidation. "I shall not attempt to conceal that I feel a considerable nervousness about the coming talks with him. His is so subjective a character, he is so empirical and unpredictable, that it is impossible to foresee what his attitude will be." Sherry feared that Cannon might, "with a personalist resentment, either refuse any settlement or pose conditions which are utterly unacceptable."[41] As expected, the meeting with Cannon—which resulted only in an exchange of position papers on conditions for reunification—was heated and upsetting. He later wrote Pablo about the whole visit: "If Marxism had a heaven, I should, I think, be in line for a sainthood for the way I kept my temper; but even so, I was 'counting to 10' so much that I reached higher mathematical levels."[42]

Sherry returned to Paris toward the end of May and found himself in an impossible financial situation. He wrote to Tony Palmer that a quarrel over style had terminated the Valéry translation; that another book tha was to produce $2500 for translating had been unexpectedly cut down to a length where he would make a total of $1400; that a second book under negotiation had been canceled; that within the fortnight he would be destitute and without any job to earn money. He had written everywhere for more work, but so far there was nothing at all. "As my 53rd birthday approaches and I find myself still on what Fred Allen termed the treadmill to oblivion, I am determined nevertheless to give it two years more and see if I cannot somehow manage my life so that I can work [write]." If this still proved impossible two years later, "then I think I'll call it a lifetime and to hell with it; but I still haven't lost hope."[43]

With no recognition for his literary efforts in the foreseeable future, Sherry increasingly felt that the political commitments that had guided him were the only source of solace in trying to evaluate the meaning of his life. Just a few weeks before his birthday he told Charles Haywood that if he had died in 1953, it would have been with much secret bitterness and a certain sense of defeat, because the current was still running against his political movement. But now, in 1957, "I could die easy, because I can see . . . the possibility of the beginnings of socialism." In answer to Haywood's question about what socialism had done "for" Sherry, as well as what it had done "to" him, Sherry responded:

"For me," it has given me a guidance and a purpose far beyond any personal one that I might have conceived, save poetry itself. "To me," yes, Chas, I know what you're getting at—it has made me pay, and pay dear. Not in terms of the lush times of using journalism as a cover-up and eating high-off-the hog; do you really think I'm the kind of man who could have stomached going on in Time, Inc. to— where would I be today? some sort of $25,000-a-year neurotic whom it would take one psychoanalyst, one vintner, and two secretaries to keep from jumping out the window? No, but in my present situation, where, escaped from death and eager to work again, I am still viewed by the people who could throw me little jobs that would make me say $3500 a year in three or four months working time as a "controversial" figure, not to be risked. Yes, Chas, that is one of the things Marxism has done to me; but I won't change one opinion one iota because of it. No USIA jobs, eh? No UNESCO nonsense. I know what I consider dishonorable work; and I have refused much of it. They all know now, and no longer offer it.

In trying to evaluate his present situation, he agreed with Haywood that it was important that he had finally emerged "out of that nightmarish swamp of 1954 in New York City and on to dry land," but his main interest in living was not to be simply a person, but also a producer. And the older he grew, the more he felt this to be true. He conjectured that "on an actuarial basis, I have perhaps twelve years left," and that could "theoretically" mean the production of twelve books. But "as things go these days, it does not mean even two. If I believed that my life would continue in its present form for the rest of it, I should, I assure you, blow out my tragically unutilized brains tonight." It was only because he believed that he could "beat the sons-of-bitches, that I can somehow find a way to keep them from castrating me, that I can wangle things around so that there is some time for me to do some honest work, that I go obstinately on."[44]

Hope for a reprieve from literary isolation came a few months later when James Laughlin, director of New Directions publishing company, passed through Paris on his way to Burma from the United States. He and Sherry dined together in order to discuss the translating and editing that Sherry was doing for the company. Sherry raised the possibility of New Directions publishing a collection of some twenty-five poems he had almost completed. Laughlin indicated that he would be interested when the financial situation of the company permitted, so in his spare time Sherry began to assemble the contents under the title "Interim Report."

However, Sherry's central concerns during the summer of 1957 were political. He wrote Joshua Epstein in late July that he was being considered for several new assignments by the Fourth International, including a secret mission to Poland to meet with dissidents who might be interested in Trotskyism. "There is conceivably a small amount of risk involved, but what the hell: I should expect to run it, I who have, after all, been in this business seriously and professionally for twenty years, old boy, not just prattling about it like dear Hannah [Arendt] for good pay." He declared that "we are heading toward the political (not social, not restorationist) revolution in the Soviet Union and its orbit" that he and his friends had long been stating to be historically inevitable. The first acts had already occurred, and "though there will be set-backs (and bloody and dreadful ones, as the October events in Hungary proved), the historical process here is irreversible. Stalinism, and bureaucratism in general, are doomed; and the restoration of Bolshevik democracy is again on the order of the day."[45]

The Polish trip was canceled when the Fourth International decided to assign Sherry to assist the Algerian rebels of the National Liberation Front (FLN) in their attempt to build a base of support in France for the Algerian revolutionary movement. Sherry reported to Epstein late in August that he was getting increasingly busy, "this time on something where I'm really sticking my neck out, so you can now justifiably feel toward me the worry you were wasting in connection with my Polish trip." The danger, he said, "makes me feel good, and alive."[46] Within a few weeks, Sherry had moved out of Paris and had settled alone in a house in Orne, deep in Normandy. He was accompanied by a Gestetner Roneo machine, which he ran only at night so as not to arouse suspi-

cion. His primary task was to produce literature for the resistance move-
ment, which he then delivered to Paris in secret assignations with the
Algerians. He also studied the political character of the revolution and
published a sharp attack on the analysis of events by the American
Trotskyist Shane Mage.

"The Truth about the Algerian Revolution" (1958) was written in
unusually vigorous and eloquent language for this sort of polemic and
was essentially a defense of the FLN against Mage's charge that it was
simply for "blind terrorism." Mage claimed that the FLN constituted the
"right wing" of the national liberation movement, in contrast to the
National Algerian Movement (MNA). Marshalling facts from all sorts of
sources, including his own personal contacts with the Algerian rebels,
Mangan argued that Mage had more or less reversed the roles of the two
organizations. In addition, he used his knowledge of the Spanish civil
war to sharply contrast the economic and political situations in the two
countries for the purpose of demonstrating the need for an appropriately
adjusted revolutionary strategy in Algeria. He conceded that "it is true
that the FLN leadership as a whole cannot be said to work consciously
for a socialist Algeria. But by developing the mass uprising more and
more broadly, by preparing and putting into effect regionally the general
arming of the whole population, it is objectively preparing the socialist
Algeria and socialist Middle East of tomorrow. It deserves unconditional
support in its fight against imperialism, and friendly criticism in working
out its politics."

The dispute has some significance for the kinds of issues that would
preoccupy radicals in the 1960s and 1970s; Mangan's approach shows
that he would have been a staunch supporter of national liberation and
anti-imperialist struggles in the rest of Africa, Latin America, and Asia.
He felt that Mage's interpretation of the MNA as the "proletarian" wing
of the revolution and the FLN as the "bourgeois" wing was based on a
sectarian view that the colonial people were unable to win victory for
themselves and must first await a revolutionary uprising by the French
working class (a view held also by Messali, leader of the MNA). To this
Mangan responded:

> Such theories are wrong in principle and unproved and irresponsible
> in practice. It is true that the proletarian vanguard in a national-
> liberation movement of a colonial country must be internationalist
> in theory and action, that it must call on the oppressed people of its
> own country not to identify the rulers of the metropolitan country
> with the exploited toilers of that country. It is also true that the
> victory of the colonial revolution will be the easier and quicker, the
> more energetically the proletariat of the metropolitan country joins
> in the fight against imperialism. But it is absolutely wrong that the

armed uprising or the revolution of the oppressed people must be subordinated in any way to the "favorable time table" for revolution . . . in the metropolitan country. On the contrary, the revolutionaries of the colonial country must audaciously forge ahead, conscious of the fact that by the blows they are striking against imperialism, *they are preparing* the revolutionary upsurge in the metropolitan country.[47]

The success of Sherry's Algerian work renewed his enthusiasm for political activities. When the Fifth World Congress of the Fourth International was held that fall, he described it to Goldstein as "the most heart-warming one I have ever attended in these now twenty years." Sherry, in fact, agreed to assume a position on the leading body of the International, the International Executive Committee, and to take charge of the publication of an English-language theoretical journal called *Fourth International*. This work was to be done under the pseudonym he had been using for the past several years, Patrick O'Daniel (he was called "Patrice" in France), and a major objective was to use the publication to assist the process of reunification with Trotskyists in the United States and other English-speaking countries. He told Goldstein that the situation in the United States was now the most critical one of all, that he could not stand idle at such a juncture. "So I have come back fully into activity, and shall help guide what now looks like one of the severest struggles we have ever faced. Fortunately, my health is now restored enough so that I can envisage such activity; and I must say that this old firehorse, smelling smoke, is pawing the ground and raring to go."[48]

Unfortunately, the work turned out to be more than Sherry had anticipated. The magazine was over a hundred thousand words, much of which Sherry had to translate and revise by himself; he also had to write certain portions and read proof on everything three consecutive times. He wrote to Haywood that "not since that awful spell in Zurich," in the winter of 1949–50, had he faced "such an uninterrupted period of over-work."[49] To Epstein he acknowledged that all his personal writing had come to a halt. The last piece to see publication was "Reminiscence from a Hilltop," another in Sherry's series of surrealist-influenced stories. Unaware that this work, as well as his earlier experimental piece "Spot Dance," was much admired by *Black Mountain Review* editor Robert Creeley and the poet Denise Levertov, he wrote to Epstein that "anything I've done will be duly recognized once the world has gone on to a more civilized stage."[50] He saw the real trouble as the lack of time to do all the other projects piled up before him. His life was now divided between "silly jobs to keep a roof over my head and bread and wine on my table, and slogging work for the movement. The four books near completion will probably never be completed." He said that he had become personally reconciled to this ridiculous situation as far as it concerned him, "but it makes me all the more furious and militant in working for a world where that can no longer happen to people like me."[51] Upon learning that one of his old Harvard friends had referred to a poem of his in a recent book review, he commented ironically to Haywood that "it is a little grotesque but true that probably more people saw Dudley Fitts' graceful reference to me in the *New York Times Book Review* than ever see my own work."[52]

Sherry and Fitts resumed their correspondence shortly after the *Times* notice. Fitts expressed incredulity at the degree of obscurity into which Sherry had fallen and his difficulties in finding a publisher for "The Mountain of Death": "I should think that a novel from you would be major news."[53] When Fitts went on to complain that, compared to Sherry's life, his own as a teacher at Phillips Academy was dull, Sherry responded that there was an irony of almost a historic nature in the fact that Fitts seemed to envy his life and he certainly envied Fitts'. "A contemporary playwright would soon set that right by thinking up some gimmick that would enable us to exchange places for a year, with results that would doubtless be, according to his special bent, broadly hilarious or sourly tragic."[54]

The exchange of letters with Fitts stirred old memories of Jack Wheelwright, and Sherry began to wonder if there might be anything he could do to help preserve his work. He soon found himself writing a letter to Charles Lynch, a fellow classicist from Harvard to whom *Cinderella Married* had been dedicated. Lynch later became a professor at Brown; he and Sherry had quarreled over politics, and Sherry satirized Lynch in his poem "Vincent Sullivan," which was published in 1949 in *New Directions 11*. Now he asked Lynch if he ever saw S. Foster Damon, who was also a teacher at Brown. He explained that a shadowy project was far in the back of his mind. In Damon's hands, "or legally I suppose in the hands of his poor mad wife, are the manuscripts of Jack Wheelwright, who, as the years pass, and there are more and more surer bases for comparison, seems to me to be one of the best poets of my generation." After he had caught up on his own long postponed work, Sherry thought he might try to get a foundation grant to spend a year digging a few books out of Wheelwright's rich disordered archives. "Don't say as much flatly to Foster, because I understand he is rather odd on the subject; but I should appreciate knowing if he still has for me a certain esteem which he used to have. That would be the first step."[55]

Still, Sherry's commitment to the magazine *Fourth International* was too strong for him to put any other work ahead of it, and in June it was decided that the next issue would be printed in Amsterdam. Sherry was required to travel there for at least two weeks before each issue to see it through the press. In the meantime, a fight had erupted among leaders of the International Secretariat of the Fourth International over how to respond to the reaction that was expected to accompany de Gaulle's ascension to power. Pablo was anxious to move the bureau (the working committee of the secretariat) to Amsterdam at once. In Paris this body had consisted of Pablo, Ernest Mandel, and Pierre Frank; in Amsterdam it would consist of Pablo and Sal Santen, and there were suspicions on the part of Mandel and Frank that this might be a maneuver to give Pablo more influence. Sherry, for his part, preferred Rome, and was even sent there to examine the appropriateness of the location's facilities. The conflicts grew bitter and Sherry fell into sharp disagreement with Pablo for the first time. Harsh words were exchanged and their friendship never recovered from it.[56]

By fall, however, Pablo had won out. The bureau was established in Amsterdam with Pablo and Santen, and they were joined for monthly meetings by Mandel, Frank, Sherry, Livio Maitan from Italy, Georg Jungclas from Germany, and, some time later, the Argentine Adolpho Gilly. Sherry's responsibilities were concentrated mainly on the magazine, but he increasingly found that the entire burden of publication was exclusively his own. In the latter part of 1958, he discovered that he had to spend seven solid weeks in Amsterdam in order to get it out. Afterward he wrote Goldstein that the issue was finally finished, "and I am damn near finished, too, as a result." Getting the magazine out had produced such a crisis in his personal affairs that he "got up on . . . hind legs at last" and formally refused any further duties beyond the all-too-numerous ones he had already accepted. "I have protested before, but always given way before the obvious emergency need for the new work to be done. But this time I would not give an inch, and I finally forced my position to be accepted, without, I think, losing any respect."[57]

Sherry felt himself at a special disadvantage because he did not work regular hours at an office or factory; he consequently appeared to be always available for political work. Unable to keep up with the editorial jobs from his dwindling number of clients—let alone seek out new clients—Sherry found himself "eating damn little, and that little on credit with the various shopkeepers."[58] To Emilio von Westphalen, a Peruvian poet and onetime Trotskyist now living in Rome, Sherry complained that the magazine and political responsibilities had encroached on all his time: "Like a man jumping off a fast-moving train, I have been running very fast just to keep from falling on my face."[59]

The only writing he was able to do in these months was an editorial about Japanese labor, "News Notes" for the magazine, and a book review of Pasternak's Dr. Zhivago for the magazine. The latter praised Pasternak as a lyric poet and cited a number of lyrically descriptive passages in the novel. But in terms that were becoming all-too-familiar in Mangan's bitter view of popular books, he expressed extreme disappointment in its content: "Dr. Zhivago turns out to be just one more novel of petty-bourgeois intellectual disillusion with life in the world as it is, like hundreds published in the West since Mr. T. S. Eliot opened the period with his tone-setting poem, *The Waste Land*."⁶⁰ He insisted to Haywood that "there's plenty of stuff in my mind that I would like to get out if ever again I had some *continuous and uninterrupted* free time for it."⁶¹ But what spare moments he did have were spent servicing his diminishing number of clients. To von Westphalen he reported: "While I write translations of Marxist theory with my right hand, I am giving the final editorial touches with my left to the manuscript of the New Directions [edition of] Gottfried Benn."⁶² One of his major clients, Elizabeth Mann Borgesse, a daughter of Thomas Mann, thought Sherry was a first-rate editor and painstakingly punctual and reliable worker. She remarked that "it is very rare to find such an extraordinarily gifted editor: most people that gifted would not bother with such jobs."⁶³

By the fall of 1959, the strain finally proved too much for Sherry. In Holland he spent fifteen days straight, working from 7:30 A. M. to 1:30 A. M., putting out the magazine. When he arrived back in Dampierre, he was in a state of prostration, but expected that he would revive after a few days of bed rest, which was his usual practice. Instead he sank deeper and deeper into exhaustion. Finally, even though he had no money, he asked the garageman to drive him to the American hospital. He started to explain his condition to the doctors, but they would not listen. They put him into a wheel chair, rolled him over to a bed, and placed him under an oxygen tent, where he lay unconscious for three days. By the time he was able to talk, the doctor told him that his exhaustion had led to heart failure and that he had got there just about in time. His heart was permanently injured, and he was ordered to be on digitalis for the rest of his life. Three systems were involved: the cardiovascular, the respiratory, and the renal (his kidneys were damaged by insufficient blood from the weakened heart). "I will have to let the magazine drop entirely for a while," he wrote Goldstein. "The friends will just have to organize it some other way. I hope to gawd they can, because I was proud of it, and I shall feel miserable if the next issue is both late and wretchedly produced. But I just can't do any more." He knew that overwork on the magazine had brought him where he was. "I am perfectly willing to die for the Revolution, but not, if possible, in such a stupid and unnecessary way."⁶⁴

In such desperate straits, Sherry was fortunate that a number of his friends responded with quick and generous actions. He had written Virgil Thomson shortly after his hospitalization that the only thing for which he now lived was the opportunity to write again:

> When I and my little oxygen tent were wandering around in outer darkness those first two or three days, looking back down on the earth in pardon and comprehension . . . I told Old Mr. Thanatos to

go away till the next time and made the effort to keep breathing deeply, as the occasional apparition of the frightened face of the special night nurse at the tent opening kept urging me to do . . . [because of the] hope, the dream, that sometime, somehow, I'd still have a year free from both hacking and political overwork to finish the books that are in process and to write the new poems that sometimes keep trying to break through into the open and have to be suppressed because, once I yielded to them, I'd never be able to force myself back to hacking. At the Quai Voltaire, you were one day expressing a well-founded recognition of what *larus* and *Pagany* represented as against *The Hound and Horn*, and also what was to me a very heartening recognition also of the level of my contribution thereto. But I am still the same person, the same poet. And with not very much time left to prove it.[65]

Thomson, moved by his friend's dilemma, used his influence to obtain him a small fellowship from the National Institute for Arts and Letters special fund.

Additionally, Richard de Rochemont obtained support for Sherry from the special fund of the Overseas Press Club; Greville Droescher, the sister of Sherry's first wife, urged him to come down to Spain and occupy her house on the Costa Brava during the winter months of 1960. Sherry accepted. Then Jacques Privas, a French Trotskyist leader with whom Sherry had become intimate in the late 1940s, repaid Sherry's friendship with extreme devotion. Privas stayed with Sherry at Dampierre during the week of preparation, when Sherry was nearly helpless, and drove him by easy stages to Spain.

Once settled in, Sherry discovered that, seated at his desk, he could do up to six and even seven hours work a day with a clear mind; but all physical activity was exhausting. Even walking required stopping every few hundred paces to hang onto something and catch his breath; bus travel was particularly tiring. Stairs had to be taken four at a time with a rest stop. There could be no bending, lifting, or carrying. His political duties were cut to the minimum. Thus he wrote Palmer: "As for Utopia Inc., I put in some 30 hours of translation and editing for the outcoming issue of the magazine, so that my conscience is clear without my health being wrecked." This reminded Sherry of a joke. The other morning, while shaving with rather black thoughts, he was meditating "on the way suicide is excluded because it would mean such an intolerable burden of tidying up for friends that I should be considered an inconsiderate and cowardly s.o.b." At that moment he suddenly realized that "there *was* a form of suicide that would leave one's memory honored, namely, to accept all the work that the little friends would be glad to give me to do. I laughed so hard that I cut myself."[66]

The months on the Costa Brava were a gentle reprieve, but before Sherry had a chance to make any headway on restructuring "The Mountain of Death," his conscience began to bother him about the *Fourth International* and his pledge to oversee its functioning in order to facilitate a reunification of the world Trotskyist movement. After learning that the latest issue was a month late and in total disarray, he dropped his paid work, moved north, and reestablished his base in Dampierre. His apartment there, which he liked to call his "rural slum tenement," had been in his possession since the 1940s. Dampierre was a small town southwest of Paris and his rooms on the first floor of a squat grey house were comfortable enough for him to host visitors. Among those who came to see him were Else, a German woman he had met in England during the war, and Kate Kurzke, his ex-wife, who was now separated from her second husband and working as a school-teacher in London.

Then, even Sherry's few moments of tranquillity at Dampierre were interrupted when it was learned that Pablo and Sal Santen had been arrested in Amsterdam in the spring of 1960. They were charged with manufacturing false identity papers and false banknotes for members of the Algerian FLN. Sherry wrote to Haywood in early July that "I am having to get out the old magazine single-handed again" and that "my tasks have been redoubled as a result." In order to protect the security of the organization, the leaders of the Fourth International also decided that its bureau should be moved to Rome and that larger monthly meetings should be held in Milan. The Italian location was quite satisfactory to Sherry because he knew that the climate would be beneficial to his health.[67] With two hundred dollars that the Italian Trotskyist leader Livio Maitan had raised from political sympathizers, Sherry managed to make the move. He drove his car over the Mont Centis Pass so that the customs inspectors would not examine the materials he was transporting, and in Florence he briefly visited Joshua Epstein, who was there examining paintings by Giotto.

Once in Rome, he found a first-story cellar on the Aventine, which solved the problem he had climbing stairs. He wrote to Tony Palmer that he had managed to land in Rome, "but like a shipwrecked mariner." Now he was faced, from the twenty-first of December until the end of January, with a period in which he could earn nothing, "what with the World Congress and the (for me, fortunately, last) issue of the magazine that must be brought out immediately thereafter." After that, the situation looked better. First of all, at that congress, Sherry intended "at last to lay down the crushing (and once nearly killing) burden I accepted at the last one, and retire from activity. I have done enough: financial catastrophe, prevention of my own work, and once nearly death. It is time I be released to pick up the pieces of my somewhat shattered life; and the friends are finally beginning to see that they must accept the fact."[68] Tony Palmer had made a modest comeback with several small books of poetry; Charles Haywood continued to publish his novels and histories; and Joshua Epstein had found a new artistic identity as a painter late in life. Sherry still hoped that he could join their company.

His plan for the last weeks of December 1960 was to wholly occupy himself with preparations for the Sixth World Congress. Then, for a few weeks after the congress, he expected to be busy preparing an issue of *Fourth International* featuring congress documents, a task that would be less laborious than usual because he already would have translated about half its contents. Then he anticipated a "new life," in which he would no longer be considered a full-time political functionary, but would restrict his political contributions to work on translations and editing for thirty to forty hours a month.

But the plan did not go as anticipated. In early December the weather in Rome turned very foul with constant rain. Sherry found himself forced to be out in it more than he had anticipated and could detect the bad effects this was having on his respiration. He grew more and more tired, but the work for the congress did not let up. December twenty-third was a particularly exhausting day for him. He was out in the rain and the crowds from dawn until dusk, running errands for the Fourth International. He finally got to bed at 1:00 A. M., but had to rise at 5:00 A. M. on the morning of 24 December to take a plane to Dusseldorf for the congress. As a result of some crossed signals, he found himself alone in the city in an unheated hotel, with no food, for about twenty-eight hours. At 8:00 P. M. on Christmas Day he was picked up by a car, but it dropped him off over three hundred yards from the hostel where the Congress was to be held. When he finished walking the three hundred yards, he was blue in the face and could scarcely speak. Two doctors among the delegates consulted, sent Sherry to bed, and appealed to the secretariat. The next morning at dawn he was protestingly removed on a stretcher to an ambulance and transported to a hospital, where he remained for the rest of the congress. Then he was driven in a heated car to the airport, taken by wheelchair to the plane, given oxygen on the plane, and flown back to Rome in the company of Livio Maitan. The diagnosis was pneumonia and Sherry was confined to his bed for the month of January. He managed to get the World Congress issue of *Fourth International* completed, but his own finances were in the worst state they had ever been.[69]

Sherry sent out emergency calls for work of any kind. Virgil Thomson arranged for him to get a small fee for translating a few poems, and Sherry wrote Thomson about the desperation with which he awaited their arrival. "Here it is mid-February, and I have not yet received the French text and music for the little translation you asked me to make for

you. . . . all three of my remaining clients have dried up on work simul-
taneously. Very awkward. I'm on a bread and wine diet."[70] As the winter
months dragged on, there was barely enough work to sustain him even
on that level. For New Directions he began three projects for which
he earned about $2.50 an hour: a translation of Chromanski's *Jealousy
and Medicine*, a revision of Danielou's translation of "Slipadikaram,"
and a revision of P. Lal's translation of Sanskrit plays. A scholarly journal
called *Vita Italiana* hired him to do translations at $1.25 an hour on a
monthly basis, but the materials never seemed to arrive on time. Finally,
on 23 May, Sherry wrote to William Rothenberg of the Carnegie Fund for
Authors, virtually begging for a financial subsidy. He explained that in
January a grave pneumonia had required a convalescence that left him in
an absolutely desperate financial situation. "It is only realistic to sup-
pose that I do not have very many years before me, and I should like,
in those that remain, at least to complete the two present works-in-
progress ["The Mountain of Death" and "Barclay Street"], as well as, if
possible, two others—one of poetry ["Interim Report"] and the other of
stories ["Alphabet in Disorder"]."[71]

On 31 May Sherry finished writing his last poem. It was called "What
Are We Listening To?" and contrasts two lovers sitting in Central Park,
listening to a performance of Beethoven's *Emperor* piano concerto. The
woman is wholly caught up in the music, while the man is distracted
by planes in the night sky, which remind him of the threat of nuclear
warfare:

1
Smack in the middle of the "Emperor," under the stars,
that plane shrieked over, deafening, and you grimaced,
you and three thousand others, till it passed,
and then forgot it utterly. While I,
my head rolled back, watched it rejoin far squadrons
(whose gibbering colored lights, in night manoeuvres,
mocked searchlights' fingers groping after them),
and pictured radars' sweeps and nikes following points,
H-bombs air-borne each hour of the day and night,
and others sheathed in lethal penciled length
on earth, below the sea, at any madman's mercy;
and turned my gaze again to watch you—rapt,
unheeding, as if the world were only music.

2
Or on that other evening when you'd grown
impatient with me for the time I'd spent
in working on the protest, and in fear of talk
that might again grow bitter, we had fled

the issue, and we were recapturing
our menaced sense of love by listening
together, sprawled on a couch, with just
our fingers touching, to the one-eleventh,
while through them love flowed back, under the spell,
and outside there were passingly sirens
(this time, just fire-sirens, but sirens still
sufficient to recall the final ones to come)
and passingly also my thought: there is
so little time to head them off, to save
all time for love and music; but when I rolled
my head upon the pillow toward you, you
were listening as if there were forever.

3
If we would still hear music, we
must also listen to the knell
tolling for music and for love.
Will it be only when I see your loved flesh turn
from red to black, and my already black
flesh is crackling, and we realize
that we had missed the epicentre, so we were not
blissfully vaporized, but must go on,
and, it being of course the moment for
the supreme kiss, will it only be when
our four lips fall together to the floor
that we shall wonder: did we always,
always in every way, with all our strength,
fight to prevent this moment, or,
were we, like all your clever friends,
just listening to Beethoven?[72]

And so Stendhal's "pistol-shot in the middle of a concert" comes full circle. Mangan's poem textualizes the dialectic of politics and art, not as irreconcilable elements but as tensions demanding a proper relationship. The complexity of this observation is enriched by the choice of the first piece of music, the *Emperor* concerto; there has been some debate about whether and in what ways this work may have been influenced by Beethoven's onetime sympathy for the French Revolution. Thus art, on one level, may have political implications, while the poem, on another level, aestheticizes the political consciousness and convictions of the poet.

Another ironic interconnection of politics and art occurs as well: deafening is the shriek of the intruding airplane, deafening the pounding of Beethoven's chords in the middle of this concerto. Even the composer became deaf. The doubleness that ran throughout Mangan's life and work—Sherry Mangan and Terence Phelan, journalist and revolutionary, poet and Bolshevik, lover and scientific socialist—appears in the poem as well. Finally, music also reappears as a literary motif, as it does in his earlier "Etudes for the Eleventh Finger" (see discussion in the Conclusion) and other writing. In this instance, music is appropriate for the elegant language with which Mangan seeks to soothe his troubled emotions; but music is also the least referential of all art forms, an effective symbol for the realm of the imagination through which he aspires to transcend his life-threatening struggle to form meaning out of obdurate reality.

On 13 June Sherry wrote Thomson that he was "in the worst yet of financial crises, due to a month's delay in receiving the rest of translations of the next issue of *Vita Italiana*. Bread and wine this week; bread and water next." On 17 June he added:"I am well, but very depressed. The bread-and-butter *Vita Italiana* translations have been postponed till 1 July . . . so that the godam fuckin' roof is going to fall in about the 12th of July. Still, my stubborness remains; and I suspect that my 'last words' will be simply 'doch doch.'"[73] On 19 June James Laughlin heard that Sherry was in deep financial trouble and mailed him a check for fifty dollars. On Thursday, 22 June, Emilio von Westphalen stopped by Sherry's apartment to ask him to dinner on the twenty-seventh. Sherry appeared to be in a good mood and not ill, but later von Westphalen learned from Sherry's part-time maid that he had already begun to feel the symptoms of some sort of attack.

On Saturday, 24 June, the maid stayed with Sherry until 11:00 A.M. An unidentified person arrived for an appointment with Sherry, but there was no answer to the doorbell ringing and knocking. The neighbors were alarmed and finally the police were called. When the door was broken in, Sherry was found dead in bed with a calm face.

That same night his body was taken to the mortuary and his apartment sealed off. There was a great deal of curiosity on the part of the police about all the boxes of papers piled up in Sherry's rooms. A witness recalls that the police kept wondering, "Had they found a poet or a dangerous subversive?"[74] Soon it was discovered that Sherry did not have sufficient funds in his possession to pay for his own burial; in fact, he had been borrowing money from the maid to live on during the preceding weeks and owed her approximately fifty dollars. A cable was sent to Joshua Epstein in the United States that he must send several hundred dollars or Sherry would be buried in a common grave. Epstein wired back enough cash for Sherry to be buried in the so-called Protestant Cemetery, which is also the location of the graves of other revolutionaries and writers—Antonio Gramsci, Antonio Labriola, John Keats, and Ronald Firbank.

In Amsterdam the trial of Pablo and Sal Santen was in progress and news of Sherry's death was suppressed so as not to upset the defendants.

The Trotskyists sent a wreath of red roses to the grave site, but only Livio Maitan, the von Westphalens, and one or two other people were present for the burial. Trotskyist newspapers in Europe and the United States carried notices of Sherry's death some time later. The only mention of it in the public media was a news report that came over a Boston radio station and a tiny obituary in his hometown newspaper in Lynn.

When Kate Kurzke learned of Sherry's death, she immediately wrote Charles Haywood, who handled his legal matters. She was anxious that something be done to preserve Sherry's books, paintings, furniture, manuscripts, and other possessions. She reflected that "indeed Sherry was a wonderful person." She thought he should have lived in the eighteenth century, "when conversations and letter-writing were truly valued. It always seems so unfair that people with exceptional gifts and vitality go so soon while dull, expendable people live on and on." She recalled that his mind was keen to the last, "but physically he turned prematurely into a decrepit old man. What he dreaded most was having a stroke and not being able to keep up his independent existence as there was no one to take care of him. Anyway, that never happened."[75]

It turned out that there was nothing but debts in the entire Mangan estate, debts amounting to thousands of dollars. Haywood soon recognized that he would not be able to preserve anything of Sherry's except the papers, which Tony Palmer had agreed to retrieve from Rome as part of a pledge he had made years before. The matter of Sherry's effects was closed the following year when Haywood wrote the American consulate in Rome that the books, furniture, clothes, and paintings would have to be auctioned off merely to pay the debt to the maid and the storage bill that had accumulated. As for the rest of the debts, Haywood concluded, there was simply no way that they could be resolved: "John Sherry Mangan, in the best literary tradition, died leaving almost nothing."[76]

The Poetics of Radical Modernism

In trying to assess the lives and careers of John Wheelwright and Sherry Mangan, my conclusion is that all of Mangan's writings after the 1930s, including those of the Bolivian period, confirm the comparative correctness of Wheelwright's strategy for resolving the fundamental problem of radical modernism: the desire to create art that is objectively elitist by virtue of its difficulty and the desire to employ art to affect the consciousness of a mass audience. For Wheelwright, literature was an instrument for teaching values that he believed appropriate to the class with which he had declared solidarity. He became an organic intellectual in Gramsci's sense, taking as his task the providing of cultural resources for the conversion of the proletariat into a consciously revolutionary class. Hence Wheelwright set about his tasks with deliberateness. For him, there was never any question of the virtue of experimentation as such, but only a question of the ends to be served. Montage, sudden shifts in perspective, and mixture of poetic modes were permissible and desirable so long as they ultimately disclosed a vision suffused with the Marxist view of social reality. The ideological tensions between scientific socialism and theology that troubled Wheelwright were resolved in practice during the Great Depression; the former proved sturdy and the latter irrelevant.

Mangan, however, failed to heal the disjuncture in his art that had set in as early as 1931, when the simple realism of his "Barclay Street" stories contrasted markedly with the aggressive obscurity of surrealist-influenced prose writings such as "Enter in Grey." His last efforts before turning to Marxism were attempts to write a post-Eliotic verse exemplified by jarring bluntness, as in "No Apology for Poetrie," or by ironic anti-intellectualism, as in "Words to Time's Winds."

In his Marxist phase, one half of Mangan's writing retained the approach of the "Barclay Street" stories; he reduced his intellectual apparatus significantly and reverted to a sensibility that echoed the romantic view of art as emotion. In some cases a faint metaphysical strain was conserved, but his main effort was devoted to forging emotive images and precise language. This approach is evident in "Activist Miliciano" (1956), which describes a Spanish Republican about to be executed by Franco's Fascists:

As he felt the wall against his back and against
the back of his head, he suddenly thought: The glint
of sun I see on those rifles is the last
glint of sun I shall see on rifles or
on anything else.

                    The thought
seemed to him too personal for this moment,
which, with three hundred others coming
after him, the counteroffensive broken, and the loss
of four towns, was more than merely individual.
But he was no theoretician, had no last words, and even
when he heard the snick of the bolts clicking
into place, all he could think was:
I did the best I could. So it's all right. But
after a life at it, it's hard not to be here
to see how it all came out.[1]

The poem's grace and lucidity, as well as its insight into the psychology of the situation, is reminiscent of Robert Graves's early poems about World War I. Mangan depicts the attitude of a soldier at the point when individual fate, normally the paramount concern, shrinks into insignificance because defeats have been so sweeping and so vast. The poem is also a personal testament; Mangan was in ill health after 1954 and suspected that he might not live to see his own life's work completed.

The rupture in his imagination between the desire to recreate "reality" and the need to subvert it is evidenced by an unfinished series of poems called "Etudes for the Eleventh Finger." Mangan worked on this series from the mid-1930s until his death. A section called "Grade 5: Seven Dives: A Sensible Dead End" was published in *New Directions* in 1948:

Take seven dives, then, Father Sargeant. Thank you. Arm your grael
with crooks before and after; traverse grim grammar's dale;
now butter Pa with torque and fistula, him gently leaven,
so Kris may sing to bairns, and you hang seven times seven.

At home, to gobble slavs, at standing Delia makes signs of
old wreckers' lights, a Satan's swarm—this vets man like a glove;
in lairs of docking whistles, elders will at billing veer,
so try for sons, blue sisters' fodder; fans will nap it queer.

But seven dives vexed the upper valley, axles breaded stark
old sleet on Pa, aching in thrall, and brought out scar and mark;
wherefrom a gladsome village rose, much longer to eat clocks
or candy, fair with glory old, and girt with building blocks.

In Hermes' name, thou oldest sound, when shall I sing it free?
Go talk thy gabble, eating go, or do embroidery.
Go get the visa, elder sot, break through the crooked wood,
and seven dives take till Slavs are tanked, and you shall have
    withstood.

Thus Milan's jags make sons our debts, to scatter granny's swing;
Father was son, though garpike with; the trap is set to spring.
Who pleases all displeases all, who drifts finds normal death;
and only you can know yourself—the rest is waste of breath.[2]

This poem illustrates the striking contrast between Mangan's approach
to modernism and that of Wheelwright. Where Wheelwright strove to
forge a subversive symbolism, Mangan created dialectics in a vacuum, a
jumble of disorderly images collapsing into esoteric allusion. The prob-
lems are not due exclusively to his strategy of dissociation; the odd
vocabulary of the poem renders it virtually opaque.

However, "Seven Dives" is not ultimately chaotic. Although some
modernists saw modernism as the expression of unmediated, disjointed
experience, Mangan retained the view that genuine freedom comes
through control, not spontaneity. His aspiration is to link immediacy
and abstraction, so the obscurity of "Seven Dives" is the product of
craftsmanship, as it is, for example, in Dylan Thomas's difficult sonnet
sequence, "Altarwise by Owl-light." The "Eleventh Finger" in the title is
the imagination, and the poem itself charts the search for self-liberation
through art in the face of hereditary social roles and the pressure to con-
form. When the poem is read in the context of Mangan's experimental
prose works of the same period, it appears that the difficulty and ob-
scurity of the poem are intended to assault the pseudo-rationality of
bourgeois society, making pseudo-irrationality or ironic "insanity" a
central theme in his work.[3]

For example, "A Night in Scranton" (1953) describes a visit by an
unnamed narrator and two associates to a distinguished Scranton geisha
house called "Eden."[4] The star of one of the acts in Eden is a man named
O'Brien. The proprietor is Joshua, who is described as a philosopher with
a problem. Even though his star performer loves wearing a turban in his
act, he no longer wants to put walnut dye on his face for his Indian rope-
trick number. So the ready-witted Joshua decides to bring O'Brien on in
an oxygen tent, with the explanation that O'Brien is dying but the show
must go on. The only explanation Mangan ever gave for this obscure
story was a remark in a letter that his main idea was to slide so smoothly
from reality to irreality and back that the mind would begin to lose
track, thus producing a very mild state of psychosis. "The piece is
essentially an attack on sanity," he observed.[5]

A similar approach characterizes "Reminiscence from a Hilltop" (1957). This piece of prose fiction begins with an unnamed narrator who is disturbed because "the region where I lived began to be much troubled by mud-geysers"; for assistance, he contacts an organization that specializes in "boring":

> Mr. Roderick Cogan, the engineer who was going to demonstrate to me these techniques in the underriver boring of the Queens-to-Eternity Tunnel, was late in calling for me, and I was watching the street below for him from the roof of my 14-story apartment-building, as I absent-mindedly played pat-a-cake with the building next door. I was, indeed, too absent-minded, for when on one of its upstrokes I patted the roof down again excessively hard, the building accordeoned too far, almost endangering its occupants, and on its rebound, was obviously going to shoot over my head. With an instinct that I immediately then after recognized as stupid, I grabbed its cornice with both hands, and it would have served me right if it had thrown me arse-over-teakettle over the Empire State Building. As it was, it sent me cartwheeling up and over several blocks, and I landed with rather a thump on the roof of the Alcatraz Hotel.[6]

Both pieces of prose, alternately jarring and oneiric, read like dream texts; yet they were intentionally constructed to create psychological effects and dramatize psychoanalytical themes (the working title of the latter was "Anal Is Not Necessarily Sadistic"). In Mangan's attack on "sanity," he wanted to undermine the pseudosanity of bourgeois society, the illusion of rationality we have when we conform to the norms of a capitalist society. Since capitalist society in Mangan's view is ultimately based on an irrational economic system (pitting social production against private ownership), he is not attacking reason in these writings but irrationality masking itself as reason. Ultimately his objective may have been to reaffirm the integral human personality in the face of atomization and alienation; his fissuring of conventional thought and perception in such writings may thus have been conceived as a politically progressive act. But at best the mystified reader is left with an agitated consciousness.

Wheelwright, and other radical modernists such as Brecht, shared similar objectives but achieved remarkably different results. In *Rock and Shell* and *Political Self-Portrait*, for example, Wheelwright was able to combine this assault on the illusions and perceptual distortions of capitalist society with a reorganization of sensibility around socialist concepts. Through a public poetry, an accessible symbolism, a distinct rhetorical voice, colloquialisms, jolts, and other devices, he aspired to evoke a revolutionary myth. Mangan, however, was incapable of such a resolution. In the 1920s, when the artistic life was his all-consuming substitute for social identity, he made initial attempts to forge myths. His most successful effort was a pattern in his poems that transposed religious motifs. In "Resurgam" and "Salutation to Valediction," for example, he declared art his god by substituting Apollo for Christ and announcing himself a poet-priest-servant, but one who violates trust, deviates from responsibilities, and risks being punished by the loss of poetic powers. In the early 1930s Mangan's myth turned into reality as his writing became blocked. At first he blamed the influence of Eliot and called for a radically new kind of poetry based on science; then he blamed literary criticism in general, urging artists to eschew critical writing; finally he turned to journalism.

Mangan's last attempt at myth in the 1930s was a long poem on Lucretius, which he worked on periodically for twenty-five years. Part of it was published in *Diogenes* in 1941. In this poem he compared himself to Lucretius, feeling a link between his own literary disorientation and a biographical gloss about Lucretius contained in the annals attributed to Saint Jerome: "While he [Lucretius] was expounding Epicurus's doctrines in verse, his wife, believing herself neglected, gave him a love potion. But, instead of burning with love, he went mad with a frenzy. Though his mind wandered, yet he tried to complete his poem. In vain. For in the forty-third year of his life he met death at his own hand."[7] "Lament for all Lucretii" is characterized by romantic irony (also present in "Valediction") in that its structure takes its own subjective origin into account: the poet's tragic condition is part of the creation. Yet both poems were only partly completed, both constituted despairing attempts to expend poetic powers on impossible tasks. If myth partly serves the function of resolving real contradictions through the use of the imagination, then Mangan was incapable of constructing an appropriate one.

Socialism seems so far removed from poetry such as "Seven Dives" and prose such as "Reminiscence from a Hilltop" that one is tempted to see their ultimate value simply in their virtuoso display of linguistic and imaginative skills. However, Mangan's realism in "Activist Miliciano" and his aborted novel about Bolivian tin miners provide the necessary complement to his artistic project. Although his experimental writing seems to depict a world bereft of transcendental meaning, the completed chapters of "The Mountain of Death" and several other works are realist in their almost scientific reproduction of concrete extensive reality from a Marxist point of view. If his anger at the alienation of capitalist society made him assault pseudosanity with "irrational" prose, a continued faith in the possibilities of reason led him to make his major effort through the realist novel, a repository of traditional rationality. Yet here he found himself unable to transcend the paradox that Wheelwright and other radical modernists had managed to overcome through experimental methods: art is necessarily selective; the more one aspires to complete fidelity in order to expose the concrete particulars of social processes obscured by myths, lies, and illusions, the more one runs the risk of driving the fictive element out of the literary work.

Mangan's writings in the realist mode did have several distinguished moments, particularly when he was able to rework the raw material of theme and plot imaginatively so that the stamp of his intriguing personality was visible. A 1940 poem called "Before the Wind Rises" provides insight into the emotional sources of his Marxist commitment. Nicholas Calas included the poem in a special number of *View* that he guest-edited, briefly hoping to turn the magazine into an American version of *Clé*. The poem expresses the tensions that Mangan felt between his politics and emotions. He begins by contrasting his feelings about political responsibilities toward humanity in the abstract with the intense personal feelings he holds toward a loved individual:

> The manifesto written, suddenly to see you,
> humanly sitting in the silence of a ticking clock;
> and in the Niagara-roar of one's own paper thunder, feel
> the cells drum hard with prescience of how soon
> there'll not be time . . .[8]

But as the class struggle (the "wind") urges him toward his political duties, he recognizes that the contradiction between his generalized sense of responsibility and his individualized love only masks a deeper relationship underneath:

> Spain   China   Minneapolis   Pacific Coast   now France
> always steel auto truckers clang clashing clarion calls.
> Nor shall we fail that cause; it is because
> we know we shall not fail that we cling
> desperate for the last gentleness, as the wind rises . . .[9]

In the closing stanza, Mangan analogizes principles and machines to forge a memorable image of the two poles of his personality: the drive toward the severity of Bolshevik discipline, with its "inhuman" demand of subordinating individuality to political principle, and intense sensitivity to the sensuality of life, the quality of the passing moments:

> before we march, bloody automata of principle,
> always remembering, tactilely, how felt
> your hand slipping from mine . . .[10]

The purpose of this book has been twofold. First, I have especially endeavored to restore Wheelwright's reputation as a poet of note. Second, I have given an account of two instances of the modern poet as Marxist revolutionary. How, the book asks, did each man reconcile the function of poetic visionary with that of political actor? In Wheelwright's case, we have a poet who successfully integrated the refinements of a strong poetic talent with revolutionary ideas. The case of Sherry Mangan contrasts with this success. Despite several remarkable poems and stories and an admirable life as a professional revolutionist, he succeeded in reconciling literature with politics only in his journalism. In poetry he rarely achieved such an integration; indeed, his life was characterized by alternate swings between total commitment to politics and total commitment to literature.

But a book like this has a function that transcends the reconstruction and analysis of the lives of the poets. The blend of Marxist politics and modernist literary techniques that we have seen in the work of Wheelwright and Mangan is nowhere acknowledged in any of the histories of American poetry. Yet this blend did exist and was widespread. These poets represent but two examples of an entire literary tendency that has been virtually forgotten.[11] Is there any hope that the present situation will be changed, that the repressed past will be acknowledged, that literary tradition as currently codified will be altered to accommodate the true scope of literary practice in the 1930s?

The irony of our present situation is precisely that such work was begun in the 1960s, when powerful new social movements inspired the exploration of many areas of our forgotten or neglected past—for example, the culture of women, minorities, workers, and several aspects of the literary left. New academic programs evolved that encouraged such studies; university presses became alert to the value of such scholarship; young scholars began to develop skills and a commitment appropriate to such research.

Since that decade, however, as the national economic situation has deteriorated, new programs have been eliminated, university presses have been cut back, and young scholars sensitive to these areas of study have not been finding new jobs or holding old ones. Although there are a few signs that the experience of the 1960s and 1970s has not been forgotten, for the most part the recorded past remains a false one. The discrepancy between literary tradition as lived and as remembered in texts about twentieth-century American poetry remains a significant barrier to our understanding of the past, as well as a disturbing sign about the nature of the institutions that are in the process of codifying the cultural experience of the present.

ABBREVIATIONS

AW   Alan Wald
B   Beinecke Rare Book and Manuscript Library, Yale University
BU   Brown University Library
CPVP Charles Patterson Van Pelt Library, University of Pennsylvania
GA   George Arents Research Library, Syracuse University
HL   Houghton Library, Harvard University
HRO Harvard University Records Office, Harvard College Clipping Sheet
JR   Joseph Regenstein Library, University of Chicago
JW   John Wheelwright
ML   Morris Library, University of Delaware
NL   Newberry Library, Chicago
SM   Sherry Mangan
WCP *Collected Poems of John Wheelwright*, ed. Alvin H. Rosenfeld (New York: New Directions, 1972)

Letters and documents not identified by a library or collection are in the possession of Alan Wald. In some cases the complete date for a letter is not available, nor is the full bibliographic citation for some book reviews and newspaper clippings preserved in the scrapbooks of John Wheelwright and Sherry Mangan.

NOTES

INTRODUCTION

1. Max Hayward and Leopold Labedz, eds., *Literature and Revolution in Soviet Russia, 1917–1962* (London: Oxford University Press, 1963), p. 71.

2. Irving Howe, *Politics and the Novel* (New York: Meridian, 1964), p. 15.

3. The quotation from Trotsky is discussed in Terry Eagleton, *Marxism and Literary Criticism* (Berkeley: University of California Press, 1976), pp. 50–51; Eagleton's description of aesthetic effect is elaborated in *Criticism and Ideology* (London: New Left Books, 1976), p. 177.

4. Granville Hicks et al., *Proletarian Literature in the United States* (New York: International Publishers, 1935), p. 148.

5. Ibid., p. 167.

6. *WCP*, p. 149.

7. Walt Whitman, *Leaves of Grass and Selected Prose* (New York: Random House, 1950), p. 225.

8. *WCP*, p. 154.

9. Ibid., pp. 138–39.

10. James T. Farrell, *A Note on Literary Criticism* (New York: Vanguard, 1936), p. 116.

11. Fredric Jameson, *Aesthetics and Politics* (London: New Left Books, 1977), p. 205.

PART I: THE LAPSE OF URIEL, 1897–1931

CHAPTER I

1. Kenneth Rexroth, *Assays* (New York: New Directions, 1961), p. 168.

2. Dudley Fitts to SM, 7 September 1958, HL.

3. Dudley Fitts to SM, 30 November 1958, HL.

4. Malcolm Cowley, *Exile's Return* (New York: Viking, 1966), p. 35.

5. Daniel Aaron, *Writers on the Left* (New York: Harcourt, Brace and World, 1961), p. 346.

6. *Time*, 14 October 1940, p. 119; Horace Gregory and Marya Zaturenska, *A History of American Poetry: 1900–1940* (New York: Harcourt, Brace and Co., 1946), p. 349; Austin Warren, "No Apology for Sherry," *Sewanee Review* 44, no. 1 (January–March 1936): 108; Kenneth Rexroth to AW, 28 June 1976.

7. V. F. Calverton to JW, January 1938, BU; *WCP*, p. 112.

8. *WCP*, p. 113.

9. Ibid., p. 151.

10. SM to Morton Zabel, 10 November 1931, JR; SM, *No Apology for Poetrie* (Boston: Bruce Humphries, 1934), p. 43.

11. SM to Morton Zabel, 10 November 1931.

12. SM to Ezra Pound, 27 August 1934, B; SM to Duncan, 1 October 1942, HL; SM to Ezra Pound, 28 January 1932, B.

13. SM, *No Apology for Poetrie*, p. 44.

14. SM, "Makes: Maker: Makes," *Bozart-Westminster 9*, no. 1 (Spring–Summer 1935): 32.

15. SM, "Walk Do Not Run," *New Republic*, 14 August 1935, p. 15.

16. *WCP*, p. 78.

17. Ibid., p. 40.

18. E. E. Cummings, *100 Selected Poems* (New York: Grove, 1959), p. 8.

19. *WCP*, p. 53.

20. Ibid., p. 244.

21. Paul Siegel, ed., *Leon Trotsky on Literature and Art* (New York: Pathfinder, 1970), p. 104.

22. Daniel Aaron, *Men of Good Hope* (New York: Oxford University Press, 1967), pp. 3–20.

23. Stephen E. Whicher, ed., *Selections from Ralph Waldo Emerson* (Boston: Houghton Mifflin Co., 1960), pp. 426–28.

CHAPTER 2

1. S. Foster Damon, *Amy Lowell: A Chronicle* (Boston: Houghton Mifflin Co., 1935), pp. 3–4.

2. Austin Warren, *New England Saints* (Ann Arbor: University of Michigan Press, 1956), p. 178; Dudley Fitts, "*Mirrors of Venus*," *New England Quarterly* 13, no. 3 (September 1940): 544; Matthew Josephson, "Improper Bostonian: John Wheelwright and His Poetry," *Southern Review* 7 (Spring 1971): 536; Mark DeWolfe Howe, "To the Editor of the *Transcript*," typed version courtesy of John Marshall.

3. Descriptions of Wheelwright are based on the author's interview with Elroy Webber, May 1977; a letter from Polly Thayer Starr to AW, 19 September 1977; a letter from Lincoln Kirstein to AW, 27 December 1978; a letter from A. Hyatt Mayor to AW, 4 August 1977; and a letter from Oliver Prescott, Jr., to AW, 13 October 1977.

4. Gregory and Zaturenska, *A History of American Poetry*, p. 348.

5. Author's interview with Muriel Rukeyser, May 1977.

6. Howe, "To the Editor of the *Transcript*"; Josephson, "Improper Bostonian," p. 510.

7. Barrett Wendell, "Edmund March Wheelwright, '76," *Harvard Graduate's Magazine*, December 1912, HRO.

8. M. A. DeWolfe Howe, ed., *Barrett Wendell and His Letters* (Boston: Atlantic Monthly Press, 1924), p. 23.

9. Martin Kaplan, ed., *The Harvard Lampoon Centennial Celebration, 1876–1973* (Boston: Little, Brown and Co., 1973), p. 59; Howe, *Barrett Wendell and His Letters*, p. 24; Robert T. Self, *Barrett Wendell* (Boston: G. K. Hall and Co., 1975), p. 32.

10. Frederic Jesup Stimson, "Edmund March Wheelwright," HRO.

11. Wendell, "Edmund March Wheelwright, '76."

12. See Edmund March Wheelwright, "A Frontier Family," *Publications of the Colonial Society of Massachusetts*, 1 (1892–94): 271–303; letter from Warren L. Wheelwright to AW, 2 October 1977; letter from Gerald M. Kelley to AW, 8 March 1978.

13. Edmund March Wheelwright to John Jay Chapman, 25 December (year unknown), HL; Melvin A. Bernstein, *John Jay Chapman* (New York: Twayne, 1964), p. 28; Wendell, "Edmund March Wheelwright, '76"; *Boston Transcript*, 16 August 1912, HRO.

14. JW to Barrett Wendell, 14 July 1919, HL.

15. Edmund March Wheelwright to Barrett Wendell, 4 September 1876, HL; Edmund March Wheelwright to Barrett Wendell, 11 June 1881, HL.

16. Oliver Prescott, Jr., to AW, 13 October 1977; interview with Dr. Austin and Mrs. Amelia (Wheelwright) Vickery, December 1977.

17. Warren, *New England Saints*, p. v.

18. Oliver Prescott, Jr., to AW, 13 October 1977. Cases similar to that of Bessie Brooks are described in Robert V. Bruce, *Bell: Alexander Graham Bell and the Conquest of Solitude* (Boston: Little, Brown and Co., 1973). The "Frog Pond" accident is the most widely believed explanation of Bessie Brooks's loss of hearing. Two other stories say that she was born deaf and that deafness came as a consequence of scarlet fever; see Polly Thayer Starr to AW, 19 September 1977, and Mary Marshall to AW, 3 September 1977.

19. Mary Marshall to AW, 3 September 1977.

20. Oliver Prescott, Jr., to AW, 13 October 1977.

21. Mary Marshall to AW, 3 September 1977.

22. Edmund March Wheelwright to Barrett Wendell, 30 May 1911, HL; Howe, *Barrett Wendell and His Letters*, p. 253. The obituaries for Ned Wheelwright mention the diagnosis of melancholia but not the suicide. However, Oliver Prescott, Jr., wrote to AW on 13 October 1977: "In middle life he [Ned] went to pieces mentally and eventually took his own life." In a letter of 3 September 1977, Mary Marshall told AW: "That Jack's father was a suicide was a universal belief among all his friends, and I never heard it questioned." Lincoln Kirstein also referred to the suicide in a 27 December 1978 letter to AW.

23. From p. 1 of an untitled twenty-five page memoir of the *Secession* magazine controversy, unpublished, BU.

24. *WCP*, p. 78.

25. Frank Merchant to AW, 29 April 1978.

26. JW, "The Good Boy Who Enjoyed the Cake," *Hound and Horn* 4 (April–June 1931): 428.

27. *WCP*, p. 243.

28. Ibid., p. 244.

29. Oliver Prescott, Jr., to AW, 13 October 1977.

30. Author's interview with Benjamin Kittridge, Jr., December 1977.

31. Bessie Wheelwright to Barrett Wendell, 21 March (year unknown), HL; author's interview with John Marshall, July 1977. Marshall recalled: "March I knew. He came back from the First World War somewhat shattered. At that time the Wheelwrights still had a big house at Medford, and March was so ill at ease with his family and their surroundings that he insisted on having his meals in the

kitchen with the servants. So there was much trouble with March. I never knew much about it. March was the older son. . . . He married an Irish girl who was regarded by his family as rather lower class. . . . March was not comfortable in his very high-born position." Some further details about March can be found in the *Harvard Class of 1914: Fiftieth Anniversary Report* (Cambridge: Harvard University, 1964), p. 563.

32. These grades were obtained from the Harvard University Registrar with permission of the Wheelwright family.

33. Clippings from *The Dragon*, St. George's.

34. Author's interview with Benjamin Kittridge, Jr., December 1977.

35. Bessie Wheelwright to Barrett Wendell, 13 August 1916, HL.

36. *WCP*, p. 57; *National Cyclopedia of American Biography* (New York: James J. White and Co., 1929), p. 459; John Nicholas Brown to AW, 27 June 1977; Byron Rushing to AW, 25 August 1978.

37. Clippings from *The Dragon*, St. George's.

38. Bessie Wheelwright to Barrett Wendell, 13 August 1916, HL.

39. JW to Barrett Wendell, 29 August 1916, HL.

40. The information about JW's grades, forced withdrawal and the text of his "nausia" note was obtained from his file at the Harvard University Registrar's Office with the permission of the Wheelwright family. The description of the chemistry class episode is from Josephson, "Improper Bostonian," *Southern Review*, p. 517.

41. Clippings from *The Dragon*, St. George's.

42. JW to Barrett Wendell, August 1916, HL.

43. Author's interview with Malcolm Cowley, July 1977; Alvin H. Rosenfeld and S. Foster Damon, "John Wheelwright: New England's Colloquy with the World," *Southern Review* 7 (April 1972): 314; Winfield Townley Scott, "John Wheelwright and His Poetry," *New Mexico Quarterly* 24, no. 2 (Summer 1954): 179.

44. JW to Benjamin Kittridge, Jr., 1921, BU.

45. Edgar Scott to AW, 2 August 1977. JW also contributed to the "Versailles Number" a poem called "The War Bride" and a satire on the new generation of expatriates called "The American Colonists."

CHAPTER 3

1. S. Foster Damon and Robert Hillyer, eds., *Eight More Harvard Poets* (New York: Brentano's, 1923), p. xii.

2. The unpublished review by Hart Crane is in JW's scrapbook, BU.

3. Milton Raison, review in the *New York Herald-Tribune*, 8 January 1923, in JW's scrapbook, BU; Hervey Allen, review in *The State*, Columbia, South Carolina, in JW's scrapbook, BU.

4. Harold Acton, *Voices: A Journal of Verse*, p. 203, in JW's scrapbook, BU; unsigned review in *The Cherwell*, 16 February 1924, in JW's scrapbook, BU.

5. Damon and Hillyer, *Eight More Harvard Poets*, p. 124.

6. *WCP*, p. 79.

7. Damon and Hillyer, *Eight More Harvard Poets*, pp. 117-18.

8. See the correspondence between JW and Amy Lowell, HL. S. Foster Damon records an encounter between JW and Amy Lowell at Harvard in *Amy Lowell*, p. 345. Damon dates the meeting as 1916; but in his "Argument" to "Dinner Call," JW states that the description should have appeared on p. 449 of Damon's book, which would have made the meeting 1918 according to Damon's chronology.

9. JW, unpublished memoir, BU.

10. According to Rosenfeld and Damon, JW "had been one of those who had defended in the *Harvard Monthly* the newly established USSR"; see "John Wheelwright," p. 316.

11. In his 1921 letter to Benjamin Kittridge, Jr., Jack wrote: "The Laski number was horrid. I had been told nothing about it although it was planned as the last whack of the old group who had such good times and such brilliant successes in the *Transcript, Cosmopolitan*, etc. . . . The dirty sheet mortified me. [That] the *Lampoon*, flesh of my flesh by inheritance, spirit of my spirit by my own work, was capable of such a thing. . . . Laski I admired. He is a great political thinker, he is a suggestive teacher, a master of knowledge. He was one of the first to appreciate and cultivate my intellect. But personally his flip fresh Jewish insolence prevented a friendship for which I yearned." Anti-Semitic remarks also occur in letters from S. Foster Damon to JW, BU.

12. JW to Malcolm Cowley, undated, NL; JW to Allen Tate, 3 November 1931, BU.

13. JW to Barrett Wendell, 2 October [1920?], HL; JW, "Life May Be Led Well," *Freeman*, 7 March 1923, p. 618; Damon and Hillyer, *Eight More Harvard Poets*, pp. xii–xiii.

14. Unpublished memoir of JW by Helen Howe, BU.

15. Lewis Mumford to AW, 27 July 1978; Susan Jenkins Brown to AW, 3 September 1978; Matthew Josephson, *Life Among the Surrealists* (New York: Holt, Rinehart and Winston, 1962), pp. 234–36; Alvin Rosenfeld, "John Wheelwright, Gorham Munson, and the 'Wars of Secession,'" *Michigan Quarterly Review* 19, no. 1 (Winter 1975): 13–40.

16. *WCP*, pp. 3–8.

17. Damon discusses the significance of Lowell's book in *Amy Lowell*, p. 478. JW mentions his admiration for this volume in his comment on an 18 May 1923 letter from Malcolm Cowley, BU.

18. JW, "Thomas Hobbes: Twin to Terror," *Freeman*, 2 November 1921, p. 171; JW, "Thomas Hobbes: Arch-Anarch," *Freeman*, 30 November 1921, p. 275.

19. JW, European notebook, undated, p. 13, BU.

20. JW to Mary Opdycke, undated, BU.

21. *WCP*, pp. 10–11.

22. Lincoln Kirstein to AW, 27 December 1978; Elroy Webber to AW, 20 November 1976; A. Hyatt Mayor to AW, 4 August 1977; JW to Malcolm Cowley, undated, NL.

23. One of JW's projects was designing a house for Robert and Dorothy Hillyer.

24. JW to Newton Arvin, 1932, BU.

25. JW calls "Evening" the third published section of a "novel" on Doubting Thomas in an undated letter to *Partisan Review*. Rutgers University Library, New Brunswick, New Jersey. The subtitle of *Mirrors of Venus* is *A Novel in Sonnets*.

26. *WCP*, pp. 13 and 230.

27. Ibid., p. 57. I am indebted to Mary M. Hendricksen's unpublished paper, "John Wheelwright's Thomas Poems," for drawing my attention to the importance of quietism and for a number of other observations.

28. *WCP*, pp. 57–58.

29. JW to Morton Zabel, 17 January 1935, NL.

30. Fredric Jameson, *Fables of Aggression* (Berkeley: University of California, 1979), pp. 2–3.

31. JW to Lincoln Kirstein, 6 August 1930, B.

32. At various times JW states that his background sources include the following: Reverend Sabine Baring-Gould, *Lost and Hostile Gospels* (London: Williams and Norgate, 1874); Rhys Davids, ed., *Manual of a Mystic*, trans. F. L. Woodward (London: Humphrey Milford, 1916); the hymnal; the psalter; the *Bhagavadgita*; the Apocryphal Acts. In his "Argument" to "Twilight," JW states that the poem is "the first of three completed workings of mine of material in Walker's translation of a Nestorian novel on the Acts of Thomas." In the "Argument" to "Evening" he states that he used material from "the Nestorian Liturgy of Malabar or St. Thomas." Alexander Walker translated *Apocryphal Gospels, Acts, and Revelations* for vol. 16 of the *Ante-Nicene Christian Library*, ed. Alexander Roberts and James Donaldson (Edinburgh: Clark, 1870). There is no evidence that any sort of "novel" existed. Nestorius, bishop of Constantinople in 428 A.D., was banished for heresies such as his separation of the divine and human nature of Christ. Most of his works were destroyed by the official church. A novel that JW may have read on this subject is James Freeman Clarke's *The Legend of Thomas Didymus* (Boston: Lee and Shepard, 1881).

33. In "The Apostle Thomas in North India," *John Rylands Library Bulletin* 10, no. 1 (January 1926): 85, J. N. Farquhar states that "the word Thomas means 'twin,' yet the Apostle receives no other name in the New Testament [except for Didymus, which is simply Greek for 'twin']. He must have had a name of his own; but he seems to have been usually called 'Twin.' At a later point we shall suggest a reason for believing that Judas was his personal name, and that he was called Judas Thomas in the document preserved at Edessa. Now Jesus had a brother named Judas. It was therefore possible to identify the twin with him." It is not known whether Wheelwright read this essay.

34. *WCP*, p. 230.

35. JW to Harriet Monroe, 18 October 1933, NL.

36. *WCP*, p. 208.

37. Ibid., p. 34.

38. Ibid., p. 58.

39. JW to Harriet Monroe, 18 October 1933, NL; JW to Morton Zabel, 17 January 1935, NL.

40. *WCP*, p. 189.

41. Ibid.

42. JW to Harriet Monroe, 6 November 1933, NL.

43. JW to Quincy Howe, 8 August 1932, BU.

44. JW, "The Frog Who Would Be an Ox," *Hound and Horn* 3 (April–June 1930): 425.

45. *WCP*, p. 59.

46. Ibid., p. 43.

47. Ibid.

48. This image of art surviving and transcending a decadent society is another example of the influence of Amy Lowell on JW. On p. 469 of *Amy Lowell*, S. Foster Damon gave the following analysis of *Can Grande's Castle*: "In *Can Grande's Castle*—particularly in 'The Bronze Horses'—she accepts Brooks Adams's theory that civilizations arise cyclically upon economic success, then decay as the racial energy runs out; she also accepts Henry Adams's theory that international crises recur more and more frequently as the speed of history accelerates. But Amy Lowell, in organizing and completing her theory, won a place of her own amongst the historical philosophers. To her, art was not only the expression of a civilization: it was life's highest achievement and its only permanence—it was almost civilization itself. The economic system is the root, the popular pleasures are the transient flower, and the arts are the seed-bearing fruit."

49. JW to Allen Tate, 3 November 1931, BU.

50. Kenneth Porter to JW, 10 June 1933.

51. JW, letter to the editor, *New Republic*, 13 July 1932, p. 238.

CHAPTER 4

1. Kate Kurzke to AW, 20 September 1974.

2. Tessa Gilbert to Russell Fraser, undated.

3. Kate Kurzke to AW, 20 September 1974.

4. Regina Arroll to AW, 4 December 1976; obituary for John Joseph Mangan from *Holy Cross Alumnus*, 1935, College of Holy Cross.

5. Neither Henry J. Donaghy nor James Kilroy, both authors of books on James Clarence Mangan, have been able to confirm or deny the possibility of a relationship. Gerald Fitzgerald, Jr., a distant cousin of Sherry Mangan, has possession of the memoirs of Owen Peter Mangan and has researched the relationship without coming up with anything conclusive. However, in a letter of 10 September 1976 to AW, Regina Arroll (a first cousin of Sherry Mangan) stated: "We are definitely direct descendants of the Irish poet James Clarence Mangan, and my father, the doctor's brother, was named after him, and also my brother—both James Clarence Mangan." A recent novel, *The Mangan Inheritance* by Brian Moore (Farrar, Straus and Giroux, 1979), depicts a character who has a number of remarkable similarities to Sherry Mangan and who also believes himself to be a descendant of James Clarence Mangan.

6. For further information on James Clarence Mangan, see Henry J. Donaghy, *James Clarence Mangan* (New York: Twayne, 1974) and James Kilroy, *James Clarence Mangan* (Lewisburg: Bucknell University Press, 1970).

7. Dorothy Haywood to AW, undated. The pilgrimages are also referred to in Sherry Mangan's fictional memoir "Snow."

8. Obituaries for Patrick Sherry from Lynn newspapers and from *Shoes and Leather Trade*, 5 September 1931, Lynn Public Library, Lynn, Massachusetts.

9. Richard Haywood to AW, 23 August 1976.

10. This information was obtained from the Harvard Registrar's Office with the permission of the Mangan family.

11. Richard Haywood to AW, 23 August 1976. Haywood gives the following

details: "It was late January or early February of my junior year in the high school and their [Charles Haywood's and Sherry Mangan's] senior year. They had the idea of writing up a little sheet about the school and the teachers and wanted me to join, which I did. It was one sheet, perhaps nine by six . . . called *The Tophet Tehelegram News*, purporting to be published in Hell and imitating the name of *The Lynn Telegram News*. . . . We were caught, of course. Our fathers stood by us. We were suspended for three days and had to apologize to each teacher. It made a slight stir in town."

12. SM's stories from the *Gazette*, courtesy of Dorothy Haywood, Lynn Public Library.

13. From SM, "Snow," HL.

14. Regina Arroll to AW, 10 September 1976.

15. A description of the Liberal Club is given by Virgil Thomson in *Virgil Thomson* (New York: Knopf, 1966), p. 65: "This was my kind of club, a fair eating place (something anyone needed in Cambridge) frequented by a mixed set, artistic and scholarly. Shortly after the war a leftist group had got together under the name Harvard Liberal Club and leased a house, their *raison d'être* being the discussion of current events. . . . Then suddenly, during my year abroad, it had expanded into a culture group."

16. SM, *No Apology for Poetrie*, p. 12.

17. Thomson, *Virgil Thomson*, p. 45; John Marshall to AW, 1 August 1974. In a 23 August 1976 letter to AW, Richard Haywood recalled that SM asked him to purchase peyote for him during a trip to the Southwest.

18. John Marshall to AW, 1 August 1974.

19. SM to Kate Kurzke, 26–27 June 1960, HL.

20. Harvard University Registrar's Office.

21. SM to John Joseph Mangan, 15 February 1926, HL. SM's letters also contain early versions of translations of poetry for his father to read. They were later published as "From Valerius Aeditus," *Commonweal*, 30 September 1925, p. 504, and "Fragments of Latin Verse from Porcius Licinius and Quintus Catullus," *Commonweal*, 10 February 1926, p. 375.

22. SM to John Joseph Mangan, 18 November 1925, HL.

23. SM to Virgil Thomson, 15 December 1960, JH; John Joseph Mangan, *Life, Character and Influence of Desiderius Erasmus of Rotterdam*, 2 vols. (New York: Macmillan Co., 1927), 1:xii.

24. A photograph of Sherry receiving the degree of Doctor of Letters on behalf of Dr. Mangan appears in the *Holy Cross Bulletin*, July 1928, p. 3. SM to Virgil Thomson, undated, HL: "I cannot, I fear, return to Paris in the Spring, principally on account of my father, who is thoroughly dependent upon me in his present condition."

25. A copy of the brochure is in the Lynn Public Library.

26. Janet Lewis to AW, 13 July 1976.

27. The second brochure is in the Lynn Public Library.

28. General information on *larus* and *Tempo* can be found in Frederick J. Hoffman et al., *The Little Magazine* (Princeton: Princeton University Press, 1947), pp. 286, 264.

29. SM, "I Fuge," *larus* 1, no. 1 (February 1927): 1.

30. Hoffman, *The Little Magazine*, p. 286.

31. SM, "*Ars Gloria Artis* versus The Cuttlefish: III," *larus* 1, no. 4 (July 1927): 2. Mangan often spoke well of Lewis's work and he knew Lewis slightly. For a political study of Lewis and other right-wing literary figures, see John R. Harrison, *The Reactionaries* (New York: Shocken Books, 1968). There is no evidence that SM was ever connected with any right-wing organizations or that he took Fascist ideas seriously. He published "Three Prayers to the Holy Ghost" in *The Nationalist Quarterly* 2, no. 3 (Spring 1937), which purported to be the organ of the Monarchist party. But by that time SM had publicly identified with the Socialist party, so either his contribution or perhaps the publication itself was intended to be tongue-in-cheek.

32. SM, "*Ars Gloria Artis* versus The Cuttlefish: II," *larus* 1, no. 3 (May 1927): 1.

33. Jameson, *Fables of Aggression*, pp. 15-17.

34. Richard Haywood to AW, 23 August 1976.

35. SM to Virgil Thomson, undated, HL.

36. Author's interview with Mary (Morris) Baird, July 1977; author's interview with Virgil Thomson, June 1976.

37. SM, "Mush," *Poetry* 39, no. 1 (October 1931): 53.

38. SM, *Cinderella Married or How They Lived Happily Ever After: A Divertissement* (New York: A. & C. Boni, 1932), p. 54.

39. Ibid., p. 301.

40. Kate Kurzke to AW, 20 September 1974.

41. See SM, "Revenant" and "Xanthocyanopia," in *No Apology for Poetrie*, pp. 42–43 and 87–88, and "Epistle to Adeimantos," *Pagany* 2, no. 3 (July–September 1931): 54–58.

42. SM, *Cinderella Married*, p. vii.

43. *New York Herald-Tribune Books*, 17 April 1935, p. 2.

44. SM to Virgil Thomson, undated, HL; SM, "Thirteen," *Atlantic Monthly* 146, no. 1 (July 1930): 63–69; SM, "The Coat," *London Mercury* 27, no. 162 (April 1933): 493–501; SM, "The Alligator and the Building Blocks," *Esquire*, August 1938, pp. 160–62, 169.

45. SM to Charles Haywood, 10 April 1952, HL.

46. SM, "Enter in Grey," *Pagany* 1, no. 4 (October–December 1930): 24–30.

PART II: THE REBEL POETS, 1931–1940

CHAPTER 5

1. JW to Hannah Josephson, 28 March 1928, BU.

2. JW to Evan Shipman, 9 January 1932, BU.

3. JW to Newton Arvin, 1932, BU.

4. See JW's undated report on the situation among radical intellectuals in the Boston area and on his own work for the Trotsky Defense Committee, probably late 1937, JHL.

5. JW to Hannah Josephson, 28 March 1928, BU. For further details about Matthew Josephson's political career, see David Shi, *Matthew Josephson: Bourgeois Bohemian* (New Haven: Yale University Press, 1981).

6. JW to Evan Shipman, 9 January 1933, BU.

7. Undated text of speech by JW, BU.

8. JW to Hannah Josephson, 28 March 1928, BU.

9. JW to Evan Shipman, 9 January 1933, BU.

10. JW, review of *The Poems of Richard Aldington, Poetry* 45, no. 1 (October 1934): 47–50.

11. JW to Evan Shipman, 9 January 1933, BU.

12. *Harvard Class of 1920: Twenty-Fifth Anniversary Report* (Cambridge: Harvard University, 1945), p. 872. The biographical material seems to be based on information from Damon.

13. See JW, "To All Branches and Local Secretaries of Massachusetts" and "Review of Literature," 15 May 1936, BU.

14. James Laughlin to AW, 21 August 1974.

15. Alfred Baker Lewis to JW, 26 December 1933, BU.

16. The fifteen-page statement is dated 17 February 1934, BU.

17. *WCP*, p. 169.

18. Obituary for Larry Trainor, *Militant*, 15 August 1975, pp. 24–25; George Weissman to AW, 17 June 1979.

19. JW to Ernest Erber and Albert Goldman, undated, BU.

20. Author's interview with Malcolm Cowley, May 1977.

21. Edward Weeks to AW, 16 August 1977.

22. Mary Marshall to AW, 18 August 1977.

23. JW to Van Wyck Brooks, 6 February 1932, CPVP.

24. See the following by JW: "Richard Upjohn, Churchman and Architect," *New England Quarterly,* 12, no. 3 (September 1939): 500–509; Book Review Section, *New England Quarterly* 13, no. 1 (March 1940): 138–45; "The New Architecture," *Modern Quarterly* 11, no. 1 (Fall 1938): 98–101; "Genevieve Taggard: Collected Poems," *Modern Quarterly* 11, no. 2 (Winter 1939): 83–85; "Fugue: or the Future of Frozen Music," in *Whither, Whither or After Sex, What?* ed. Walter S. Hankel (New York: The Macaulay Company, 1930), pp. 168–89.

25. See JW's reviews of books by the following poets: Laura Riding, *Poetry* 40, no. 5 (August 1932): 288–91; Walter Lowenfels, *Poetry* 42, no. 1 (April 1933): 48–50; Christopher LaFarge, *Poetry* 45, no. 4 (January 1935): 228–31; Edgar Lee Masters, *Poetry* 48, no. 1 (April 1936): 41–43; Alice Very, *Poetry* 50, no. 2 (May 1937): 113–15; Leonard Bacon, *Poetry* 52, no. 4 (July 1938): 229–31; Archibald MacLeish and Alfred Kreymborg, *Poetry* 54, no. 3 (June 1939): 164–67; Stephen Leacock, *Poetry* 50, no. 4 (July 1937): 210–15; Robert Frost, *Poetry* 49, no. 1 (October 1936): 45–48; Kenneth Porter, *Poetry* 42, no. 3 (June 1933): 168–70; Ernest Walsh, *Poetry* 46, no. 6 (September 1935): 349–51; Richard Aldington, *Poetry* 45, no. 1 (October 1934): 47–50.

26. See the following by JW in the *New Republic*: "Sailors and a Soldier," 3 December 1930, pp. 78–79; "Religion and Theology," 4 March 1931, pp. 79–80; "Existence Justified," 16 March 1932, p. 134; "Truth Against the World," 29 June 1932, p. 186; "Eakins: The Painter at Work," 10 July 1933, p. 50; "Hillyer's Collected Verse," 28 March 1934, p. 191; "Kirstein: Verse and Prose," 11 March 1936, pp. 145–46.

27. JW, "Remington and Winslow Homer," *Hound and Horn* 7, no. 4 (July–September 1933): 630–31.

28. JW, "Art and the Leisure Class," *New Republic*, 13 July 1932, p. 238.

29. James Laughlin to AW, 21 August 1974; author's interview with Elroy Webber, May 1977; Mary Marshall to AW, 3 September 1977.

30. Fairfield Porter to AW, 5 August 1974; Kenneth Porter, "Political Self-Portrait," *New England Quarterly* 14, no. 1 (March 1941): 146–53.

31. Gus Tyler to AW, 17 July 1978.

32. Frank Merchant to AW, 27 April 1978.

33. Author's interview with Muriel Rukeyser, December 1977.

34. Richard Eberhart to AW, 6 February 1977.

35. Samuel French Morse to AW, 11 September 1974.

36. Author's interview with Muriel Rukeyser, December 1976.

37. SM to Kate Kurzke, 8 June 1942, HL.

38. Author's interview with Elroy Webber, May 1977.

39. Author's interview with Matthew Josephson, May 1977; author's interview with Malcolm Cowley, May 1977.

40. Polly Thayer Starr to AW, 20 December 1977.

41. Howard Nemerov to AW, 1 September 1977.

42. JW to Albion, undated, BU.

43. Lee Baxandall and Stefan Morawski, *Marx and Engels on Literature and Art* (St. Louis: Telos, 1973), pp. 121, 148.

44. Harvey Swados, *A Radical's America* (Boston: Little, Brown and Co., 1962), p. xvi.

45. JW to Morton Zabel, August 1934, JR.

46. JW, "Pure Poetry," *New Republic*, 21 July 1937, pp. 315–16.

47. JW to Newton Arvin, 1932, BU.

48. Fairfield Porter to AW, 5 August 1974.

49. Mary Marshall to AW, 18 August 1977.

50. JW to Van Wyck Brooks, 6 February 1932, CPVP.

51. JW, "Christian Rebels," *Poetry* 42 (June 1933): 168.

52. JW, "Meet Six Nihilists," *Arise* 1 (April 1935): 26–27.

53. *WCP*, p. 119.

54. Isaac Deutscher, ed., *The Age of Permanent Revolution* (New York: Dell, 1964), p. 14.

55. Letter from JW reprinted in Jack Weber's "March of Events" column in the *Militant*, 1 September 1934, p. 2.

56. Edward Thompson, "Romanticism, Utopianism and Moralism: The Case of William Morris," *New Left Review*, no. 99 (September–October 1976): 85.

CHAPTER 6

1. *WCP*, p. 231.

2. Ibid., p. 230.

3. Ibid., pp. 54–55.

4. JW to Van Wyck Brooks, 6 February 1932, CPVP.

5. *WCP*, p. 56.

6. Ibid., p. 97.

7. Ibid., p. 100.

8. Ibid., p. 58.

9. Edmund S. Morgan, *Visible Saints* (New York: New York University Press, 1963), p. 66.

10. For a number of these insights I am indebted to William Loizeaux's unpublished paper, "John Wheelwright's *Rock and Shell*: Spiritual Autobiography With a Twist."

11. Morgan, *Visible Saints*, pp. 70–71.

12. *WCP*, p. 58.

13. Ibid., p. 38.

14. Ibid., pp. 39–40.

15. Ibid., p. 41.

16. Ibid., p. 154.

17. Ibid., pp. 59–60.

18. Ibid., p. 45.

19. Ibid., p. 46.

20. Ibid.

21. JW to Robert Fitzgerald, undated, JHL.

22. *WCP*, p. 43.

23. Ibid., pp. 44–45.

24. Ibid., p. 59.

25. Ibid., p. 60.

26. "The New England Notebook of John Wheelwright," *New England Quarterly* 4 (December 1972): 572.

27. *WCP*, p. 47.

28. Ibid., p. 60.

29. Ibid., p. 50.

30. Ibid., p. 60.

31. JW to Bruno Fischer, 12 October 1934, BU; "Walled in this Tomb," foreword to pamphlet, courtesy of John Poulos.

32. See the following reviews: Eda Lou Walton, "Poetry with Footnotes," *Nation*, 10 October 1934, p. 418; Horace Gregory, "Poet of New England," *New Republic*, 16 January 1935, p. 283; Morton Zabel, "American Poetry: 1934," in JW's scrapbook, BU; Muriel Rukeyser, *New Masses*, 10 July 1934, p. 28; R. P. Blackmur, "See Byron First," *Poetry* 44, no. 5 (August 1934): 282–86. Also see R. P. Blackmur, Note to *John Wheelwright: Selected Poems* (New York: New Directions, 1941), p. 2.

33. *WCP*, p. 156.

34. Horace Gregory and Marya Zaturenska, *A History of American Poetry: 1900–1940* (New York: Harcourt, Brace and Co., 1946), p. 349.

35. SM, "A New New England Poet," unpublished, BU.

36. JW to Horace Gregory, undated, GA.

37. JW to Horace Gregory, undated, GA; JW to Willard Maas, 6 April 1936, JR.

38. See the following reviews in JW's scrapbook, BU: Paul Rosenfeld, "Also in Memoriam," *Nation*, 15 October 1938, pp. 384–85; Kenneth Patchen, review in *Books and Writers* (California: Jewish Community Press), 28 October 1938; Muriel Rukeyser, "Group of Poets," *New Republic*, 8 March 1938; Merrill Moore, "A Story Told in the Form of Sonnets," *Boston Transcript*, 28 August 1938; Harry Roskolenko, "Sound or Meaning," *Voices* (date unknown); Louis MacNeice, *Commonsense*, June 1939.

39. JW to Harry Roskolenko, undated, GA.
40. *WCP*, p. 92.
41. See Lemuel Johnson, *The Devil, the Gargoyle, and the Buffoon: The Negro as Metaphor in Western Literature* (Port Washington, N.Y.: Kennikat Press, 1971), pp. 156–72.
42. *WCP*, p. 100.
43. *Harvard Bulletin*, 4 April 1918, HRO; S. Foster Damon to JW, 4 February 1921, BU.
44. William H. Whalen (Assistant, Harvard University Archives) to AW, 26 July 1978; Robert Fitzgerald to AW, 23 May 1979.
45. *WCP*, p. 66.
46. Ibid., p. 67.
47. Ibid., p. 68.
48. Ibid.
49. Ibid., p. 69.
50. Ibid.
51. Ibid., p. 70.
52. Ibid., p. 71.
53. Ibid., p. 75.
54. Ibid., p. 78.
55. Ibid., p. 96.
56. Ibid., p. 64.
57. Ibid., p. 100.
58. JW to Van Wyck Brooks, undated, CPVP.

CHAPTER 7

1. Samuel Hynes, *The Auden Generation* (New York: Viking, 1977), p. 65.
2. Virgil Thomson, *Virgil Thomson* (New York: Knopf, 1966), p. 161; Kenneth Rexroth to AW, 28 June 1976.
3. SM, *Pagany* 1, no. 2 (April–June 1930): 23.
4. Ezra Pound, *Pagany* 2, no. 3 (January–March 1931): 105.
5. Stephen Halpert (with Richard Johns), ed., *A Return to Pagany* (Boston: Beacon Press, 1969), pp. 215–17.
6. SM to Richard Johns, 18 March 1932, ML.
7. Kate Kurzke to AW, 11 September 1976; Richard Carline to AW, 8 December 1976. Kate Kurzke also recalls that a degree of half-serious bickering characterized the relations between JW and R. P. Blackmur. JW would kid Blackmur about his family's lack of distinction and Blackmur's lack of a college education. He also said that Helen Blackmur had a baleful look like a girl in a fairy story who had toads fall out when she opened her mouth, and that Dick's mouth was too small for long words. JW claimed that Blackmur also reminded him of a tale in which someone had a mouth so small he had to feed himself with a pin. For more details about the relationships among Mangan, Wheelwright, and Blackmur, see Russell Fraser, *A Mingled Yarn: The Life of R. P. Blackmur* (New York: Harcourt, Brace, Jovanovich, 1981).
8. SM to Richard Johns, 14 April 1930, ML; SM to Richard Johns, 18 March

1932, ML; SM to Ezra Pound, 28 January 1932, B. For Lincoln Kirstein's version of the beginnings and objectives of *Hound and Horn*, see his "Crane and Carlsen: A Memoir, 1926–1934," *Raritan* 1, no. 3 (Winter 1982): 6–40.

9. SM, *Fantasy* 6, no. 1 (1938): 28.

10. SM to Samuel Putnam, 16 January 1931, Princeton University Library, Princeton, New Jersey; SM to Ezra Pound, 28 January 1932, B.

11. SM, *No Apology for Poetrie*, p. vi.

12. Ibid., p. 28.

13. Ibid., p. 80.

14. Ibid., pp. 83–84.

15. Ibid., p. 89.

16. The Benét and Fitzgerald articles are in SM's scrapbook, HL: William Rose Benét, "No Apology for Poetrie," *Saturday Review of Literature*, 29 December 1934, p. 404; "No Apology for Poetrie," *Breeze*, January 1935, p. 19; and "No Apology for Poetrie," *Boston Transcript*, 23 March 1935; William Fitzgerald, "No Apology for Perfection," *Anathema*, April–June 1935.

17. Austin Warren, "No Apology for Sherry," *Poetry* 45, no. 6 (March 1935): 108.

18. Howard Blake, "Thoughts after Sherry," *New Frontier*, July 1935, pp. 34–36, in SM's scrapbook, HL; John Wheelwright, "From Mist We Breathed," *Poetry* 45, no. 6 (March 1935): 339–42.

19. SM to Virgil Thomson, 18 June 1930, HL.

20. SM to Virgil Thomson, undated but marked "Mallorca," HL.

21. SM to Virgil Thomson, Lady's Day 1927, HL.

22. SM to "Little Eagle," 14 May 1950, HL.

23. SM, *Salutation to Valediction* (Boston: Bruce Humphries, 1938).

24. Ibid.

25. Ibid.

26. SM to Charles Haywood, 3 June 1957, HL.

27. Sean Niall and Katherine Mangan, "Mexico—Tierra Triste," *North American Review* 241, no. 1 (Spring 1937): 65–79. Sean Niall was a pseudonym SM used at various times in his journalism career.

28. SM to Ezra Pound, 23 August 1934, B.

29. Author's interview with Robert Fitzgerald, June 1976.

30. John Cheever to AW, 30 July 1977.

31. SM to Virgil Thomson, 13 February 1933, HL; SM to Virgil Thomson, 13 November 1935, HL.

32. Richard Haywood to AW, 23 August 1976; "Opinions of the Supreme Judicial Court: Commonwealth Vs. John J. S. Mangan, 3 February 1936," HL.

33. SM to Virgil Thomson, 10 August 1936, HL.

34. Cuthbert Daniel to AW, 12 July 1976.

35. JW to Horace Gregory, undated, GA.

36. Fairfield Porter to AW, 5 August 1974. Fairfield Porter, JW, and SM all had political and literary associations after 1934, but Porter moved away from Trotskyism as the other two moved toward it. He eventually became a disciple of Paul Mattick's "Council Communism."

37. SM also translated a large part of a semisurrealist book on Mexican art: *The Cloud and the Chronometer* by Louis Cardoza y Aragon. The manuscript has been lost.

38. SM to JW, 27 December 1936, JHL; SM to JW, 29 December 1936, BU; SM to JW, 30 December 1936, BU.
39. SM to Virgil Thomson, 15 October 1933, HL.
40. SM to Virgil Thomson, 19 March 1938, HL.
41. James P. Cannon to the International Secretariat of the Fourth International, 25 June 1938, Library of Social History, New York City.

CHAPTER 8

1. JW to John Marshall, 14 September 1936, John Marshall Papers.
2. JW to Max Shachtman, undated, BU.
3. JW to Martin Abern, 13 August 1934, BU; John McDonald to JW, 25 September 1934, BU.
4. Felix Morrow to JW, 16 August 1938, BU.
5. JW to James Burnham, 12 July 1939; James Burnham to JW, 16 August 1938, BU.
6. JW to the editor of the *Socialist Appeal*, 14 December 1937, BU.
7. JW to Philip Rahv, undated, Rutgers University Library, New Brunswick, New Jersey.
8. JW to George Novack, 26 January 1938, BU.
9. JW to Max Shachtman, 12 March 1938, BU.
10. James P. Cannon to JW, 17 January 1940, BU.
11. JW to James P. Cannon, undated, Library of Social History.
12. JW, "Not Soviet Patriotism, but Bolshevist Renaissance," *Internal Bulletin* (Socialist Workers Party) 2, no. 12 (February 1940), p. 1.
13. JW to James P. Cannon, undated, Library of Social History.
14. Lawrence Trainor to AW, 18 December 1974.
15. JW to Robert Fitzgerald, undated, BU.
16. George Weissman to AW, 17 June 1979.
17. JW to Harry Roskolenko, undated, GA.
18. Dwight Macdonald to JW, 24 April 1939, BU.
19. JW quarreled with Roskolenko and eventually withdrew from Exiles Press. The radio poetry readings were broadcast on Friday at noon from the Miles Standish Hotel in Boston. In addition to JW and SM, participants included John Peale Bishop, Merrill Moore, May Sarton, S. Foster Damon, Kenneth Porter, Austin Warren, Ada Russell, and Helen Howe.
20. JW, "U.S. 1," *Partisan Review* 4, no. 4 (March 1938): 54–56.
21. *WCP*, p. 156.
22. JW, "U.S. 1," p. 56.
23. *WCP*, p. 103.
24. Ibid., p. 104.
25. Ibid., p. 114.
26. Ibid., p. 152.
27. Ibid., p. 149.
28. Cited in Antonio Gramsci, *Prison Notebooks* (New York: International Publishers, 1973), p. 126.
29. JW to SM, identified as received in 1939. Additional confirmation of JW's

rejection of religion at the end of his life comes from the following: Quincy Howe to AW, 1 August 1974; author's interview with Austin Warren, May 1976; Dudley Fitts to James Laughlin, 26 September 1940.

30. *WCP*, p. 153.

31. Ibid., p. 154.

32. Ibid., p. 135.

33. Ibid.

34. Ibid.

35. Ibid., p. 102.

36. Ibid., p. 142.

37. Ibid.

38. Ibid., p. 143.

39. Matthew Josephson, "Improper Bostonian: John Wheelwright and His Poetry," *Southern Review* 7 (Spring 1971): 512.

40. Charles Francis Adams, *Three Episodes of Massachusetts History*, vol. 2 (Boston: Houghton Mifflin Co., 1892).

41. Stanley Elkins, *Slavery* (Chicago: University of Chicago Press, 1968), p. 175.

42. These and all subsequent quotations from the "Fast-Day Sermon" are from Adams, *Three Episodes of Massachusetts History*, 2:439–40. For further information on Antinomianism in Massachusetts, see David D. Hall, ed., *The Antinomian Controversy* (Middletown: Wesleyan University Press, 1968); and Kai Erikson, *The Wayward Puritans* (New York: John Wiley and Sons, 1966).

43. *WCP*, pp. 115–16.

44. David Herreshoff, *The Origins of Marxism in America* (New York: Monad, 1973), p. 41.

45. Charles and Mary Beard, *The Rise of American Civilization*, vol. 2 (New York: Macmillan Co., 1930), p. 54. Further discussions of this concept can be found in Staughton Lynd, *Intellectual Origins of American Radicalism* (New York: Vintage, 1968), p. 3; and George Novack, ed., *America's Revolutionary Heritage* (New York: Pathfinder, 1976), p. 250. The following references are useful for situating the Antinomian controversy in the development of capitalism on the North American continent: Herbert Aptheker, *The Colonial Era* (New York: International Publishers, 1974), p. 94; Larzer Ziff, *Puritanism in America* (New York: Viking, 1973), p. 75; Vernon L. Parrington, *The Colonial Mind* (New York: Harcourt, Brace and World, 1954), p. 27; James Truslow Adams, *The Founding of New England* (Boston: Little, Brown and Co., 1949), pp. 146–74. A useful analysis of the diverse elements involved in the bourgeois revolution in England and the United States can be found in George Novack, *Democracy and Revolution* (New York: Pathfinder, 1971), p. 51.

46. *WCP*, p. 137.

47. JW to Marya Zaturenska, identified as received in mid-1940, GA.

48. Howard Nemerov to AW, 1 September 1977.

49. Ruben Gotesky to JW, 9 December 1938, BU; V. F. Calverton to JW, 19 February 1938, BU.

50. JW to Kenneth Porter, 26 February 1940.

51. "Journal Report for 24 Hours," Boston Police Department, Eighteenth Division.

52. Frank Merchant, "Elegy," typed version courtesy of Austin Warren.

PART III: MANGAN IN EXILE, 1938–1961

CHAPTER 9

1. SM to JW, 1 June 1938, BU.

2. SM to JW, 30 September 1938, BU. According to a letter from SM to Charles
Haywood, 10 July 1954, SM also wrote the preface to a book of etchings by Gabor
Peterdi called *Black Bull*.

3. James P. Cannon to SM, 5 October 1938, Library of Social History, New York
City; SM to James P. Cannon, October 1938, Library of Social History. Trotsky
praises SM's work in Naomi Allen and George Breitman, eds., *Writings of Leon
Trotsky (1938–1939)* (New York: Pathfinder, 1974), p. 237.

4. SM to JW, 26–27 November 1938, BU. Information on SM's activities at this
time in the International Federation for Independent Revolutionary Art can be
found in Georges Hugnet, *Pleins et déliés: Témoignages et souvenirs, 1926–1970*
(Paris: Editions Guy Authier, 1972), pp. 312–13, 402–6. Hugnet reports that SM
defended him and protested to Trotsky when Breton expelled him from the
organization.

5. SM to James P. Cannon, 9 December 1938, Library of Social History; SM to
Rose Karsner, 2 February 1939, Library of Social History. A *Time* credential was
obtained for Cannon by SM.

6. SM to the Political Committee of the Socialist Workers party, 8 May 1939,
Library of Social History; Minutes of the International Secretariat, 9 July 1939,
Library of Social History.

7. Stefan Lamed to AW, 21 July 1979.

8. SM to JW, Easter Day 1939, BU.

9. SM, "Paris Letter," *Partisan Review* 6, no. 1 (Fall 1938): 101–5.

10. SM, "Paris Letter," *Partisan Review* 6, no. 2 (Winter 1939): 100–105.

11. SM, "Paris Letter," *Partisan Review* 6, no. 3 (Spring 1939): 100–105.

12. Dwight Macdonald to SM, 22 July 1939, HL.

13. SM, review of James Joyce's *Finnegan's Wake*, *Time*, 8 May 1939, p. 78.

14. SM, interview with Julian Gorkin and M. Casanova, *Socialist Appeal*, 3
March 1939, p. 1.

15. Virgil Thomson, *Virgil Thomson* (New York: Knopf, 1966), pp. 297–99.
When SM moved into Paris, he turned his Dampierre apartment over to Robert
McAlmon. McAlmon, in turn, permitted others to stay there; some visitors were
rather destructive, so this became the source of friction between SM and McAl-
mon.

16. Annette Kraeutler to AW, 1 December 1976.

17. Author's interview with David and Susie Rousset, May 1978.

18. SM to David Hulburd, 1 July 1940, University of Nanterre, Nanterre, France.
Neal O'Hara's column, "Take It From Me," undated, in scrapbook belonging to
SM.

19. *New York Times*, 13 August 1940, p. 10, col. 5.

20. SM to Kate Kurzke, 8 June 1942, JL. Joseph Hansen, who was present when
Trotsky was murdered, recalled that he first met SM late in 1940 in Boston.
According to a December 1977 interview with Joseph Hansen, SM insisted that he

go over all the details of the assassination and exclaimed that it was hard for him to believe it could have happened.

21. SM to Albert Goldman, 1940, Library of Social History.

22. Robert Alexander, *Trotskyism in Latin America* (Stanford: Hoover Institution, 1973), p. 56.

23. Nahuel Moreno to AW, 30 June 1977.

24. Alexander, *Trotskyism in Latin America*, pp. 53–59.

25. Nahuel Moreno to AW, 30 June 1977.

26. Alexander, *Trotskyism in Latin America*, pp. 56–57; clippings of articles in scrapbook belonging to SM.

27. SM, "State of the Nation: Minority Report," *Fortune* 28, no. 5 (November 1943): 137–41, 254–56, 259, 260, 262.

28. SM, "The End of French Democracy," *Fourth International* 2, no. 3 (March 1941): 79.

29. SM, "How Paris Fell," *Fourth International* 2, no. 6 (June 1941): 146–49.

30. SM, "A Reminder: How Hitler Came to Power," *Fourth International* 4, no. 2 (February 1943): 39.

31. SM, "Woodrow Wilson and Bolshevism," *Fourth International* 4, no. 4 (April 1943): 106; SM, "What the Peacemakers Did to Europe," *Fourth International* 4, no. 5 (May 1943): 141.

32. Frank Lovell [Frederick J. Lang], *Maritime: A Historical Sketch and Workers Program* (New York: Pioneer, 1943), p. ix; Frank Lovell to SM, 26 March 1943, HL.

33. Art Sharon to AW, 10 January 1977; Charles Curtiss to AW, 27 August 1976.

34. SM to Karl Goldstein, 15 July 1943.

35. Felix Morrow to SM, 27 September 1942, HL.

36. SM to Felix Morrow, 3 August 1943, HL.

37. SM to Felix Morrow (not sent), 10 May 1943, HL.

38. Author's interview with John Archer, June 1978; author's interview with Sam Gordon, June 1978; Pierre Frank to AW, 12 August 1976. Jean van Heijenoort recalled that "on the political plane he was quite modest," but he had the impression "that there was in Sherry Mangan a deep and burning intellectual exile"; Jean van Heijenoort to AW, 20 June 1976.

39. George Anthony Palmer to SM, 14 August 1954; Kate Kurzke to AW, 11 September 1976. In an interview with the author in June 1978, John and Mary Archer recalled that SM was criticized for his relatively high standard of living by some of the British Trotskyists who disagreed with him.

40. Author's interview with Sam Gordon, June 1978.

41. SM to Marguerite Mangan, 5 March 1944, HL.

42. SM to Marguerite Mangan, 29 January 1944, HL; SM to Marguerite Mangan, 12 May 1944, HL.

43. SM to Marguerite Mangan, 4 January 1944, HL; Hart Preston to AW, 15 October 1979.

44. SM to Marguerite Mangan, 13 April 1944, HL.

45. SM to Marguerite Mangan, 9 May 1944, HL.

46. SM to Marguerite Mangan, 19 May 1944, HL.

47. SM to Marguerite Mangan, 15 August 1944, HL.

48. SM to Marguerite Mangan, 10 October 1944, HL.

49. Rodolphe Prager to AW, 8 January 1978.

50. From a transcription of interviews with Michel Pablo by Rodolphe Prager, 15 and 17 October 1977; author's interview with Sam Gordon, June 1978.

51. Author's interview with George Weissman, May 1977.

52. Author's interview with Jacques Gremblat, May 1978; from a transcription of an interview with Ernest Mandel by Rodolphe Prager, 12 November 1977; author's interview with Ernest Mandel, May 1978.

53. Michel Pablo, "Our Friend Sherry, Our Comrade Patrice," *Fourth International* (European edition), no. 15 (May–July 1962): 3–4; author's interview with Michel Pablo, June 1978; author's interview with George Breitman, May 1977; author's interview with George Weissman, May 1977.

54. Pablo, "Our Friend Sherry," pp. 3–4.

55. Charles Curtiss to AW, 27 August 1976.

56. Pierre Frank to AW, 30 July 1979.

57. Alice B. Toklas, *Letters* (New York: Liveright, 1973), pp. 77–78.

58. Author's interview with Joel Carmichael, May 1977.

59. SM to Charles Haywood, 22 June 1946, HL.

60. SM to Winifred Scott, 6 October 1945, HL.

61. SM to Marguerite Mangan, 20 July 1947, HL.

62. Mina Curtiss to SM, dated only "Saturday noon."

63. John Hersey to AW, 28 August 1978.

64. SM to Charles Haywood, 22 April 1948, HL.

65. SM to Charles Haywood, 13 May 1948, HL.

CHAPTER 10

1. SM to Marguerite Mangan, 2 May 1948, HL.

2. SM to Marguerite Mangan, 5 May 1948, HL.

3. SM to Marguerite Mangan, 9 May 1948, HL.

4. SM to Mina Curtiss, 17 November 1948.

5. Mina Curtiss to SM, 25 November 1948.

6. SM to Mina Curtiss, 15 May 1949.

7. Ibid.

8. Ibid.

9. Mina Curtiss to SM, 2 May 1949.

10. SM to Mina Curtiss, 11 November 1949.

11. SM, "The Outlook for France's Jews: The National Crisis Threatens Their Security," *Commentary* 4, no. 11 (November 1947): 441–47.

12. SM, "France: Is de Gaulle Fascist?" *Commentary* 5, no. 1 (January 1948): 8–16.

13. SM, "Is Europe's Middle Class Finished? The Political Future of the 'Third Force,'" *Commentary* 6, no. 7 (August 1948): 99–107.

14. George Lichtheim and Irving Howe, letters to the editor, *Commentary* 6, no. 10 (September 1948): 283-84.

15. Clement Greenberg to SM, 2 June 1949, HL.

16. SM, "The French Intellectual Merry-Go-Round," *Commentary* 7, no. 6 (June 1949): 550–58.

17. SM, "The French Turn to Psychoanalysis: Freud Breaches Reason's Citadel,"

Commentary 9, no. 2 (February 1950): 182–88.

18. SM to Joshua Epstein, 8 June 1950, HL.

19. George Weissman to AW, 17 June 1979.

20. SM to Joshua Epstein, 8 June 1950, HL.

21. SM to Joshua Epstein, 5 August 1951; SM to George Anthony Palmer, 3 June 1950, HL.

22. SM to Joshua Epstein, 8 October 1950, HL.

23. SM to Joshua Epstein, 8 August 1950, HL.

24. SM to George Anthony Palmer, 3 June 1951, HL.

25. SM to Charles Haywood, 7 March 1951, HL; SM to Karl Goldstein, 25 February 1951.

26. SM to George Anthony Palmer, 3 June 1951, HL.

27. SM to Catherine Carver, 8 May 1957, HL.

28. SM, "Breath," *Argosy* 335, no. 1 (July 1952): 29, 67–70.

29. SM, "A Costume for Carnival," *Arizona Quarterly* 14, no. 1 (Spring 1958): 35–49.

30. SM to Karl Goldstein, 29 May 1951.

31. SM to Virgil Thomson, 23 June 1951, HL.

32. SM to Charles Haywood, 28 June 1951, HL.

33. SM to Charles Haywood, 15 March 1952, HL.

34. SM, "Snow," p. 51, HL.

35. SM to Charles Haywood, 15 July 1951, HL.

36. SM to Charles Haywood, 19 July 1951, HL.

37. SM to Charles Haywood, 6 August 1951, HL.

38. SM to Karl Goldstein, 20 March 1951.

39. SM to Karl Goldstein, 25 April 1951.

40. SM to Virgil Thomson, 23 June 1951, HL.

41. SM to Charles Haywood, 19 August 1952, HL.

42. SM to Karl Goldstein, 14 April 1953.

43. SM to Charles Haywood, 13 May 1953, HL.

CHAPTER II

1. SM to Virgil Thomson, 4 June 1953, HL.

2. SM to Karl Goldstein, 29 June 1953.

3. SM to Mina Curtiss, 28 October 1953.

4. SM to Virgil Thomson, 22 November 1953, HL.

5. SM to Norman Dodge, 13 September 1954, HL.

6. SM, "A Question of Principle," *Harpers* 213, no. 1274 (July 1956): 70–77; SM to Charles Haywood, 12 January 1954, HL.

7. SM to Charles Haywood, 15 February 1954, HL.

8. SM to Charles Haywood, 1 March 1954, HL.

9. SM to Charles Haywood, 21 April 1954, HL.

10. SM to Karl Goldstein, 15 April 1954.

11. Dorle J. Soria to AW, 6 July 1976.

12. SM to Charles Haywood, 15 April 1954, HL. Feitelson does not recall ever agreeing to marriage, according to a 15 June 1977 letter to AW. In a May 1977

interview, Joshua Epstein recalled that Feitelson considered SM a "magnificent journalist" and a "professional writer," but was alarmed by his drinking, inability to find steady work, and attitudes that she considered male chauvinist.

13. SM to Karl Goldstein, 16 March 1934.

14. Author's interview with Bert Cochran, January 1978.

15. SM to Charles Haywood, 11 May 1954, HL.

16. SM, "Blackness of a White Night," HL.

17. SM, "Last Will and Testament of Sherry Mangan, 1954"; revoked, 11 April 1957.

18. SM to Charles Haywood, 17 July 1954, HL.

19. George Anthony Palmer to SM, undated, HL; SM to George Anthony Palmer, 11 May 1955, HL.

20. SM to Karl Goldstein, 17 March 1955.

21. SM to Karl Goldstein, 22 April 1955.

22. SM to Karl Goldstein, 21 May 1955.

23. Gunther von Fritsch to AW, 9 June 1976.

24. Pearl Kazin Bell to AW, 30 June 1976.

25. SM to Karl Goldstein, 19 June 1955.

26. SM, "Thoughts on Approaching Fifty," *Arizona Quarterly* 19, no. 1 (Spring 1963): 50.

27. SM to Charles Haywood, 28 December 1955, HL.

28. SM to Charles Haywood, 8 May 1955, HL.

29. SM to Charles Haywood, 9 July 1956, HL.

30. SM to George Anthony Palmer, 29 January 1956, HL.

31. SM to Charles Haywood, 1 September 1956, HL.

32. SM to Charles Haywood, 23 February 1956, HL.

33. SM to George Anthony Palmer, 2 January 1957, HL.

34. SM to George Anthony Palmer, 16 July 1956, HL.

35. SM to Joshua Epstein, 21 October 1956, HL.

36. SM to Joshua Epstein, 22 May 1956, HL.

37. SM, "Impeccable is Perhaps Too Strong a Word," *Arizona Quarterly* 12, no. 2 (Summer 1956): 112–36; SM to Joshua Epstein, 21 October 1956, HL. A companion story, "A Costume for Carnival," appeared in *Arizona Quarterly* 14, no. 1 (Spring 1958): 35–49.

38. SM to Michel Pablo, 31 March 1957, HL.

39. Pierre Frank to AW, 30 July 1979; SM to Michel Pablo, 24 April 1957, HL.

40. Much material on the conflict from the point of view of the Socialist Workers party is contained in James P. Cannon, *Speeches to the Party* (New York: Pathfinder, 1973). According to George Novack, who had served as the Socialist Workers party's representative in Europe before the split with Pablo, Cannon's followers did not regard SM as an authentic leader of significant stature in either the American or European Trotskyist movement. Novack offered the following assessment in an 8 June 1979 letter to AW: "Politically, he had the misfortune of coming into the movement from the top and staying there. There is no evidence . . . of his participation in the everyday activities of branch and party building, the essential groundwork for a leader. That element was missing from his political personality and experience and asserted itself at critical turning points in his career. . . . His status as a deracinated revolutionist enabled him to perform

valuable and indispensable services to the international movement. But it deprived his development and capacities of a necessary dimension, imparting an intellectualistic bent to his judgments. . . . As a freelance operator, he was akin to Pablo who likewise suffered from not being controlled by or responsible to the membership and leadership of a strong section."

41. SM to Michel Pablo, 24 April 1957, HL.
42. SM to Michel Pablo, 17 May 1957, HL.
43. SM to George Anthony Palmer, 16 June 1957.
44. SM to Charles Haywood, 3 June 1957, HL.
45. SM to Joshua Epstein, 23 July 1957, HL.
46. SM to Joshua Epstein, 25 August 1957, HL.
47. SM, "The Truth about the Algerian Revolution," *Fourth International* no. 2 (Spring 1958): 41–50.
48. SM to Karl Goldstein, 9 October 1957.
49. SM to Charles Haywood, 6 March 1958, HL.
50. SM, "Reminiscence from a Hilltop," *Black Mountain Review* 3, no. 7 (Autumn 1957): 63–82; Robert Creeley to AW, 7 July 1978; Denise Levertov to AW, 24 August 1977.
51. SM to Joshua Epstein, 21 February 1958, HL.
52. SM to Charles Haywood, 6 March 1958, HL.
53. Dudley Fitts to SM, 7 September 1958, HL.
54. SM to Dudley Fitts, 16 June 1959, HL.
55. SM to Charles Lynch, 5 February 1958, HL.
56. Pierre Frank to AW, 30 July 1979.
57. SM to Karl Goldstein, 19 June 1958.
58. SM to Charles Haywood, 18 December 1958, HL. According to Pierre Frank in a 30 July 1979 letter to AW, the Trotskyist leaders were not aware of the extent of Sherry's financial problems. He recalls an incident in Amsterdam when SM was hesitant to join Frank and Georg Junclas for lunch in a restaurant because he lacked money; but Sherry gave the impression that his difficulties were only temporary.
59. SM to Emilio von Westphalen, 22 July 1959, HL.
60. SM, review of Boris Pasternak's *Dr. Zhivago*, *Fourth International*, no. 2 (Spring 1958): 65–66.
61. SM to Charles Haywood, 18 December 1958, HL.
62. SM to Emilio von Westphalen, 3 May 1959, HL.
63. Elizabeth Mann Borgesse to AW, 9 August 1977.
64. SM to Karl Goldstein, 9 November 1959, HL.
65. SM to Virgil Thomson, 28 December 1958, HL.
66. SM to George Anthony Palmer, 13 April 1960, HL.
67. SM to Charles Haywood, 3 July 1960, HL.
68. SM to George Anthony Palmer, 12 December 1960, HL.
69. Interview with Ernest Mandel, May 1978; interview with Livio Maitan, May 1978.
70. SM to Virgil Thomson, 15 February 1961, HL.
71. SM to William Rothenberg, 23 May 1961, HL.
72. SM, "What Are We Listening To?" *Pembroke Magazine* 8 (Spring 1977): 98–99.

73. SM to Virgil Thomson, 13 June 1961, HL; SM to Virgil Thomson, 17 June 1961, HL.

74. Anne Marie Satta to AW, 10 November 1978.

75. Kate Kurzke to Charles Haywood, 6 August 1961.

76. Charles Haywood to John Brown, 1 October 1962.

CONCLUSION

1. SM, "Activist Miliciano," *Western Review* 21, no. 1 (Autumn 1956): 33.

2. SM, "Grade 5: Seven Dives: A Sensible Dead End," *New Directions 11* (New York: New Directions, 1949), p. 331.

3. Mangan possibly had a view of reification similar to that of the Frankfurt School Marxists. See Fredric Jameson, *Aesthetics and Politics* (London: New Left Books, 1977), p. 212, and "Reification and Utopia in Mass Culture," *Social Text* 1, no. 1 (Winter 1979): 130–48.

4. SM, "A Night in Scranton," *New Directions 14* (New York: New Directions, 1953), pp. 153–56.

5. SM to George Anthony Palmer, 9 April 1951, HL.

6. SM, "Reminiscence on a Hilltop," *Black Mountain Review* 3, no. 7 (Autumn 1957): 63.

7. SM, "Lament for All Lucretii," *Diogenes* 1, no. 3 (Autumn 1941): 87.

8. SM, "Before the Wind Rises," *View* 1, nos. 7–8 (October–November 1941): 4.

9. Ibid.

10. Ibid.

11. For further documentation of this claim, see Alan Wald, "Erasing the Thirties," *New Boston Review* 6, no. 1 (February 1981): 20–22.

Civil War, 10, 12, 98, 109, 166, 171–72; compared with Whitman, 11–12; use of modernism, 11, 12; antiwar poetry, 12, 166–67; compared with Auden, 12; assessment of, 17–18, 21, 31, 32–34, 124, 132, 156, 165, 241, 244, 246–47; compared with Emerson's "Uriel," 21–22, 34; regional influences on, 25, 29–32, 37, 51, 55, 61, 102, 107, 108, 117, 118, 165, 166, 168, 172, 173; physical description and personal qualities of, 37–39, 45–46, 55–56, 100–102, 160, 172–73; consciousness about family history, 39; influence of Marxism on, 38–39; influence of religion on, 39, 45, 47, 53, 55, 60–67, 103–4, 112, 114–15, 131–32, 156–57, 164; Brahmin influence on, 43, 55–56; relation to father, 44–45, 147; impact of father's suicide on, 44, 47; religious conversion, 44; change of middle name, 44; desire to become Anglican priest, 44, 49; resemblance to father, 45, 47; school and college attendance of, 46–47, 48–50; expulsion from Harvard, 48; early political views of, 49–50, 59; enlistment in Harvard Reserve Officer's Training Corps, 49; impact of World War I on, 49–50; Harvard poems of, 51–56; use of pseudonym Dorian Abbot, 52; view of Eliot, 54–55; early sympathy for Russian Revolution, 56, 255 (n. 10); association with expatriates, 56–60; nicknamed "Wheels," 57; editor of *Secession*, 57; contributions to *Aesthete 1925*, 57; residence in Italy, 59–60; sexuality of, 59, 60, 64, 101–2, 130; attends architectural school at M. I. T., 60; practices architecture, 60, 255 (n. 22); impact of Great Depression on, 62, 66–69, 106–7, 110, 166–67, 122; compared with Harry Crosby, 67; attitude toward Puritan tradition, 67, 112; joins Socialist party, 68; early political views of, 89; attitude toward

Leninism, 90, 94, 104, 105; view of fascism, 90; view of the Communist party, 90; view of the working class, 90–91, 117, 132; view of the Socialist party, 90–91; remarks on intellectuals and socialism, 91–92; activities in the Socialist party, 92–96; and first contact with the Trotskyists, 93–96; as supporter of united front, 94; early view of the USSR, 94; early criticisms of Trotskyism, 96; reviews for *Poetry*, 97; writer for *New Republic*, 97; association with *Hound and Horn*, 97–99; finances, 99; debate with Granville Hicks, 98–99; view of the function of criticism, 98–99; relation to mother, 99; guest at Yaddo, 100; bohemian side of, 100; relations with Blackmur, 103, 120–21, 263 (n. 7); depression of, 101–2; relation of his art to personality, 102–3; and comparison of Communists to Puritans, 104, 173; and tension between Marxism and religion, 104, 106, 156, 162–66, 241; influence of Trotsky on, 105–6; quietism of, 109, 112; explanation of symbols "rock" and "shell," 110–11; compared with Hart Crane, 116; and creation of more public poetry, 109–22; criticism of Mangan's poetry, 147; friendship with Mangan, 152; and offer of "Correspondence Course on the Form and Content of Rebel Poetry," 153; political influence on Mangan, 153–55; as founding member of Socialist Workers party; view of World War II, 156, 167–68; controversy with *Socialist Appeal* over *Partisan Review*, 157–58; correspondence with Cannon, 158–60; attitude during Cannon-Shachtman dispute, 159–60; attitude toward Trotsky, 160–61; and poetry readings on radio, 161, 265 (n. 19); later view of the USSR, 167–68; contributions to American radicalism, 165; abandonment of Anglican beliefs,